United States Edition

2024 Year B

Workbook for Lectors, Gospel Readers, and Proclaimers of the Word®

María Enid Barga

Stephen Lampe

Eric J. Wagner, CR

Suzanne Nawrocki

LTP

LITURGY TRAINING PUBLICATIONS

CONTENTS

Advent

Christmas Time

Ordinary Time

Lent

Paschal Triduum

Easter Time

In "The Ministry of Proclamation," Rita Ferrone contributed to the first paragraph, which is about *Spiritus Domini*.

(continues on next page)

Ordinary Time

Liturgy Training Publications,
3949 South Racine Avenue,
Chicago, IL 60609; 800-933-1800;
fax: 800-933-7094;
orders@ltp.org; www.LTP.org.

Cover art: Barbara Simcoe

This book was edited
by Christina N. Condyles.
Michael A. Dodd was
the production editor,
Anna Manhart was the designer,
and Kari Nicholls was the
production artist.

Printed in the United States
of America

ISBN: 978-1-61671-710-0

WL24

In accordance with c. 827,
permission to publish was
granted on March 30, 2023 by
Most Rev. Robert G. Casey, Vicar
General of the Archdiocese of
Chicago. Permission to publish
is an official declaration of
ecclesiastical authority that the
material is free from doctrinal
and moral error. No legal
responsibility is assumed by
the grant of this permission.

THE MINISTRY OF PROCLAMATION

The lay liturgical ministry of proclaiming the Scripture readings during Mass has recently undergone a significant change. Historically, the laity have not always had the privileged ministry of lectoring available to them. When the *Constitution on the Sacred Liturgy* at Vatican II (1963) affirmed that lay people were able to carry out liturgical ministries in their own right, lay men began to read in church. In 1970, the Vatican clarified that women could read the readings too, and they undertook this ministry. Pope Paul VI's motu proprio *Ministeria quaedam* (1972, MQ) invited the laity to the instituted ministry of lector, which was previously referred to as a minor order and was solely for seminarians. But he limited the instituted ministry of lector to men. Both men and women continued to serve as readers, but only a few became instituted lectors, and all of these were male. In 2021, Pope Francis updated MQ with the apostolic letter *Spiritus Domini*. Canon law was revised with this letter, updating canon 230§1 to open the instituted ministry of lector to both men and women. The Church continues to have lay readers, as we have since the Second Vatican Council. But more of these may now become instituted lectors, who make a more formal commitment to serve in the ministry of the Word and are commissioned by the bishop. In addition to proclaiming the readings in church, instituted lectors may also be called upon to train others in this ministry, break open the Word with catechumens, lead celebrations of the Word with children, and more. What a privilege that a diversity of voices—male and female, young and old—can be heard proclaiming God's Word!

Throughout Scripture, God calls individuals to carry out his will in particular ways. Consider the vast array of characters the Bible reveals and their vastly different roles as they serve God. The unique gifts you bring to the ministry of proclamation help equip you to respond to Jesus' call to spread the Good News far and wide. You lend your voice to bring God's Word, fresh and new, to the assembly. By your proclamation, you are embodying the incarnational aspect of the Gospel itself.

Although it is essential that you be trained properly in your ministry so that you can effectively proclaim the Word of God, the underlying, most fundamental principle of your ministry is that you are a person with a deep devotion to Scripture and the liturgy, and that you desire a spirituality that is profoundly shaped by it. Your presence in the sanctuary should be consistent with your presence in the

---

Thus faith comes from what is heard, and what is heard comes through the word of Christ. (Romans 10:17)

---

community. You proclaim the Word on Sunday, and your life reveals it the rest of the week—a responsibility not to be taken lightly.

What the Scriptures Reveal

The Scriptures have always been foundational to the Church and to the life of its members. While Catholics can readily affirm that Christ is really present in the Eucharist, the Church also teaches that Christ is present in his Word—that is, in the Scriptures (*Constitution on the Sacred Liturgy*, 7 and *General Instruction of the Roman Missal*, 29). Through sacred Scripture, God communicates his love and mercy to every generation. As it is proclaimed in the liturgy, the Word of God makes God's presence known and enters into every time and place. God's Word for God's people.

During Mass, a lectionary is used instead of a Bible. The lectionary is a set of readings from the Bible that were particularly selected to be used in the liturgy, with attention given to the way the readings reflect upon the rhythm of the liturgical year. This too is a reflection of Christ, since the seasons of the liturgical year mark his life, death, and resurrection. The privilege of reading at Mass demands preparation, including familiarity with all of the day's readings, not just the one(s) for which you will be responsible, since they all contribute to our understanding of the meaning of Scripture in connection with the liturgical celebration. The *Lectionary for Mass* follows a three-year cycle for the Sunday readings: Year A, Year B, and Year C. This year's edition of *Workbook* is for Year B, which draws most of its Gospel readings from Mark, as well as including some from John.

The first reading typically comes from the Old Testament and is connected to the Gospel, amplifying it, foretelling an aspect of it, or complementing it. The Church reads the Old Testament in light of Christ's paschal mystery, which is the fullness and completion of all salvation history (see *Dei Verbum*, 14–16). This understanding does not mitigate the importance of the first reading on its own merits, for it has an interpretive value that preceded Jesus' incarnation. Additionally, the historical roots found in the Old Testament are still important today. Often, the responsorial psalm corresponds with the first reading, helping to illuminate the reading's theme.

The responsorial psalm is usually sung by a cantor, but there could be times when a reader is called upon to proclaim the psalm instead. The psalms are poetic, emotionally expressive prayers, often having a rhythmic or songlike quality even when they are spoken instead of sung. One common literary structure of the psalms is parallelism, a synonymous repetition of thought. Proclaim the richness of the imagery in the psalm like a prayer. As you look toward the assembly for the psalm response, your arms should rise with invitational confidence.

For most of the year, the selection of the second reading is semi-continuous, which means that for several Sundays in a row, the same book will be used. Looking back to the previous week's second reading and looking forward to the following week's second reading can help you better understand the context of the current day's reading. If verses are missing in your assigned reading, you might prepare by reading the entire passage in your Bible.

During the liturgical seasons outside of Ordinary Time, the Church used the principle of theme harmony to select readings for Advent, Christmas Time, Lent, and Easter Time. The Scripture selections are specifically chosen to accompany the tone of the season, not a rotation through the biblical books. Through this approach, the Church is able to use the readings to highlight the particular aspect of the mystery of Jesus' life that is being celebrated in the liturgical season. As you proclaim throughout the liturgical year and use this book, you will experience the richness of Scripture and the way it draws us deeper into our faith.

Although we use the same readings every three

> Yet just as from the heavens / the rain and snow come down / And do not return there / till they have watered the earth, / making it fertile and fruitful . . . / So shall my word be / that goes forth from my mouth. (Isaiah 55:10–11)

years, the Scriptures are ever new. While the stories might be familiar, the Scriptures are heard in a new time and a new place, by new people in new situations, proclaimed by new voices with new experiences— the interpretation of a text as fresh and enlightening results from being proclaimed alongside its contemporary cultural setting. New sensibilities come to light. Consider, for example, how the creation accounts in Genesis are heard in light of current environmental concerns and theology. What other contemporary concerns come to mind as you hear the readings throughout the year? Despite this newness, God's saving message remains the same. What changes is the way that we receive it, how we apply it to our lives and respond to its call.

Understanding Literary Styles

Identifying the literary style—the genre—of your reading helps to shed light on the tone you should use and the meaning of the Scripture passage. Think of the ease with which you read different parts of a newspaper. You easily identify what is an ad, a cartoon, an editorial, a weather report, or a news story. A literary form addresses "how" an utterance expresses itself. The following paragraphs provide a brief overview of some of the more frequently used literary styles in the lectionary. Keep in mind that one reading can include different styles.

A narrative tells a story that involves characters, places, and action. Narratives answer some particulars of who, what, where, and when. Identifying the parts of a narrative as you prepare can help ensure that the assembly can hear them.

A parable is a type of narrative that delivers a moral lesson. One does not have to look hard for a parable. Often, the narrator will announce it within the Scripture reading itself. Mark's Gospel has quite a few parables. Parables have distinctive features that challenge social expectations: a situation is turned on its head for shock value, an unearned gift is received, a story is left open-ended so that you can find yourself in it, the lowly ones are raised up. Through the parable story, our previous ideas about God, his kingdom, and the world are transformed.

A prophetic text arouses the conscience of the people with emotional words and vivid descriptions that are often contrary to the dominant culture. You can read strong emotional words with emphasis. Passion is contagious, and the assembly will hear deeply words that are proclaimed with intensity. Anger is often associated with volume, sadness with a softer, slower delivery. Communication theorists since Aristotle acknowledge that passion (pathos) aids persuasion, and modern communication experts add that passion aids memory.

Scripture can be didactic, or a teaching text. A statement is put forward, and a case will be made to support it—a deductive approach. Alternatively, a specific premise will build to a conclusive teaching —an inductive approach. Jesus is known for his teaching in the Gospels, as is Paul in his many letters.

An exhortatory text is a reading that is a call to action and accountability. It often includes an underlying sense of urgency. Exhortatory texts could be addressed from God to the people, or from the people in prayer to God. These texts are frequently found in the writings of the Old Testament prophets, the Gospels (especially John), and the New Testament letters.

Scripture contains many other literary forms: apocalyptic, genealogies, hymns, history, poems, law codes, wisdom, dreams, myths, prayers, and songs. No matter the genre, understanding the literary form helps us determine what God is telling us and, in turn, communicate that meaning to the assembly.

Emphasizing the Text

Our bodies are integrally involved in the delivery of the lectionary reading. The more naturally you use your unique voice, the easier the reading's meaning will be grasped. To read naturally means to read with the same emphasis, phrasing, and inflection that you easily use in ordinary conversation. Studying everyday speech patterns is not to be confused with acting but is respectful to the listening assembly by providing speech patterns that are easy to hear and understand.

Indeed, the word of God is living and effective, sharper than any two-edged sword, penetrating even between soul and spirit, joints and marrow, and able to discern reflections and thoughts of the heart. (Hebrews 4:12)

There are several ways to emphasize specific parts of the text. A change in tempo or pacing, for example, adds emphasis. The keyword here is "change." If you speak at a fast pace, slowly delivered words will stand out. If you are speaking slowly and suddenly speed up, perhaps to indicate excitement, the words that are quickly spoken will have increased attention. As you prepare, be intentional about your tempo. Decide where the most important sections are and how you will draw attention to them.

Pausing is a form of pacing, whether to show sentence structure or to allow you to take a breath. Pausing can give the listener a chance to digest what they just heard. The length of a reading will vary, and pausing can help with both short readings and long readings. For example, a second reading from one of Paul's letters could be just two or three verses, yet pausing in the midst of a long, run-on philosophical sentence will give the listener time to grasp the meaning. When Scriptures are read too fast, without some intentional pauses, the listener, who is trying to comprehend the text, will momentarily stop listening while thinking, losing even more ground before again tuning back in.

Pauses can also be used to note a scene change or introduce a new part of the story. Some narratives announce scene changes with temporal markers (for example, "The next day . . . "). You can follow these markers with a pause to help the listener prepare for what comes next. Similarly, pauses can be used to prepare a listener for a character's dialogue. For example, in Genesis 1:3, we read, "Then God said: Let there be light." Using pauses, it could be read as, "Then God said: / (indicates pausing) Let there be light." A slight pause gives the listener's internal voice time to prepare to hear what God's performative word is going to do. Marking pauses in this book is a helpful way to practice.

Using different tones can help the listener distinguish who is speaking. For example, a subdued, even, and steady tone can draw attention to a narrator's voice. A narrator's voice should read background information consistently enough to be easily recognized as separate from a character's voice. Sometimes the narrator in the reading is emotionally invested rather than subdued, but the same rule applies; the listener should easily recognize who is speaking or acting.

Stressing and subduing word combinations is another way to add emphasis. A new idea is stressed the first time it appears and subdued when repeated (it is now an old idea). This rule of thumb might seem confusing, but it happens naturally in conversational English. The idea of dampening the old idea the second time it is read holds true for synonyms as well. The closely related words are already in the listener's mind; new ideas need to come forth. If you are not sure whether the synonym is a substantial substitution, exchange one word for the other and check for consistency in the sentence's meaning.

An "old idea" might also appear as a pronoun. Stress the noun and then subdue the following pronoun. If a reading is lengthy, the initial idea might need reemphasis. Reemphasize the word or phrase and subdue its following usages again as you continue along in the passage.

When you compare or contrast two things, both parts are usually stressed. Again, this is a common practice in conversational English and done automatically. It needs to be applied to our proclamation. *Workbook* will often **boldface** the items in a comparison or contrast. A couple of examples might help.

Example 1: Stress the first and second items in contrasts or opposites.

> But now we must celebrate and rejoice, because your brother was **dead** and has come to **life** again; he was **lost** and has been **found**. (Luke 15:32)

Example 2: Stress the new idea and subdue the ideas when repeated.

> And the younger son said to his father, "Father, give me the share of your **estate** that should come to me." So the father divided the property between them. After a few days, the younger son collected all his belongings and set off to a distant country where he **squandered** his inheritance on a life of **dissipation**. (Luke 15:12–13)

In this example, "Father" (the one being addressed) and "me" (the one speaking) are established. **Estate** is the new idea, and "property" and "inheritance" are synonyms. **Squandered** and **dissipation** are new ideas. The same conversational pattern applies to reading verbs and adverbs. New ideas or contrasting ideas are stressed.

Guidelines for proclaiming are guidelines. You are the reader and, ultimately, the determination of how to proclaim the message is up to you. If you are also the homilist, you know the focus of your homily and can proclaim the text accordingly.

Preparing Your Proclamation

Before preparing the practical aspects of your reading and proclamation, it is important to prepare spiritually. One way to do this is through the practice of lectio divina. Lectio divina, or divine reading, is an ancient practice that combines reading, meditation, and prayer. You can easily find step-by-step instructions for this practice online. In general, you read the text silently and out loud several times with stillness between the recitations, allowing your heart and mind to be open to the Spirit's promptings. Consider what words resonate with you and how God might be using this word to speak to your situation. Silence, peace, and stillness are not always easy, but this type of prayer helps to internalize God's Word as he speaks it to us now, in this moment.

Once you are ready to turn to the practical side of preparing, there are several things to consider. Fundamentally, your spiritual preparation informs your practical preparation because your own engagement with the text will come through in your voice. For example, a flat delivery shows that you know how to read, but that you are not inspired by the gravity of the words you are reading. Monotone voices are easily recognized, so much so that they are mocked in secular media. Think of the cartoonish, flat tone used to represent the teacher in the Peanuts cartoons. Flat delivery is not a neutral delivery. Instead, it says that each word is as insignificant as the last. Your tone of voice and other qualities can help you deliver a reading that effectively communicates God's Word to others.

But how can they call on him in whom they have not believed? And how can they believe in him of whom they have not heard? (Romans 10:14)

Direct eye contact is an embodied communication channel that varies by culture. In Western cultures, eye contact is a sign of trust and authenticity. Practice in front of a mirror to determine whether you are frequently looking up and out at the assembly. Is your eye contact sufficient to encompass the entire space without resting on an individual? It should also not be scattered, which would make you appear nervous. Load your short-term memory with content and then look up to deliver. Some verses are more easily remembered than others. Deliver as much as you can looking out at God's people. This practice is not about encouraging memorization but familiarity. Most readers look up at the end of a verse. Reverse this practice. Look out at assembly to deliver a line and down to "reload." The margin notes in *Workbook* will help you to recognize opportunities to make eye contact, as well as provide information about unfamiliar words and shifts in ideas or narratives.

If you have not yet mastered looking up at the congregation during the proclamation, you can at least look directly at the assembly during the opening rubric, "A reading from . . . " You have practiced and you know what book you are reading from. Looking toward the community will confirm that the congregation is settled and ready to listen. Your first words give the listener the chance to hear the quality of your voice; they are essential. Pause and begin. When finished, pause before issuing the closing rubric. The pause gives the assembly time to savor the last words of the reading before giving thanks. After the assembly responds, pause again, and leave the ambo with the same steady and measured reverence with which you entered.

Practicing in your sacred space is invaluable, both for beginner and veteran liturgical ministers. Once in the space, you will be able to judge the angle of the ambo's surface, the height of it, and how the microphone is positioned in relation to it. You will also get a sense of the lighting in the space. All of these things can affect your proclamation, how you shift your focus from the text to the assembly, how your voice is amplified, and the way the assembly sees your natural embodiment of speech. During this practice time, you could also record yourself on video and review it. This will help you hear how you sound and see how your facial expressions and head movements connect with the text. Remember that, before you begin reading, you should neutralize your expression and movement, a visible signal that you are about to begin. Once you start, your facial expression should change naturally to reflect the message of the reading.

While all of this preparation is important, keep in mind that practicing in an empty space will not entirely prepare you for the Sunday assembly since a packed church demands more voice projection than when you practice alone. Control what you can, but most importantly, be prepared for your experience when you enter the ambo; if you are unprepared, it will come through in your proclamation, expressions, and mannerisms. Your practiced embodiment of the reading reveals authenticity, which invites the listener into a deeper relationship with God. Be open to feedback, and approach your ministry with humility: it is God's Word that is being proclaimed, and the Spirit is moving within this space.

Suzanne Nawrocki

The Authors

María Enid Barga holds PHD, MPHIL, and MA degrees in biblical studies from the Catholic University of America (Washington, DC) and an undergraduate degree in classical archeology, French, and Spanish from Mercer University (Macon, GA). Recent publications include contributions to the Routledge volume *Reading the Gospels in Islamic Context* and to Brill's *A Companion to Comparative Theology*. She currently holds the position of assistant professor at the University of St. Mary of the Lake/ Mundelein Seminary in Illinois, where she teaches biblical studies courses that incorporate elements of comparative Scripture and address suffering in the Bible.

Fr. Stephen Lampe is a retired associate professor of biblical studies at Cardinal Stritch University in Milwaukee, Wisconsin, and is currently the assisting priest at Divine Savior Congregation (Fredonia) and Our Lady of the Lakes Catholic Congregation (Random Lake). He earned his licentiate (SSL) at the Pontifical Biblical Institute and his doctorate (STD) at the Pontifical Gregorian University. In addition to serving as pastor of two parishes and assisting priest at five parishes, he taught for fifteen years at St. Francis Seminary and thirteen years at Cardinal Stritch University. As well as producing written ministerial resources in English and Spanish, he has spoken across the Midwest on biblical and ministerial topics.

Eric J. Wagner, CR, holds a BA in architecture (Washington University, St. Louis), an MA in theology and an MDIV (Aquinas Institute of Theology), and a PHD in biblical studies (Catholic University of America). Ordained a priest in the Congregation of the Resurrection (2010), Wagner has taught Scripture and catechism classes on the theology faculty at the Pontifical College Josephinum (2018–2022). Currently, he is an adjunct professor at St. Louis University, where he teaches courses on the Old Testament. He also serves as a parochial vicar at Immaculate Conception parish in Columbia, Illinois.

Dr. Suzanne Nawrocki holds business degrees from St. Mary's College, an MA and an MDIV from St. Mary's Seminary, Houston, and a DMIN from the Aquinas Institute of Theology. She has spoken at the Los Angeles Religious Education Congress and has consulted with the Notre Dame Marten Preaching Program. Her past work with the United States Conference of Catholic Bishops, Notre Dame, and Creighton demonstrates her passion for the implementation of *Laudato si'*. Currently she consults with the Dallas Homiletic Institute, teaching workshops and offering private coaching. She uses her background in embodiment studies to train lectors so that their proclamation helps bring to life the Word of God in the hearts of listeners.

The authors' initials appear at the end of the Scripture commentaries.

An Option to Consider

The third edition of *The Roman Missal* encourages ministers of the Word to chant the introduction and conclusion to the readings ("A reading from . . . "; "The word of the Lord"). For those parishes wishing to use these chants, they are demonstrated in audio files that may be accessed either through the QR codes given here (with a smartphone) or through the URL indicated beneath the code. This URL is case sensitive, so be careful to distinguish between the letter l (lowercase L) and the numeral 1.

The first QR code contains the tones for the first reading in both a male and a female voice.

http://bit.ly/l2mjeG

The second QR code contains the tones for the second reading in both a male and a female voice.

http://bit.ly/krwEYy

The third QR code contains the simple tone for the Gospel.

http://bit.ly/iZZvSg

The fourth QR code contains the solemn tone for the Gospel.

http://bit.ly/lwf6Hh

A fuller explanation of this new practice, along with musical notation for the chants, is provided in a downloadable PDF file found at http://www.ltp.org /t-productsupplements.aspx. Once you arrive at this web page, scroll until you find the image of the cover of *Workbook*, click on it, and the PDF file will appear.

Recommended Works

Find a list of recommended reading and assistance in considering and implementing chanted introductions and conclusions to the readings in download-able PDF files at http://www.ltp.org/products/details /WL24.

Pronunciation Key

bait = bayt
cat = kat
sang = sang
father = FAH-ther
care = kayr
paw = paw
jar = jahr
easy = EE-zee
her = her
let = let
queen = kween
delude = deh-LOOD
when = hwen
ice = īs
if = if
finesse = fih-NES

thin = thin
vision = VIZH*n
ship = ship
sir = ser
gloat = gloht
cot = kot
noise = noyz
poison = POY-z*n
plow = plow
although = ahl-THOH
church = cherch
fun = fuhn
fur = fer
flute = floot
foot = foot

Shorter Readings

In the Scripture readings reproduced in this book, shorter readings are indicated by brackets and a citation given at the end of the reading.

FIRST SUNDAY OF ADVENT

LECTIONARY #2

READING I   Isaiah 63:16b–17, 19b; 64:2–7

A reading from the Book of the Prophet Isaiah

> You, LORD, are **our father**,
>> our **redeemer** you are named **forever**.
> Why do you let **us wander**, O LORD, from your **ways**,
>> and **harden** our **hearts** so that we **fear you not**?
> **Return** for the **sake** of your **servants**,
>> the tribes of your heritage.
> Oh, that you would **rend the heavens** and **come down**,
>> with the **mountains quaking** before you,
> while you wrought **awesome deeds** we could **not hope** for,
>> such as they had **not heard** of from of **old**.
> **No ear has ever heard**, no **eye** ever **seen**, any **God** but you
>> doing such deeds for those who **wait** for him.
> Would that you might **meet** us doing **right**,
>> that we were mindful of you in our ways!
> Behold, you are **angry**, and **we are sinful**;
>> all of us have become like unclean people,
>> all our **good deeds** are like **polluted rags**;
> we have all **withered like leaves**,
>> and our **guilt** carries us **away** like the **wind**.
> There is **none** who calls upon your name,
>> who rouses himself to cling to you;
> for you have **hidden your face** from us
>> and have delivered us up to our **guilt**. »

Isaiah = ī-ZAY-uh

Prayerful reflection on the readings can include listening to music that uses quotes from the Scripture passages. With this reading, for example, you could listen to "Eye Has Not Seen," by Marty Haugen. Although the text of this song is based on 1 Corinthians 2:9–10, Paul refers to Isaiah 64:3 in that passage. The song's imagery can help to remind us of the enormity of what Isaiah is trying to convey.

Note the changes of emotion throughout: praise, longing, pleading, remorse, and gratitude.

Deliver image-driven words slowly.

READING I   Today's reading from Isaiah marks the beginning of our Advent journey toward the birth of Christ. The passage begins and ends with an emphasis on God as our father, providing a relational framework for understanding the rest of the reading. Unfortunately, it is a relationship that is marked by brokenness. Isaiah contrasts the reality of Israel wandering and turning away from God with the recognition that God is deserving of our awe and reverence. Indeed, if the mountains quake in God's presence, how much more should we respond with awe to God's presence in our lives?

Not only does Isaiah point to nature as an indicator of what is owed to God, he also speaks of the "awesome deeds" that God performed on behalf of his people. This is a reference to the exodus out of Egypt and God's providence during the wilderness wanderings, including the giving of the commandments on Mount Sinai. Despite this overwhelming evidence of God's majesty and power, the Israelites have turned away from God in their sins. As a result, God has justifiably "hidden" his face from them. The "hidden God" motif is common in the Psalms and depicts a breakdown in the relationship between God and his people. Yet, the reading does not end on this negative note. Instead, Isaiah calls God father for a second time, recalling that all of Israel is God's creation and that he continues to fashion them according to his will.

This language of penitential piety calls us to engage likewise in repentance and return to God during this Advent season as we prepare our hearts to celebrate the incarnation of Christ. Do we actively remember the times that God has performed

1

This is true for us today—we, too, claim a filial relationship with the Father, and we are the work of God's hands.

Note the inclusiveness of God's handiwork.

Yet, O LORD, you are **our father**;
  we are the **clay** and you **the potter**:
  we are **all** the **work of your hands**.

For meditation and context:

RESPONSORIAL PSALM   Psalm 80:2–3, 15–16, 18–19 (4)

R. **Lord, make us turn to you; let us see your face and we shall be saved.**

O shepherd of Israel, hearken,
  from your throne upon the cherubim,
    shine forth.
Rouse your power,
  and come to save us.

Once again, O LORD of hosts,
  look down from heaven, and see;
take care of this vine,
  and protect what your right hand
    has planted,
  the son of man whom you yourself
    made strong.

May your help be with the man of your
    right hand,
  with the son of man whom you yourself
    made strong.
Then we will no more withdraw from you;
  give us new life, and we will call upon
    your name.

READING II   1 Corinthians 1:3–9

Corinthians = kohr-IN-thee-uhnz

A reading from the first Letter of Saint Paul to the Corinthians

Brothers and sisters:
Grace to you and **peace** from **God** our Father
  and the **Lord Jesus Christ**.

Recall a moment when you were overcome with gratitude to God for other Christians in your life. Paul is expressing this gratitude for the people of Corinth.

Paul's lengthy sentence needs phrasing. Practice pausing to aid understanding.

I **give thanks** to my God always on **your account**
  for the **grace** of God **bestowed** on you in Christ Jesus,
  that in him you were **enriched** in every way,
  with all **discourse** and all **knowledge**,
  as the **testimony** to Christ was confirmed among you,
  so that you are **not lacking** in any **spiritual gift**
  as you **wait** for the **revelation** of our Lord Jesus Christ.

"awesome deeds" in our own lives? In what ways do we allow God to shape our lives and inform our actions in our day-to-day lives?

[READING II] Today's second reading continues with the theme of God's providence and care for his people. Like Isaiah, Paul calls God "our Father," reminding the community of their familial relationship with God and, consequently, each other. In keeping with the theme of the letter as a whole, Paul highlights God's

initiative in calling each member to him in Jesus Christ.

At the beginning of this reading, Paul requests the fullness of God's blessing ("grace" and "peace") upon the community while offering thanksgiving for God's goodness in his care of his people. For Paul, thanksgiving and petition go hand in hand: in recognizing God's activity in our lives (thanksgiving), we can be confident in his continued action in our lives (petition). For this reason, Paul not only speaks of what God has done for the community in the past, he also expresses trust in God's con-

tinued providence as he looks toward Christ's second coming.

Paul likewise emphasizes that "God is faithful," reinforcing the basis for our trust in God's continued care. In the same breath, we are reminded that God called us "to fellowship with his Son, Jesus Christ our Lord." This fellowship has ramifications for our relationship with God and with those around us. We are called to participate actively in these relationships, inspired by God's loving care and strengthened by Christ's testimony, rather than remain passive.

He will **keep** you **firm** to the end,
   irreproachable on the day of our Lord Jesus Christ.
God is faithful,
   and by him you were **called to fellowship** with his Son,
Jesus Christ our Lord.

GOSPEL   Mark 13:33–37

A reading from the holy Gospel according to Mark

Jesus said to his **disciples**:
"**Be watchful**! Be alert!
You do **not know** when the **time** will come.
It is like a **man traveling** abroad.
He leaves home and **places** his **servants in charge**,
   each with his own work,
   and orders the **gatekeeper** to be on the **watch**.
Watch, therefore;
   you do not know when **the lord** of the house **is coming**,
   whether in the evening, or at midnight,
   or at cockcrow, or in the morning.
May he not come suddenly and **find you sleeping**.
What I say to you, I say to all: '**Watch!**'"

The First Sunday of Advent marks the beginning of a new liturgical year. This year we are in Year B, in which the Gospel readings are drawn primarily from Mark. Announce the Gospel clearly and slowly.

Letting your guard down is reckless. Vigilance is mandatory.

The last words heard are often the most remembered. Let the final warning resonate before the concluding rubric.

This call to active participation in our relationship with God and our community complements the call to repentance and transformation in the first reading. As we reflect on the ways God is calling us to turn toward him, we recognize that this conversion leads us deeper into our relationship with God and those around us as expressed through concrete actions.

GOSPEL   Today's Gospel reading like-wise calls us to participate actively, remaining alert for Jesus' coming. A series of imperatives ("Be watchful! Be alert!," "Watch, therefore," and "Watch!")

gives a sense of urgency to the need to be on our guard and actively on the lookout for Jesus. In this reading, Jesus describes the attitude we should have during this time between Jesus' resurrection and his second coming.

Jesus provides the reason we should be alert: we "do not know when the time will come." He explains further that we are not just waiting passively for his coming; rather, we have been entrusted with work, God's work, each according to his or her ability. We are responsible for fulfilling our set tasks with the implication that we will need to give an account of ourselves when

Jesus returns. Since he could return at any time, we need to be prepared to recount our work for the kingdom of God at the drop of a hat.

While the context of the passage refers to the second coming of Jesus, this reading is appropriate as we prepare to commemorate Jesus' coming into this world on Christmas day. Like the "lord of the house" in today's Gospel, Jesus' incarnation came at the least expected time and manner possible, as a baby boy resting in a lowly manger. Will Christmas day find us ready for our Lord? M.B.

THE IMMACULATE CONCEPTION OF THE BLESSED VIRGIN MARY

LECTIONARY #689

READING I   Genesis 3:9–15, 20

Genesis = JEN-uh-sihs

A narrator voice sets the scene.

The changing tone of the dialogue partners needs to be captured in your proclamation.

A reading from the Book of Genesis

After the man, **Adam**, **had eaten** of the **tree**,
  the Lord God **called** to the man and asked him,
    "**Where are you**?"
He answered, "I heard you in the garden;
  but I was **afraid**, because I was **naked**,
  so I **hid** myself."
Then he asked, "**Who told you** that you were naked?
You have eaten, then,
  from the tree of which I had **forbidden** you to eat!"
The man replied, "The **woman** whom **you put here** with me—
  she gave me fruit from the tree, and so I ate it."
The Lord God then asked the woman,
  "**Why** did you do such a thing?"
The woman answered, "The **serpent tricked** me into it,
  so I ate it."

Adam's false bravado here could be understood as him implying that God is partly to blame ("The woman whom *you* put here with me").

Make it clear who God is talking to; the conversation shifts here.

Then the Lord God said to the serpent:
  "Because you have done this, you shall be **banned**
    from all the animals
    and from all the wild creatures;
  on your **belly** shall you **crawl**,
    and **dirt** shall you **eat**
    all the **days** of your life.

READING I   Today's first reading from Genesis highlights the consequences for the initial act of disobedience in the Garden of Eden. In particular, the focus rests on Eve's relationship with the serpent and with all of creation. First, the curse upon the serpent involves a shift in its relationship with Eve wherein hostility is the predominant feature. Not only is there now enmity between the two, but the hostilities will also continue between their offspring for the rest of time. This is our struggle against sin. This conflict is brought to a resolution in the persons of Mary and in her divine son, Jesus.

The second relationship highlighted in this reading is that of Eve with the rest of creation. Until this point in the narrative, Eve did not have a personal name but was referred to only as "woman." Now she is named Eve, and the meaning for the chosen name is provided: "because she became the mother of all the living." In Hebrew, there is a close connection between the name "Eve" and the verb "to live," which is the basis for the explanation behind Eve's name in the reading. Therefore, we see that in the midst of the tragic fallout of disobedience, there is an element of hope resting in the life-giving quality of Eve. This life-giving quality continues in Mary and leads us to reflect on what we celebrate today.

Through her immaculate conception, Mary is singularly prepared for responding to God's call to be Jesus' mother. Because God saved her, from the moment of her conception, from the stain of original sin, Mary is able to say yes to the fullness of life God is entrusting to her in the person of Jesus. In her "yes" to God's plan found in today's Gospel reading, she not only gave

4

As you prepare, imagine Mary as she is often depicted in art, standing on a serpent.

I will put enmity between you and the woman,
> and between your offspring and hers;
he will **strike at your head**,
> while you strike at his heel."

Adam changes from calling her "woman" to calling her "Eve." Names are important.

The man **called his wife Eve**,
> because she became the **mother** of **all the living**.

For meditation and context:

RESPONSORIAL PSALM   Psalm 98:1, 2–3ab, 3cd–4 (1a)

R. Sing to the Lord a new song, for he has done marvelous deeds.

Sing to the LORD a new song,
> for he has done wondrous deeds;
His right hand has won victory for him,
> his holy arm.

The LORD has made his salvation known:
> in the sight of the nations he has
> revealed his justice.

He has remembered his kindness and
> his faithfulness
> toward the house of Israel.

All the ends of the earth have seen
> the salvation by our God.
Sing joyfully to the LORD, all you lands;
> break into song; sing praise.

READING II   Ephesians 1:3–6, 11–12

Ephesians = ee-FEE-zhuhnz

A reading from the Letter of Saint Paul to the Ephesians

Brothers and sisters:
Blessed be the **God** and **Father** of our **Lord Jesus Christ**,
> who has **blessed us** in Christ
> with every spiritual blessing in the heavens,
> as he **chose us** in him, before the foundation of the world,
> **to be holy** and without blemish before him.
In love he **destined us for adoption** to himself through
> Jesus Christ,
> in accord with the favor of **his will**,
> for the **praise** of the glory of his **grace**
> that he granted us in the beloved. »

Read long verses slowly to aid comprehension.

birth to Jesus but also to the potential of a new, restored life for every member of the human family through Jesus Christ. Through her immaculate conception, Mary's preserved state of grace is divinely granted in anticipation of the salvific actions of her son, Jesus. Although we honor Mary for her important role in cooperating with God's plan of salvation, we must always be focused on the paschal mystery of Christ, through which the enemy of sin and death was conquered so that our relationship with God might be restored.

READING II   In this reading from Ephesians, Paul emphasizes what God has done for his people, namely, blessed us. And what does this blessing consist of? It consists of being chosen by God. By highlighting that it is God who chooses us, and not vice versa, Paul recognizes that it is always God who takes the initiative in his salvific plan. In choosing us, God invites believers to respond to and participate in his plan of salvation.

God not only invites us to participate, but he also prepares us to do so. He chose us "to be holy and without blemish before

him" and lovingly adopts us through Jesus Christ. In this instance, we can read "holy" as "set apart" and not "virtuous," as we might initially think. In doing so, the stress falls again on God's action, setting us apart to stand before him without guilt or stain. Paul notes that this new relationship with God through Jesus Christ allows us to live solely and completely praising God's glory.

Mary's life reflects this reality that we experience now through our baptism. While we are called to stand before God "without blemish," Mary was able to stand without stain before God's messenger by the grace

Each one of us is chosen and loved. What joy!

In him we were also **chosen**,
  destined in accord with the purpose of the One
  who **accomplishes all things** according to the intention
    of his will,
  so that we might exist for the praise of his glory,
  we who first hoped in Christ.

GOSPEL   Luke 1:26–38

A reading from the holy Gospel according to Luke

The **angel Gabriel** was **sent from God**
to a town of Galilee called Nazareth,
  to a virgin betrothed to a man named Joseph,
  of the house of David,
  and the **virgin's name** was Mary.
And coming to her, he said,
  "**Hail, full of grace! The Lord is with you.**"
But she was greatly troubled at what was said
  and pondered what sort of greeting this might be.
Then the angel said to her,
  "**Do not be afraid**, Mary,
  for you have found **favor** with God.

Clearly distinguish which character is speaking: the narrator or the angel.

Familiar words from the Hail Mary prayer can be heard here.
The narrator voice should reflect Mary's "troubled" spirit.

of her immaculate conception. She was set apart by God from the moment of her conception. This prepared her to praise his glory through her affirmative response to his invitation to participate in his plan for salvation. Mary is a model of what we are called to do now through the grace of our baptism: we are to live praising God's glory in every aspect of our lives by responding affirmatively to his invitation of salvation. Because God takes the initiative, we have confidence in our being chosen and set apart by God.

Paul's statement that we are "destined" for adoption presents a point of confusion for many readers today. His use of "destined" here does not in any way take away from humanity's free will. We are all free at any point to respond with cooperation to God's plan of salvation or to reject it. The grace God gives us in being set apart and in our adoption gives us strength to choose to say yes in the face of sin. Likewise, Mary's immaculate conception did not lock her into God's plan that she be Jesus' mother. She had the choice to say no to God's invitation. Because she chose to

say yes, the Church honors Mary for that on the Solemnity of the Annunciation of the Lord on March 25.

GOSPEL   In today's Gospel, the account of Mary's cooperation with God's salvific plan is retold. The angel's first words to Mary describing her as "full of grace" call to mind the blessing Paul spoke of in the second reading: "the glory of his [God's] grace that he granted to us in the beloved [Christ]." We know through our theological tradition that this grace that Mary received included the

Use a strong upward inflection to reflect Mary's bewilderment.

This would be astonishing news to Mary.

Mary's response is a profound statement of trust. Can we, like Mary, graciously agree to God's plan?

Behold, you will **conceive** in your womb and bear a son,
    and you shall **name him Jesus**.
He will be **great** and will be called Son of the **Most High**,
    and the Lord God will give him the **throne** of David
        his father,
    and he will **rule** over the house of Jacob forever,
    and of his **Kingdom** there will be **no end**."
But Mary said to the angel,
    "**How can this be**,
    since I have **no relations** with a **man**?"
And the angel said to her in reply,
    "The **Holy Spirit** will **come** upon **you**,
    and the power of the Most High will overshadow you.
Therefore the **child** to be **born**
    will be **called holy**, the **Son of God**.
And behold, **Elizabeth**, your relative,
    has also **conceived** a son in her **old age**,
    and this is the sixth month for her who was called **barren**;
    for **nothing** will be **impossible for God**."
Mary said, "**Behold, I am the handmaid of the Lord.**
May it be done to me **according** to your **word**."
Then the angel **departed** from her.

grace of her immaculate conception. Mary, however, did not have this self-knowledge and was confused by the angel's greeting.

The angel's next words are of comfort and reassurance. He tells her not to be afraid and then provides the basis for his reassurance: she has "found favor with God." To be thus chosen by God is cause for peace of mind rather than unease, and Mary responds accordingly. After the angel describes the manner in which God is inviting her to participate in his plan of salvation, Mary's only question to the angel is a practical one, given her marital and virginal state. The angel's further proclamation builds upon the astonishing nature of his previous statements, giving Mary a precise answer to her query and further adding the good news of her cousin Elizabeth's unexpected pregnancy.

The angel's last words to Mary are "for nothing will be impossible for God." This statement is echoed in the second reading when Paul declares that God "accomplishes all things according to the intention of his will." The assertion by the angel is a final reassurance to Mary of God's presence and activity in the world and, consequently, in her life. Mary chooses to participate in God's plan, and her words reflect her decision to live completely and solely for God's glory. As we praise God today for his grace in Mary's life, we too participate in our own calling to be holy and set apart before God.
M.B.

SECOND SUNDAY OF ADVENT

LECTIONARY #5

READING I   Isaiah 40:1–5, 9–11

A reading from the Book of the Prophet Isaiah

> **Comfort**, give comfort to my people,
>   says your God.
> **Speak** tenderly to Jerusalem, and proclaim to her
>   that her **service is at an end**,
>   her **guilt** is expiated;
> indeed, she has **received** from the hand of the LORD
>   double for all her **sins**.
>
>   A voice cries out:
> In the **desert prepare the way** of the LORD!
>   **Make straight** in the wasteland a highway for our God!
> Every **valley** shall be **filled** in,
>   every **mountain** and hill shall be made **low**;
> the rugged land shall be made a plain,
>   the rough country, a broad valley.
> Then the **glory of the LORD** shall be **revealed**,
>   and all **people shall see it together**;
>   for the mouth of the LORD has spoken.

Isaiah = ī-ZAY-uh

Note the musicality of this reading. It begins in a soothing tone, then builds intensity with incredulous imagery and joyful proclamation, and finally returns us to a soothing tone at the end.

expiated = EK-spee-ayt*d

Emphasize the theme of preparedness. It will be repeated in the Gospel.

"All people shall see it together": The image of solidarity, so important for today's world, should be emphasized.

READING I Today's reading from Isaiah begins with the word "comfort." God's people, referred to collectively as "Jerusalem," are comforted because a new beginning is on the horizon: "her [Jerusalem's] service is at an end, her guilt is expiated." Their comfort lies in God's redemptive actions toward his people. There is also comfort in the continuity of God's presence among them. The phrases "my people" and "your God" in the first sentence recall the covenant formula that would have been familiar to the people: "I will be your God and you will be my people." This covenant relationship is recalled and renewed throughout the Old Testament.

Isaiah then continues by depicting what this new beginning looks like through geographical topography that shifts to such a degree that even the earth manifests God's glory and none can ignore it. In this new era, all people will be united before God in praise and worship. The restoration of God's people to this new life full of glorifying God is such good news that it needs to be proclaimed from the highest mountaintop to desert paths; everyone must hear the "glad tidings."

God's people are exhorted to share this joyous communication. In this reading, Isaiah refers to God's people as both Jerusalem and as Zion. Isaiah repeats the call using both names: "Zion, herald of glad tidings . . . Jerusalem, herald of good news!" This double reference to God's people in these terms is significant. Even though both terms refer to the same geographic location, in this context the term "Zion" has religious connotations while "Jerusalem" has political connotations.

Go up onto a high mountain,
　　Zion, herald of glad tidings;
cry out at the top of your voice,
　　Jerusalem, herald of **good news**!
Fear not to cry out
　　and say to the cities of Judah:
　　Here is your **God**!
Here comes with **power**
　　the Lord GOD,
　　who rules by his **strong** arm;
here is his reward with him,
　　his recompense before him.
Like a shepherd he **feeds** his flock;
　　in his arms he **gathers** the lambs,
carrying them in his bosom,
　　and leading the ewes with care.

Despite God's strength, he holds us in tender care.

For meditation and context:

RESPONSORIAL PSALM　Psalm 85:9–10, 11–12, 13–14 (8)

R. Lord, let us see your kindness, and grant us your salvation.

I will hear what God proclaims;
　　the LORD—for he proclaims peace to
　　his people.
Near indeed is his salvation to those who
　　fear him,
　　glory dwelling in our land.

Kindness and truth shall meet;
　　justice and peace shall kiss.
Truth shall spring out of the earth,
　　and justice shall look down from heaven.

The LORD himself will give his benefits;
　　our land shall yield its increase.
Justice shall walk before him,
　　and prepare the way of his steps.

Their use together in this passage highlights the impact of the news on the totality of God's people, affecting all aspects of their lives.

As members of God's people today, we are invited to likewise share in the comfort spoken of by Isaiah. Our comfort lies in our redemption through Christ, who is the new and eternal covenant. The birth of Christ, which we will celebrate in a couple of weeks, marks a new beginning for us and all of humanity. As God's people, we are heralds of these glad tidings as we, like Jerusalem/Zion, cry out: "Here is your God!"

READING II In a life marked by seasons and time, the author of this letter reminds us today that time is not an issue for God. We read that "with the Lord one day is like a thousand years and a thousand years like one day." God's plan unfolds according to his will and in the fullness of his timing.

Knowing that God's time is different from our own provides us with the context for the way Peter addresses the concerns of a community that expected Jesus' second coming ("the day of the Lord") to occur during the time of the apostles. The community anxiously awaited the second coming to put an end to the persecution they were enduring. Peter instead provides a positive reason for the perceived delay. God is patiently waiting (not delaying), giving time so that as many people as possible can repent and receive salvation. God's timing for the second coming is therefore an act of divine mercy and a comfort to God's people.

Like we heard in the Gospel reading last Sunday, Jesus' second coming will "come like a thief" when least expected. When he does come, it will be sudden and

Proclaim slowly. A reading from 2 Peter is used only once in the regular Sunday readings of Year B.

This image of time passing is frequently used in songs because it vividly captures the enormity of what Peter is trying to convey to us about God's nature.

Consider using a rising inflection to communicate inquisitiveness, then pausing slightly to give time for the listener to have an internal response, and then continuing on with the reading.

READING II   2 Peter 3:8–14

A reading from the second Letter of Saint Peter

Do not ignore this one fact, **beloved**,
    that with **the Lord one day** is like a **thousand years**
    and a thousand years like one day.
The Lord does not delay his promise, as some regard "delay,"
    but he **is patient** with you,
    not wishing that any should perish
    but that all should come to repentance.
But the day of the Lord will **come like a thief**,
    and then **the heavens** will **pass away** with a mighty roar
    and the elements will be dissolved by fire,
    and the earth and everything done on it will be found out.

Since **everything** is to be dissolved in this way,
    what sort of persons ought you to be,
    conducting yourselves in **holiness** and **devotion**,
    waiting for and hastening the **coming of the day** of God,
    because of which the heavens will be dissolved in flames
    and the elements melted by fire.
But **according** to his **promise**
    we await new heavens and a new earth
    in which righteousness dwells.
Therefore, **beloved**, since you await these things,
    be eager to be found **without** spot or **blemish** before him,
        at peace.

decisive. The author therefore provides a template for how to be prepared for that long-awaited moment. We are to conduct ourselves "in holiness and devotion" so that we may "be found without spot or blemish before him, at peace." When we live each day actively engaged in repentance and following the way of the Lord, we will experience the peace and comfort that only comes with being in right relationship with God and the community. This peace is rooted in the knowledge that no matter when Jesus comes again, we will be found ready to stand before him.

During Advent, we prepare for the coming of the Lord. While many people might emphasize the preparation of our celebration of Jesus' birth, awaiting Jesus' second coming is also an integral part of the Church's theology of the season of Advent. We are called during this season to make sure that we are in right relationship with God so that on Christmas day we are at peace knowing that we have oriented our lives toward God and are ready to stand before him.

GOSPEL   The very first line of the Gospel reading prepares us for how we should understand the events immediately following. We are about to hear the Good News of Jesus, called Christ (the "anointed" one of God) and Son of God. The messianic and divine character of Jesus is revealed here and is bookended by the centurion's acclamation at the foot of the cross in Mark 15:39: "Truly this man was the Son of God!" From the outset of this reading, we are equipped with information that breaks open the significance of the rest of Mark's Gospel.

Isaiah = ī-ZAY-uh

Part of the quotation Mark is using comes from today's first reading.

Make clear the multiple voices: the narrator, the quotation from the prophet, and John the Baptist.

What John eats and wears creates a vivid image, but the focus should be on the proclamation he makes. John understands the urgency of his message.

Let John's humility be heard. He never wavers from his role in God's plan.

GOSPEL   Mark 1:1–8

A reading from the holy Gospel according to Mark

The **beginning** of the **gospel** of **Jesus Christ the Son** of **God**.

As it is written in **Isaiah** the prophet:
   *Behold, **I am sending my messenger** ahead of you;*
      *he will **prepare** your way.*
   A voice of one crying out in the desert:
      *"Prepare the way of the **Lord**,*
      make straight his paths."
John the Baptist appeared in the desert
   proclaiming a baptism of repentance for the
      forgiveness of sins.
People of the whole Judean countryside
   and all the inhabitants of Jerusalem
   were **going out** to him
   and were being baptized by him in the Jordan River
   as they **acknowledged** their **sins**.
John was clothed in camel's hair,
   with a leather belt around his waist.
He fed on locusts and wild honey.
And this is what he proclaimed:
   "**One mightier** than I **is coming** after me.
I am **not worthy** to stoop and loosen the thongs of his sandals.
I have **baptized you** with **water**;
   he will baptize you with the **Holy Spirit**."

Immediately following this revelatory statement about Jesus, Mark synthesizes passages from Exodus, Malachi, and Isaiah in the quote he attributes solely to Isaiah, part of which we read in today's first reading. After telling of the coming of a herald who will cry out, "Prepare the way of the Lord," John the Baptist appears on the scene as the long-awaited herald of the Good News. The "way of the Lord" is the journey of discipleship. In fact, in Acts 9:2 Christians are said to belong to "the Way," clearly marking those who follow the "Way" of Jesus as true disciples.

John's ministry gives us an early glimpse of what the journey of discipleship entails, which will be perfectly and fully embodied by Jesus. First, we see discipleship involves the need to repent, which is central to John the Baptist's message. Second, the way of discipleship includes proclaiming the Good News. John exemplifies this aspect of discipleship as he prepares the people for the coming of Jesus; he always points to Jesus, who is coming after him and who is greater than him. This Good News is a comfort to those who have been awaiting the coming of the Messiah.

It is not only words of comfort to the people, but also a call to action, to repent and reorient themselves toward God. We also are called to this way of discipleship as we prepare for the coming of Christ during Advent. M.B.

THIRD SUNDAY OF ADVENT

LECTIONARY #8

READING I Isaiah 61:1–2a, 10–11

A reading from the Book of the Prophet Isaiah

Isaiah = ī-ZAY-uh

Notice the abundance of personal pronouns. As you prepare, appropriate them to yourself—we are chosen servants of the Lord.

Give these directives equal attention; each one starts with "to."

> The **spirit of the Lord** God is **upon me**,
>   because the Lord has **anointed** me;
> **he has sent me** to bring **glad tidings** to the **poor**,
>   to heal the **brokenhearted**,
> to proclaim **liberty to the captives**
>   and **release to the prisoners**,
> to **announce** a year of **favor** from the Lord
>   and a day of vindication by our God.

Emphasize "rejoice." This sentiment is echoed in the responsorial psalm and the second reading.

The reference to clothes and jewelry is image-driven metaphorical language. The theology that is being communicated is about God's salvific plan and our response of praise.

diadem = DĪ-uh-dem = crown

> I **rejoice** heartily in the Lord,
>   in my God is the joy of my soul;
> for he has **clothed** me with a robe of **salvation**
>   and wrapped me in a mantle of **justice**,
> like a bridegroom adorned with a diadem,
>   like a bride bedecked with her jewels.
> As the earth brings forth its plants,
>   and a garden makes its growth spring up,
> so will the Lord God make justice and **praise**
>   spring up before **all** the **nations**.

READING I On this third Sunday of Advent, the reading from Isaiah adds to our sense of joy on this Gaudete (meaning "rejoice") Sunday. The greater part of the Book of Isaiah focuses on the impending destruction of the kingdom of Judah for their transgressions against God. Yet doom is not the final word for God's people. In today's reading, Isaiah rejoices in God because he has received salvation and justice from God. After a period of captivity and suffering, God grants his favor not only upon the prophet but also on all his people.

In fact, Isaiah is called to "bring glad tidings to the poor," the brokenhearted, and the captives. The marginalized and imprisoned are singled out to emphasize the magnitude and graciousness of God's redemptive activity that allows them to have new life in him. This revival of God's people is represented by the new life of "justice and praise" that springs from the ground: God's people have been shackled and now are set free that they too might rejoice in the Lord.

We rejoice today in our new life in proper relationship with God that was ushered in by Jesus' incarnation. We recognize God's salvific activity in every aspect of our lives. Like Isaiah and the ancient Israelites, God's redemptive movement in our lives has enlivened us so that we are free to praise God "before all the nations."

For meditation and context:

RESPONSORIAL PSALM   Luke 1:46–48, 49–50, 53–54 (Isaiah 61:10b)

R. My soul rejoices in my God.

My soul proclaims the greatness of the Lord;
  my spirit rejoices in God my Savior,
for he has looked upon his lowly servant.
  From this day all generations will call
  me blessed.

The Almighty has done great things for me,
  and holy is his Name.

He has mercy on those who fear him
  in every generation.

He has filled the hungry with good things,
  and the rich he has sent away empty.
He has come to the help of his servant Israel
  for he has remembered his promise
  of mercy.

READING II   1 Thessalonians 5:16–24

A reading from the first Letter of Saint Paul to the Thessalonians

Thessalonians = thes-uh-LOH-nee-uhnz

Brothers and sisters:
Rejoice always. **Pray without ceasing**.
In all circumstances **give thanks**,
  for this is the **will of God** for you in **Christ Jesus**.
Do not quench the Spirit.
Do not **despise prophetic utterances**.
Test everything; retain what is good.
Refrain from every kind of **evil**.

In this teaching text, Paul shares some dos and don'ts of the Christian life. After each phrase, pause to let the assembly absorb the instruction.

Pause to introduce the second section: God's promises to us.

May the God of peace make you **perfectly holy**
  and may you entirely, spirit, soul, and body,
    be preserved blameless for the **coming** of our **Lord**
      Jesus Christ.
The one who calls you is **faithful**,
  and he will also accomplish it.

READING II Today's second reading continues the themes of rejoicing and thanksgiving. Paul commands us with a series of imperatives: "Rejoice always," "Pray without ceasing," and "In all circumstances give thanks." In the verses preceding this passage, Paul emphasized aspects of our relationship with other people but here the focus is completely on our relationship with God. Through each of these exhortations, Paul highlights three major aspects of prayer: adoration, petition, and thanksgiving. It is by engaging in adoration, petition, and thanksgiving that God accomplishes his will for us.

It is important to keep in mind that the exhortation to offer thanksgiving "*in* all circumstances" does not mean that we need give thanks *for* all circumstances. Amid our suffering or loss of a loved one, for example, we can continue to give thanks to God while not feeling particularly grateful for the circumstances in which we find ourselves at that time. When we suffer, God is filled with compassion and suffers with us; he does not inflict it upon us but wills our good.

Additionally, Paul models yet another aspect of prayer, this time invocation, beginning with his words "May the God of peace make you perfectly holy." Paul reminds us that God is faithful and continually calls us to holiness and to a life of prayer, which will lead to peace in him. This is what we can give thanks for in all circumstances.

GOSPEL   John 1:6–8, 19–28

A reading from the holy Gospel according to John

A man named **John was sent** from **God**.
He came **for testimony**, to testify to the **light**,
    so that all might **believe through** him.
He was **not** the light,
    but came to testify to the light.

And this is the testimony of John.
When the **Jews** from **Jerusalem sent priests and Levites** to him
    to ask him, "**Who are you?**"
    he admitted and did not deny it,
    but admitted, "**I am not the Christ.**"
So they asked him,
    "**What** are you then? Are you **Elijah**?"
And he said, "I am **not**."
"Are you the Prophet?"
He answered, "No."
So they said to him,
    "**Who are you**, so we can give an **answer** to those who sent us?
What do you have to say for yourself?"
He said:
    "I am *the **voice** of one crying out in the **desert**,*
    *'**Make straight** the way of the Lord,'*
    as Isaiah the prophet said."
Some **Pharisees** were **also sent**.
They asked him,
    "**Why** then do you **baptize**
    if you are not the Christ or Elijah or the Prophet?"

A narrator voice introduces John and sets the scene of the passage.

Notice that some of the religious hierarchy are sent to question John the Baptist.

Use an upward inflection for all of the interrogatives. Continue the questioning with increasing exasperation as the leaders' frustration builds.

The persistent questioning shows the obtuse nature of those seeking answers.

GOSPEL   Today's Gospel highlights our sense of anticipation for Jesus' birth next week. In these verses from the beginning of John's Gospel, we hear more about who John the Baptist is, or is not, with tantalizing allusions to Jesus. First of all, John's role is described as being sent from God to "testify to the light." John is clearly characterized as "not the light," thus highlighting Jesus as the light to whom John is a witness. This is reinforced later in the Gospel when Jesus states, "I am the light of the world" (John 8:12).

If John's role is to testify, then we must reflect on the content of his testimony. It is about the one whose sandals John is "not worthy to untie." It is important to keep in mind that untying sandals was a servant's task. This statement gains significance when we see that John not being worthy of such a lowly task would be shocking to those around him who were asking if he was either the Christ, Elijah, or the Prophet. They mention here three figures who play a prominent role in their religious understanding. They wait in hope for the Messiah (the Christ) to restore the people and bring about the kingdom of God. Elijah, a major prophet in ancient Israel, was thought to return at the end of times, which the people were also anticipating. And the reference to the "Prophet" is to the long-expected prophet-like-Moses promised in Deuteronomy 18:15. Thus, John is confused for long-awaited, important,

John the Baptist's humble attitude remains steadfast. Reflect on your own attitude as you approach Jesus in the Eucharist.

John answered them,
   "I baptize with **water**;
   but there is **one** among you whom **you do not recognize**,
   the one who is coming after me,
      whose sandal strap I am not worthy to untie."
This happened in Bethany across the Jordan,
   where John was baptizing.

and noteworthy figures, yet John says there is another greater than he who is coming. So much greater, in fact, that he is not even worthy to be this person's servant!

   Like the crowds, we are left with a heightened sense of expectation and hope by the end of this Gospel reading. We remain in joyful expectation of the birth of the light of the world, Jesus Christ, in a little over a week. M.B.

DECEMBER 24, 2023

FOURTH SUNDAY
OF ADVENT

LECTIONARY #11

READING I 2 Samuel 7:1–5, 8b–12, 14a, 16

A reading from the second Book of Samuel

When **King David** was settled in his **palace**,
    and the Lord had given him **rest** from his **enemies**
        on every side,
    he said to **Nathan the prophet**,
    "Here I am living in a house of cedar,
    while the **ark of God dwells in a tent**!"
Nathan answered the king,
    "**Go**, **do** whatever you have in mind,
    for the **Lord is with you**."
But **that night** the **Lord spoke** to Nathan and said:
    "Go, tell my servant David, 'Thus says the Lord:
    Should you build me a house to dwell in?

"'It was I who **took you** from the **pasture**
    and from the care of the flock
    to be **commander** of my **people Israel**.
I have been **with you** wherever you went,
    and I have **destroyed all your enemies** before you.
And I will **make you famous** like the great ones of the earth.
I will fix a place for my people Israel;
    I will plant them so that they may dwell in their place
    without further disturbance.

READING I Today's reading describes the establishment of the Davidic dynasty. After years of struggle and fighting, David has finally attained relative peace as king of Israel, yet this peace was granted to him by God himself: "the Lord had given him rest from his enemies on every side." This statement is important for understanding God's pronouncements to David a few verses later. It reminds us that all that David has achieved thus far has been secured by God himself and should not be attributed to David's credit.

David, while pious, lost sight of this fact, as seen in his concern to build a house (meaning a temple) for the ark of God. Although the prophet Nathan originally sanctions David's plans, he later receives a divine message for David that changes everything. God's words to David remind him that it is God who makes a place for his people and not vice versa. God begins with a rhetorical question which, by the end of the message, we know should be answered in the negative. God reminds David and us that he is the one who called David from his task as a shepherd in a field to rule over

Israel. Furthermore, God reaffirms that he has constantly been with David, guiding him and guaranteeing his victories.

God does not only speak of his past care for David, but he also goes on to assure David of his continued presence in years to come, not only with David but all of Israel. He begins by stating that he will make a place for his people, which is consistent with God's past interventions with David. Also in keeping with past actions, God says he will give Israel rest from all their enemies.

16

An intimate filial relationship is being established. It is echoed in the responsorial psalm.

Neither shall the **wicked** continue to **afflict them** as they did
of old,
since the time I first appointed judges over my people Israel.
I will **give you rest** from all your enemies.
The LORD also reveals to you
that he will establish a house for you.
And when your time comes and you **rest** with your ancestors,
I will **raise up** your heir after you, sprung from your loins,
and I will make his kingdom firm.
I will be a father to him,
and he shall **be a son** to me.
Your house and your kingdom **shall endure forever** before me;
your throne shall stand firm forever.'"

For meditation and context:

RESPONSORIAL PSALM   Psalm 89:2–3, 4–5, 27, 29 (2a)

R. For ever I will sing the goodness of the Lord.

The promises of the LORD I will sing forever;
through all generations my mouth shall
proclaim your faithfulness.
For you have said, "My kindness is
established forever";
in heaven you have confirmed
your faithfulness.

"I have made a covenant with my chosen one,
I have sworn to David my servant:
forever will I confirm your posterity
and establish your throne for
all generations."

"He shall say of me, 'You are my father,
my God, the rock, my savior.'
Forever I will maintain my kindness
toward him,
and my covenant with him stands firm."

Finally, we have God's promise to David to establish not only his rule, but also his family line. When God says he will make a house for David, "house" in this context means "dynasty." Thus, the Davidic dynasty is established with God promising to be with David's heir, describing their relationship as that between father and son.

We are reminded today that God makes a place for us as he did for David and for his people, Israel. Our salvation is secured by God alone and not through any merit of our own. Like David, we are blessed by God's continued presence in our lives.

On this Fourth Sunday of Advent, we are on the verge of celebrating Jesus' birth as the fulfilment of God's promises to David. Jesus fulfills the promises God makes in this reading, as he is the temple of God that is raised again in three days and is from the house of David, the heir whose father is God.

READING II This doxology (a hymn of praise to God) from Romans marks the conclusion of Paul's letter and echoes themes found throughout the letter such as the call to an "obedience of faith." Other themes from the letter highlighted in

this passage are God's power, God strengthening believers, the Gospel (Good News), God's revelation manifested, prophetic writings, and the only, wise God.

Paul sees the revelation of the Gospel as the pinnacle of salvation history. Paul particularly praises God for manifesting salvation through Jesus Christ. It is Jesus who reveals that which has been both long-hidden and communicated in the prophetic writings. In the first reading from 2 Samuel, we heard of Nathan's prophetic message to David that is completely fulfilled only in Jesus. This is just one of the prophetic

READING II   Romans 16:25–27

A reading from the Letter of Saint Paul to the Romans

Brothers and sisters:
To him who can **strengthen** you,
    according to **my gospel** and the **proclamation of Jesus Christ**,
    according to the **revelation of the mystery** kept secret
        for long ages
    but now manifested through the prophetic writings and,
    according to the command of the eternal God,
    made known to all nations to bring about the **obedience**
        of faith,
    to the only **wise** God, through Jesus Christ
    be **glory forever** and ever. Amen.

God's new revelation in Christ is articulated in each phrase that begins with the word "according."

The revelation of God's promise of salvation is being made known to all peoples.

GOSPEL   Luke 1:26–38

A reading from the holy Gospel according to Luke

The **angel Gabriel** was **sent from God**
    to a town of Galilee called **Nazareth**,
    to a **virgin betrothed** to a man named **Joseph**,
    of the house of David,
    and the virgin's name was **Mary**.
And coming to her, he said,
    "**Hail, full of grace! The Lord is with you.**"
But she was greatly **troubled** at what was said
    and pondered what sort of greeting this might be.
Then the angel said to her,
    "**Do not be afrai**d, Mary,
    for you have found **favor** with God.

Resist the temptation to rush through this familiar reading.

Clearly distinguish which character is speaking: narrator, angel, or Mary.

Familiar words from the Hail Mary prayer can be heard here.

The narrator voice should reflect Mary's "troubled" spirit.

---

writings that demonstrates God's salvific design laid out and "kept secret for long ages." The full extent of God's words to David remained a mystery until Jesus' coming. Through Jesus' birth, life, death, and resurrection (the paschal mystery), God's plan of salvation is revealed and made evident "to all nations."

While the first reading speaks of God's salvific plan for David and Israel, the second reading broadens the recipients of God's salvation to all humanity. Paul notes that God has commanded everything through his wisdom to bring us all to faith. As we

prepare to celebrate Christmas tomorrow, we remember that it is God who strengthens us in our faith. Today we join Paul in his doxology, praising God for his providential care of us in bringing about our salvation through his Son, Jesus Christ.

GOSPEL   The angel's announcement to Mary in today's Gospel reading echoes and builds upon the themes found in the first and second reading, those of the fulfillment of God's plan of salvation and the call for a response of an obedience of faith. One of the first things we learn

about Mary is that she is engaged to a man from the lineage of David. Our minds immediately go the first reading, where David's lineage is established and preserved by God. The angel's greeting to Mary likewise echoes God's continual presence with David and his people seen in the first and second readings: "The Lord is with you."

The angel then proceeds to lay out God's plan for all humanity to bring them back into right relationship with him. In revealing God's plan, the angel also describes Jesus in no uncertain terms. He will be "great," "Son of the Most High,"

Use a strong upward inflection to reflect Mary's bewilderment.

Mary's response is a profound statement of trust. Pause to let the significance of Mary's "yes" resonate before ending with the narrator voice announcing the angel's departure.

"Behold, you will **conceive** in your womb and bear a son,
  and you shall **name him Jesus**.
He **will be great** and will be called **Son of the Most High**,
  and the Lord God will **give** him the **throne** of David
    his father,
  and he will **rule** over the house of Jacob forever,
  and of his **kingdom** there will be **no end**."
But Mary said to the angel,
  "**How can this be**,
  since I have **no relations** with a man?"
And the angel said to her in reply,
  "The **Holy Spirit will come upon you**,
  and the power of the Most High will overshadow you.
Therefore the **child** to be **born**
  will be called **holy**, the **Son of God**.
And behold, **Elizabeth**, your relative,
  has also conceived a son in her **old age**,
  and this is the sixth month for her who was called **barren**;
  for **nothing will be impossible for God**."
Mary said, "**Behold, I am the handmaid of the Lord**.
May it be done to me **according to your word**."
Then the angel departed from her.

"holy," and "Son of God," as well as the recipient of the Davidic throne. With these words, we see the fulfillment of God's promises to David recorded in 2 Samuel 7 and alluded to in Romans, from the inheritance of David's throne to the filial relationship with God.

As with David, God's future actions in this reading are confirmed by his previous acts on behalf of his people. The angel's pronouncement of the miracle of Elizabeth's pregnancy is a sign to Mary that God has and will continue to have mercy on his people. It also serves as evidence of God's power and might in order to affirm that "nothing will be impossible for God." Thus reassured, Mary gives her ready assent to her role in God's plan that is not only for her but for all humanity.

Mary's yes to God points to her "obedience of faith" to which we are all called. Mary is the first human to await the proximate birth of Christ and the ushering in of salvation. For a short while, she is the only one who knows the extent of God's faithfulness in fulfilling his promises to David and his people. As such, her response to the angel serves as a model for our own response to the birth of Christ. Like Mary, we should assent to God's salvific activity in our own lives, entrusting our entire being to God's plan and providential care. In so doing, our entire life can become a doxology that continually recognizes and praises the glory of God and his power manifested in our lives. M.B.

THE NATIVITY OF THE LORD (CHRISTMAS): VIGIL

LECTIONARY #13

READING I   Isaiah 62:1–5

A reading from the Book of the Prophet Isaiah

> For **Zion's sake I** will **not** be **silent**,
>   for Jerusalem's sake I will not be quiet,
> until her **vindication shines** forth like the dawn
>   and her victory like a burning torch.
>
> **Nations** shall **behold** your vindication,
>   and all the **kings** your **glory**;
> you shall be **called** by a **new name**
>   pronounced by the mouth of the LORD.
> You shall be a **glorious crown** in the hand of the LORD,
>   a royal diadem held by your God.
> **No more** shall people call you "**Forsaken**,"
>   or your land "**Desolate**,"
> but you shall be called "My **Delight**,"
>   and your land "**Espoused**."
> For the LORD **delights in you**
>   and makes your land his **spouse**.
> As a young man marries a virgin,
>   your Builder shall marry you;
> and as a bridegroom rejoices in his bride
>   so shall your **God rejoice in you**.

Isaiah = ī-ZAY-uh

Bring the tempo and tone of sharing exciting news to this reading.

When reading a couplet, stress the first stanza—which is a new idea—and subdue the second.

God is making something so glorious a new name is needed.

diadem = DĪ-uh-dem = crown

With great joy announce that God delights in us. Deliver this line looking directly at the assembly.

There are options for today's readings. Contact your parish staff to learn which readings will be used.

READING I Today's first reading emphasizes God's promises of restoration to Jerusalem/Zion. Isaiah speaks to a people scarred by their experience of the Babylonian exile. The language in this passage highlights the positive shift in the people's lives and their relationship with God. From being called "Forsaken" and their land "Desolate" during the exilic period, they will now be known as "My Delight" and their land "Espoused." These new names point toward the restoration of Jerusalem/Zion's glory. Her glory, as represented by the "glorious crown" and "royal diadem," is given by God and not acquired by her own merit. Additionally, the "royal diadem" alludes to the Davidic monarchy, further reinforcing God's rule in his kingdom.

Jerusalem/Zion's restoration is on such a grand scale that all the nations and kings will recognize the legitimacy of her vindication and glorification. In this way, Jerusalem/Zion becomes a beacon to the other nations, leading them to recognize the power of God, who is the sole source of Jerusalem/Zion's glory. The references to light "shining" and "burning" become synonymous with salvation described as "vindication" and the glory given by God alone.

In this passage, Isaiah not only states the divine intent to restore Israel, but he also clearly indicates the intimate level of connection between God and his people. The metaphor utilized in this passage is of a marital relationship where the groom/God rejoices in his bride/God's people. Furthermore, the image of Jerusalem/Zion

For meditation and context:

RESPONSORIAL PSALM   Psalm 89:4–5, 16–17, 27, 29 (2a)

R. For ever I will sing the goodness of the Lord.

I have made a covenant with my
    chosen one,
    I have sworn to David my servant:
forever will I confirm your posterity
    and establish your throne for
    all generations.

Blessed the people who know the
    joyful shout;
in the light of your countenance,
    O Lord, they walk.

At your name they rejoice all the day,
    and through your justice they are exalted.

He shall say of me, "You are my father,
    my God, the rock, my savior."
Forever I will maintain my kindness
    toward him,
    and my covenant with him stands firm.

READING II   Acts of the Apostles 13:16–17, 22–25

A reading from the Acts of the Apostles

When **Paul** reached Antioch in Pisidia and entered the **synagogue**,
    he stood up, motioned with his hand, and said,
    "Fellow Israelites and you others who are God-fearing, **listen**.
The **God** of this people Israel **chose our ancestors**
    and **exalted** the people during their sojourn in the land
        of Egypt.
With **uplifted arm** he **led** them out of it.
Then he **removed Saul** and **raised up David** as **king**;
    of him he testified,
    'I have found **David**, son of Jesse, a man after my own heart;
    he will **carry out my** every wish.'
From this man's **descendants** God, according to his promise,
    has brought to Israel **a savior, Jesus**.
John heralded his coming by proclaiming a baptism of repentance
    to all the people of Israel;
    and as John was completing his course, he would say,
    'What do you suppose that I am? **I am not he**.
Behold, **one is coming** after me;
    I am not worthy to unfasten the sandals of his feet.'"

Antioch = AN-tee-ahk

Pisidia = pih-SID-ee-uh

Imagine Paul assertively entering the synagogue, motioning for silence, and directing this teaching text to Jews and Gentiles alike.

sojourn = SOH-jern (exile)

Paul makes historical connections throughout, this time more recently with the ministry of John the Baptist. The Gospel will continue the theme of connecting the past to the present.

---

receiving her crown from God likewise reinforces the bridal imagery, as crowns were a part of the adornments worn by both the bride and the groom.

This reading is appropriate as we celebrate the birth of the Messiah who restores humanity to a proper relationship with God. Jesus, son of David, Son of God, reconciles us with God and makes us a new people. The image of Jesus as bridegroom and the Church as bride likewise corresponds with the intimate relationship between God and his people seen in this passage. As we rejoice at the coming of Christ into the world, God similarly rejoices in us in our restored state, made possible through Christ and generously given to us by God. As the bride of Christ, we share in the light of salvation that is Christ. By means of our baptism and discipleship in Christ, we become beacons of light drawing others to God and salvation.

READING II   Paul's address to the Antiochians in Acts of the Apostles continues the theme of salvation for all nations, including both Jews and God-fearing Gentiles. These "God-fearers" were those who frequented the synagogues but were not Israelites. They were familiar with the Jewish Scripture and remained obedient to its ethical commandments. As such, they, too, recognized Israel's history as it was summarized by Paul in this passage. Paul's summary serves as a reminder of God's past interventions in human history, confirming and affirming his continued salvific actions in Jesus Christ.

Additionally, Paul reinforces the belief that Jesus is the fulfillment of God's promise to David in 2 Samuel 7:12b–14a: "I will raise up your offspring after you, sprung

GOSPEL   Matthew 1:1–25

A reading from the holy Gospel according to Matthew

The book of the **genealogy** of **Jesus** Christ,
    the son of **David**, the son of **Abraham**.

Abraham became the **father** of **Isaac**,
    Isaac the father of **Jacob**,
    Jacob the father of **Judah** and **his brothers**.
Judah became the father of **Perez** and **Zerah**,
    whose **mother** was **Tamar**.
Perez became the **father** of **Hezron**,
    Hezron the father of **Ram**,
    Ram the father of **Amminadab**.
Amminadab became the father of **Nahshon**,
    Nahshon the father of **Salmon**,
    Salmon the father of **Boaz**,
    whose **mother** was **Rahab**.
Boaz became the father of **Obed**,
    whose mother was **Ruth**.
Obed became the father of **Jesse**,
    Jesse the father of **David the king**.

David became the father of **Solomon**,
    whose mother had been the **wife of Uriah**.
Solomon became the father of **Rehoboam**,
    Rehoboam the father of **Abijah**,
    Abijah the father of **Asaph**.
Asaph became the father of **Jehoshaphat**,
    Jehoshaphat the father of **Joram**,
    Joram the father of **Uzziah**.
Uzziah became the father of Jotham,
    Jotham the father of Ahaz,
    Ahaz the father of **Hezekiah**.

Practice this reading repeatedly to master the ancient names. Stress the first mention and subdue the second.

Build with excitement as you read through the generations and then slow to announce the birth of Jesus. The change in tempo will draw attention to the most important part of the genealogy. Matthew is providing evidence that Jesus is the fulfillment of the Jewish tradition.

Judah = JOO-duh
Perez = PEE-rihz or PAYR-ez
Zerah = ZEER-uh
Tamar = TAY-mahr
Hezron = HEZ-ruhn
Ram = ram
Amminadab = uh-MIN-uh-dab
Nahshon = NAH-shon or NAH-shuhn
Salmon = SAL-muhn
Boaz = BOH-az
Rahab = RAY-hab
Obed = OH-bihd

Jesse = JES-ee

Solomon = SOL-uh-muhn
Uriah = yoo-RĪ-uh
Rehoboam = ree-huh-BOH-uhm
Abijah = uh-BĪ-juh
Asaph = AY-saf
Jehoshaphat = jeh-HOH-shuh-fat
Joram = JOHR-uhm
Uzziah = uh-ZĪ-uh
Jotham = JOH-thuhm
Ahaz = AY-haz
Hezekiah = hehz-eh-KĪ-uh

---

from your loins, and I will establish his kingdom. He it is who shall build a house for my name, and I will establish his royal throne forever. I will be a father to him, and he shall be a son to me." Jesus is the long-awaited Messiah, the son of David. God's fidelity to his promises is a central theme of Acts of the Apostles and is a source of hope and assurance to both Jews and God-fearing Gentiles.

    Another important aspect of Paul's summary is the distinction between John the Baptist and Jesus. While John the Baptist is the prophet who heralds the imminent arrival of the Messiah, it is Jesus who is the realization of God's promise to David and all God's people. John the Baptist preaches a baptism of repentance to prepare Jews and God-fearing Gentiles to be ready when they encounter Jesus. If they are not ready, they run the risk of being set aside as Saul was set aside in favor of David. Thus, John the Baptist's baptism is not the same as baptism in Jesus' name, which restores humanity to God and bestows both life and spirit upon the recipient.

    Like the Antiochians in today's second reading, we hear Paul's summary of salvation history and rejoice in the Good News of the coming of Jesus and the kingdom of God. We spent Advent mindful of the need to repent that we might be receptive to Jesus' presence and message. Now, at the celebration of Christmas, we move from repentance to rejoicing at Jesus' birth and the fulfillment of God's salvific activity in human history. But it does not end here. By virtue of our baptism, we are equipped to proclaim to others God's goodness and fidelity to his promises, just as Paul does in this reading.

Manasseh = muh-NAS-uh

Amos = AY-m*s

Josiah = joh-SĪ-uh

Jechoniah = jek-oh-NĪ-uh

Shealtiel = shee-AL-tee-uhl

Zerubbabel = zuh-ROOB-uh-b*l

Abiud = uh-BĪ-uhd

Eliakim = ee-LĪ-uh-kihm

Azor = AZ-zohr

Zadok = ZAD-uhk or ZAY-dok

Achim = AY-kihm

Eliud = ee-LĪ-UHD

Eleazar = el-ee-AY-zehr

Matthan = MAT-uhn

Hezekiah became the father of **Manasseh**,
    Manasseh the father of **Amos**,
    Amos the father of **Josiah**.
Josiah became the father of **Jechoniah** and his brothers
    at the **time** of the **Babylonian exile**.

After the Babylonian exile,
    Jechoniah became the father of Shealtiel,
    Shealtiel the father of Zerubbabel,
    Zerubbabel the father of **Abiud**.
Abiud became the father of **Eliakim**,
    Eliakim the father of **Azor**,
    Azor the father of **Zadok**.
Zadok became the father of Achim,
    Achim the father of Eliud,
    Eliud the father of **Eleazar**.
Eleazar became the father of Matthan,
    Matthan the father of **Jacob**,
    Jacob the **father of Joseph**, the **husband of Mary**.
Of her was **born Jesus** who is **called the Christ**.

Thus the **total number** of **generations**
    from Abraham to David
    is **fourteen** generations;
    from **David** to the Babylonian **exile**,
    fourteen generations;
    from the Babylonian exile to the **Christ**,
    fourteen generations.

The genealogy ends and the narrative starts. Pause before the scene change.

Now [this is how the **birth** of **Jesus** Christ came about.
When his **mother Mary** was **betrothed** to **Joseph**,
    but **before they lived together**,
    she was found **with child** through the **Holy Spirit**.
Joseph her husband, since he was a **righteous** man,
    yet **unwilling to expose her to shame**,
    decided to **divorce** her quietly. »

GOSPEL   The genealogy in today's Gospel announces who Jesus is. In the very first line we see that Jesus is the Christ, the Greek rendering of "messiah." Jesus as the Messiah is further reinforced by his identification as son of David. "Son of David" was a standard messianic title connected with God's promises to David in 2 Samuel 7 (as mentioned in the commentary on today's second reading). This title connects Jesus to his Jewish ancestry and the foundational covenant with David that Jesus fulfills.

While the identification "son of David" points to Jesus as a true Israelite, the reference to Jesus as "son of Abraham" points to the salvation of the Gentiles as part of God's plan. Abraham was a Gentile by birth and is described as the father of many nations in later Jewish literature. Scripture notes that through Abraham, all the nations of the earth will be blessed (for example, in Genesis 12:3; 18:18 and Matthew 28:19). Furthermore, Paul sees Abraham as the father of all who have faith (as in Romans 4:1–25 and Galatians 3:6–29). Matthew's genealogy of Jesus is a continuation not

only of biblical history, but also of salvation history. It is proof of the legitimacy of Jesus' identification as "son of David" and "son of Abraham."

After the genealogy there is a description of Jesus' birth, beginning with the angel's proclamation to Joseph in a dream. Thus, the second half of today's Gospel focuses on Jesus' identity as "son of God." Joseph is addressed as "son of David" by the angel, further establishing Jesus' messianic connection through his foster father. It is in Joseph's dream that another name is attributed to Jesus: Emmanuel ("God is with

Read this phrase with intentionality. Listeners will hear the echo of the same words from the angel at the annunciation.

When the angel finishes, use a steady even tone for the narrator. Use a strong voice for the prophet's words and return to the narrator voice to conclude.

Such was his intention when, behold,
    the **angel of the Lord appeared** to him in a **dream** and said,
    "Joseph, son of David,
    do not be afraid to take **Mary** your **wife** into your home.
For it is **through the Holy Spirit**
    that this child has been conceived in her.
She will bear a son and you are to **name him Jesus**,
    because he will **save his people** from their **sins**."
All this took place to fulfill
    what the Lord had said through the prophet:
      Behold, the virgin shall conceive and bear a son,
        and they shall name him **Emmanuel**,
    which means **"God is with us."**
When Joseph awoke,
    he did as the angel of the Lord had commanded him
    and **took his wife into his home.**
He had **no relations** with her **until she bore a son**,
    and he **named him Jesus**.]

[Shorter: Matthew 1:18–25 (see brackets)]

us"). The emphasis on this name is consistent with Matthew's theme of God's continued presence in the Church until the end of time (Matthew 28:20) and corresponds with Paul's insistence on God's continued fidelity to his promises in the second reading.

Adding to the way this passage continues to ground the circumstances of Jesus' birth in salvation history, Joseph's dream matches the Old Testament annunciation pattern: "behold," announcement, child's name, further details of child's identity (see Genesis 17:19, 1 Chronicles 22:9-10, 1 Kings 13:2, and Isaiah 7:14). In fact, the scriptural

quote that is made in this Gospel reading, regarding a virgin who will conceive a son named Emmanuel, comes from Isaiah 7:14 in the Greek Septuagint, which is the source of most of the Old Testament quotes and allusions in the New Testament.

This passage also highlights the way Joseph's righteousness minimizes any scandal associated with Mary's unexpected pregnancy. This righteousness is reinforced when Joseph "did as the angel of the Lord had commanded." This language also reflects a typical Old Testament fulfillment formula.

Joseph's trust in the angel's message and in God's past interventions in human history lays the groundwork for his obedience to the angel's command. In a similar way, we are called to be like Joseph in receiving the Good News today. Like Joseph, we are aware of God's previous salvific actions on behalf of his people. These past actions are foundational for understanding how God continues his plan of salvation in Jesus Christ. Our confidence in God's fidelity to his promises provides the basis for our rejoicing in the birth of our Lord Jesus Christ today. M.B.

THE NATIVITY OF THE LORD (CHRISTMAS): NIGHT

LECTIONARY #14

READING I   Isaiah 9:1–6

A reading from the Book of the Prophet Isaiah

Isaiah = ī-ZAY-uh

Emphasize the contrasts of darkness and light.

> The **people** who **walked** in **darkness**
>   have seen a great **light**;
> upon those who dwelt in the land of gloom
>   a light has shone.
> You have brought them **abundant joy**
>   and great rejoicing,
> as they rejoice before you as at the harvest,
>   as people make merry when dividing spoils.
> For the **yoke** that **burdened** them,
>   the pole on their shoulder,
> and the rod of their taskmaster
>   you have smashed, as on the day of Midian.
> For every boot that tramped in battle,
>   every cloak rolled in blood,
>   will be burned as fuel for flames.
> For a **child is born to us**, a **son is given** us;
>   upon his shoulder **dominion rests**.
> They name him **Wonder-Counselor**, **God-Hero**,
>   **Father-Forever**, **Prince of Peace**. »

Emphasize "yoke" and subdue the synonyms, "pole" and "rod."

Midian = MID-ee-uhn

Change the tone from the images of oppression and war to reflect joy and amazement at the dawn of a new day for Israel.

These are descriptors of the ideal king of the future.

There are options for today's readings. Contact your parish staff to learn which readings will be used.

READING I In this reading, Isaiah speaks of a people walking in darkness who now see a "great light." During the time of Isaiah, the "darkness" referred to the exilic period, and the people addressed were the survivors of the Babylonian conquest and exile. Now, the people experience a restoration of their land and of their relationship with God. This restora-tion, brought about by God, is the reason for their rejoicing, which is depicted in agricultural terms and images of military victory. For example, the reference to the "day of Midian" could be an allusion to Gideon's victory in Judges 7:1–25. Although God decreased the size of Gideon's army from 32,000 to 300 men, they were still able to defeat the Midianites and didn't even strike a single blow! The victory belonged solely to God's power and might. In a similar way, the restoration of the people living in darkness can only be attributed to God's fidelity and power. The last line of today's reading reinforces the fact that God is the ultimate source of all these great occurrences.

The Gospels refer to this passage and its themes in connection with Jesus' salvific activity. In Luke 1:78–79, Zechariah prophe-sies concerning what God will do for his people through Jesus Christ, ultimately leading the people to the path of peace. Likewise, Matthew cites these verses at the beginning of Jesus' ministry in Galilee when he preached that the kingdom of God is at hand (Matthew 4:15–16). Jesus is the "great light" that restores humanity to a

To aid in your spiritual preparation to proclaim, you can listen to the first part of Handel's *Messiah* (that focuses on Advent and Christmas Time). Some of the lyrics are directly drawn from today's Scripture passage.

His **dominion is vast**
   and **forever peaceful**,
from David's throne, and over his kingdom,
   which he confirms and sustains
by **judgment** and **justice**,
   both **now and forever**.
The **zeal** of the LORD of hosts will do this!

For meditation and context:

RESPONSORIAL PSALM   Psalm 96:1–2, 2–3, 11–12, 13 (Luke 2:11)

R. Today is born our Savior, Christ the Lord.

Sing to the LORD a new song;
   sing to the LORD, all you lands.
Sing to the LORD; bless his name.

Announce his salvation, day after day.
   Tell his glory among the nations;
   among all peoples, his wondrous deeds.

Let the heavens be glad and the
   earth rejoice;
   let the sea and what fills it resound;
   let the plains be joyful and all that is
     in them!
Then shall all the trees of the forest exult.

They shall exult before the LORD,
   for he comes;
   for he comes to rule the earth.
He shall rule the world with justice
   and the peoples with his constancy.

READING II   Titus 2:11–14

Titus = Tī-tuhs
Announce the reading carefully; readings from Titus don't occur that frequently.

Notice the inclusivity of God's grace. Read with energy and excitement without speeding.

Feel the abundance of God's grace; his salvific love purifies us so we can be his own.

A reading from the Letter of Saint Paul to Titus

Beloved:
The **grace of God** has **appeared**, **saving all**
   and training us to **reject godless ways** and **worldly desire**s
   and to **live temperately, justly,** and **devoutly** in this age,
   as we **await** the blessed hope,
   the appearance of the glory of our great God
   and savior Jesus Christ,
   who **gave himself** for **us** to **deliver** us from all lawlessness
   and to **cleanse** for himself a people as his own,
   eager to **do** what is **good**.

proper relationship with God. Peace comes to the people when righteous justice prevails, which is brought about by Jesus.

The imagery of darkness and light in this reading is especially powerful as it is assigned to our celebration of Jesus' nativity at Mass during the night. We celebrate the birth of our Lord Jesus Christ who continues to shine his light in our lives. Like the ancient Israelites returning from exile, we rejoice in the fulfillment of God's plan of salvation and our restoration to himself. He alone is our light and our life.

READING II   The second chapter of Titus focuses on how Christians in different states of life should live out the Gospel. The verses that we read today provide a foundation for living the Christian life of virtue. The reason for this way of living is founded on God's works on behalf of his people, as demonstrated and fulfilled in the person of Jesus and his salvific life, death, resurrection, and ascension. Jesus gave himself over to cleanse us and deliver us from "all lawlessness." To be delivered from lawlessness is to experience freedom.

This freedom is the freedom of love that is exhibited through loving service to others.

Not only are we saved by God, but we are also trained by him in this freedom of love so that we might reject evil ways and desires. This "training" leads to three positive effects that pertain to us, our relationship with others, and our relationship with God. First, we learn self-control through temperate living. Second, we act "justly" in relation to others. Finally, we act "devoutly" in our worship, building up our relationship with God. God's love for us empowers us to

GOSPEL   Luke 2:1–14

A reading from the holy Gospel according to Luke

In those days a **decree** went out from **Caesar Augustus**
    that the whole world should be enrolled.
This was the first enrollment,
    when Quirinius was governor of Syria.
So all went to be enrolled, each to his own town.
And **Joseph** too went up from **Galilee** from the town of Nazareth
    to Judea, to the city of **David** that is called **Bethlehem**,
    because he was of the house and family of David,
    to **be enrolled with Mary**, his betrothed, who was **with child**.
While they were there,
    the **time came** for her to have her **child**,
    and she gave birth to her **firstborn** son.
She wrapped him in swaddling clothes and laid him in a manger,
    because there was no room for them in the inn.

Now there were **shepherds** in that region **living in the fields**
    and keeping the **night watch** over their flock.
The angel of the **Lord appeared** to them
    and the **glory** of the Lord **shone around them**,
    and they were struck with **great fear**.
The angel said to them,
    "**Do not be afraid**;
    for behold, I proclaim to you good news of **great joy**
    that will be for all the people.
For today in the city of David
    a **savior has been born** for you **who is Christ** and Lord. »

Caesar Augustus = SEE-zehr aw-GUHS-tuhs

Avoid "telegraphing" the assumption that everyone knows the outcome of the story. Read it with fresh energy for this time and place. Scripture is ever new.

Quirinius = kwih-RIN-ee-uhs

Judea = joo-DEE-uh or joo-DAY-uh

Add tenderness to your tone as you describe this scene.

Pause between the multiple scene changes.

Although it is common for people in Scripture to respond to the presence of angels with fear, don't gloss over this reaction.

The angel's voice should be reassuring.

do good deeds: loving God, others, and ourselves as we should. This call to do good emphasizes that we are not merely passive recipients of God's love, but that salvation enables us to actively do good. In rejecting evil and worldly desires, we make a choice in light of the gift of salvation and love that we receive from God. The celebration of Jesus' birth commemorates this salvific gift. When we recall God's immense love for us in sending his Son to save us, it inspires our calling to show God's love to others.

GOSPEL   In Luke's account of Jesus' birth, he is careful to highlight the global impact of Jesus' birth by situating it within the context of a census of the "whole world." While the exact historical data does not neatly match up (Herod died in 4 BC while Augustus reigned from 27 BC to AD 14 and Quirinius was governor from AD 6–7), the significance of including these figures is to stress the historical nature of Jesus' birth. Jesus comes to the world at a discrete moment in history, at the fullness of time, to bring salvation to humanity. Luke's accounting of time could also be a corrective to the view of Augustus as a savior and a god, as he is described in some Greek inscriptions. Instead, it is Jesus who is the true savior of the world.

Along with situating Jesus' birth in global history, Luke also situates his birth within Israelite history with the references to Joseph as a descendant of David. Reporting that Joseph is of "the house and family of David" accomplishes two things. First, Luke provides the reason for Joseph and Mary to travel to Bethlehem, the city of David. Second, he also connects Jesus, as the adopted son of Joseph, to God's promise

What great imagery a "sudden" multitude of celestial beings evokes. Their message should be read strongly to help the assembly recognize the words joyfully sung earlier in the liturgy.

And this will be a sign for you:
    you will find an infant wrapped in swaddling clothes
    and lying in a manger."
And **suddenly** there was a **multitude of the heavenly host**
    with the angel,
    praising God and saying:
  "**Glory to God in the highest**
    and on **earth peace** to those on **whom his favor rests**."

of establishing the Davidic throne and the coming of the Messiah (2 Samuel 7:12–16).

Furthermore, the description of Joseph and Mary's poverty highlights an important theme in Luke's Gospel: the "Great Reversal," in which the lowly are brought high and the lofty are brought low. This theme continues with the annunciation of Jesus' birth to the shepherds. They are considered lowly; however, they are the first to receive the Good News of Jesus' birth. The shepherds provide yet another connection to David, who was a shepherd before being anointed as king of Israel and thus a shepherd to the entire nation of Israel.

The annunciation of the angels to the shepherds includes most of the elements of the typical Old Testament pattern: angel appears, shepherds fear, message is conveyed with assurances to not fear, and a sign is given as assurance of the message. The sign given is Jesus himself, "an infant wrapped in swaddling clothes and lying in a manger." In this way, Jesus is both the sign and that which is signified, "a savior . . . who is Christ and Lord."

Today, we, like the shepherds, receive the Good News of Jesus' birth and rejoice at the coming of the Christ, our Lord and savior. We also join in the angel's proclamation of "Glory to God in the highest" when we acclaim the Gloria toward the beginning of Mass! M.B.

THE NATIVITY OF THE LORD (CHRISTMAS): DAWN

LECTIONARY #15

READING I Isaiah 62:11–12

A reading from the Book of the Prophet Isaiah

> See, the LORD **proclaims**
>   to the ends of the **earth**:
> say to daughter Zion,
>   **your savior comes**!
> Here is his reward with him,
>   his **recompense** before him.
> They shall be called the **holy people**,
>   the redeemed of the LORD,
> and you shall be called "**Frequented**,"
>   a **city** that is **not forsaken**.

Isaiah = ī-ZAY-uh

Read joyfully!

The assembly will easily associate the prophecy of Isaiah with the incarnation of Christ.

recompense = REK-uhm-pens = compensation for wrongs suffered

"Frequented" is an unlikely term. Think of the holy people as being sought out, no longer ignored.

For meditation and context:

RESPONSORIAL PSALM Psalm 97:1, 6, 11–12

R. A light will shine on us this day: the Lord is born for us.

The LORD is king; let the earth rejoice;
  let the many isles be glad.
The heavens proclaim his justice,
  and all peoples see his glory.

Light dawns for the just;
  and gladness, for the upright of heart.
Be glad in the LORD, you just,
  and give thanks to his holy name.

There are options for today's readings. Contact your parish staff to learn which readings will be used.

READING I | Today's first reading, from Isaiah, describes the joy of God's people upon seeing the coming of their salvation. "Daughter Zion" refers to God's people who have suffered through the Babylonian exile and are now the recipients of the promises of their liberation and restoration. Upon the arrival of the savior, God's people are recognized as holy and

set apart. Their holiness is not an inherent quality; rather, it is a description of their new state as a result of the restoration of their relationship with God. Consequently, all of God's people are called to a life of dedicated service to him. Additionally, the people are now acknowledged to be "the redeemed of the LORD." This further reinforces the fact that the new state of holiness comes from God's salvific act which is freely given to them. As we celebrate Christ's birth today, this reading reminds us that we too are set apart and made holy through Jesus Christ. Like the ancient

Israelites, we rejoice at his coming, recognizing our savior who redeems us.

READING II | In this reading from Titus, Paul highlights God's love and mercy in saving humanity and at the same time connects our salvation to our baptism. Moreover, God's salvific work provides a positive motivation for our behavior as baptized Christians. While we did nothing to merit our salvation, we are still called to live out our renewed life in the Spirit through good works and righteous acts.

Titus = Tī-tuhs
Announce the reading carefully; readings from Titus don't occur that frequently.

Read with joy as we reflect on our justification: we didn't earn it! We received it through God's gift of mercy.

Pay special attention to the commas in this passage. They help to organize Paul's thoughts and your proclamation.

READING II   Titus 3:4–7

A reading from the Letter of Saint Paul to Titus

Beloved:
When the **kindness** and generous **love**
    of God our savior appeared,
not because of any righteous deeds we had done
    but because of his **mercy**,
he saved us through the **bath of rebirth**
    and **renewal** by the **Holy Spirit**,
whom he richly poured out on us
    through Jesus Christ our savior,
so that we might be **justified by his grace**
    and become **heirs** in hope of **eternal life**.

Read this familiar passage with fresh energy.

Distinguish between the voice of the shepherds and the voice of the narrator.

GOSPEL   Luke 2:15–20

A reading from the holy Gospel according to Luke

When the **angels went away** from them to heaven,
    the **shepherds** said to one another,
    "Let us **go**, then, to **Bethlehem**
    to see this thing that has taken place,
    which the **Lord has made known** to us."
So they went in **haste** and **found Mary** and **Joseph**,
    and the **infant lying** in the manger.
When they saw this,
    they made known the **message**
    that had been **told them** about this child.
All who heard it were **amazed**
    by what had been told them by the shepherds.

God's love for us is the perfect model we must follow in loving others.

In this passage, both God and Jesus are referred to as "savior," and the Holy Spirit renews the baptized members of the community. Thus, Paul emphasizes here the Trinity's role in our salvation and the role of our baptism. He also goes on to tell us the reason for our salvation. Contrary to what some may think, God pours forth his love and salvation on us, not because of anything we have done or might do, but "because of his mercy." His purpose in so doing is that we might "become heirs in

hope of eternal life." God's past interventions in human history lay the foundation for our hope of his continued presence in our lives that leads us to eternal life in him.

GOSPEL   The shepherds in today's Gospel publicly proclaim the Good News of Jesus' birth that they received from the angels. They waste no time in going to see this newborn infant and proclaiming to others what they heard and saw. As they return to work, the shepherds echo the song of the angels glorifying God and giving him praise. The shepherds

present a model of proclaiming the Good News amid their daily tasks.

The shepherds' reaction to the Good News is one of three reactions presented in today's Gospel. The second reaction is that of everyone who heard their proclamation. We are told that they "were amazed" but no further information is provided regarding what they did upon hearing the shepherds' words. This amazement parallels the wonder and astonishment of the people at Zechariah's restored speech in Luke 1:66, when they said, "What, then, will this child be?" While the people do not make

The shepherds found the Holy Family and responded with great joy. Place yourself in this scene: how would the encounter change your evangelizing efforts?

And **Mary kept all these things**,
 reflecting on them in her heart.
Then the shepherds returned,
 glorifying and praising God
 for all they had heard and seen,
 just as it had been told to them.

a similar statement here, Luke clearly implies that a similar question applies in this instance.

The third reaction is Mary's, as she "kept all these things, reflecting on them in her heart." While Mary is the ideal disciple, it is also clear that she does not fully understand the events that are unfolding. Her reaction presents a contrast to that of the shepherds. She models private reflection while the shepherds model public proclamation of the Good News. Mary's reaction also differs from that of the people who are amazed but give no indication of belief.

As seen in her *fiat*, her yes to the angel's proclamation in Luke 1:26–38, and in her canticle in Luke 1:46–55, known today as the Magnificat, Mary trusts and believes in God's continued work in human history.

What is our reaction to the news of Jesus' birth that we celebrate today? Perhaps while we rejoice today, we are simultaneously called to publicly proclaim, privately reflect, and sit in amazed wonder at the Good News we have received. M.B.

THE NATIVITY OF THE LORD (CHRISTMAS): DAY

LECTIONARY #16

READING I   Isaiah 52:7–10

Isaiah = ī-ZAY-uh

With great excitement we proclaim that God is king. Notice the plethora of action words: "bring," "announcing," "bearing," "hark," "shout," and so on.

A reading from the Book of the Prophet Isaiah

How **beautiful** upon the mountains
    are the feet of him who brings **glad tidings**,
announcing peace, bearing good news,
    announcing **salvation**, and saying to Zion,
    "Your God is King!"

Hark! Your **sentinels raise a cry**,
    together they **shout** for joy,
for they see directly, before their eyes,
    the LORD restoring Zion.
Break out together in song,
    O ruins of Jerusalem!
For the LORD **comforts his people**,
    he **redeems** Jerusalem.
The LORD has **bared** his holy **arm**
    in the sight of **all the nations**;
all the ends of the earth will behold
    the **salvation** of our God.

The kingdom is universal, not nationalistic or tribal. Emphasizing the last line will help listeners hear it repeated in the responsorial psalm.

There are options for today's readings. Contact your parish staff to learn which readings will be used.

READING I Leading up to the verses in today's reading from Isaiah, the prophet is inviting the people to action following their inactivity during the Babylonian exile. Now they are called upon to witness to God's glory in bringing about their salvation as the messenger announces that "Your God is King!" Isaiah's message is one of peace, goodness, and salvation, all of which are accomplished through God's reign.

Zion's deliverance bears testimony to God's power and mercy. As such, Isaiah encourages the people to rejoice and break into song in light of their approaching restoration. What is interesting here is that the people should sing God's praises in the midst of their ruinous state: "Break out together in song, O ruins of Jerusalem." They are not to wait for their full restoration to begin exalting God's name. Their songs of praise come not from a place of ease and peace but from darkness and desolation. The very knowledge that God *will* redeem them is enough motivation for their great joy. Furthermore, their imminent redemption brings comfort to a people who suffered exile from their homeland.

Along with God's people witnessing to his power as he redeems them, all nations—"all the ends of the earth" in fact—also see and can testify to God's salvific power. In so doing, they are led to recognize the kingship of God over all nations. Thus, God's redemption is not limited to Israel but encompasses all of humanity.

For meditation and context:

RESPONSORIAL PSALM   Psalm 98:1, 2–3, 3–4, 5–6 (3c)

R. All the ends of the earth have seen the saving power of God.

Sing to the LORD a new song,
  for he has done wondrous deeds;
his right hand has won victory for him,
  his holy arm.

The LORD has made his salvation known:
  in the sight of the nations he has
    revealed his justice.
He has remembered his kindness and
    his faithfulness
  toward the house of Israel.

All the ends of the earth have seen
  the salvation by our God.
Sing joyfully to the LORD, all you lands;
  break into song; sing praise.

Sing praise to the LORD with the harp,
  with the harp and melodious song.
With trumpets and the sound of the horn
  sing joyfully before the King, the LORD.

READING II   Hebrews 1:1–6

A reading from the Letter to the Hebrews

Brothers and sisters:
In times past, **God spoke** in **partial** and various ways
  to our ancestors through the **prophets**;
  in these last days, he has spoken to us **through the Son**,
  whom he **made heir** of all things
  and through whom he **created** the **universe**,
    who is the refulgence of his glory,
      the very **imprint** of his being,
    and who **sustains** all things by his mighty word.
    When he had accomplished **purification** from sins,
    he took his seat at **the right hand** of the Majesty on high,
    as far superior to the angels
    as the name he has inherited is more excellent than theirs.

For to which of the angels did God ever say:
  You are my son; *this day I have begotten you?*
Or again:
  I will be a father to him, and he shall be a son to me?
And again, when he leads the firstborn into the world, he says:
  *Let all the **angels** of God **worship him**.*

"Brothers and sisters" is a vocative, a form of address. Use a tone of fondness.

Christ is God's final and complete Word to the world.

refulgence = rih-FUHL-j*nts = radiance or brilliance

Paul is using a bit of humor, exaggerating to make a point.

Today we celebrate the incarnation and birth of Jesus who redeemed all peoples, restoring humanity to a proper relationship with God. It is for this reason that Paul refers to this passage in Romans 10:15 in his exhortation to Christians to proclaim the Good News of Jesus to others. Today, we hear that Good News and receive joy and comfort from the knowledge that we are redeemed in Jesus Christ. In our times of joy and in our times of sorrow, we should break into songs of praise, recognizing that Jesus Christ is our savior and king.

READING II Today's second reading places an emphasis on God's spoken word by contrasting the way God communicated in the past with the way God communicates through Christ. In the past, God spoke through the prophets and now he speaks through his Son, who is greater than the prophets. Whereas God spoke to his people in the past "in partial and various ways," God speaking through his Son is the final word. To reinforce this point, the passage focuses on Jesus' divine majesty, his redemptive work, and his glori-

ous exaltation. Furthermore, it is Jesus' "mighty word" that "sustains all things."

Jesus' three roles come into focus in this passage. Being the final word, Jesus' role as prophet, indeed the ultimate prophet, is emphasized. His role as priest is likewise stressed in his purification of the people from their sins. Finally, Jesus' enthronement "at the right hand of the Majesty on high" calls attention to his role as king, as the authority over all. We have seen how Jesus is superior to other prophets but here it is also clearly stated that he

GOSPEL   John 1:1–18

A reading from the holy Gospel according to John

[In the **beginning was** the Word,
     and the Word was **with** God,
     and the Word **was God**.
He was in the beginning with God.
   All things came to be through him,
     and without him **nothing** came to be.
What came to be **through** him was **life**,
     and this life was the **light** of the **human race**;
   the light shines in the darkness,
     and the darkness has not overcome it.]
A man named **John** was **sent** from God.
He came for **testimony**, to testify to the light,
   so that all might **believe** through him.
He was **not** the light,
   but came to testify to the light.
[The true light, which enlightens everyone,
     was coming into the world.
   He was **in the world**,
     and the world came to be **through him**,
     but the world did **not** know him.
   He came to what was **his own**,
     but his own **people did not accept** him.

These familiar verses have a parallel structure. Read the opening verses with a steady, firm, and deliberate voice.

The hymn celebrates the preexistent Word and his role in creation.

Pause before starting this new section on John the Baptist.

Another shift, now talking about Jesus, the light of the world.

The author is shockingly honest about those who reject Jesus. Read it as such.

---

is exceedingly superior to angels. Thus, he is above all on earth and all in heaven.

     The first two biblical quotes in this passage come from Psalm 2:7 and 2 Samuel 7:14, respectively. Both quotes point toward the people's messianic hopes. It is important to note that in Hebrews, "son" is not simply adoptive language but instead indicates a distinctive and eternal relationship with God the Father. The third biblical quote is a combination of Deuteronomy 32:43 and Psalm 97:7 (in the Septuagint translation). The passage from Deuteronomy comes from Moses' last words prophesying

the defeat of Israel's enemies, while Psalm 97 is a song of praise exalting God above all other supposed gods. In this way, Hebrews highlights Jesus' defeat of death and evil while praising and exalting him above all other beings. He is truly the Son of God and as such participates in the creation of the universe and the salvation of humanity and receives the glorious worship that belongs to God alone.

     God continues to speak to us today through his Son, Jesus. As we celebrate the birth of Jesus, we recognize that he is the ultimate prophet, priest, and king who

cleanses us from our sins and redeems us. Similar to the message in the first reading, we follow the model of the angels and worship him, praising and glorifying his name.

GOSPEL   Today's Gospel also proclaims the theme of Jesus as God's Word. In this prologue of John's Gospel account, John provides a profound theological treatise on Jesus as the preexistent Word of God. As in the second reading, Jesus' role in the creation of the universe comes to the forefront in this passage. Furthermore, Jesus is the light that "shines

An immediate contrast is offered about those who did believe.

But to those who **did accept** him
    he gave **power** to become **children** of God,
    to those who believe in his name,
    who were born not by natural generation
    nor by **human choice** nor by a man's decision
    but of God.
      And the **Word became flesh**
        and made his **dwelling** among us,
        and we **saw** his glory,
        the glory as of the Father's only Son,
        full of grace and truth.]

Stress the first mention of "us." This reading is very personal.

John testified to him and cried out, saying,
    "This was he of whom 1 said,
    'The one who is coming after me ranks ahead of me
    because he existed before me.'"
From his fullness we have all **received**,
    grace in place of grace,
    because while the **law** was given through **Moses**,
    grace and **truth** came **through Jesus** Christ.
No one has ever **seen God**.
The only **Son**, God, who is at the Father's side,
    has **revealed** him.

Pause briefly again before returning to John the Baptist. What John testified to is made manifest anew on this Christmas Day.

[Shorter: John 1:1–5, 9–14 (see brackets)]

---

in the darkness" to guide all people to the Father. As the exiled Israelites were in darkness in the first reading, all of humanity was in darkness before the incarnation, exiled from God, and only restored to him through the light that is Jesus. The response of humanity to God's revelation of light and the Word incarnate is mixed: some "did not know him" and others "did not accept him," but there were some who accepted him and believed, thereby becoming children of God. The prologue finishes by reinforcing Jesus, the only Son of the Father, as the object of their belief.

The description of Jesus as the "Word [become] flesh" stresses both that he communicates and reveals God in the world and that he is fully human. He is God's tangible presence in the world, revealing the glory of God the Father. While the people received an initial gift of the law through Moses, Jesus perfects this gift through the gifts of grace and truth. The rest of John's Gospel narrates how Jesus accomplished all of this.

The uniqueness of Jesus is emphasized by the comparison between him and John the Baptist. In this passage, their respective roles are clearly defined. John

the Baptist's role as herald of the Good News of Jesus reinforces Jesus' superiority over all other beings, as was depicted in today's second reading. Jesus is not simply another prophet in a long line of prophets. He is more; he is the Son of God and he alone reveals the Father to humanity.

In the context of our celebration of Christmas today, this reading invites us to recognize Jesus, the Word of God made flesh, as fully human and fully divine. He is the light in the world that dispels the darkness around us, guiding us in grace and truth to the Father. M.B.

THE HOLY FAMILY OF JESUS, MARY, AND JOSEPH

LECTIONARY #17

READING I   Genesis 15:1–6; 21:1–3

A reading from the Book of Genesis

The word of the **Lord** came to **Abram** in a vision, saying:
  "**Fear not**, Abram!
    I am your **shield**;
    I will make your **reward** very **great**."
But Abram said,
  "**O Lord GOD**, what good will your gifts be,
  if I keep on being **childless**
  and have as **my heir** the **steward** of my house, **Eliezer**?"
Abram continued,
  "See, you have **given me no offspring**,
  and so one of my servants will be my heir."
Then the word of the LORD came to him:
  "No, that one shall **not** be your heir;
  your **own issue** shall be **your heir**."
The Lord took Abram outside and said,
  "**Look** up at the **sky** and **count** the **stars**, if you can.
Just so," he added, "shall your **descendants** be."
Abram put his **faith in the LORD**,
  who credited it to him as an act of righteousness.

Genesis = JEN-uh-sihs
Notice the gap in the Scripture citation. As you prepare, take time to read some of the story that is not included in today's reading.
Make sure to distinguish between the character voices: narrator, Abram, and the Lord.

This is a cry of anguish and fear. Infertility is a heartbreaking situation, even in today's time.

Imagine the scene: the Lord leads Abram outside to gaze at the heavens. Use a tone of assurance as God dispels Abram's fear.

There are options for today's readings. Contact your parish staff to learn which readings will be used.

| READING I | **Genesis.** Today's first reading begins with the word of the Lord coming to Abraham (formerly called Abram). This description matches subsequent prophetic events in the Bible. As such, we should not be surprised that God's message to Abraham contains a prophetic message concerning the reward being granted to him. God's message to

Abraham begins with a promise of continued protection ("I am your shield") followed by a promise of a reward. What today's reading does not convey is the reason for this reward. Just prior to this passage, Abraham's generosity toward Melchizedek is narrated along with his rejection, per God's command, of riches from the king of Sodom. Abraham's generosity and obedience lead to the scene we encounter in today's reading.

For the first time in Abraham's story, we have actual dialogue between him and God. This conversation is marked by its intimate and friendly qualities. Abraham honestly tells God that any material reward would be pointless since he has no heir to inherit it. Furthermore, he actually places the blame for the lack of an heir at God's feet. And God does not refute the accusation. Instead, he reassures Abraham that he will have an heir. In fact, God states that Abraham's descendants will be as numerous as the stars! The abundant generosity of God shines forth in this reading. Abraham's righteousness stands out here because he believes based solely on God's word. By the end of the reading, we see the

The LORD took note of **Sarah** as he had said he would;
he did for her as he had **promised**.
Sarah became pregnant and bore **Abraham a son in his old age**,
at the set time that God had stated.
Abraham gave the name **Isaac** to this son of his
whom Sarah bore him.

Or:

READING I   Sirach 3:2–6, 12–14

A reading from the Book of Sirach

God sets a **father** in honor **over** his **children**;
a **mother's authority** he confirms over her **sons**.
Whoever honors his father **atones for sins**,
and preserves himself from them.
When he **prays**, he is **heard**;
he stores up **riches** who **reveres** his **mother**.
Whoever honors his father is **gladdened by children**,
and, when he prays, is heard.
Whoever reveres his father will live a **long life**;
he who obeys his father brings **comfort** to his mother.

My son, **take care** of your father when he is **old**;
grieve him not as long as he lives.
Even if his **mind fail**, be considerate of him;
revile him not all the days of his life;
kindness to a father will **not be forgotten**,
firmly planted against the debt of your sins
—a house raised in **justice** to you.

Sirach = SEER-ak or Sī-ruhk

A didactic reading that seeks to establish right family relationships. Eye contact is important as you connect this reading to the listening families.

"My son" is an endearing vocative. Dole out the timeless wisdom of Sirach tenderly. Patience and kindness are necessary for care of our aged parents.

fulfillment of God's promise as Sarah conceives and gives birth to Isaac. God is not only generous, but he is also faithful to his promises, and Abraham's faith proves to be well-placed.

As we celebrate the Holy Family today, the story of Abraham, Sarah, and Isaac gives us an example of what it means to trust God with the protection and blessing of our family. God does not simply do these things, he does them with abundance. In light of Abraham's faith and obedience, we too are called to form families of faith who trust and believe in God's promise of his

continued presence in our lives. This faith provides the foundation for our obedience as we continually discern God's will for ourselves and our families.

Sirach. Today's first reading from Sirach describes ideal family dynamics. Both mothers and fathers have authority over their offspring. As a result, Sirach exhorts children to honor and revere their parents. In addition to the inherent good of honoring parents, there are other benefits to doing so. These benefits include atonement for and preservation from sins as well as prayers being heard and the storing up

of riches—whether material or spiritual is left to the interpretation of the reader. Other potential rewards for children honoring their parents include offspring of their own, long life, and bringing comfort to their mothers.

The second half of the reading describes what honoring one's parents looks like. It is a way of life that continues from childhood into adulthood. As parents age and may become senile, children are to exhibit patience and care for them. Children are therefore meant to provide both material and moral support to their

For meditation and context:

RESPONSORIAL PSALM   Psalm 105:1–2, 3–4, 5–6, 8–9 (7a , 8a)

R. The Lord remembers his covenant for ever.

Give thanks to the LORD, invoke his name;
    make known among the nations
        his deeds.
Sing to him, sing his praise,
    proclaim all his wondrous deeds.

Glory in his holy name;
    rejoice, O hearts that seek the LORD!
Look to the LORD in his strength;
    constantly seek his face.

You descendants of Abraham, his servants,
    sons of Jacob, his chosen ones!
He, the LORD, is our God;
    throughout the earth his
        judgments prevail.

He remembers forever his covenant
    which he made binding for a thousand
        generations
which he entered into with Abraham
    and by his oath to Isaac.

Or:

For meditation and context:

RESPONSORIAL PSALM   Psalm 128:1–2, 3, 4–5 (1)

R. Blessed are those who fear the Lord and walk in his ways.

Blessed is everyone who fears the LORD,
    who walks in his ways!
For you shall eat the fruit of your handiwork;
    blessed shall you be, and favored.

Your wife shall be like a fruitful vine
    in the recesses of your home;
your children like olive plants
    around your table.

Behold, thus is the man blessed
    who fears the LORD.
The LORD bless you from Zion:
    may you see the prosperity of Jerusalem
        all the days of your life.

READING II   Hebrews 11:8, 11–12, 17–19

A reading from the Letter to the Hebrews

Brothers and sisters:
By **faith Abraham obeyed** when he was **called** to go out
    to a place
        that he was to receive as an **inheritance**;
        he went out, **not knowing** where he was to go.

Abraham's faith is praised. Have you acted in faith even when you were unsure of where God was leading you?

---

parents. By acting in this way, children are respecting their parents and keeping God's commands. Therefore, we can see this passage as providing commentary on the fourth commandment, as in Exodus 20:12 and Deuteronomy 5:16, where honoring one's parents leads to a long life. The commandments show us that love of God leads to love of others—in this case, one's parents.

Though this reading is primarily addressed to children, it also has implications for parents. Parental authority should be a reflection of divine authority which is ultimately rooted in love and seeking the

good of those under their authority. For people who have not experienced healthy family relationships, this reading could be challenging to hear. We are invited to look past the negatives of our familial relationships to the divine love and goodness of God as the parent who cares for us, protects us, and always acts for our good.

READING II   **Hebrews.** In this reading from the Letter to the Hebrews, the themes of Abraham and Sarah's faith and obedience continue. Key moments in their lives are marked by the

faith they exhibited. First, their faith led them to a foreign land promised to them by God. Then, their faith is the distinguishing characteristic of their ability to conceive Isaac. Their age and sterility should have precluded such an event, yet through their faith and trust in God's promise they "received power to generate." Finally, when asked to sacrifice the son through whom God's promise of numerous descendants was to be fulfilled, Abraham's faith allowed him to trust completely in God's plan. The author explains that Abraham had so much faith that he was certain of God's

Shift your tone from the desolation of infertility to awe at unfathomable fertility.

By **faith** he received **power to generate**,
    even though he was past the normal age
    —and **Sarah** herself was **sterile**—
    for he thought that the one who had made the promise
        was trustworthy.
So it was that there came forth from one man,
    himself as good as dead,
    descendants as numerous as the **stars** in the sky
    and as **countless as the sands** on the seashore.

Paul recounts God's promise to Abraham. The references to elements of creation ("stars" and "sand") emphasize the magnitude of God's promise.

Hardship and trials await us despite our strong faith.

By faith Abraham, when put to the **test**, offered up Isaac,
    and he who had received the promises was ready to offer his
       only son,
    of whom it was said,
    "Through **Isaac** descendants shall bear your **name**."
He reasoned that **God** was able to **raise** even from the dead,
    and he received Isaac back as a symbol.

Or:

READING II   Colossians 3:12–21

A reading from the Letter of Saint Paul to the Colossians

Colossians = kuh-LOSH-uhnz

Brothers and sisters:
[Put on, as **God's chosen ones, holy and beloved,**
    heartfelt **compassion, kindness, humility, gentleness,**
      and **patience,**
    bearing with one another and **forgiving** one another,
    if one has a grievance against another;
    as the **Lord has forgiven you**, so must you also do.
And over all these put on love,
    that is, the bond of perfection.
And let the **peace** of **Christ** control your **hearts**,
    the peace into which you were also called in one body. »

Look directly at the assembly to deliver, "God's chosen ones, holy and beloved." Pause briefly as you work through the list, allowing the listener to "try on" the instructions. Paul has used the image of clothing.

ability to raise Isaac from the dead if needed to fulfill the promises God made to Abraham and Sarah.

The inclusion of Sarah in the discussion of Abraham's faith reinforces the communal character of faith. As a family, they believed and trusted in the Lord. Their barrenness was essentially like being dead: there was no heir to inherit their material possessions nor to carry on and remember their names. These were the closest thing to eternal life in their understanding since there was no concept of an afterlife at that point in their history. Through their joint faith, Abraham and Sarah brought life out of death as a type of foreshadowing of Jesus' resurrection.

The sacrifice of Isaac brings all members of their family into the sphere of obedience and faith. Abraham and Sarah trusted in God's life-giving power in the conception of their son, and this faith is put to the test when Abraham is asked to sacrifice Isaac. Here we note a connection between this biblical family and Jesus, who was actually sacrificed and restored to life through his resurrection. Isaac's rescue from Abraham's knife is symbolic of the deliverance experienced by the Christian faithful through Jesus' sacrifice.

The faith of Abraham, Sarah, and Isaac provides a model for all families to trust in God's providence and presence in every moment of their lives, especially at pivotal moments of discernment or crisis. The story of Abraham, Sarah, and Isaac also shows us how to recognize that every good we have comes from God and ultimately belongs to him.

Colossians. In today's reading from Colossians, Paul provides the community with guidance on how to live out their

Tone changes from instruction to thankfulness, and then back to instruction on household behavior

And be **thankful**.
Let the **word of** Christ dwell in you richly,
    as in all **wisdom** you teach and **admonish** one another,
    singing psalms, **hymns**, and spiritual **songs**
    with gratitude in your hearts to God.
And whatever you do, in word or in deed,
    do everything in the **name** of the Lord Jesus,
    giving thanks to God the Father through him.]

Wives, be subordinate to your husbands,
    as is proper in the Lord.
Husbands, love your wives,
    and avoid any bitterness toward them.
Children, **obey** your **parents** in everything,
    for this is pleasing to the Lord.
Fathers, do not **provoke** your **children**,
    so they may not become discouraged.

[Shorter: Colossians 3:12–17 (see brackets)]

GOSPEL   Luke 2:22–40

A reading from the holy Gospel according to Luke

Use a narrator voice to set the scene.

[When the days were completed for their **purification**
    according to the **law of Moses**,
    they took him up to **Jerusalem**
    to **present him** to the Lord,]
    just as it is written in the law of the Lord,
Every *male that opens the womb shall be* **consecrated**
    to the Lord,
    and to offer the **sacrifice** of
    a pair of turtledoves or two young pigeons,
    in accordance with the dictate in the law of the Lord.

Christian vocation, turning to particular advice for spouses and children. Paul begins by identifying the community as chosen by God, holy, and beloved; they are holy (set apart for God) and beloved by virtue of being chosen by God. These characteristics inform and shape their behavior toward God and each other. Paul emphasizes that these are not mere dispositions but actions. Their "compassion, kindness, humility, gentleness, and patience" is manifested in tolerance and forgiveness, as the Lord has already forgiven them. Above all, they are called to live out their Christian

vocation in love. As God has loved them in choosing them and making them holy, so too should Christians love each other. Thus, divine actions are the guiding principle for our own actions.

God's mercy and goodness in choosing, sanctifying, and loving us leads naturally to heartfelt gratitude and praising God in both word and deed. Paul addresses the entire community in this call to worship God. He then moves to more particular counsel in the last third of the reading, directing his speech to wives, husbands, children, and fathers.

Fear of the Lord is the motivation for the proper behavior of each person/role Paul names. This fear is one of awed recognition of God's greatness in loving us. All conduct is therefore subordinate to Jesus and based on love. The commands to submit oneself to another are paired with commands of obligation for the other party that negates abuse or misuse of the commands of submission. As husbands, men are prohibited from being overbearing and considering themselves superior to their wives, instead loving them as Jesus loves. Likewise, fathers are forbidden to provoke their

Mary, Joseph, and Simeon are examples of piety as they fulfill the law. Their devotion is evident in their actions. Later, the reading will also use Anna as an example of faith-filled devotion.

Now there was a man in Jerusalem whose name was **Simeon**.
This man was **righteous** and devout,
    awaiting the consolation of Israel,
    and the **Holy Spirit** was upon him.
It had been revealed to him by the Holy Spirit
    that he should **not see death**
    before he had **seen** the **Christ** of the Lord.
He came in the Spirit into the temple;
    and when the **parents brought** in the child **Jesus**
    to perform the custom of the law in regard to him,
    he **took him into his arms and blessed** God, saying:
        "Now, Master, you may **let your servant go**
            in peace, according to your **word**,
        for my eyes have seen your **salvation**,
            which you **prepared** in sight of all the peoples,
        a light for revelation to the Gentiles,
            and glory for your people Israel."

Use a tender and reverent tone. Imagine what it must have been like for Simeon to hold Jesus, whom he recognizes as God's promise fulfilled. This is a sacred moment.

The child's **father** and **mother** were **amazed** at what was said
    about him;
    and **Simeon blessed them** and said to Mary his mother,
    "Behold, this child is **destined**
    for the fall and rise of many in Israel,
    and to be a sign that will be contradicted
    —and you yourself a **sword will pierce**—
    so that the thoughts of many hearts may be revealed."

Despite the remarkable events in Mary and Joseph's life thus far, they continue to be amazed. Capture their amazement and parental pride.

There was also a **prophetess**, **Anna**,
    the daughter of Phanuel, of the tribe of Asher.
She was **advanced** in years,
    having lived seven years with her husband after her marriage,
    and then as a **widow** until she was eighty-four.
She **never left** the temple,
    but **worshiped** night and day with **fasting** and **prayer**.
And coming forward at that very time,
    she gave **thanks** to God and spoke about the child
    to all who were **awaiting the redemption** of Jerusalem. »

children with thoughtless or undisciplined behavior that does not model divine love but places burdens on the children. Wives are to submit to their husbands, but only "as is proper in the Lord," modeling their actions and attitudes on Christ's. Children are to honor and obey their parents, an exhortation like that found in the first reading from Sirach. The motivation of all these commands lies in pleasing the Lord and avoiding behavior that discourages others and leads them away from God's love.

GOSPEL   Today's Gospel presents Jesus within the context of his family and the social world. The first thing that we know is that his parents are obedient to the law of Moses. In fact, references to the "law" apear five times in this section out of the total of nine occurrences in Luke's Gospel. Clearly, observing the law of the Lord is an important characteristic of the Holy Family. They are faithful to God's commands and are thus solidly situated within the Jewish traditions of their time. As such, they offered a sacrifice of two turtledoves or pigeons, the sacrifice required

of those who were poor and could not afford more costly sacrificial offerings per the "law of the Lord." From these brief observations, then, we know that Mary and Joseph were devout, pious Jews and were poor.

Luke next describes their encounter with two prophets in the temple, Simeon and Anna, who are both depicted as righteous and holy people. These two prophets shed further light on the Holy Family, and Jesus in particular. Simeon's prophecy is fulfilled on the spot as he sees Jesus and recognizes him to be the long-awaited Christ

References to Jesus' youth are scarce. Read the last lines slowly so the image of Jesus maturing can be savored.

[When they **had fulfilled** all the prescriptions
  of the law of the Lord,
  they returned to Galilee,
  to their own town of Nazareth.
The **child** grew and **became strong**, filled with **wisdom**;
  and the **favor** of God was **upon** him.]

[Shorter: Luke 2:22, 39–40 (see brackets)]

who brings salvation to God's people. Simeon continues by addressing Mary, describing Jesus' upcoming ministry as well as her own future sorrow. This moment is a bittersweet combination of rejoicing and sorrow in the lives of the Holy Family. As the reading then turns to Anna, we come back to the joyous aspect of the event. While we do not have specific words attributed to Anna, she is one of the first to evangelize, proclaiming the Good News to everyone in the temple and thanking and praising God for fulfilling his promise of salvation.

This passage ends with a return to normal domestic life for the Holy Family and the attributes of the child Jesus as he grew. We know three things about Jesus during this period of his life: he became strong in the Lord, he was "filled with wisdom," and he received God's favor. These descriptions allude to holy people in the Old Testament, such as the judges and prophets, especially Solomon in his wisdom. Jesus' ministry exceeds all those who came before him, and his childhood is an indicator of this fact.

The Holy Family is the ideal family; surpassing the other families depicted in the various readings today and embodying the paradigm for faith-centered family life. They model devout living rooted in God's love in everyday life and in caring for each other. M.B.

MARY, THE HOLY MOTHER OF GOD

LECTIONARY #18

READING I   Numbers 6:22–27

A reading from the Book of Numbers

The **LORD said** to **Moses**:
    "**Speak to Aaron** and his sons and tell them:
    This is **how** you shall bless the Israelites.
Say to them:
      The **LORD bless you** and **keep** you!
      The LORD let his **face shine** upon
          you, and be **gracious** to you!
      The LORD look upon you **kindly** and
          give you **peace**!
So shall they invoke my **name** upon the Israelites,
    and I will bless them."

"You" now refers to the people.

Emphasize "face shine" by smiling as you proclaim this line. This phrase will be repeated in the responsorial psalm.

For meditation and context:

RESPONSORIAL PSALM   Psalm 67:2–3, 5, 6, 8 (2a)

R. May God bless us in his mercy.

May God have pity on us and bless us;
    may he let his face shine upon us.
So may your way be known upon earth;
    among all nations, your salvation.

May the nations be glad and exult
    because you rule the peoples in equity;
    the nations on the earth you guide.

May the peoples praise you, O God;
    may all the peoples praise you!
May God bless us,
    and may all the ends of the earth
      fear him!

READING I The first reading provides the priestly blessing that the Lord gave to Moses in order that there would be a uniform blessing bestowed upon the Israelites. This blessing is probably what Zechariah would have been expected to say upon leaving the Temple in Luke's Gospel, except that he emerged mute from his encounter with the angel Gabriel (see Luke 1:21–23).

This blessing repeatedly emphasizes God as the source of the power to enact the blessings. While the priests are holy people, set apart for service to God, they themselves have no power to actualize the blessings stated. God is the initiator and actor every time. The first half of each line describes God's movement toward his people while the second half of each line delineates God's action on their behalf.

The first line of the blessing sets the general foundation for the rest of the actions described: "The LORD bless you and keep you." To "bless" here goes beyond material prosperity and wealth. It encompasses fertility and posterity, health, military victory, strength, and peace. It touches upon every aspect of life. The reference to "keep" points to God's guidance of his people and his fidelity to the covenant with them.

The whole blessing concludes with God granting the people peace. Similar to "bless," the concept of "peace" here extends beyond freedom from military conflict or finding inner tranquility. It entails wholeness in all areas of life: health, material, familial, societal, and religious.

READING II Today's reading from Galatians explains how we, as baptized Christians, became children of God. Through our salvation in Jesus Christ,

Galatians = guh-LAY-shuhnz

Read personal pronouns carefully so that the Son of God is distinct from the sons that we are to become as adoptive children.

Paul is stressing Jesus' human nature.

READING II   Galatians 4:4–7

A reading from the Letter of Saint Paul to the Galatians

Brothers and sisters:
When the **fullness of time** had come, **God sent** his **Son**,
    born of a **woman**, born **under** the **law**,
    to ransom those under the law,
    so that we might **receive adoption** as **sons**.
As **proof** that you are sons,
    God sent the **Spirit** of his Son into our **hearts**,
    crying out, "**Abba**, Father!"
So you are **no longer** a **slave** but a son,
    and if a son then also an **heir**, through God.

we entered into the intimate relationship between Jesus and God the Father and therefore can be called God's children. Being a child of God is the highest dignity offered to us and entails the right of inheritance.

The passage reminds us that this gift comes to us solely through God's initiative, just as God is the source of the power in the priestly blessing in the first reading. Paul describes the surprising actions that God takes to make this gift possible for us. Instead of sending the Son to the world as an exalted worldly prince, God acts through rather humble circumstances: Jesus was

"born of a woman" and "born under the law." Being born of a woman highlights human fragility and provides the basis for everyone's capacity to receive God's adoption. Being born under the law means that the Son of God submits to an external norm so that he might ransom those under that same law.

Through Jesus, we are now adopted children of God; however, this is not merely a change in legal status. God's life is communicated to each baptized individual. This effects a real change in the person. Nevertheless, an important point to keep in mind

is that all human beings are created in the image and likeness of God. In this sense, then, all human beings are children of God. Through baptism, however, Christians enter into a deeper and unique relationship with God that involves the right of inheritance as described in today's second reading.

The blessing described in the first reading and the way God's actions on behalf of humanity are described in this reading point to the way that God initiates and effects our salvation.

GOSPEL Luke 2:16–21

A reading from the holy Gospel according to Luke

The **shepherds** went in **haste** to **Bethlehem** and found **Mary**
     and **Joseph**,
and the **infant** lying in the **manger**.
When they saw this,
     they made known the message
     that had been told them about this child.
All who heard it were **amazed**
     by what had been **told** them by the shepherds.
And Mary kept all these things,
     reflecting on them in her heart.
Then the shepherds **returned**,
     glorifying and **praising** God
     for all they had heard and seen,
     just as it had been told to them.

When **eight days** were completed for his **circumcision**,
     he was **named Jesus**, the name given him by **the angel**
     before he was conceived in the womb.

This reading will be very familiar to you and the congregation. Upon careful study, what strikes you as new? Attempt to make it fresh, for this time and place.

God's message energizes the shepherds to share the Good News. When have you been energized to share your faith? Let your proclamation reflect this energy.

Pause before the scene change. The narrator ends with Jesus' parents fulfilling the prescriptions of the law and the naming of Jesus as previously instructed.

GOSPEL In Luke's Gospel, we find Mary described in terms of a woman of faith. As Jesus was "born under the law" in the second reading from Galatians, it makes sense that he undergoes circumcision according to the law. Mary and Joseph are clearly observant Jews and raise Jesus according to the Jewish laws and faith.

Today's reading emphasizes Mary's reaction to the shepherds' recounting of the events that led them to seek Jesus (see Luke 2:8–15). Her response here is similar to her reaction at finding Jesus in the temple when he was twelve years old ("his mother kept all these things in her heart," Luke 2:51b). She senses that there are deeper implications to the events around her and reflects privately upon them. It seems that she does not fully understand all that is happening, but she observes quietly and guards these memories in her heart.

Mary's reflection and her observance of the Jewish religious custom of circumcision for her infant son portray Mary as a devout and pious woman. Despite not fully understanding all that she sees and hears, she obediently follows God's will for her and her family. This is also implied in the naming of Jesus according to the angel's message. The honor of being the holy mother of God comes not from some grandiose quality but from her simple and sincere acceptance of God's work in her life. Mary remains a maternal model for us who are baptized children of God. Like Mary, we need to remain attentive to God's presence in our lives. We might even recognize his activity through unexpected and humble avenues, such as Mary did in her encounter with the shepherds. M.B.

THE EPIPHANY OF THE LORD

LECTIONARY #20

READING I   Isaiah 60:1–6

A reading from the Book of the Prophet Isaiah

Isaiah = ī-ZAY-uh

Be energized in your delivery. This is an exciting prophecy that is fulfilled in Jesus Christ!

Notice the light–dark–light pattern and the verbs throughout this reading. Action words help the listeners feel the transformation from darkness to the majesty and magnitude of the light.

Become familiar enough to deliver this line ("Raise your eyes . . .") while looking directly at the assembly.

Slow down and use a tender tone.

Isaiah's prophecy prefigures the Magi. Read it with excitement so when the Gospel is proclaimed the assembly will hear the connection.

dromedaries = DROM-eh-dayr-ees = single-humped camels

Midian = MID-ee-uhn

Ephah = EE-fuh

Sheba = SHEE-buh

> **Rise up** in **splendor**, Jerusalem! Your **light** has come,
>   the glory of the Lord shines upon you.
> See, **darkness covers** the **earth**,
>   and thick clouds cover the peoples;
> but upon you the LORD shines,
>   and over you appears his glory.
> **Nations** shall walk by your light,
>   and **kings** by your shining **radiance**.
> Raise your eyes and look about;
>   they all gather and come to you:
> your sons come from afar,
>   and your **daughters** in the **arms** of their nurses.
>
> Then you shall be **radiant** at what you see,
>   your **heart shall throb** and overflow,
> for the riches of the sea shall be emptied out before you,
>   the wealth of nations shall be brought to you.
> **Caravans** of **camels** shall fill you,
>   **dromedaries** from **Midian** and **Ephah**;
> all from Sheba shall come
>   bearing **gold** and **frankincense**,
>   and proclaiming the **praises** of the LORD.

READING I This reading from Isaiah comes from a section that focuses on the glory of the new Jerusalem/Zion. Having been restored and made new, Jerusalem becomes the locus of God's reign over the entire world. The darkness mentioned refers to the experience of conquest and exile of Israel. Juxtaposed with the darkness is the light imagery that brings the hope of God's coming to his people. This light is not a natural light but a supernatural light; it is the glory of God made manifest in the world. Jerusalem shines forth like a beacon to foreign nations, drawing them to recognize the universal kingship of God.

This universal kingship is further emphasized by the description of luxury goods brought by land and sea to Jerusalem from the surrounding nations. The Midianites were known as camel traders while Ephahites were descendants of Midian's son, and Sheba was Midian's nephew. Sheba was also known in the Old Testament as a source of exotic and valuable goods. More importantly, these nations will also come praising and worshiping God. The reference to frankincense alludes to this worship because it was used Jewish temple worship.

Today we celebrate the fulfillment of Isaiah's prophecy as we hear in today's Gospel of people from foreign nations who come bearing gold, frankincense, and myrrh (all luxury goods) to pay homage to the newborn king of the Jews, the locus of God's power and glory.

READING II This short reading from Paul's letter to the Ephesians highlights the Gentiles as recipients of God's salvific action. Paul has been

For meditation and context:

RESPONSORIAL PSALM   Psalm 72:1–2, 7–8, 10–11, 12–13 (11)

R. Lord, every nation on earth will adore you.

O God, with your judgment endow the king,
    and with your justice, the king's son;
he shall govern your people with justice
    and your afflicted ones with judgment.

Justice shall flower in his days,
    and profound peace, till the moon be
        no more.
May he rule from sea to sea,
    and from the River to the ends of
        the earth.

The kings of Tarshish and the Isles shall
        offer gifts;
    the kings of Arabia and Seba shall
        bring tribute.
All kings shall pay him homage,
    all nations shall serve him.

For he shall rescue the poor when he
        cries out,
    and the afflicted when he has no one
        to help him.
He shall have pity for the lowly and the poor;
    the lives of the poor he shall save.

Ephesians = ee-FEE-zhuhnz

READING II   Ephesians 3:2–3a, 5–6

A reading from the Letter of Saint Paul to the Ephesians

Brothers and sisters:
You have **heard** of the **stewardship** of **God's grace**
    that was **given** to me for **your benefit**,
    namely, that the **mystery** was made **known** to me by **revelation**.
It was **not** made known to people in **other generations**
    as it has **now** been revealed
    to his holy **apostles** and **prophets** by the **Spirit**:
    that the **Gentiles are coheirs**, members of the same body,
    and **copartners** in the **promise** in **Christ Jesus** through
        the **gospel**.

Now is the time! Previous generations were not privy to the revelation of God's plan of salvation in Jesus Christ. We are beneficiaries of this revelation. Read this with power and conviction.

Gospel means "good news."

GOSPEL   Matthew 2:1–12

A reading from the holy Gospel according to Matthew

When **Jesus** was born in **Bethlehem** of Judea,
    in the days of King **Herod**,
    behold, **magi** from the east arrived in **Jerusalem**, saying,
    "**Where** is the newborn **king of the Jews**? »

Read this beloved story with fresh energy for this time and place. The Scriptures are ever new.

---

entrusted by God to proclaim the Good News for the benefit of others. The "mystery" he refers to is God's plan of salvation that is now revealed through Jesus Christ and the Gospel. Since this message was previously unknown to past generations, the revelation of this mystery could be misconstrued as a Christian innovation. Paul clarifies that this is not an innovation, but rather a fulfillment of God's plan.

Paul refers to apostles and prophets as holy people. Indeed, Paul regards all Christians as holy, meaning set apart by and for God. Holiness entails a close rela-

tionship with God, a fact that is especially true of the apostles and prophets. Since the revelation of Jesus was made known to all people, now Gentiles are included in this call to holiness.

To explain how faith in Christ transforms the Gentile believers, Paul describes three distinctive roles that they take on in their faith. First, he calls them "coheirs." As baptized Christians, they too are adopted children of God who now have the right of inheritance of God's grace and salvation (see the second reading for January 1, Galatians 4:4–7, for more about

this). Second, he refers to the Gentiles as "members of the same body." As members of the body of Christ, they cannot be treated like second-class citizens, just as part of the body cannot be relegated as inferior to other parts of the body since all work together to help us live. Finally, Paul states that they are "copartners in the promise in Christ Jesus through the gospel." Just as Paul was entrusted with the proclamation of the Good News, the Gentiles likewise share in his ministry and commission from God. This equal participation of

Watch for the shift in scenes. Pause between them.

We saw his **star** at its **rising**
    and have come to do him **homage**."
When King Herod heard this,
    he was **greatly troubled**,
    and all **Jerusalem with him**.
Assembling all the **chief priests** and the **scribes** of the people,
    he inquired of them **where** the **Christ** was to be **born**.
They said to him, "In Bethlehem of Judea,
    for thus it has been written through the **prophet**:
        And you, Bethlehem, land of Judah,
            are by no means least among the rulers of Judah;
        *since from you shall come a **ruler**,*
            *who is to **shepherd** my people Israel.*"

Change your volume to represent secrecy and intrigue. Herod's words are insincere.

Then Herod called the magi **secretly**
    and ascertained from them the **time** of the **star's** appearance.
He sent them to Bethlehem and said,
    "**Go** and **search** diligently for the child.
When you have found him, **bring me word**,
    that I too may go and **do him homage**."
After their audience with the king they set out.
And behold, the star that they had seen at its rising
        preceded them,
    until it came and stopped over the place where the child was.
They were **overjoyed** at seeing the star,
    and on entering the house
    they saw the **child** with **Mary** his mother.

Unlike the insincerity of Herod mentioned above, the Magi are sincere and share gifts of great importance.

They **prostrated** themselves and did him **homage**.
Then they opened their **treasures**
    and offered him gifts of gold, frankincense, and myrrh.
And having been **warned** in a **dream** not to return to Herod,
    they departed for their country by **another way**.

Herod's plan is thwarted—stress "another way."

the Gentiles emphasizes the fact that everyone is a new creation in Jesus Christ.

| GOSPEL | In today's Gospel, we encounter the Magi who come to pay homage to Jesus. Jesus' birth in Bethlehem evokes his Davidic kingship and messianic role. Traditionally, it was initially thought that the Magi were part of the Persian priestly class. Now, they are considered to be astrologers or astronomers who charted major events based on their study of the stars and planetary movements. They could be Persians, but what is

most important for us theologically is that they were clearly Gentiles.

Their reference to the "newborn king of the Jews" clearly agitated Herod, who already bore the title "king of the Jews." Fearing the advent of a rival to his throne, the help Herod offered the Magi was insincere and a ploy to discover this rival and do away with him. Yet we see God's hand guiding the Magi. God's plan of salvation cannot be thwarted by human endeavors to the contrary, and the Gentile Magi prove themselves attentive and open to God's guidance.

The gifts of gold and frankincense allude to today's first reading, wherein Gentile nations bring luxury goods and their worship to Jerusalem in recognition of God's universal kingship. Today's Gospel presents the Magi meeting with the false king of the Jews, Herod, and then encountering the true king of the Jews, Jesus. They pay homage to him, indicating their submission to Jesus' authority and the proper attitude toward God. The Magi are the first Gentiles to worship Christ, prefiguring the Gentiles in the second reading and fulfilling the prophecy in the first reading. M.B.

SECOND SUNDAY IN ORDINARY TIME

LECTIONARY #65

READING I   1 Samuel 3:3b–10, 19

A reading from the first Book of Samuel

Samuel was **sleeping** in the **temple** of the Lord
    where the **ark of God** was.
The Lord **called to Samuel**, who answered, "**Here I am**."
Samuel **ran** to **Eli** and said, "Here I am. **You called** me."
"I did **not** call you," Eli said. "**Go back to sleep**."
So he **went** back to sleep.
Again the Lord **called** Samuel, who rose and **went** to Eli.
"Here I am," he said. "You called me."
But Eli answered, "I did **not** call you, **my son**. Go back to sleep."

At that time Samuel was **not familiar** with the Lord,
    because the Lord had not **revealed anything** to him as yet.
The Lord called Samuel again, for the **third** time.
Getting up and going to Eli, he said, "Here I am. You called me."
Then Eli **understood** that the Lord was calling the youth.
So he said to Samuel, "Go to sleep, and if you are called, reply,
    '**Speak**, Lord, for your **servant is listening**.'"
When Samuel went to sleep in his place,
    the Lord **came and revealed his presence**,
    calling out as before, "**Samuel**, Samuel!"
Samuel answered, "Speak, for your **servant is listening**."

Samuel grew **up**, and the Lord was **with him**,
    not permitting any **word** of his to be without effect.

What an image! Sleeping in the temple where the ark of God was kept. Pause before starting the dialogue and then be clear which characters are speaking: the Lord, Samuel, Eli, and the narrator.

Emphasize the first time a repeated phrase appears and subdue the others.

Eli = EE-lī

"Son" implies a familiar relationship; Eli (the temple priest in charge of Samuel) does not seem to be irritated that he has been repeatedly awakened. Use a calm voice for Eli's replies.

As you prepare, use Samuel's response as your own prayer: "Speak, Lord, for your servant is listening."

The double negative found in the last phrase can be confusing. Practice to read clearly.

READING I   Today's reading from 1 Samuel presents the call narrative of Samuel. Prior to this passage, we learn that Samuel's birth is a result of God hearing his mother's plea for a child after years of barrenness. Thus, Samuel's birth is viewed as a divine act of mercy, and his mother subsequently consecrates her son to temple service. This is why we encounter Samuel here sleeping in the Lord's temple, ready to serve at a moment's notice.

Samuel's readiness to serve is evidenced by his quick response to what he perceives as a summons from the priest, Eli. He runs to Eli and says quite simply, "Here I am." At no point does Samuel demonstrate annoyance at being told three times in succession that Eli did not call him and to go back to sleep; he is ready and willing to obey each summons. When Eli finally realizes it is the Lord calling Samuel, he prepares Samuel with the proper response to attend to the Lord's call, which Samuel obediently follows. At the fourth call, then, Samuel responds to the Lord instead of going to Eli. God then establishes Samuel as a prophet.

Although we see Samuel as one of the great Old Testament prophets, this story of his call reveals to us that Samuel does not initially recognize that it is God calling to him. The learning curve exhibited by Samuel continues as he matures both physically and spiritually, aided by the presence of the Lord ("Samuel grew up, and the Lord was with him"). God's continuing presence ensures the effectiveness of Samuel's prophetic words.

Are we like Samuel, needing to fine tune our spiritual ears to God's call? And when we do hear God's call, what is our

For meditation and context:

RESPONSORIAL PSALM   Psalm 40:2, 4, 7–8, 8–9, 10 (8a and 9a)

R. Here am I, Lord; I come to do your will.

I have waited, waited for the LORD,
　　and he stooped toward me and
　　　　heard my cry.
And he put a new song into my mouth,
　　a hymn to our God.

Sacrifice or offering you wished not,
　　but ears open to obedience you gave me.
Holocausts or sin-offerings you sought not;
　　then said I, "Behold I come."

"In the written scroll it is prescribed for me,
to do your will, O my God, is my delight,
　　and your law is within my heart!"

I announced your justice in the
　　vast assembly;
　　I did not restrain my lips, as you,
　　　　O LORD, know.

Corinthians = kohr-IN-thee-uhnz

Paul uses dense philosophical language. Read slowly to aid comprehension. Paul's point is important: It is countercultural to claim our bodies are temples of the Holy Spirit.

READING II   1 Corinthians 6:13c–15a, 17–20

A reading from the first Letter of Saint Paul to the Corinthians

Brothers and sisters:
The **body** is **not** for **immorality**, but for the **Lord**,
　　and the Lord is for the body;
　　God raised the Lord and will also raise **us** by his **power**.

Do you not know that your bodies are **members of Christ**?
But whoever is **joined** to the Lord becomes one **Spirit** with him.
Avoid immorality.
Every other **sin** a person commits is **outside** the **body**,
　　but the immoral person sins against his **own** body.
Do you not know that your body
　　is **a temple** of the **Holy Spirit** within you,
　　whom you have from God, and that you are not your own?
For you have been **purchased** at a **price**.
Therefore **glorify God** in your body.

Speak as if these were two separate questions (the first ending with "you have from God," the second ending with "your own"). Use a rising inflection for questions and give the listener's internal voice time to answer.

response? Are we ready to respond humbly and at a moment's notice? Or do we say, "Now is not a good time, God, come back later when I am not so busy"?

READING II In this reading from 1 Corinthians, Paul focuses on God's call to sexual purity. For the Gentiles of this newly formed Christian community, this kind of sexual ethics was new and presented a steep learning curve. To explain this new way of living, Paul emphasizes that their "bodies are members

of Christ" and as such their union with Christ is a bodily one, not just a spiritual union.

Building upon this connection between body and soul, Paul remarks that the "body is a temple of the Holy Spirit within you." The relationship they have with God is spiritual, but it is also a physical reality that they are called to live out. Because of their connection with God, their body, now united to Christ, is no longer their own. Paul affirms that they were purchased through the blood of Christ; as such they are now called to praise and honor God with their entire being, not just their mind

or their soul. So strong is this response that Paul states it as an imperative: "glorify God in your body."

We are encouraged by this reading to reflect on our response to God's calling for our total gift of self to him. This reading reminds us that chastity reflects the glory of God and can be pursued regardless of our state in life. Jesus gave himself over to death on the cross, body and blood, for our salvation. Not only that, but he also comes to us, Body and Blood, in the Eucharist. Are we willing to offer in kind to God what he offers to us?

GOSPEL   John 1:35–42

A reading from the holy Gospel according to John

John was standing with two of his disciples,
    and as he **watched Jesus walk by**, he said,
    "Behold, **the Lamb of God**."
The two disciples **heard** what he said and **followed** Jesus.
Jesus turned and **saw** them following him and said to them,
    "**What are you looking for?**"
They said to him, "**Rabbi**"—which translated means **Teacher**—,
    "where are you **staying?**"
He said to them, "**Come**, and you will **see**."
So they **went** and saw where Jesus was staying,
    and they **stayed** with him that day.
It was about four in the afternoon.
Andrew, the brother of **Simon Peter**,
    was one of the two who heard John and followed Jesus.
He first found his own brother **Simon** and told him,
    "We have **found** the **Messiah**" —which is translated **Christ**—.
Then he **brought** him to Jesus.
Jesus **looked** at him and said,
    "You are Simon the son of John;
    you will be **called Cephas**"—which is translated **Peter**.

Speak John's prophetic words with conviction: the listening disciples, intrigued by John's words, followed Jesus.

Note all of the names used for Jesus: Lamb of God, Rabbi, Teacher, Messiah, Christ.

Temporal markers indicate a scene change. Pause briefly before beginning the new section.

Naming is of great importance. Peter's new name foreshadows his importance.

Cephas = SEE-fuhs

GOSPEL | Today's Gospel reading describes the calling of Jesus' first disciples. In the verses preceding this passage, the focus was on John the Baptist as witness and herald to the coming of Jesus. John had already seen Jesus once before and testified to Jesus being "the Lamb of God, who takes away the sin of the world" (John 1:29). In today's reading, John gives the same witness, this time to the two disciples who are with him.

Upon hearing John's words, the two disciples followed Jesus, yet it is Jesus who takes the initiative in turning to them and speaking first, asking, "What are you looking for?" True discipleship flows from Jesus' initiative. He speaks to us first, and we then have a choice in how we respond. The two disciples respond by remaining with him, and then one of them, Andrew, goes a step further by sharing his encounter with Christ with his brother Simon, who is later known as Peter/Cephas.

Though it is Andrew who brings Simon to Jesus, it is Jesus who again speaks first. With one sentence, Jesus reveals that he already knows who Simon is. Furthermore, he also knows who Simon will be after embarking on his journey of discipleship. While in the first reading we are told that Samuel matures in the presence of the Lord, Simon's future maturation is implied in Jesus' renaming him at their first encounter.

Like the disciples, our relationship with God is a result of God's initiative and calling. We can choose whether to heed his call and follow or turn a deaf ear to his voice. M.B.

THIRD SUNDAY
IN ORDINARY TIME

LECTIONARY #68

READING I   Jonah 3:1–5, 10

A reading from the Book of the Prophet Jonah

The **word** of the LORD **came** to **Jonah**, saying:
  "**Set out** for the great city of **Nineveh**,
  and **announce** to it the message that I will **tell** you."
So Jonah made ready and **went** to Nineveh,
  according to the LORD's bidding.
Now Nineveh was an enormously **large city**;
  it took **three days** to go through it.
Jonah began his journey through the city,
  and had gone but a single day's walk **announcing**,
  "**Forty days more** and Nineveh shall be **destroyed**,"
  when the people of Nineveh **believed God**;
  they proclaimed a **fast**
  and **all** of them, great and small, put on **sackcloth**.

When God **saw** by their actions how they **turned** from their
    evil way,
  he **repented** of the evil that he had **threatened** to do to them;
  he **did not** carry it out.

Jonah = JOH-nuh
To prepare, read all of Jonah 3, including the verses omitted from today's lectionary reading.
Nineveh = NIN-uh-vuh
Distinguish the character voices: the narrator, the Lord, and the prophet Jonah.

This is an important verse. The people heed God's warning and repent. The theme of repentance will be heard again in the Gospel.

God is compassionate and merciful. These themes are echoed in the responsorial psalm.

READING I This passage from Jonah highlights the need to turn one's life completely toward God. God's word comes to Jonah, now for a second time, with a message for Nineveh. In the chapters preceding today's reading comes the well-known story of Jonah's attempt to avoid God's commission and his subsequent stint in the belly of the whale. We do not learn until later why Jonah did not want to fulfill his prophetic duties: he did not want the Ninevites to experience God's mercy. Jonah hated the Ninevites because Nineveh was the capital of the Assyrian empire, which had destroyed the northern kingdom of Israel, killed many of its inhabitants, and sent the survivors into exile. Jonah's hatred shapes most of the action in the Book of Jonah.

In today's reading, God comes to Jonah again but does not reproach him for his previous disobedience. Jonah goes as commanded but does the bare minimum to accomplish what God has commanded. He does not even make it halfway into the city proclaiming God's message! Up to this point in the book, we did not know the content of the message but finally we hear that Nineveh has forty days before it will be destroyed. Forty days is a typical period of testing and waiting. For example, Moses spent forty days in supplication to the Lord for his mercy after the Israelites made an idol of a golden calf (see Deuteronomy 9:15–19).

Despite Jonah's deficient preaching, the people's hearts are changed. They repent, wearing sackcloth and fasting to indicate the sincerity of their repentance. They also changed their way of living and "turned from their evil way." As a result, God stayed his hand and they were not destroyed.

For meditation and context:

RESPONSORIAL PSALM   Psalm 25:4–5, 6–7, 8–9 (4a)

R. Teach me your ways, O Lord.

Your ways, O Lord, make known to me;
    teach me your paths,
guide me in your truth and teach me,
    for you are God my savior.

Remember that your compassion, O Lord,
    and your love are from of old.

In your kindness remember me,
    because of your goodness, O Lord.

Good and upright is the Lord;
    thus he shows sinners the way.
He guides the humble to justice
    and teaches the humble his way.

READING II   1 Corinthians 7:29–31

Corinthians = kohr-IN-thee-uhnz

The lack of time suggests a sense of urgency.

Rhetorical negations can be confusing. Emphasize the first mention of what is negated and the negative, and subdue the second mention. The bolding will help you see the pattern.

Pause before the last line.

A reading from the first Letter of Saint Paul to the Corinthians

I tell you, **brothers** and **sisters**, the **time** is running **out**.
From now on, let those having wives act as **not** having them,
    those **weeping** as **not** weeping,
    those **rejoicing** as **not** rejoicing,
    those **buying** as **not** owning,
    those **using** the **world** as **not** using it fully.
For the **world** in its present form is **passing** away.

GOSPEL   Mark 1:14–20

Don't rush the cryptic mention of John's arrest. It's a reminder—prophets don't have an easy life.

The theme of repentance from the first reading is repeated.

A reading from the holy Gospel according to Mark

After John had been **arrested**,
    Jesus came to Galilee **proclaiming** the **gospel** of God:
    "This is the time of **fulfillment**.
The kingdom of God is at hand.
Repent, and **believe** in the gospel." »

The prophecies of doom and destruction, such as the one found in today's reading, are not meant to be the final word. Instead, they are an invitation to the recipients to change their lives and reorient themselves towards God. We see the Ninevites accept this invitation as they "believed God," repented, and turned from doing evil.

READING II In these verses from 1 Corinthians, Paul likewise warns his audience that "time is running out." Here Paul is referring to the second coming of Christ, which will come when it is least

expected. Thus, believers should live as if Christ could return that very day. Following this warning, Paul gives advice about how believers should live out their Christian identity with this eschatological attitude.

However, it is important to understand that in these verses Paul is speaking rhetorically and not literally. For example, his statement about those who are married does not mean that they should live celibately, as this would go against his advice to married couples earlier in the letter (1 Corinthians 7:2–6). Nor does he mean that one can really keep from weeping in

moments of grief. The rhetorical force of these words emphasizes that our focus should be on things that last rather than on things that do not have lasting value: "For the world in its present form is passing away."

This reading reminds us of the eschatological tension in which we live today. We are called to live in the "now" with the end in mind. We are to reexamine our relationship to the world on all levels: social, personal, and commercial. Are we too focused on the things of this world such that they draw us away from being prepared to stand

Jesus doesn't leave the disciples to their own devices. He assures them that he will make them fishers of people.

Zebedee = ZEB-uh-dee

Mark's account has the disciples drop everything and follow. In general, Mark's Gospel has a breathless, urgent quality. Read the actions of the disciples slightly more quickly than your normal pace to reflect the haste with which they respond to Jesus' invitation.

As he **passed** by the **Sea** of **Galilee**,
　　he saw **Simon** and his brother **Andrew** casting their **nets**
　　　into the sea;
　　they were **fishermen**.
Jesus said to them,
　　"**Come** after me, and I will **make you** fishers of **men**."
Then they **abandoned** their nets and **followed** him.
He walked along a little farther
　　and saw **James**, the son of **Zebedee**, and his brother **John**.
They too were in a boat **mending** their nets.
Then he **called** them.
So they **left** their **father Zebedee** in the boat
　　along with the **hired men** and **followed** him.

before God when Jesus comes again? In other words, have we turned our lives completely over to God as we saw the Ninevites do in the first reading?

GOSPEL Today's Gospel reading presents examples of those whose relationship to earthly things is second to their relationship with God. The first person in this passage who has completely given his life over to God is John the Baptist, so much so that he has been arrested because he spoke the truth of God to others. Next, we hear Jesus' preaching that

includes a call to conversion. Jesus' words calling for repentance remind us of Jonah's proclamation to Nineveh, but Jesus goes further and speaks of the kingdom of God and the need to believe in the Gospel, the good news of God's salvation for all. Jesus' message demands a change in one's attitude and life.

Other people exemplifying a complete turn toward God include Simon, Andrew, James, and John. Jesus calls to them and, without asking for explanations or looking for excuses, all four men immediately obey Jesus and follow him. Their actions fore-

shadow Jesus' words later about the path of discipleship, in which one has to leave all behind for the sake of the Gospel (Mark 10:28–29). It is crucial to realize that this does not mean that disciples must completely break from their families. In fact, a few verses after today's readings, we read about Jesus going to Simon and Andrew's house and healing Simon's mother-in-law (1:29–31). Like Paul's words to the Corinthians, the concern here is about having a proper disposition toward our earthly relationships so that we are not distracted from our primary relationship with God. M.B.

FOURTH SUNDAY IN ORDINARY TIME

LECTIONARY #71

READING I Deuteronomy 18:15–20

A reading from the Book of Deuteronomy

Moses spoke to all the **people**, saying:
"A **prophet** like me will the LORD, your God, **raise** up for you
from among your own **kin**;
to him you shall **listen**.
This is exactly what you **requested** of the LORD, your God,
at **Horeb**
on the day of the assembly, when you said,
'Let us **not again hear** the voice of the LORD, our God,
nor see this great fire any more, **lest we die.**'
And the LORD said to me, 'This was **well said**.
I will **raise up** for them a **prophet** like you from among their kin,
and will put my **words** into his mouth;
he shall tell them all that I **command** him.
Whoever will **not listen** to my words which he speaks
in my name,
I myself will make him **answer** for it.
But if a prophet **presumes to speak** in my name
an **oracle** that I have **not commanded** him to speak,
or speaks in the name of other gods, he shall **die.**'"

Deuteronomy = d<u>oo</u>-ter-AH-nuh-mee or dy<u>oo</u>-ter-AH-nuh-mee

As you begin, notice the numerous quotations. Help the assembly understand who is speaking.

Horeb = HOHR-eb

The Lord approves of the sense of reverence the people have for the divine. Convey a sense of pride and satisfaction.

The reading concludes with two stern warnings: one for the prophet and one for the listener.

READING I In today's first reading, we hear of the promise of a prophet-like-Moses who will come to lead the people. In the Gospels, Jesus is identified as the promised prophet-like-Moses. While Moses' prophetic role is highlighted in this reading, Moses is never called a prophet in any of the books of the Pentateuch. This is the closest he comes to that designation, and here his prophetic role is described as an intermediary between God and God's people. Moses reminds the people that they requested the establishment of this role because they feared direct interac-

tions with God (see Deuteronomy 5:22–27). Today's reading emphasizes the establishment of a permanent channel of communication between God and his people.

It describes how prophets will act and how they communicate the message of God. God's promise, "[I] will put my words into his [the prophet-like-Moses'] mouth," affirms the prophet as God's spokesperson and envoy. The prophets are chosen by God and are given his words to speak. They should only speak God's word to the people. However, this reading also warns against two types of false prophecy. First,

we see that there can be false oracles presented by the prophet as God's words. Second, false prophets might proclaim oracles from other gods. God will condemn both types. Additionally, those who do not heed the prophet when he conveys God's words will answer to God himself.

This reading from Deuteronomy assures us of God's continual efforts to communicate with us and his commitment to ensuring that his message arrives to us without distortion. For our part, we need to listen to God's words, especially those communicated through and in Jesus Christ,

For meditation and context:

RESPONSORIAL PSALM   Psalm 95:1–2, 6–7, 7–9 (8)

R. If today you hear his voice, harden not your hearts.

Come, let us sing joyfully to the LORD;
  let us acclaim the rock of our salvation.
Let us come into his presence
    with thanksgiving;
  let us joyfully sing psalms to him.

Come, let us bow down in worship;
  let us kneel before the LORD who made us.

For he is our God,
  and we are the people he shepherds,
    the flock he guides.

Oh, that today you would hear his voice:
  "Harden not your hearts as at Meribah,
    as in the day of Massah in the desert,
  where your fathers tempted me;
    they tested me though they had seen
      my works."

READING II   1 Corinthians 7:32–35

A reading from the first Letter of Saint Paul to the Corinthians

Corinthians = kohr-IN-thee-uhnz

Paul's overarching concern is to mitigate anxieties. Many early Christians believed that the Lord's return was imminent. What advice could he offer the people of Corinth?

Subdue "unmarried" and "married" to reflect the more important theological message that we all need to stay focused on the Lord no matter our vocational status.

Brothers and sisters:
I should like you to be **free of anxieties**.
An unmarried man is **anxious** about the **things** of the **Lord**,
  how he may **please** the Lord.
But a married man is anxious about the things of the **world**,
  how he may **please** his **wife**, and he is **divided**.
An unmarried woman or a virgin is anxious about the things
    of the Lord,
  so that she may be **holy** in both **body** and **spirit**.
A married woman, on the other hand,
  is anxious about the things of the **world**,
  how she may **please** her husband.
I am telling you this for your own **benefit**,
  not to impose a **restraint** upon you,
  but for the sake of **propriety**
    and **adherence** to the Lord **without distraction**.

Paul's tone softens as he explains the reasoning behind his teaching.

---

the Word of God made flesh, and integrate them into our lives.

READING II Paul's concerns for freedom from anxiety motivates his words in today's second reading. For Paul, anxiety takes our attention away from prayer and service to the Church. With these words, Paul reflects on the ways the social situations and commitments according to a person's state of life may pull him or her away from devoting time to God. However, even those who have more flexibility of time do not always use their time in this way.

In this passage, Paul expresses a preference for the celibate life, not because he believes it is the only possible state of life for Christians, but because he sees it as more conducive to being free from the cares of the world and its values. It is true that married couples ought to pay attention to the needs of their spouse and, if they have any, their children. We should keep in mind that Paul is not saying that married life is inferior or that married couples are not as holy. This would contradict Paul's words earlier in the letter when he says that every believer is the temple of the Holy Spirit

(1 Corinthians 6:19). Paul's preference comes from his desire that we devote all our time and energy to prayer and service to God and others. He sees this most easily accomplished through the celibate state, yet it is crucial to note that prior to expressing these views, Paul clarifies that he is presenting his opinion on the matter and not issuing a command (1 Corinthians 7:25).

Regardless of our state in life, our primary vocation granted through our baptism calls us to devote ourselves to prayer and serving God. All other concerns will fall into their proper place when we do so.

GOSPEL   Mark 1:21–28

A reading from the holy Gospel according to Mark

Then they came to Capernaum,
     and on the sabbath **Jesus** entered the **synagogue** and **taught**.
The **people** were **astonished** at his teaching,
     for he taught them as one **having authority** and **not** as
          the **scribes**.
In their synagogue was a **man** with an **unclean spirit**;
     he cried out, "**What have you to do with us, Jesus of Nazareth**?
Have you **come to destroy us**?
I **know who you are**—the **Holy One** of God!"
Jesus **rebuked** him and said,
     "**Quiet**! Come out of him!"
The unclean spirit **convulsed** him and with a **loud cry** came
          out of him.
All were **amazed** and asked one another,
     "**What is this**?
A **new** teaching with authority.
He commands **even** the unclean spirits and they **obey** him."
His **fame spread** everywhere throughout the whole
          region of Galilee.

Capernaum = kuh-PER-nee-*m or kuh-PER-nay-*m or kuh-PER-n*m

Emphasize "not as the scribes"; this is surprising. The scribes were viewed by the people as experts and teachers of the Jewish law.

The authoritative nature of Jesus bookends the reading.

"Rebuke" is a strong word. Jesus' performative language should be commanding.

Imagine yourself witnessing an exorcism. Bring that amazement to the reaction of the crowd.

GOSPEL This passage from Mark's Gospel picks up where we left off in last Sunday's reading. The disciples travel with Jesus to Capernaum, the center of Jesus' Galilean ministry. There they witness Jesus' power and authority, providing a basis for their following Jesus. In fact, Jesus' authority is such that it surpasses that of the scribes, the experts on the Law. We are reminded of the promised prophet-like-Moses from the first reading, who conveys God's words with authority.

The exorcism account in this passage highlights the distinction between the holi- ness of Jesus and the uncleanliness (mean- ing "unholiness") of the spirit. "Holiness" here is not a moral designation but refers to "sacred," set apart by and for God. The demon recognizes Jesus' holiness and becomes defensive in response, revealing special knowledge about Jesus, which is why Jesus rebukes him. Jesus casts out the demon by the power of his word alone. Once again, Jesus reveals himself as the prophet-like-Moses whose authority to teach and exorcise has a divine source. In Jesus, God continues to communicate him- self to his people by giving to us the Word of God incarnate.

Today's Gospel invites us to recognize Jesus' power and authority. Because Jesus is the fullness of God's message to us, we need to be attuned to how Jesus communi- cates himself to us on a continual basis: through Scripture, by the actions and words of those around us, and most especially, in the Eucharist. M.B.

FIFTH SUNDAY
IN ORDINARY TIME

LECTIONARY #74

READING I Job 7:1–4, 6–7

A reading from the Book of Job

Job spoke, saying:
Is not **man's life** on earth a **drudgery**?
    Are not his days those of **hirelings**?
He is a **slave** who longs for the **shade**,
    a hireling who waits for his **wages**.
So I have been **assigned** months of **misery**,
    and troubled **nights** have been allotted to me.
If in bed I say, "**When** shall I **arise**?"
    then the **night drags** on;
I am filled with restlessness until the dawn.
My **days** are **swifter** than a weaver's shuttle;
    they come to an end **without hope**.
Remember that my life is like the wind;
    I shall **not see happiness again**.

Job = johb

Job describes the misery of life itself before turning to his own despair.

Consider slowing down "night drags on" and speeding up for "days are swifter". Let the words represent what they express.

Don't overdo the woe in these lines. Some of your listeners might feel as Job does, but although this reading is mostly negative, Job's faith in God prevails in the whole Book of Job. By your tone, prepare the listener for the joy of God's enduring promise that is proclaimed in the responsorial psalm.

READING I In these verses, Job muses on the purpose of life, in particular his own life of misery and suffering. In his current state, Job projects a sense of the futility of life; however, we should keep in mind that Job is not proposing a philosophy of life. He rather speaks from the depths of his suffering. The references to "a hirelings" further highlight Job's dejection as he sees no real purpose to hard labor.

There is a connection between Job's musings on hard labor and Adam's punishment in Genesis 3:17: "Cursed is the ground because of you! In toil you shall eat its yield all the days of your life." Both Job and the curse in Genesis point toward a brokenness in the human experience. While Job dwells on the misery caused by this brokenness, Genesis 3 provides us an explanation for why this brokenness exists to begin with. As a result of original sin, no human can avoid experiencing tragedy and the struggles of life.

Along with bemoaning hard labor, Job laments the brevity of life. He sees his life coming to an end in this miserable state as another layer of suffering. While he speaks of his life ending "without hope," the last sentence of this reading reveals that Job is not really hopeless. He asks God to "remember," to heed him in his misery. If Job did not think there was a purpose to God's attention, he would not seek it but would truly despair and not speak.

Job's rhetoric in this reading reflects the reality that suffering comes to us all. When it does, we turn to God for answers and the hope that he will alleviate our suffering. Sometimes the answer is not what we expect or want, as we see by the end of the Book of Job; yet God does heed our cries.

For meditation and context:

RESPONSORIAL PSALM Psalm 147:1–2, 3–4, 5–6 (3a)

R. Praise the Lord, who heals the brokenhearted.
or
R. Alleluia.

Praise the LORD, for he is good;
    sing praise to our God, for he is gracious;
    it is fitting to praise him.
The LORD rebuilds Jerusalem;
    the dispersed of Israel he gathers.

He heals the brokenhearted
    and binds up their wounds.

He tells the number of the stars;
    he calls each by name.

Great is our Lord and mighty in power;
    to his wisdom there is no limit.
The LORD sustains the lowly;
    the wicked he casts to the ground.

Corinthians = kohr-IN-thee-uhnz

Paul uses somewhat dense philosophical statements. Watch the punctuation.

recompense = REK-uhm-pens = compensation

As challenging as inclusivity is, Paul tries to ensure his actions and words are able to communicate the Gospel to as many as possible. Do our evangelization efforts reflect the same wide reach?

READING II 1 Corinthians 9:16–19, 22–23

A reading from the first Letter of Saint Paul to the Corinthians

Brothers and sisters:
If I **preach** the **gospel**, this is **no reason** for **me** to **boast**,
    for an **obligation** has been **imposed** on me,
    and **woe** to me if I do **not** preach it!
If I do so **willingly**, I have a **recompense**,
    but if **un**willingly, then I have been entrusted with
        a **stewardship**.
What then is my **recompense**?
That, when I preach,
    I offer the gospel **free** of charge
    so as not to make full use of my right in the gospel.

Although I am free in regard to all,
    I have made myself a **slave** to all
    so as to **win over** as **many** as possible.
To the **weak** I became weak, to win over the weak.
I have become **all things** to all, to save at least **some**.
All this I do for the sake of the **gospel**,
    so that **I** too may have a **share** in it.

READING II In today's second reading, Paul speaks of a different kind of labor. For Paul, preaching the Gospel is an "obligation" divinely imposed on him. Paul's conviction that it is not an option for him to not preach echoes similar words from Jeremiah (Jeremiah 20:8–9), affirming Paul's words as expressing a prophetic experience. It also reminds us of Jonah's futile attempt to escape his prophetic commission.

Paul's labor is to preach the Gospel, yet it is not a paid job. He emphasizes that he offers the Gospel "free of charge" to ensure that he does not misuse his authority in the Gospel. By preaching without pay, Paul is free to serve others and is not hindered or distracted by financial obligations; hence Paul's emphasis on being "free in regard to all." His goal is to bring salvation to all. However, in stating he does so "to save at least some," he also recognizes that not everyone will accept the Gospel.

Paul's reward for preaching is the preaching of the Gospel. While this may seem like circular reasoning, in preaching salvation Paul likewise partakes in salvation. Like a muscle that needs to be used to remain strong, preaching the Gospel strengthens and confirms Paul's faith in it.

A possible point of confusion is Paul saying he became "all things to all." This does not mean that he changes to please others. In fact, Paul usually comes down against trying to please others (for example, see 1 Thessalonians 2:4 and Galatians 1:10). Instead, he gives himself completely to preaching the Good News. Paul's approach presents a model for our own preaching of the Gospel. We joyfully and freely share the Good News because we have received it

Be aware of the multiple scene changes in this reading and pause before each. The shifts occur at the temporal markers: "When it was evening" and "Rising very early before dawn."

News of the miracle spreads quickly. Convey the anxiousness and fervent hope people had as they brought their maladies before Jesus.

Jesus is confirming his role to the disciples. Read this with strength. Jesus is renewed from his solitude and prayer.

GOSPEL   Mark 1:29–39

A reading from the holy Gospel according to Mark

On **leaving** the **synagogue**
    Jesus entered the **house** of **Simon** and **Andrew** with **James**
        and **John.**
Simon's **mother-in-law** lay **sick** with a fever.
They immediately **told** him **about her.**
He **approached**, **grasped** her hand, and **helped** her **up.**
Then the fever **left** her and she **waited** on them.

When it was **evening**, after sunset,
    they **brought** to him **all** who were **ill** or possessed by **demons.**
The whole town was **gathered** at the **door.**
He **cured** many who were sick with various diseases,
    and he **drove out** many demons,
    not permitting them to **speak** because they **knew** him.

Rising very early before dawn, he **left**
    and went off to a **deserted place**, where he **prayed.**
Simon and those who were with him **pursued** him
    and on finding him said, "**Everyone is looking for you.**"
He told them, "Let us **go** on to the nearby **villages**
    that I may **preach** there also.
For this **purpose** have I come."
So he went into their **synagogues**,
    preaching and **driving out demons** throughout the whole
        of Galilee.

free of charge. The Gospel is a gift that we need to share with others.

GOSPEL Today's Gospel conveys a sense of immediacy and urgency in Jesus' ministry. The people's need for the Good News is great, and there is no time to waste in proclaiming and witnessing to it. This resonates with Paul's compulsion to preach the Gospel in the second reading.

Jesus' ministry of prayer, healing, preaching, and exorcising is displayed in this reading. While in last week's Gospel Jesus' power was manifested through his words, today we see Jesus' power revealed by his touch alone. When he takes Simon's mother-in-law by the hand, the fever departs, and she begins to serve Jesus and the disciples. In serving them, she confirms the healing and presents a model of true discipleship which consists of humble service to others.

We also see Jesus going off to a deserted place to pray. Here we see the theme of the desert as a place to pray and connect with God. This passage also draws the connection between prayer and ministry. Jesus constantly prays throughout his ministry, and he teaches his disciples how to pray by example and through instruction.

The Gospel today presents a model for our own Christian ministry, which we are all called to live out in our daily lives and in our own unique way. First, we are reminded of the urgency to preach the Good News and not put it off for a more convenient time or occasion. Next, we see that our sharing of the Good News should be manifested in our service to others, as Simon's mother-in-law demonstrated. And finally, our whole Christian life and ministry is rooted in constant prayer. M.B.

SIXTH SUNDAY IN ORDINARY TIME

LECTIONARY #77

READING I   Leviticus 13:1–2, 44–46

A reading from the Book of Leviticus

Leviticus = lih-VIT-ih-kuhs

The **LORD** said to **Moses** and **Aaron**,
  "If someone has on his **skin** a scab or pustule or blotch
  which appears to be the sore of **leprosy**,
  he shall be **brought** to Aaron, the **priest**,
  or to one of the priests among his descendants.
If the man is leprous and **unclean**,
  the priest shall **declare** him unclean
  by reason of the sore on his head.

"The one who **bears** the sore of leprosy
  shall keep his garments **rent** and his head **bare**,
  and shall muffle his **beard**;
  he shall **cry out**, 'Unclean, **unclean**!'
As **long** as the sore is on him he shall declare himself unclean,
  since he is in fact unclean.
He shall dwell **apart**, making his abode **outside** the camp."

leprosy = LEP-ruhs-see

Don't overemphasize the description of the illnesses.

leprous = LEP-ruhs

Those who are diseased are ostracized and must publicly declare it. Having to live apart from the community compounds this sense of separation. Have you ever felt cut off from your community?

READING I In today's reading from Leviticus, the prescriptions regarding dealing with skin disorders are listed in detail. Such ailments were not trivial matters to the ancient Israelites. Those suspected of chronic skin disease were required to appear before the priest, who would declare a person clean or unclean. If the disease was of a temporary nature, then the afflicted person was deemed clean, but if the priest found that it was a chronic skin disease, then the person was deemed unclean and was treated like a corpse. The reason for this was that bodily impurity was associated with the forces of death, as opposed to God's covenantal commandments, which represented the forces of life.

Since contact between the sacred and the unclean was avoided at all costs, permanent banishment was a very real possibility for those suffering chronic skin disorders. In such cases, the afflicted person had to tear his garments, a sign of mourning, and announce his proximity to all so that others could avoid coming near him. Chronic skin disease was a significant social and religious barrier between the afflicted and the rest of the community. The only way to be reintegrated into the community was for the priest to verify that the person had been cured from the disease and to perform the prescribed rituals described in Leviticus 14:1–20.

READING II In this reading from 1 Corinthians, Paul exhorts believers to do everything for the glory of God, including not giving offense to others. Paul specifically refers to eating and drinking in this context because the Corinthians were struggling with whether they could

For meditation and context:

RESPONSORIAL PSALM　Psalm 32:1–2, 5, 11 (7)

R. I turn to you, Lord, in time of trouble, and you fill me with the joy of salvation.

Blessed is he whose fault is taken away,
　whose sin is covered.
Blessed the man to whom the Lord imputes
　not guilt,
　in whose spirit there is no guile.

Then I acknowledged my sin to you,
　my guilt I covered not.
I said, "I confess my faults to the Lord,"
　and you took away the guilt of my sin.

Be glad in the Lord and rejoice, you just;
　exult, all you upright of heart.

Corinthians = kohr-IN-thee-uhnz

READING II　1 Corinthians 10:31—11:1

A reading from the first Letter of Saint Paul to the Corinthians

Brothers and sisters,
Whether you eat or drink, or **whatever you do**,
　do everything for the **glory** of **God**.
Avoid giving **offense**, whether to the **Jews** or **Greeks** or the
　　church of God,
　just as I **try** to **please** everyone in every way,
　not seeking my own **benefit** but that of the many,
　that they may be saved.
Be **imitators** of me, as I am of **Christ**.

Sensitivity to other cultures is a timeless message of tolerance and inclusivity.

Are we confident enough in our faith to invite others to follow our Christlike living?

---

purchase and eat food that had been offered to idols. Paul's command to "Avoid giving offense" does not mean to avoid hurting others' feelings. Instead, to "give offense" meant either to impede someone's acceptance of the Gospel or to estrange a believer.

As we heard in the second reading last Sunday, Paul again states that he tries to please everyone. Paul means by this that he is careful in preaching and in living out his Christian vocation so that nothing he does turns others away from the Gospel. Instead, Paul is like transparent glass through which the Gospel is seen. Paul imi-

tates Christ so that all that the people see is Christ and not Paul. Paul encourages believers to emulate his imitation of Christ so only Christ is seen in them.

Earlier in this letter, Paul states that Christ died for weak members of the community (8:11). As imitators of Christ, we should die to ourselves for the sake of others for their salvation. This does not mean being dictated to by others' conscience, but rather that it takes careful discernment and prayer to distinguish our own preferences, habits, and opinions

from what is absolutely necessary for attaining salvation.

GOSPEL　As seen in today's first reading, chronic skin disease resulted in the afflicted person's marginalization from the rest of the community. While these chronic disorders were seen as punishment for sin, it was also clear that the cure of such diseases was a divine prerogative, like raising the dead (Numbers 12:10–12; 2 Kings 5:7).

Jesus demonstrates that he has this divine prerogative in his healing of the

GOSPEL   Mark 1:40–45

A reading from the holy Gospel according to Mark

A **leper** came to **Jesus** and **kneeling** down **begged** him and said,
   "If you **wish**, you can make me **clean**."
Moved with pity, he stretched out his **hand**,
   touched him, and said to him,
   "I do **will** it. Be made **clean**."
The leprosy left him **immediately**, and he was made clean.
Then, warning him **sternly**, he **dismissed** him at once.

He said to him, "See that you **tell no one** anything,
   but **go**, show yourself to the **priest**
   and **offer** for your cleansing what Moses prescribed;
   that will be **proof** for them."

The man went away and began to **publicize** the whole matter.
He **spread** the report abroad
   so that it was **impossible** for Jesus to enter a town openly.
He remained **outside** in **deserted** places,
   and **people** kept **coming** to him from everywhere.

The leper bravely approaches Jesus. Think of a time that you knelt in prayer and begged God for healing. Bring the intensity of that prayer to the reading.

Read Jesus' actions and performative words slowly and tenderly. Jesus is answering the man's deepest prayer for healing.

Jesus repeats this request for secrecy throughout the Gospel of Mark. Here, and in other places, it is ignored.

leper. Not only does he go against Levitical purity laws by touching the leper, he cures him through the power of his word and touch. Here Jesus combines in one healing event both word and deed, each method having been demonstrated separately in the miracles seen in the two previous Sunday Gospel readings. After the healing, Jesus follows Levitical legislation, telling the former leper to show himself to the priest and offer sacrifice as prescribed by the religious law.

As in today's second reading, there is a concern for following the letter of the law. However, the overriding concern here is reintegrating the marginalized into the community that they, too, might be saved. By the end of this reading, the healed man is not only restored in health and in society, he also participates in Jesus' ministry by proclaiming the Good News of Jesus Christ to all. M.B.

ASH WEDNESDAY

LECTIONARY #219

READING I   Joel 2:12–18

A reading from the Book of the Prophet Joel

Even now, says the LORD,
  return to me with your whole **heart**,
  with **fasting**, and **weeping**, and **mourning**;
Rend your hearts, **not** your **garments**,
  and return to the LORD, your **God**.
For **gracious** and **merciful** is he,
  slow to anger, **rich in kindness**,
  and relenting in punishment.
Perhaps he will again **relent**
  and **leave** behind him a **blessing**,
Offerings and **libations**
  for the LORD, your God.

Blow the trumpet in Zion!
  proclaim a fast,
  call an **assembly**;
Gather the people,
  notify the congregation;
Assemble the **elders**,
  gather the **children**
  and the **infants** at the breast;
Let the **bridegroom** quit his room
  and the bride her chamber.

Although we are entering a penitential season, these practices can be read with excitement. God has given us concrete actions to help conform our hearts, minds, and spirits to him.

Notice the comprehensive nature of who Joel is addressing—everybody.

READING I | As we begin this Lenten journey, today's first reading invites us to renew our biblical faith and revisit those religious practices in which we may have become lax. The prophet Joel highlights our relationship with God as the center of our biblical faith and emphasizes that we are to invest in that relationship with our entire heart. Joel's use of the phrase "with your whole heart" recalls the fundamental expression of biblical faith known as the *Shema*, which appears in Deuteronomy 6:4–5. Following Moses' restatement of the ten commandments,

God, through Moses, tells the people "Hear [*shema*], O Israel! The LORD is our God, the LORD alone! Therefore, you shall love the LORD, your God, with your whole heart, and with your whole being, and with your whole strength." Like devout Jews today, who still recite this prayer multiple times every day, Jesus quotes the *Shema* when asked to identify the first and most fundamental law given by God in Torah (see Mark 12:28–30). From a biblical perspective, to love God *with your whole heart* is not simply about fostering emotional affection for the Lord. Rather, it entails mindful loving since in the

Bible (especially the Old Testament) "heart" refers to the mind. Thus, we might say that when Joel calls us to renew our love for God, emotionally engaged thinking is in order. Joel invites us to thoughtful and intentional love of God—we are to love God with our whole being. We act in this way because God first extends gracious, merciful, and steadfast love to us.

Attentive to the call to whole-hearted faith, Joel turns to traditional religious practices: fasting, weeping, mourning, offering sacrifices, and assembling God's people. All of these behaviors focus on the movement

We add our own plea for God's mercy and presence. Proclaim this prayer clearly so the congregation can make it their own.

Between the porch and the altar
    let the **priests**, the **ministers** of the LORD, **weep**,
And say, "**Spare**, O LORD, your people,
    and make not your heritage a reproach,
    with the nations ruling over them!
Why should they say among the peoples,
    '**Where** is their God?' "

Then the LORD was stirred to **concern** for his **land**
    and took **pity** on his people.

For meditation and context:

RESPONSORIAL PSALM   Psalm 51:3–4, 5–6ab, 12–13, 14 and 17 (3a)

R. Be merciful, O Lord, for we have sinned.

Have mercy on me, O God,
    in your goodness;
    in the greatness of your compassion
      wipe out my offense.
Thoroughly wash me from my guilt
    and of my sin cleanse me.

For I acknowledge my offense,
    and my sin is before me always:

"Against you only have I sinned,
    and done what is evil in your sight."

A clean heart create for me, O God,
    and a steadfast spirit renew within me.
Cast me not out from your presence,
    and your Holy Spirit take not from me.

Give me back the joy of your salvation,
    and a willing spirit sustain in me.
O Lord, open my lips,
    and my mouth shall proclaim your praise.

READING II   2 Corinthians 5:20—6:2

A reading from the second Letter of Saint Paul to the Corinthians

Corinthians = kohr-IN-thee-uhnz

Brothers and sisters:
We are **ambassadors** for **Christ**,
    as if God were appealing through us.
We implore you on behalf of Christ,
    be **reconciled** to **God**.
For **our** sake he made him to be **sin** who did **not** know sin,
    so that we might become the **righteousness** of God in him. ❯❯

Announce the first lines with pride. Ambassadors have a connotation of importance. You, too, are an ambassador for Christ.

Practice until you are comfortable with the pronouns. Listeners have only one chance to understand.

of making a return to the Lord. The basic notion of making a return to the Lord, which can be misunderstood at times, is less about pressuring God to act mercifully toward us (something God always does) and more about taking up those practices that lead to the transformation of our hearts. Penitential practices, like those mentioned by Joel and those that we take up in this Lenten season, make us more aware of God's constant compassion for us.

READING II When Paul and his companion (Timothy) claim to be God's "go-betweens" (ambassadors), they make clear that their message originates in God, not themselves. At its core, this message calls us to grow in our awareness of what God has done for us in Christ. The message consists of perennial elements of the Christian call, first and foremost of which is that we are to "be reconciled to God." Interestingly, the verb here in the original Greek is a passive imperative form. This grammatical construction suggests that the command to "be reconciled to God" fundamentally entails letting God act upon us. In other words, our reconciliation with God—a focus of every Lent—begins with God's work upon us and on our behalf. God initiates the reconciliation process. In turn, we offer an increasingly generous response to God as we come to recognize God's grace at work in our lives.

To help us grow in our awareness and understanding of that grace, Paul succinctly describes what God has done in Christ: the sinless one became sin itself. While Paul does not explicitly connect the dots for us here, we can recognize that by Christ becoming sin, he put our sins to death on the cross. Consequently, Paul

Working together, then,
    we **appeal** to you not to receive the grace of God in **vain**.
For he says:

> In an acceptable time ***I heard you***,
>   and on the day of salvation ***I helped*** you.

Behold, **now** is a very acceptable **time**;
    behold, now is the day of **salvation**.

GOSPEL   Matthew 6:1–6, 16–18

A reading from the holy Gospel according to Matthew

Jesus said to his **disciples**:
    "Take care **not** to perform **righteous deeds**
    in order that people may **see** them;
    otherwise, you will have **no recompense** from your
        heavenly **Father**.
When **you give alms,**
    do not blow a trumpet before you,
    as the **hypocrites** do in the synagogues and in the streets
    to win the **praise** of others.

Amen, I say to you,
    they have **received** their **reward**.
But when you give alms,
    do **not** let your **left hand** know what your **right** is doing,
    so that your **almsgiving** may be **secret**.
And your Father who sees in **secret** will **repay** you.

shows us that Christ opens up for us a privileged experience and otherwise unimaginable status with God. We, in Christ, can claim to be both God's co-workers and God's embodied righteousness in the world. In light of these observations, Paul also offers a wise reminder that we are to take our unmerited status with God seriously, not in vain. The language of "vanity" that Paul uses here echoes the biblical wisdom tradition and gives him the opportunity to provide yet another perennial Christian truth: it is always opportune to recognize that the moment of salvation is *now*. And

so, as we enter *this* Lent, we recognize what God has done and continues to do for us in Christ, and we respond in kind.

GOSPEL   Jesus' message in the Gospel, like the first reading, offers a two-fold reminder to attend to our religious practices and our interior dispositions that accompany those practices. In talking with the disciples about different spiritual practices they might engage in, Jesus highlights almsgiving, prayer, and fasting as preeminent examples. Called the "pillars" of Lent for good reason, these tra-

ditional practices call us to reconciliation and to a renewal of justice (giving God and others their due). For example, by diligently giving alms, we stand to recognize anew how much God has given us, become more aware of our attachments to material goods, let go of tendencies to "keep up" with others (covetousness), renew our responsibility to share our resources, and ultimately advance toward being better stewards of the gifts we have. Broadly speaking then, almsgiving fosters a renewal of justice with our neighbors, especially those in most need. Prayer animates and

"When **you pray**,
   do **not** be like the hypocrites,
   who love to **stand** and pray in the **synagogues** and on
      street corners
   so that **others** may **see** them.
Amen, I say to you,
   they have received their reward.
But when you pray, go to your **inner room**,
   close the door, and pray to your Father in **secret**.
And your Father who **sees** in secret will **repay** you.

"When you **fast**,
   do not look **gloomy** like the hypocrites.
They **neglect** their appearance,
   so that they may appear to others to be fasting.
Amen, I say to you, they have received their reward.
But when **you** fast,
   anoint your head and **wash** your face,
   so that you may not appear to be **fasting**,
   except to your **Father** who is **hidden**.
And your Father who sees what is hidden will repay you."

renews our devotion to God and can lead us to the experience of reconciliation in the sacrament of penance. Fasting, when performed as a spiritual practice, reminds us of our vulnerability and ultimate dependence on God. As such, it can help us to reorder our priorities, thus renewing justice within us so that we may be in right relationship with God.

Yet, for all the good that almsgiving, prayer, and fasting (or any spiritual practice) can bring, a deeper commitment to spiritual acts also entails critical attentiveness. Jesus reminds us that, without proper discernment, spiritual practices can be done for the wrong reasons. Those disordered motivations undermine the purpose of these spiritual practices and draw undue attention to us, instead of leading others to God. Jesus' proposed remedy is to perform spiritual practices in a self-effacing, non-attention-grabbing way. So, whatever specific spiritual practices we undertake this Lent, the instruction of Jesus is clear: our works should transform our interior disposition toward greater selflessness and direct attention toward God. E.W.

FIRST SUNDAY OF LENT

LECTIONARY #23

READING I Genesis 9:8–15

A reading from the Book of Genesis

Genesis = JEN-uh-sihs

This is a familiar story. Your proclamation helps others hear it anew. Pause after the narrator announces God will speak, giving the listeners time to prepare for God's words.

God said to **Noah** and to his **sons** with him:
"See, I am now **establishing** my **covenant** with **you**
and your **descendants** after you
and with **every living creature** that was with you:
all the birds, and the various tame and wild animals
that were with you and came out of the **ark**.
I will establish my covenant with you,
that **never again** shall all bodily **creatures** be **destroyed**
by the waters of a **flood**;
there **shall not** be another flood to **devastate the earth**."
God added:

God's word is amplified with a physical sign. Hear me and see my promise.

"This is the **sign** that I am giving for all ages to come,
of the **covenant** between me and you
and every living **creature** with you:
I set my **bow** in the clouds to serve as a sign
of the covenant between me and the **earth**.
When I bring clouds over the earth,
and the bow appears in the clouds,
I will **recall** the covenant I have made
between me and you and all living beings,
so that the **waters** shall **never** again become a **flood**
to **destroy** all mortal beings."

bow = boh

God's covenant is not just with humans but with all of creation. Ecological concerns are not a new issue. God has provided for creation from the beginning.

READING I This reading—the first of three exploring baptismal imagery—comes from the end of the flood account in Genesis where God establishes the first unequivocal covenant (*berit* in Hebrew) with humanity. Covenants establish deep bonds between/among the parties that enter into them, and they always consist of explicit terms (usually behavior based) that benefit all parties involved. In most cases, signs or symbolic actions establish the covenant and/or remind participants of the covenant in the future. The covenant of Christian marriage, for example, is established in the sacramental celebration of matrimony and is recalled in the sign of wedding rings worn by the couple.

In the case of the biblical flood, God anticipates the covenant made in today's reading before the flood with a promise to protect Noah, his descendants, and all living things on the earth, as well as every food (Genesis 6:18–21). In view of this promised covenant, Noah remains faithful to God's commands (Genesis 6:22) by building and filling the ark. Today's first reading then demonstrates God's faithfulness through the establishment of the foretold covenant. Noah, his descendants, and every living thing on the earth will never again be subject to a global flood. Moreover, and notably, only God's actions are restricted by the terms of this covenant, despite the fact that humanity's sins wrought the flood (Genesis 6:5–8). It is thus possible to see in today's first reading a type or precursor of baptism in which, through water, God restricts the divine power to enact justice in order to show forth the divine power to extend mercy to sinners in need of forgiveness.

For meditation and context:

RESPONSORIAL PSALM   Psalm 25:4–5, 6–7, 8–9 (10)

R. Your ways, O Lord, are love and truth to those who keep your covenant.

Your ways, O Lord, make known to me;
    teach me your paths,
guide me in your truth and teach me,
    for you are God my savior.

Remember that your compassion, O Lord,
    and your love are from of old.

In your kindness remember me,
    because of your goodness, O Lord.

Good and upright is the Lord,
    thus he shows sinners the way.
He guides the humble to justice,
    and he teaches the humble his way.

First Peter is rarely used during Year B. Announce the book distinctly.

READING II   1 Peter 3:18–22

A reading from the first Letter of Saint Peter

Beloved:
Christ suffered for **sins once**,
    the **righteous** for the sake of the **un**righteous,
    that he might **lead** you to **God**.

The Spirit that animates Jesus animates us.

Put to **death** in the **flesh**,
    he was brought to **life** in the **Spirit**.
In it he also went to preach to the spirits in **prison**,
    who had once been **disobedient**

Read "patiently" slowly.

    while God **patiently waited** in the days of **Noah**
    during the **building** of the **ark**,
    in which a few persons, eight in all,
    were **saved** through water.
This prefigured **baptism**, which **saves you now**.
It is **not** a **removal of dirt** from the body

Read through to the end with energy. God's majesty is on display.

    but an appeal to God for a clear **conscience**,
    through the **resurrection** of Jesus Christ,
    who has **gone** into **heaven**
    and is at the **right hand of God**,
    with **angels**, **authorities**, and **powers subject** to him.

READING II | This passage from Peter's first letter explores baptismal imagery by interpreting the Noah story in light of Christ's paschal mystery. The passage speaks of Jesus' descent to the realm of the dead and his proclamation of the Gospel to all those who died before his incarnation. This preaching in the realm of the dead, for Peter, was a manifestation of God's patience toward those who were disobedient in prior generations, especially the generation of Noah. Peter then extends the connection he makes between Noah and Christ's saving activity to baptism—

another washing with water that, although it is experienced outwardly as a washing, has an internal aim of cleansing and reconciling our consciences. Similar to the way that the flood called for God to be patient while Noah completed and filled the ark, so baptism calls for God to be patient with us as we journey either toward forgiveness of sins in baptism (as the elect do during this Lenten season) or toward a deeper realization of our baptismal call to conversion (as baptized Christians do in their reception of reconciliation this Lent). Thus, for Peter, baptism is an act of inquiry, a polite but

strenuous appeal to God imploring patient mercy. And, knowing of God's faithfulness and patient mercy in the covenant forged with Noah, we have assurance that our appeal to the Lord for mercy in the sacraments of forgiveness (baptism and penance) will be fulfilled.

GOSPEL | Mark's Gospel passage today is characteristically short, swift, and action-packed. Just after his baptism, Jesus is driven by the Spirit into the wilderness. This connects Jesus' baptism (and ours) with a purpose-filled

Pause after "beasts." It will contrast with "angels."

Pause for the scene change. Don't rush through John's plight.

Read Jesus' words with energy and convey immediacy. Pause after "repent," which helps emphasize "gospel."

GOSPEL   Mark 1:12–15

A reading from the holy Gospel according to Mark

The **Spirit drove Jesus** out into the **desert**,
　　and he **remained** in the desert for **forty days**, **tempted**
　　　　by Satan.
He was among wild **beasts**,
　　and the **angels ministered** to him.

After John had been **arrested**,
　　Jesus came to **Galilee** proclaiming the gospel of God:
　　"**This is the time of fulfillment**.
The kingdom of God is at hand.
Repent, and **believe** in the **gospel**."

mission. He does not remain on the shores of the Jordan but goes immediately to the wilderness to contend with Satan's temptations. Mark does not mention the nature or number of those temptations. Rather, he highlights the length of Jesus' stay—forty days—and the inhabitants Jesus encounters —wild beasts and angels. These subtle cues highlight Jesus' triumphant inversion of the meaning and power of wilderness temptations. Unlike the temptations of doubt and despair that tempted and overtook God's people in the wilderness upon hearing a mixed report of forty days of spy-

ing out the promised land (Numbers 13–14), Jesus's forty-day sojourn leaves him untouched by spiritual and physical threats in this perilous region. In fact, God's messengers care directly for Jesus while he is in the wilderness, and his mission follows immediately from his experience there. Jesus returns to Galilee and proclaims the Gospel, which is comprised of a few key elements. First, the nature of our temporal age has changed. Jesus' coming means we live in a time of fulfillment rather than a time of promise. Second, the fulfillment of our age is marked by the proximity of God's

kingdom; it is at hand in Jesus. Finally, this new age and the closeness of God's kingdom call for a two-fold response: repentance and belief. Still today, Jesus transforms our present place and time to call us to respond accordingly with acts of repentance and belief. E.W.

SECOND SUNDAY OF LENT

LECTIONARY #26

READING I Genesis 22:1–2, 9a, 10–13, 15–18

A reading from the Book of Genesis

God put **Abraham** to the **test**.
He called to him, "Abraham!"
"**Here I am**!" he replied.
Then God said:
    "Take **your son Isaac**, your **only one**, whom **you love**,
    and **go** to the land of **Moriah**.
There you shall **offer** him up as a **holocaust**
    on a height that I will point out to you."

When they came to the place of which God had told him,
    Abraham built an **altar** there and arranged the wood on it.
Then he reached out and took the knife to slaughter his son.
But the LORD's messenger called to him from heaven,
    "Abraham, **Abraham**!"
"Here I am!" he answered.
"**Do not lay your hand on the boy**," said the messenger.
"Do **not** do the **least thing** to him.
I know now how **devoted** you are to God,
    since you did not withhold from me **your** own beloved **son**."
As Abraham looked about,
    he spied a ram caught by its horns in the thicket.
So he went and took the **ram**
    and **offered it up** as a holocaust in place of his son. »

Genesis = JEN-uh-sihs

This reading can be challenging. In your preparation, read all of Genesis 22:1–18, including the verses missing from the lectionary reading. God is not asking for child sacrifice (a pagan practice) but is asking for faith and trust.

Moriah = moh-RĪ-uh

Heighten the story by emphasizing "your son", "only one," and "you love." The idea of a beloved son is heard again in the Gospel reading.

Read the command to do no harm with great intentionality.

READING I In this abridged account of the "Binding of Isaac" (*Akedah* in Hebrew), God tests Abraham by asking him to sacrifice his beloved son, Isaac. Abraham obediently gathers all the necessary sacrificial implements and travels with Isaac to a mountain in the land of Moriah where, at the last instant, God intervenes by sending a messenger who alters the instructions, thus sparing the boy. With Abraham's faith having been clearly demonstrated, a ram is sacrificed instead of Isaac. The story closes with God, again through a messenger, blessing Abraham with many valorous descendants who will bring blessing to all earth's nations.

Although this is a familiar story to many of us, it still raises many questions that we can prayerfully ponder as we renew and deepen our habit of prayer this Lent. Why did God, who knows Abraham's faith, test him in the first place? Why test his obedience and not some other area of potential weakness? Why test him in this way, with an invitation to sacrifice his beloved son? And, once Abraham demonstrates obedience, why wait until Abraham sacrifices a ram to bless him? Hadn't he already passed the test? Such questions highlight an important reality revealed in this story: our relationship with God entails sacrifice. In time, and based on the type found in Isaac, Jesus offers the perfect sacrifice on the cross reconciling us with God. Christ's sacrifice is fully efficacious for our salvation. At the same time, as Christians, we are called to imitate Christ. Thus, we might ponder how our relationship with God is calling us to sacrifice and how our interior disposition toward God might need to change to better respond to God with Abraham-like faith and generosity.

The abundance of God's blessing is described in various ways.

Again the **LORD's messenger called** to Abraham from **heaven**
    and said:
"I **swear** by myself, declares the LORD,
that because you acted as you did
in not **withholding** from me your beloved son,
I will **bless** you **abundantly**
and make your **descendants** as **countless**
    as the stars of the sky and the sands of the seashore;
your descendants shall take **possession**
    of the gates of their enemies,
and in your descendants **all the nations** of the earth
    shall find blessing—
all this because you **obeyed** my command."

Abraham exemplifies a faithful servant. The responsorial psalm will echo the willingness to serve faithfully.

For meditation and context:

RESPONSORIAL PSALM   Psalm 116:10, 15, 16–17, 18–19 (9)

R. I will walk before the Lord, in the land of the living.

I believed, even when I said,
    "I am greatly afflicted."
Precious in the eyes of the LORD
    is the death of his faithful ones.

O LORD, I am your servant;
    I am your servant, the son of your
        handmaid;
    you have loosed my bonds.

To you will I offer sacrifice of thanksgiving,
    and I will call upon the name of the LORD.

My vows to the LORD I will pay
    in the presence of all his people,
in the courts of the house of the LORD,
    in your midst, O Jerusalem.

READING II   Romans 8:31b–34

A reading from the Letter of Saint Paul to the Romans

Paul is not seeking information but is confirming an obvious conclusion using the rhetoric of questioning. Use a rising inflection for each question.

Brothers and sisters:
If **God** is for **us**, who can be **against** us?
He who **did not spare** his own **Son**
    but handed him over for us all,
        how will he not also give us everything else along with him?

READING II | This passage from the letter to the Romans highlights how the willing, sacrificial death of Jesus, his resurrection, and his ascension to God's right hand change the whole logic of human existence, especially for God's chosen people. Prior to Jesus, God's chosen people were to live by the law and the sacrificial system given at Mount Sinai. In this context, when the law was violated, God could justly condemn individual members or the entire chosen people, but a sacrifice could be made to rectify the ruptured relationship with God. But when Jesus offers himself as a sacrifice for our sake on the cross, he effectively makes a sacrifice that functions in advance for all future infractions. Thus, those who enter into Jesus' death and resurrection through baptism enjoy a relationship with God that was not previously possible. Now, thanks to the sacrifice that God has made for us in Jesus, we have assurance that the debt of sacrifice we owe to God has been paid—not by us or our ancestors, but by God. Consequently, when Paul poses his bold rhetorical questions in this reading, we can prayerfully ponder his questions in light of our faith in Jesus. We know that God will give his chosen ones everything along with Jesus, that any charge brought against God's people will not require a sacrifice greater than that of Jesus, and that ultimate condemnation cannot be leveled against God's people because God has acquitted them.

GOSPEL | On the second Sunday of Lent each year, an account of the transfiguration is proclaimed and the version in the Gospel we read from today in Mark is paradigmatic. Jesus takes Peter, James, and John up a high mountain alone,

Who will bring a **charge** against God's **chosen** ones?
　　It is God who **acquits** us, who will condemn?
Christ Jesus it is who **died**—or, rather, was **raised**—
　　who also is at the **right hand** of God,
　　who indeed **intercedes** for us.

The right hand implies the position of honor.

GOSPEL   Mark 9:2–10

A reading from the holy Gospel according to Mark

Jesus took Peter, **James**, and **John**
　　and led them up a high **mountain** apart by themselves.
And he was **transfigured** before them,
　　and his clothes became dazzling **white**,
　　such as no fuller on earth could bleach them.
Then **Elijah appeared** to them along with **Moses**,
　　and they were **conversing** with Jesus.
Then Peter said to Jesus in reply,
　　"**Rabbi, it is good** that we are **here**!
Let us make **three tents**:
　　one for you, one for Moses, and one for Elijah."
He hardly knew what to say, they were so **terrified**.
Then a **cloud came**, casting a **shadow** over them;
　　from the cloud came a voice,
　　"**This is my beloved Son. Listen to him.**"
Suddenly, looking around, they **no longer saw** anyone
　　but **Jesus alone** with them.

As they were coming **down** from the mountain,
　　he charged them **not** to relate what they had **seen** to anyone,
　　except when the **Son of Man** had **risen** from the **dead**.
So they kept the matter to **themselves**,
　　questioning what rising from the dead meant.

A narrator sets the scene but quickly gets caught up in the excitement of what he is describing.

fuller = FUHL-her = A fuller prepares wool to be made into cloth.

Elijah = ee-LĪ-juh

Peter momentarily gets hold of himself enough to speak. Stumbling on what to say, he offers . . . housing? The energy-charged situation increases with the appearance of the cloud.

Change from Peter's trembling tone to God's commanding voice.

Pause for the scene change. End with the even tone of a narrator.

gloriously transfigures, is accompanied by Elijah and Moses, and converses with them. Peter suggests raising tents (*skēnē* in Greek) for Jesus, Elijah, and Moses. The proposal recalls the tent or tabernacle in which God dwelt with his people from the revelation at Sinai until the completion of Solomon's temple. This proposal, albeit praiseworthy, highlights the uniqueness of Jesus. First, Elijah and Moses were prophets, while God alone occupied the tabernacle. Second, as the content of God's message makes clear, God's revelation in Jesus is fundamentally new and different from all prior revelation. Jesus is the beloved Son to whom the disciples are to listen. The word "listen" (*akouō* in Greek) recalls God's initial mandate to "hear" (*shema* in Hebrew), the great commandment in Deuteronomy 6:4. So, atop this mountain surrounded by another sacred cloud, Jesus' disciples are led to understand that Jesus is the incarnate law, not another prophet. Third, the abrupt end of the transfiguration signals that the high point of God's revelation in Jesus is yet to come. Finally, Jesus' instruction to keep the matter secret until the resurrection indicates that the transfiguration is an interpretive key for the more fundamental revelation accomplished in Jesus' death and resurrection. So, Peter's tent-building proposal may have been commendably pious, but the call to ponder the meaning of rising from the dead is the core take-away from this transfiguration account. After all, Jesus reveals that this mystery—the paschal mystery—is the goal of our journey through Lent and life. E.W.

THIRD SUNDAY
OF LENT

LECTIONARY #29

READING I   Exodus 20:1–17

A reading from the Book of Exodus

[In those days, **God delivered** all these **commandments**:
"I, the **LORD**, am **YOUR GOD**,
who **brought** you out of the land of **Egypt**, that place of **slavery**.
You shall **not** have **other gods** besides **me**.]
You shall not **carve idols** for yourselves
in the shape of anything in the sky **above**
or on the earth below or in the waters beneath the earth;
you shall not **bow** down before them or worship them.
For I, the LORD, your God, am a **jealous** God,
inflicting **punishment** for their **fathers' wickedness**
on the **children** of those who hate me,
down to the third and fourth generation;
but bestowing **mercy** down to the **thousandth generation**
on the children of those who **love me** and **keep**
my commandments.

["You shall not **take** the **name** of the LORD, your God, in **vain**.
For the LORD will not leave unpunished
the one who **takes** his name in vain.

"Remember to keep **holy** the **sabbath day**.]
Six days you may labor and do all your work,
but the **seventh** day is the sabbath of the LORD, your God.

Exodus = EK-suh-duhs

The even tone of a narrator turns to the voice of one giving a command: firm yet kind. The familiarity with the commands might encourage rushing. Resist. Let each command settle on the assembly so they can appropriate it into their behavior.

The consequences of sin have a ripple effect on families.

There are options for today's readings. Contact your parish staff to learn which readings will be used.

READING I The law, the temple, and God's oneness constitute the fundamental institutions for God's chosen people. These three are the bedrock of their religious beliefs and traditions. The meaning of each is on full display in today's Liturgy of the Word. The Exodus reading consists of the ten commandments and treats the law and God's oneness. As *the*

fundamental laws given by God to the chosen people, the ten commandments organize and summarize Torah's many laws, making them tantamount to an abridged version of the whole Torah. They are so important that Moses reiterates them (slightly differently) in Deuteronomy 5, prior to the people's entry into the promised land. For the sake of focus, we will attend to the first commandment: "I, the LORD, am your God. . . . You shall not have other gods besides me." This commandment, along with the next two, treats God's nature and

what it means to be in right relationship with God.

The chosen people are not to have any image or anything that takes the place of God. Why? Because God is God alone. The idolatrous practices of the chosen people that follow the giving of the commandments indicate that the meaning of this commandment would take time to grasp. As the reading continues, we learn that the one true God rightly manifests jealousy toward the chosen people. Often mistaken as envy (a vice), jealousy means God protects the chosen people as a rightful

No work may be done then either by you, or your son or daughter,
   or your male or female slave, or your beast,
   or by the alien who lives with you.
In six days the LORD **made** the **heavens** and the **earth,**
   the **sea** and all that is **in** them;
   but on the seventh day he rested.
That is why the LORD has **blessed** the sabbath day and made
   it holy.

["**Honor** your **father** and your **mother,**
   that you may have a long **life** in the land
   which the LORD, your God, is giving you.
You shall not kill.
You shall not **commit adultery.**
You shall not **steal.**
You shall not bear **false witness** against your **neighbor.**
You shall not **covet** your neighbor's house.
You shall not covet your neighbor's **wife,**
   nor his male or female **slave,** nor his **ox** or **ass,**
   nor anything **else** that belongs to him."]

[Shorter: Exodus 20:1–3, 7–8, 12–17 (see brackets)]

Emphasize the new information and subdue the words when repeated. For further explanation on emphasizing and subduing, see the introduction to the *Workbook*.

For meditation and context:

RESPONSORIAL PSALM   Psalm 19:8, 9, 10, 11 (John 6:68c)

R. Lord, you have the words of everlasting life.

The law of the LORD is perfect,
   refreshing the soul;
the decree of the LORD is trustworthy,
   giving wisdom to the simple.

The precepts of the LORD are right,
   rejoicing the heart;
the command of the LORD is clear,
   enlightening the eye.

The fear of the LORD is pure,
   enduring forever;
the ordinances of the LORD are true,
   all of them just.

They are more precious than gold,
   than a heap of purest gold;
sweeter also than syrup
   or honey from the comb.

---

possession. Envy, by contrast, would amount to God desiring someone or something that rightfully belongs to another—this is impossible since the whole earth belongs to God (see Exodus 9:29). Understood in this way, God's jealous protection of the chosen people is on display even when God promises intergenerational punishment of the wicked. After all, rather than punish families overrun by wickedness and hatred to the thousandth generation, which would match the scope of mercy extended to obedient families, God promises to protect those who are unborn (the fifth gener-

ation and on) from divine punishment bound to afflict a wicked generation. In this way God, who alone can curb divine power, protects future generations of the chosen people by refraining from divinely established consequences of sin. Thus, God's law draws us into pondering God's oneness in today's passage from Exodus.

READING II Continuing the first reading's focus on God's oneness, the passage from 1 Corinthians highlights how God confounds expectations of divine behavior. To make his point,

Paul contrasts how Jews and Greek Gentiles expected God to act. According to Paul, Jews of his day expected God to manifest power in signs. Evidently, such signs were deeds thought to be something only God could perform. Thus, when signs were perceived, Jews considered God to be nearby and active. Alternatively, Greeks, according to Paul, expected God to act in accord with wisdom. That is, God should behave in a way that conforms to reason and in accord with predictable, discernible rules governing the universe.

Corinthians = kohr-IN-thee-uhnz

Paul is trying to bring this insight to a world that is not looking for a crucified savior.

Practice to keep the integrity of the parallel structures intact.

READING II   1 Corinthians 1:22–25

A reading from the first Letter of Saint Paul to the Corinthians

Brothers and sisters:
Jews demand signs and **Greeks** look for **wisdom**,
   but we proclaim **Christ crucified**,
   a stumbling **block** to **Jews** and **foolishness** to **Gentiles**,
   but to those who are called, Jews and Greeks alike,
   Christ the power of God and the wisdom of God.
For the **foolishness** of God is **wiser** than **human wisdom**,
   and the **weakness** of God is stronger than human **strength**.

Set the scene with a narrator's voice and then increase your pace with Jesus' rising anger. A whip, spilled coins, and crashing tables create a loud, frenetic scene. Jesus wants better for us.

GOSPEL   John 2:13–25

A reading from the holy Gospel according to John

Since the **Passover** of the **Jews** was **near**,
   Jesus went up to **Jerusalem**.
He found in the **temple** area those who **sold oxen**, **sheep**,
      and **doves**,
   as well as the **money changers** seated there.
He made a **whip** out of cords
   and **drove** them all **out** of the temple area, with the sheep
      and oxen,
   and **spilled** the **coins** of the money changers
   and **overturned** their **tables**,
   and to those who sold doves he said,
   "Take these out of here,
   and **stop making my Father's house a marketplace."**
His **disciples** recalled the words of Scripture,
   Zeal for your house will **consume me**.
At this the **Jews** answered and **said** to him,
   "What **sign** can you show us for doing this?"

Yet, as Paul notes, God sends Christ to die on a cross. By both Jewish and Greek standards of Paul's time, God's definitive action in Christ baffles. By sending Christ to die on the cross, God's action simultaneously manifests total weakness and absurdity. In Jesus' crucifixion, God does not subdue powerful oppressors as had been the case with Pharaoh in Egypt. Nor does God overcome human sin by ushering in universal training in and practice of virtue, as a good Greek might propose. Instead, by manifesting the fullness of grace in Jesus' violent death on the cross, God reveals

how God alone can manifest power and act wisely in apparent displays of abject weakness and insanity. Ultimately, Paul sees God's sovereign plan that is worked out in Christ's death quite apart from any concern about weakness or power, wisdom or folly. Only the one true God could act with such sovereignty.

GOSPEL   In today's Gospel, Jesus' relationship with all three fundamental institutions of the Jewish faith—the temple, the law, and God's oneness—comes into view as he cleanses

the temple. All four Gospels recount Jesus' cleansing of the temple with similar basic elements. Near the time of Passover, Jesus entered the temple, that is, the outer precinct where Gentiles could go, and sacrificial animals could be bought and sold to perpetuate the temple sacrificial system. During a pilgrimage festival like Passover, this area of the temple would have been bustling with more devout Jews who had made their way to Jerusalem to offer sacrifice for such occasions. The commerce unfolding in this area was normative activity that helped pilgrims fulfill their obliga-

Jesus is speaking metaphorically, and the Jews, listening literally, misunderstand him. Use a narrator voice as John interprets for his readers what Jesus meant.

Pause before the concluding scene. Jesus wants us to be in a relationship with him. He doesn't want to be used just for his power.

Jesus answered and said to them,
     "**Destroy** this **temple** and in **three days** I will **raise it up**."
The Jews said,
     "This temple has been under construction for **forty-six years**,
     and you will raise it up in three days?"
But he was **speaking** about the **temple** of his **body**.
Therefore, when he was raised from the dead,
     his disciples **remembered** that he had said this,
     and they **came to believe** the **Scripture**
     and the word Jesus had spoken.

While he was in Jerusalem for the feast of Passover,
     many began to believe in his **name**
     when they **saw** the signs he was doing.
But **Jesus would not trust himself to them** because he **knew**
          them all,
     and did not need anyone to **testify** about **human nature**.
He himself **understood** it well.

tions to the sacrificial laws of Torah, especially those in Leviticus. Having entered this quasi-commercial context, Jesus drives out buyers and sellers and, according to John, overturns tables of the money changers, which certainly caused a stir.

Jesus' disruptive behavior is then justified in each Gospel based on biblical tradition. In the synoptic Gospels (Matthew, Mark, and Luke), Jesus justifies his actions by citing Isaiah 56:7—"my house shall be called a house of prayer for all peoples" —and Jeremiah 7:11—"Has this house which bears my name become in your eyes a den of thieves?" In John's Gospel, the disciples justify Jesus' actions by recalling Psalm 69:9, translated in the Gospel as "Zeal for your house will consume me."

In the synoptics, Jesus' actions suggest that he held contempt for the temple and the (sacrificial) law, which hastens his arrest and passion. In John's Gospel, by contrast, the cleansing of the temple is among Jesus' earliest signs and occasions a confused exchange with Jewish leaders in Jerusalem who think his actions and claim (to raise the temple from a state of destruction in three days) amount to antagonism toward the temple, the law, *and* the one true God. After all, God had not yet facilitated the temple's completion after more than forty years. Jesus, however, makes a more audacious and obscure claim: as the one true God and incarnate word, Jesus will fulfill the chosen people's fundamental institutions when the temple of his body rises from the dead on the third day. Jesus' resurrection makes his claim intelligible and leads the disciples to a more deeply held belief of Scripture and Jesus' word. E.W.

THIRD SUNDAY
OF LENT, YEAR A

LECTIONARY #28

READING I   Exodus 17:3–7

A reading from the Book of Exodus

In those days, in their **thirst for water**,
    the **people grumbled** against **Moses**,
    saying, "**Why** did **you** ever make **us** leave Egypt?
Was it just to have us **die** here of **thirst**
    with our **children** and our **livestock**?"
So Moses **cried** out to the LORD,
    "What shall I **do** with this people?
A little more and they will **stone** me!"
The LORD answered Moses,
    "Go over there in **front** of the **people**,
    along with some of the **elders** of **Israel**,
    holding in your hand, as you go,
    the **staff** with which you struck the **river**.
I will be **standing** there in **front of you** on the **rock** in **Horeb.**
Strike the rock, and the **water** will flow from it
    for the people to **drink**."
This Moses did, in the presence of the elders of Israel.
The place was called Massah and Meribah,
    because the Israelites **quarreled** there
    and **tested** the LORD, saying,
    "Is the LORD in our **midst** or not?"

Exodus = EK-suh-duhs

Use rising inflections for all the questions and pause slightly before the answers.

The people are scapegoating Moses for their hardship. Emphasize "you" and "us" with an accusatory tone.

When Moses turns to God for advice, God will once again show the people his power through Moses in a manner that can't help but remind them of the life-and-death drama of crossing the Red Sea.

Horeb = HOHR-eb

Massah = MAS-uh
Meribah = MAYR-ih-bah

The Israelites questioned if the Lord was in their midst. Do we act like the Lord is in our midst?

There are options for today's readings. Contact your parish staff to learn which readings will be used.

READING I The scrutinies of the third, fourth, and fifth Sundays of Lent are when the elect make final preparations for entering the Church's sacramental life at the Easter Vigil. These critical examinations help the elect grow in faith, determine their commitment to God and God's Church, and remove any obstacles hindering their acceptance of life in the sacraments. Since the elect only participate in the Liturgy of the Word at Mass, these Sundays include readings designated for the occasion (these are the readings found in Year A). For the first scrutiny, the readings explore the free gift (grace) of God's life-giving love available to those who participate in Christ through the sacraments. Using water imagery and the language of outpouring, the readings anticipate the baptism, confirmation, and Eucharist awaiting the elect at the Easter Vigil.

The reading from Exodus unfolds after the people's departure from Egypt but before the giving of the law at Sinai. It portrays the chosen people complaining and requesting water in the wilderness. They are concerned that, by following God's servant Moses into the wilderness, they, their children, and their livestock will die of dehydration. Moses, for his part, worries that the complaints may lead to an uprising that will lead to his execution by stoning if the people decide to take justice into their own hands. Moses' concern is genuine for two reasons: the people's lack of water and lack of law in the Sinai wilderness are both real. Strikingly, prior to providing them with

For meditation and context:

TO KEEP IN MIND
On the Third, Fourth and Fifth Sundays of Lent, the readings from Year A are used when the scrutinies—prayers for purification and strength—are celebrated with the elect, those who will be baptized at the Easter Vigil.

Address the assembly with intentionality. We are brothers and sisters in Christ. Practice until you are comfortable with the phrasing and the plethora of pronouns. Select a few statements that can be delivered while looking directly at the assembly.

The gravity of these words should go deep. How do you remind yourself daily of Christ's paschal mystery?

RESPONSORIAL PSALM   Psalm 95:1–2, 6–7, 8–9 (8)

R. If today you hear his voice, harden not your hearts.

Come, let us sing joyfully to the LORD;
   let us acclaim the Rock of our salvation.
Let us come into his presence with
   thanksgiving;
   let us joyfully sing psalms to him.

Come, let us bow down in worship;
   let us kneel before the LORD who
   made us.

For he is our God,
   and we are the people he shepherds, the
   flock he guides.

Oh, that today you would hear his voice:
   "Harden not your hearts as at Meribah,
   as in the day of Massah in the desert,
where your fathers tempted me;
   they tested me though they had seen
   my works."

READING II   Romans 5:1–2, 5–8

A reading from the Letter of Saint Paul to the Romans

Brothers and sisters:
Since we have been **justified by faith**,
   we have **peace** with God through our **Lord Jesus Christ**,
   through whom we have gained **access** by **faith**
   to this grace in which we stand,
   and we **boast** in **hope** of the **glory** of **God**.

And hope does **not disappoint**,
   because the **love** of God has been **poured** out into our **hearts**
   through the **Holy Spirit** who has been given to us.
For Christ, while we were still **helpless**,
   died at the appointed time for the **ungodly**.
Indeed, only with **difficulty** does one **die** for a **just person**,
   though perhaps for a good person one might even find **courage**
     to die.
But God proves his **love** for us
   in that while we were **still sinners** Christ **died** for us.

---

the law, the Lord quenches the people's thirst and does so by the very means with which they seemed to threaten Moses' life. To keep the people from striking Moses with rocks, God instructs Moses to strike the rock so that, through God's power, water might flow from it for the people.

Exodus conveys that Moses did as God commanded, and we are left to understand that the people's thirst was slaked. But the scene ominously closes with an account of how the place became associated with the people's quarreling as they wondered whether or not the Lord was in

their midst. This question is, in the scrutinies, now appropriately redirected toward those who would follow God, both the elect and the whole congregation: do we trust that the Lord is in our midst?

READING II In the second reading, Paul reflects on the meaning of faith in God's love that was embodied for us in Christ. Paul begins by speaking of being justified by faith—a summary of his argument in prior chapters of this letter to the Romans. Effectively, Paul's argument claims that faith in Christ amounts to trust-

ing that our obligations to God under the law are fulfilled in Christ. The basis of that faith lies in Christ's sacrifice on the cross and his glorious resurrection. A natural outcome of faith in Christ's death and resurrection is the unmerited gift (grace) of enjoying peace with God now and hoping in our own future glory, our own resurrection. So, faith in Christ begets ultimate peace and hope.

With the implications of faith in Christ established, the remainder of this passage explores the value of those implications. That value, according to Paul, is difficult to

Use the pronouns carefully. Help the assembly understand the back and forth of the dialogue.
Samaria = suh-MAYR-ee-uh
Sychar = SĪ-kahr or SIH-kahr or sih-KAHR

Samaritan = suh-MAYR-uh-tuhn

Notice the sharp contrast between the practical speech of the woman and Jesus' spiritual insights. Can we relate to the woman? Do we keep our faith practical and avoid going deep?

GOSPEL   John 4:5–42

A reading from the holy Gospel according to John

[**Jesus came** to a town of **Samaria** called **Sychar**,
    near the **plot** of land that **Jacob** had given to his **son Joseph**.
Jacob's **well** was there.
Jesus, **tired** from his **journey**, **sat** down there at the **well**.
It was about **noon**.

A **woman** of **Samaria** came to draw water.
Jesus said to her,
    "**Give me** a **drink**."
His **disciples** had **gone** into the town to buy food.
The Samaritan woman said to him,
    "How can **you**, **a Jew**, **ask me**, a **Samaritan woman**,
        for a drink?"
—For Jews use **nothing** in common with Samaritans.—
Jesus answered and said to her,
    "If you **knew** the **gift** of God
    and **who is saying** to you, 'Give me a drink,'
    you would have asked him
    and he would have **given** you **living water**."
The woman said to him,
    "**Sir**, **you do not** even have a **bucket** and the **cistern** is **deep**;
    where then can you get this living water?
Are you **greater** than our father Jacob,
    who gave us this cistern and drank from it himself
    with his children and his flocks?"
Jesus answered and said to her,
    "**Everyone** who drinks this **water** will be **thirsty again**;
    but whoever drinks the water I shall give will **never** thirst;
    the water I shall give will become in him
    a spring of water welling up to **eternal life**."

imagine. To show the cost of Christ's self-sacrifice for the ungodly, he compares it to other examples in which someone might lay down his life for another. Dying for a just person is, for Paul, only done with difficulty. For example, few people jump at the chance to serve as bodyguards for efficient, high-level judges prone to death threats. And while dying for someone we deem admirable and generally worthy of emulating—"a good person"—might be easier to imagine, the prospect of doing so remains tenuous at best, as Paul's "perhaps" (*tácha* in Greek) suggests. Thus, the scenario in Christ is

stunning. He died for us while we were still sinners, neither just nor good. In doing so, Christ made the great scope of God's love apparent: it is unconditional.

Recognizing Paul's understanding of God's love, we may note that at the heart of this passage he talks of God's love being poured (*ekchéo* in Greek) into our hearts through the Holy Spirit. This word for "pouring" is relatively rare in Scripture. Among Paul's letters it only appears here. Elsewhere, this word has sacrificial significance, appearing notably in Jesus' institution of the Eucharist in the synoptic Gospels when he

says the cup of his blood will be poured out (Matthew 26:28; Mark 14:24; Luke 22:20). Given this sacrificial significance, we might say that, for Paul, the outpouring of the Holy Spirit into Christian hearts is of a piece with the Lord's work in the Eucharist. For the elect seeking the sacraments of initiation at the Easter Vigil, Paul's language offers assurance that what lies on their sacramental horizon is the reception of God's freely given, unearned Holy Spirit.

| GOSPEL | The story of the woman at the well was read for the |

The woman said to him,
  "**Sir**, **give me** this water, so that I may **not** be thirsty
  or have to keep coming here to draw water."]

Jesus said to her,
  "Go call your **husband** and **come back**."
The woman answered and said to him,
  "I **do not have** a husband."
Jesus answered her,
  "You are **right** in saying, 'I do not have a husband.'
For you have had **five** husbands,
  and the one you have now is **not** your husband.
What you have said is **true**."
The woman said to him,
  ["Sir, I can see that you are a **prophet**.
Our **ancestors worshiped** on this mountain;
  but **you people** say that the place to worship is in **Jerusalem**."
Jesus said to her,
  "**Believe me**, woman, the hour is coming
  when you will **worship** the **Father**
  neither on this **mountain nor** in Jerusalem.
You people worship what you do **not understand;**
  we worship what we understand,
  because **salvation** is **from** the **Jews**.
But the hour is coming, and is **now** here,
  when **true worshipers** will worship the Father in **Spirit**
    and **truth;**
  and indeed the Father **seeks** such people to worship him.
God is **Spirit**, and those who worship him
  must worship in Spirit and truth." »

The Jews were prejudiced against the Samaritans. "You people" shows the dislike was reciprocal. Use an accusatory tone.

first scrutiny in antiquity. It is an unflinching inquiry in two directions. A Samaritan woman seeks to grasp Jesus' identity, while Jesus works to reveal herself to her and also himself as the Messiah. It is a scrutiny in story form.

The story begins with Jesus entering an obscure Samaritan town adjacent to significant biblical geography, which provides a meaningful context for the Gospel story. The land that Jacob gave Joseph recalls primordial memories of fraternal hatred among Jacob's sons and the origins of Israel's servitude in Egypt (see Genesis 37

and 47). But it is also an icon of hope since Joseph reconciled with his brothers and father (Genesis 45–46). Jacob's well reminds us that God provides throughout multiple generations. Finally, the scene unfolds in the shadow of Mount Gerizim, which was a traditional worship site designated by God in Torah as a place to ritually enact the covenant (see Deuteronomy 11:29; 27:1–8, 11–14; and Joshua 8:30–35). Gerizim remained important from the time of the Judges (Judges 9:7) to Jesus' day, when the Samaritans considered it the proper place to worship the Lord. As the woman will

point out, the place was of such religious significance that it constituted a fundamental point of discord between Jews and Samaritans.

In this contentious context, Jesus' initial phrase can seem harsh—"Give me a drink." But the same expression appears on the thirsty lips of God's people in the wilderness just prior to today's first reading (Exodus 17:2). In effect, the Lord turns an ancient test on this woman. She neither rejects nor accepts his command, but considers it a question to which she poses her own—how can a Jewish man ask a

Imagine telling someone that what they have been waiting to hear for their entire life is right in front of them. Jesus reveals himself slowly so the woman can grasp it.

The mood changes when the disciples return. Use a narrator voice to read the internal voice of the disciples.

Use some excitement. She leaves her jug and her despondency behind. She is changed and her energy is contagious. Can you remember an epiphany in your faith life?

"Meanwhile" shifts and links the scenes together.

The woman said to him,
"I **know** that the **Messiah is coming**, the one called
the **Christ**;
when he comes, he will tell us **everything**."
Jesus said to her,
"**I am he**, the one speaking with you."]

At that moment his **disciples returned**,
and were **amazed** that he was **talking** with a woman,
but still **no one said**, "What are **you** looking for?"
or "**Why** are you talking with her?"
The **woman** left her water jar
and **went** into the town and said to the people,
"**Come see** a **man** who told me everything I have done.
Could he possibly **be the Christ**?"
They went out of the town and came to him.
Meanwhile, the disciples urged him, "**Rabbi, eat**."
But he said to them,
"I have **food** to eat of which you do **not know**."
So the disciples said to one another,
"Could **someone** have **brought** him something to eat?"
Jesus said to them,
"My **food** is to do the **will** of the one who sent me
and **to finish his work**.
Do you not say, 'In four months the **harvest** will be here'?
I tell you, **look up** and see the fields **ripe** for the harvest.
The **reaper** is already **receiving** payment
and gathering crops for **eternal life**,
so that the **sower** and reaper can **rejoice** together.
For here the saying is verified that '**One** sows and **another** reaps.'

Samaritan woman for a drink? As far as she (and the narrator) is concerned, their respective backgrounds preclude them from speaking. Yet, the woman's response demonstrates her willingness to engage in dialogue with Jesus, a disposition necessary for a scrutiny. So, Jesus responds to her openness with a theologically robust reply in which he calls himself God's gift (*dō reá* in Greek) and offers living water. His "gift" language matches one of Paul's bold descriptions of Jesus (Romans 5:15–17), but the woman, perhaps unprepared for a serious theological back-and-forth, focuses on material concerns. The water of which Jesus speaks entices her, but his lack of a bucket confounds. Nonetheless, she continues to engage in conversation with a question about how Jesus might rate relative to the great Jacob. With the conversation left open, Jesus continues it by speaking of the perpetual, soul-quenching water he has to offer, which finally hooks the woman and occasions her to take up his initial command: "Sir, give me this water." With his words now in her mouth, Jesus advances against the obstacle keeping her from fully engaging him (and others)—a pattern of broken marital relationships. When her story comes to light, she recognizes him as a prophet and moves directly toward the matter of theological significance that seemingly divides them—the place of right worship. Her concern provides an opportunity for Jesus to reframe the division by stating that true worship of the Father is done in spirit and in truth. With such core rifts so swiftly mended, the woman ponders aloud about the Messiah's coming. With uncommon candidness, Jesus tells her that he is the Messiah. Immediately, she becomes a witness to Jesus for her

I **sent you** to reap what you have **not worked** for;
others have done the work,
and you are sharing the fruits of their work."

[Many of the **Samaritans** of that town began to believe in him
because of the **word** of the **woman** who testified,
"He told me everything I have done."
When the **Samaritans** came to him,
they invited him to **stay** with them;
and he stayed there two days.
Many more began to **believe** in him because of his **word**,
and they said to the woman,
"We **no longer believe** because of **your** word;
for we have **heard** for **ourselves**,
and we know that this is **truly** the **savior** of the **world**."]

[Shorter: John 4:5–15, 19b–26, 39a, 40–42 (see brackets)]

The Samaritan woman was an evangelist; she brought others to Christ. This Lent, reflect on the way your testimony can bring others to Christ.

whole town. Her message of guarded optimism prompts their response to Jesus, and more conversion follows.

The mutual openness and steady scrutiny of the woman and Christ result in personal and communal transformation. Similarly, this Sunday's scrutiny advances the elect toward Christ by relinquishing guardedness and getting at the heart of any anguish that may hinder serious, unflinching engagement with Christ in the sacraments. E.W.

FOURTH SUNDAY OF LENT

LECTIONARY #32

READING I 2 Chronicles 36:14–16, 19–23

A reading from the second Book of Chronicles

In those days, all the **princes of Judah**, the priests, and the **people**
  added infidelity to infidelity,
    practicing all the abominations of the nations
  and **polluting** the LORD'S **temple**
    which he had **consecrated** in **Jerusalem**.

Early and **often** did the LORD, the **God** of **their fathers**,
  send his **messengers** to them,
    for he had **compassion** on his people and his dwelling place.
But they **mocked** the messengers of God,
    despised his warnings, and scoffed at his prophets,
  until the **anger** of the LORD against **his people** was so inflamed
    that there was no **remedy**.
Their **enemies burnt** the **house** of **God**,
  tore down the walls of Jerusalem,
  set all its palaces afire,
  and **destroyed** all its precious **objects**.
Those who **escaped** the sword were carried **captive** to **Babylon**,
  where they became **servants** of the king of the **Chaldeans**
    and his sons
  until the kingdom of the **Persians** came to power.

Margin notes

Chronicles = KRAH-nih-k*ls

Announce the name of the book carefully. This is the only time the book is used in Year B.

Judah = JOO-duh

Look for the distinct parts of the narrative: sinful behavior, sending of the prophets, the description of punishment, and the decree to return. Plan your pauses for a scene change.

Capture the callous and contemptuous tone the people had for their prophets.

Chaldeans = kal-DEE-uhnz or kahl-DEE-uhnz

There are options for today's readings. Contact your parish staff to learn which readings will be used.

READING I   The first reading recounts two remarkable moments in the history of God's people—the destruction and restoration of Jerusalem. The catastrophic destruction of Jerusalem and its temple at the hands of Babylonians was a pivotal and dark moment in biblical history. God's apparent dwelling place on earth was thought to be unassailable. Its destruction led to questions about God's omnipotence. Could God not protect the chosen place? But, as this passage from 2 Chronicles indicates, the destruction of Jerusalem and its temple was anticipated. God sent prophets with warnings and invitations to repentance—expressions of divine compassion to the people. Jeremiah rendered such warnings (see Jeremiah 7 and 26), and before him, Micah (see Micah 3:12). Yet despite these warnings, the people did not repent. Their wrongdoing continued, especially with regard to temple rituals. So, according to Chronicles, the people's persistent wrongdoing occasioned Jerusalem's destruction and the Babylonian exile. Servitude ensued for many of God's people in Babylon, who lived along waterways that likely amounted to little more than drainage ditches, as suggested by the prophet Ezekiel (1:1 and 3:15) and Psalm 137.

But Jerusalem's destruction and the Babylonian exile did *not* constitute God's total abandonment of the people. Alongside today's account of Jerusalem's destruction is an account of one of the brightest moments in the history of God's people—the promise of return to and res-

All this was to **fulfill** the word of the LORD spoken by **Jeremiah**:
"Until the **land** has **retrieved** its **lost sabbaths**,
during all the time it **lies waste** it shall have rest
while **seventy years** are fulfilled."

In the first year of **Cyrus**, **king** of Persia,
in order to fulfill the word of the LORD spoken by Jeremiah,
the **LORD inspired** King Cyrus of Persia
to issue this **proclamation** throughout his kingdom,
both by word of mouth and in writing:
"Thus says Cyrus, king of Persia:
All the kingdoms of the earth
the LORD, the **God of heaven**, has **given** to me,
and he has also **charged m**e to **build** him a house
in Jerusalem, which is in Judah.
Whoever, therefore, among you belongs to any part
       of **his people**,
let him **go up**, and may his **God be with him**!"

Cyrus = Sī-ruhs

A king of another nation was inspired by God. The demonstration of the universality of God's jurisdiction outside of Israel is an important lesson. Are we open to the wisdom of those outside our tradition? Our borders?

Announce the king's proclamation to release the Israelites with the solemnity of a government decree.

For meditation and context:

RESPONSORIAL PSALM   Psalm 137:1–2, 3, 4–5, 6 (6ab)

R. Let my tongue be silenced, if I ever forget you!

By the streams of Babylon
    we sat and wept when we
        remembered Zion.
On the aspens of that land
    we hung up our harps.

For there our captors asked of us
    the lyrics of our songs,
and our despoilers urged us to be joyous:
    "Sing for us the songs of Zion!"

How could we sing a song of the LORD
    in a foreign land?
If I forget you, Jerusalem,
    may my right hand be forgotten!

May my tongue cleave to my palate
    if I remember you not,
if I place not Jerusalem
    ahead of my joy.

---

toration of Jerusalem, beginning with the temple. Remarkably, this bright moment comes not through the patronage of a Davidic king but through Cyrus of Persia. This most unlikely restorer—a foreign king from east of Mesopotamia—is called an anointed one or messiah in Isaiah 45:1. Through Cyrus, God faithfully maintains the covenant forged with the people despite their unfaithfulness.

In the first reading, then, we find an invitation to see that God responds to unfaithfulness with not only justice but abiding faithfulness. As such, we might say

that the first "move" of today's Liturgy of the Word is a call to repentance and conversion, trusting that God is prepared to offer us compassion and mercy.

READING II Continuing the theme of the first reading, Paul begins by announcing that God "is rich in mercy" and abundantly loving toward us. He makes this assertion based on what God has done for us in Christ. In view of Christ's death, resurrection, and ascension in glory, Paul proclaims that our state of being has been changed. Once destined for

death on account of sin, God's saving work in Christ destines us for life. By being sacramentally initiated into and abiding in his passion, death, resurrection, and ascension, we experience "the immeasurable riches" of God's grace. No longer aiming at judgment, we enjoy the promise of abiding union (communion) with God in Christ.

Typical of Paul, he emphasizes how our new and blessed state was brought about: "by grace you have been saved." This phrase echoes like a refrain throughout this reading, making it clear that we have not earned and cannot earn God's

Ephesians = ee-FEE-zhuhnz

When proclaiming an address ("Brothers and sisters"), use a falling inflection.

God continues to choose us and to love us despite our sinfulness. As you prepare to proclaim Paul's exhortatory text, listen to the traditional hymn "Amazing Grace." We should strive to keep the spirit of amazement and gratitude alive each day.

God has lovingly and intentionally created each one of us. Let your proclamation communicate that sentiment.

Nicodemus = nihk-uh-DEE-muhs

Read Numbers 21:4–9 to understand the Old Testament reference here.

READING II Ephesians 2:4–10

A reading from the Letter of Saint Paul to the Ephesians

Brothers and sisters:
God, who is rich in **mercy**,
  because of the **great love** he had for us,
  even when we were **dead** in our **transgressions**,
  brought us to **life** with **Christ**—by **grace** you have
    been **saved**—,
  raised us up with him,
  and **seated** us with him in the **heavens** in Christ Jesus,
  that in the **ages** to come
  he might show the **immeasurable riches** of his grace
  in his **kindness** to us in Christ Jesus.
For by grace you have been **saved through faith**,
  and this is **not from you**; it is the **gift** of God;
  it is **not** from **works**, so no one may **boast**.
For we are his **handiwork**, created in Christ Jesus for the
    good works
  that **God has prepared** in advance,
  that we should live in them.

GOSPEL John 3:14–21

A reading from the holy Gospel according to John

Jesus said to **Nicodemus**:
  "Just as **Moses lifted** up the **serpent** in the **desert**,
  so must the **Son of Man** be lifted up,
  so that **everyone** who **believes** in him may **have eternal** life."

kindness toward us. In our transgressions we were dead, but in Christ we live in God's grace, that is, God's freely given mercy and love. Consequently, we enjoy the hope that only God can give—a genuine answer to the question of what happens when we die. Of course, to enjoy this hope entails a response of steady, ongoing conversion, of continually turning our attention toward God. Such conversion is work that we are especially called to during Lent as we prepare to celebrate Easter. Paul's message today aligns us well with our Lenten call to repent, to turn back to God in all things.

Paul reminds us that we do not do this work to earn God's love but to respond generously to the love and mercy he has already extended to us in Christ.

GOSPEL Today's Gospel is best understood in its broader context. Nicodemus, a pharisee, leader, and teacher among the Jews, comes to Jesus at night to have a conversation about who Jesus is (John 3:1–2, 10). As a pharisee, Nicodemus believes in the resurrection. As a leader and teacher, he represents and influences the broader Jewish community

of his day. In coming to Jesus at night, he cautiously opens himself to the Lord and initiates a conversation on behalf of those he represents. He begins by stating what was apparently accepted about Jesus—" we know that you are a teacher who has come from God" (John 3:2). His claim to knowledge quickly evaporates as Jesus confounds him with talk of needing to be reborn. Nicodemus imagines literal rebirth from the womb. Jesus means rebirth through "water and Spirit" (John 3:5), which clarifies nothing for Nicodemus. Despite being a learned Jewish leader,

Don't rush this familiar verse. In this passage, "so" means "in this way," not the adverbial "to such a great extent." Reflect on how this changes the meaning.

The frequent use of "not" can be confusing. Practice so that it makes sense to you, and in turn, the assembly's comprehension will improve. Use a compassionate tone to communicate God's mercy.

Use the Johannine theme of light and dark to examine your conscience. We aren't just proclaiming these words to others; we are meant to hear them and take them into our hearts as well.

For **God so loved** the world that he **gave** his only **Son**,
　　so that **everyone** who **believes** in him might **not perish**
　　but might have eternal life.
For God did **not send** his Son into the **world** to **condemn**
　　　the world,
　　but that the **world** might be **saved** through him.
Whoever believes in him will not be condemned,
　　but whoever does not believe has already been condemned,
　　because he has not believed in the name of the only Son
　　　of God.
And this is the **verdict**,
　　that the **light** came into the world,
　　but people preferred **darkness** to light,
　　because their **works** were **evil**.
For **everyone** who does **wicked** things **hates** the light
　　and **does not** come **toward** the light,
　　so that his works might not be exposed.
But whoever lives the **truth** comes to the light,
　　so that his works may be clearly **seen** as done in God.

Nicodemus remains confused and seemingly irritates Jesus, who asks Nicodemus how he can be a teacher and not understand this (John 3:10). To instruct Nicodemus, Jesus explains what he means by rebirth and why it matters.

This brings us to today's Gospel. In it, Jesus compares Moses' lifting up the serpent in the desert to heal the Israelites (see Numbers 21:4–9) to himself. In doing so, he means to explain that the exchange between heaven and earth, between God and the people, is fulfilled in him. Jesus completes the exchange between heaven and earth by being lifted up on the cross, rising from the dead, and ascending into heaven. Importantly, there is one reason for Jesus' exchange: "God so loved the world that he gave his only Son, so that everyone who believes in him might not perish but might have eternal life." This core Gospel message is often invoked in the crowds at large sporting events on posters reading simply "John 3:16." This is an important message about our faith because it reframes what it means to approach God. Through faith in Jesus, we can approach God with confidence that he promises salvation rather than judgment and condemnation. Consequently, Jesus continues his conversation with Nicodemus by declaring that faith in him fosters confidence to take up open pursuit of God "in daylight," as it were, rather than in private nighttime conversations. Thus, today's Gospel closes with a challenge to take up open public pursuit of our faith. In doing so, we more firmly abide in Christ's death, resurrection, and ascension, into which we were initiated in our baptismal rebirth. E.W.

FOURTH SUNDAY OF LENT, YEAR A

LECTIONARY #31

READING I   1 Samuel 16:1b, 6–7, 10–13a

A reading from the first Book of Samuel

The LORD said to **Samuel**:
  "Fill your **horn** with **oil**, and be on **your way**.
I am sending you to **Jesse** of **Bethlehem**,
  for I have **chosen** my **king** from among his **sons**."

As Jesse and his sons came to the **sacrifice**,
  Samuel looked at **Eliab** and thought,
  "Surely the LORD's **anointed** is here before him."
But the LORD said to Samuel:
  "Do **not judge** from his **appearance** or from his lofty stature,
  because I have rejected him.
Not as man sees does God see,
  because man sees the appearance
  but the LORD **looks into the heart**."
In the same way Jesse presented seven sons before Samuel,
  but Samuel said to Jesse,
  "The LORD has **not chosen** any one of these."
Then Samuel asked Jesse,
  "Are these **all** the sons you **have**?"
Jesse replied,
  "There is still the **youngest**, who is tending the **sheep**."
Samuel said to Jesse,
  "**Send** for him;
  we will not begin the sacrificial **banquet** until he arrives here."

The Lord speaks and Samuel obeys.
Use a strong voice for the Lord's directives.

Jesse = JES-ee

Eliab = ee-Lī-uhb
Use a self-satisfied tone for Samuel's observation.

Practice this verse so that you can deliver it looking out at the assembly.

TO KEEP IN MIND
On the Third, Fourth and Fifth Sundays of Lent, the readings from Year A are used when the scrutinies—prayers for purification and strength—are celebrated with the elect, those who will be baptized at the Easter Vigil.

There are options for today's readings. Contact your parish staff to learn which readings will be used.

READING I   The first reading for the second scrutiny (celebrated on the fourth Sunday of Lent) is an abridged account of God's election of David and his anointing by Samuel. The scene highlights David's origins, God's mode of discerning and choosing persons for a role in the divine plan, and something of God's own heart.

By sending Samuel to Jesse of Bethlehem to anoint a new king, God decisively moves the primordial monarchy away from the house of Saul, who had originally been chosen and anointed as king. Considering how things unfold in this story, we do well to recall that when Saul is first introduced in Scripture he is repeatedly described as handsome and that he stands "head and shoulders" above others (1 Samuel 9:2). In other words, Saul has a pleasing "look," which seems to be a potential asset for a king who would interact publicly with leaders of the tribes of the chosen people.

While contemporary readers might be reticent to admit it, Scripture accepts the simple truth that a person's size and physique can significantly influence how that person is received and, as a consequence, the ability to lead. This truth seems to guide Samuel's observations of Jesse's sons. Beginning with Eliab, Jesse's eldest son, Samuel thinks he has identified God's chosen. But God cautions him not to be fooled by his tall stature, reflective of Saul. God does not choose Eliab. The next seven sons of Jesse are similarly rejected by God. It is not until Jesse's youngest son, David,

ruddy = RUHD-ee = having a reddish complexion

Finally, the chosen one has been found! Use a cheerful tone to convey the Lord's satisfaction.

Use a narrator voice for the conclusion of the story.

Jesse sent and had the young man brought to them.
He was ruddy, a youth **handsome** to behold
    and making a splendid appearance.
The Lord said,
    "There—**anoint him**, for this is the one!"
Then Samuel, with the horn of oil in hand,
    anointed **David** in the presence of his brothers;
    and from that **day on**, the **spirit** of the Lord **rushed**
        upon David.

For meditation and context:

RESPONSORIAL PSALM   Psalm 23:1–3a, 3b–4, 5, 6 (1)

R. The Lord is my shepherd; there is nothing I shall want.

The Lord is my shepherd; I shall not want.
    In verdant pastures he gives me repose;
beside restful waters he leads me;
    he refreshes my soul.

He guides me in right paths
    for his name's sake.
Even though I walk in the dark valley
    I fear no evil; for you are at my side
with your rod and your staff
    that give me courage.

You spread the table before me
    in the sight of my foes;
you anoint my head with oil;
    my cup overflows.

Only goodness and kindness follow me
    all the days of my life;
and I shall dwell in the house of the Lord
    for years to come.

Ephesians = ee-FEE-zhuhnz

Notice the many contrasts Paul uses, and emphasize them.

"Try" points to the fact that this way of life is a learning process for all Christians. During the celebration of this week's scrutiny, we pray that the elect will hear and experience the continued call to conversion as they prepare for their baptism.

READING II   Ephesians 5:8–14

A reading from the Letter of Saint Paul to the Ephesians

Brothers and sisters:
You were once **darkness**,
    but now you are **light** in the Lord.
Live as **children** of light,
    for light produces every kind of **goodness**
        and **righteousness** and **truth**.
Try to **learn** what is **pleasing** to the Lord. »

---

is summoned from his shepherding duties that God reveals the chosen one to Samuel. And while David is also considered "handsome," it is by virtue of being anointed by Samuel "in the presence of his brothers" that day that David is endowed with God's spirit.

Of critical import in David's anointing is the distinction God makes when communicating with Samuel: human beings might look upon appearances but "the Lord looks into the heart." This principle of divine discernment is a centerpiece of God's election, and to understand its meaning explains

both the rationale of David's appointment and our own call to follow God in Christ. Based on the text, we can conclude that the Lord does not mean to express a preference for those who are homely. David, after all, is handsome. Rather, the phrase means that the Lord looks into David's mind. That is, God scrutinizes the habitual ways in which David thinks. As David's story unfolds and patterns of his decision making emerge, we get a glimpse of what God sees at the outset of his reign.

To summarize one of those patterns broadly, we can say that David has a heart

bent on deferential and passionate love for others. For example, despite multiple opportunities, David's love and regard for Saul, who was also God's anointed, keeps him from executing his embattled predecessor. Additionally, David's relationships with women, like Bathsheba and Abigail, and his care expressed toward his children, like Amnon, reveal an overly indulgent lover and father. He takes to himself women who are the wives of other men, and he spares the life of a son who rapes one of his daughters (Tamar). A similar (overly?) deferential love stays David's hand toward select

Take no part in the **fruitless works** of darkness;
   rather **expose** them, for it is shameful even to mention
   the things done by them in secret;
   but everything exposed by the light becomes visible,
   for everything that becomes visible is light.
Therefore, it says:
   "**Awake**, O **sleeper**,
   and **arise** from the dead,
   and **Christ** will **give** you **light**."

GOSPEL   John 9:1–41

A reading from the holy Gospel according to John

[As **Jesus** passed by he **saw** a **man blind** from **birth**.]
His **disciples** asked him,
   "Rabbi, **who sinned**, this man or his parents,
   that he was born blind?"
Jesus answered,
   "**Neither** he nor his parents sinned;
   it is so that the **works** of **God** might be made **visible**
      through him.
We have to do the works of the one who sent me while it is **day**.
Night is coming when **no one** can **work**.
While I am in the **world**, I am the **light** of the world."
When he had said this, [he **spat** on the ground
   and made **clay** with the saliva,
   and smeared the clay on his eyes, and said to him,
   "Go **wash** in the Pool of **Siloam**"—which means Sent—.
So he went and washed, and came back able to see.

His **neighbors** and those who had seen him earlier
     as a **beggar** said,
   "Isn't this the one who used to sit and beg?"

The disciples are trying to learn from their teacher. His answer surprises them.

Rabbi = RAB-ī

Many ancient cultures thought that saliva had medicinal properties. Read like a clinician would describe a medical protocol.

Siloam = sih-LOH-uhm

individuals who ultimately incur capital punishment by Solomon at the outset of his reign (see 1 Kings 2).

In addition to revealing David's heart and the way that God scrutinizes his chosen ones, we learn here something about God's own heart. When expressing displeasure with and rejection of Saul, Samuel proclaims that the Lord will seek "a man after his own heart" (1 Samuel 13:14). So, in David's heart we glimpse God's heart, which loves to the point of being embarrassing.

READING II   Continuing with the readings for the second set of scrutinies, we encounter Paul articulating a provocative metaphor in which he identifies the early Christians in Ephesus with the fundamental categories of creation: darkness and light. These categories frame Paul's multi-faceted exhortation in which he calls on the Christian community at Ephesus to live and learn the good life and to avoid and expose unfruitful and shameful behavior. Paul's message is an important one for the elect to hear as they approach the second scrutiny.

By identifying Christians as being in darkness before being transformed into light in the Lord, Paul highlights the depths at which a relationship with Christ operates. Paul's theme of darkness and light recalls for us the creation account of Genesis 1; it equates the Ephesians with the first elements of creation. Before their relationship with Christ, they did not yet rise to the level of something created since, on the first day of creation, the Lord said, "Let there be light" (Genesis 1:3). Only then was light separated from darkness. So, when Paul tells the Ephesians that, in the

Some said, "It is,"
   but others said, "No, he just looks like him."
He said, "**I am.**"]
So they said to him, "How were your eyes opened?"
He replied,
   "The man called Jesus made clay and anointed my eyes
   and told me, 'Go to Siloam and wash.'
So I went there and washed and was **able to see**."
And they said to him, "Where is he?"
He said, "I don't know."

[They brought the one who was once blind to the Pharisees.
Now Jesus had made clay and opened his eyes on a sabbath.
So then the Pharisees also asked him how he was able to see.
He said to them,
   "He put clay on my eyes, and I washed, and now I can see."
So some of the **Pharisees** said,
   "This man is **not from God**,
   because he does **not keep** the **sabbath**."
But others said,
   "How can a **sinful man** do such signs?"
And there was a **division** among them.
So they said to the blind man again,
   "What do you have to say about him,
   since he opened your eyes?"
He said, "He is a **prophet**."]

Now the **Jews did not believe**
   that he had been blind and gained his sight
   until they summoned the **parents** of the one who had gained
      his sight.
They asked them,
   "Is this your son, who you say was **born blind**?
How does he now see?"
His parents answered and said,
   "We know that this is our son and that he was born blind. **»**

The unnamed man credits Jesus for the miracle.

Pause for the scene change.

Is the man getting irritated repeating himself? Or does the story grow with each telling?

Imagine you have been blind from birth and experiencing sight for the first time. What tone would you use describing the person who made it possible? Despite the inquisition, he doesn't back down from his testimony.

The Jewish authorities are obstinate in their belief. They widen their inquiry.

Lord, they are light, he is effectively telling them that in the Lord they came into existence. For the elect, to whom the Church addresses this reading this Sunday, questions emerge: Have they moved beyond thinking about moral questions—concerns about right and wrong—to ponder existential and ontological matters like who they are and what it means to exist? Are they coming to understand that, at the level of their existence and identity, their relationship with God is their foundation? Following Paul's cue in this passage from Ephesians,

questions of existence precede questions of ethics.

After inviting his audience to recognize that the Lord is the fundamental ground of their existence, Paul shifts to matters of morality: "Live as children of light." For Paul, the fruit of light is anything good, right, or true. Those who have come to know themselves as members or children of God's creation—children of the light—resonate with all things that work in accord with their fundamental nature. Light is drawn to light. Good to good. Right to right. At the same time, they avoid and

unmask what is not in accordance with the light. For the elect who undergo their second scrutiny today, Paul invites them to allow the light of Christ to expose any darkness and shamefulness so that Christ's light may radiate from them all the more.

GOSPEL | Following the tradition of the early Church, John's account of the healing of the blind man is read on the occasion of the second scrutiny. When the disciples question Jesus at the outset of the story, they frame an aspect of the elect's discernment this

We do **not know how** he sees now,
    nor do we know **who** opened his eyes.
Ask him, he is of age;
    he can **speak** for **himself**."
His parents said this because they were **afraid**
    of the Jews, for the Jews had already agreed
    that if anyone acknowledged him as the Christ,
    he would be **expelled** from the **synagogue**.
For this reason his parents said,
    "He is of age; question him."

So a **second time** they called the man who had been blind
    and said to him, "Give **God the praise**!
We know that this man is a sinner."
He replied,
    "If he is a sinner, I do not know.
One thing I do know is that **I was blind** and now I see."
So they said to him,
    "**What** did he do to you?
    How did he open your eyes?"
He answered them,
    "I **told you already** and you did not **listen**.
Why do you want to hear it again?
Do you want to **become** his **disciples**, too?"
They **ridiculed** him and said,
    "**You** are that man's disciple;
    we are disciples of **Moses**!
We know that God spoke to Moses,
    but we do not know where **this one** is from."
The man answered and said to them,
    "This is what is so **amazing**,
    that you do not know where he is from, yet he opened my eyes.
We know that God does **not listen** to **sinners**,
    but if one is devout and does his will, he listens to him.
It is unheard of that anyone ever opened the eyes of a person
        born blind.

The narrator interjects with the parents' motive.

His frustration turns into sarcasm.

Using a demonstrative pronoun, "this one," distances them from Jesus and betrays a condescending attitude. They believe they are better than Jesus.

Sunday: when someone finds themselves in a woeful condition beyond their control, who is to blame? The disciples' vision of the world is such that they regard any and all deficiencies as the result of wrongdoing, so the logical inclination is to assign blame and sin to all occasions in which things are not right. In the case of the man who was born blind, someone must have sinned —the man or his parents. For a contemporary audience familiar with modern science, the disciples' reasoning can seem illogical. The right tests would likely determine the natural cause of the man's blind-

ness. But even today, the human quest to find causes for things is still prone to turn to human moral agency for explanation. For example, it is common enough for us to hear someone stricken with a serious illness or injury to ask what they did to deserve it. In recognizing that confusion about moral agency and culpability is more typical than we might like to admit, we turn to Jesus' response to the disciples' question in today's reading. For Jesus, the disciples' logic must be turned on its head. The man's blindness is not a reason to find fault or assign blame. Rather, it is an opportunity

for the manifestation of God's works in the world.

Interestingly, we never learn the blind man's name. Rather, the defining feature of this man's identity is his blindness. By giving the man sight, Jesus transforms his fundamental identity from a blind beggar to an ordinary man. As a new man with visual and social capacity (he no longer needs to beg), the man becomes an instrument for God's work in his community. Everyone who previously crossed his path is tested by his new vision and how it came about. They repeatedly question the man, who is

Pause for the scene change.

Jesus' interrogation of the man is not accusatory but invitational.

"Lord": he correctly identifies Jesus.

Emphasize "are we" to make it personal to those gathered in your assembly.

Study the inversion in these lines. Practice to clearly convey Jesus' message.

If this man were not from God,
  he would not be able to do anything."
[They answered and said to him,
  "You were **born** totally in **sin**,
  and are you trying to **teach us**?"
Then they **threw** him out.

When **Jesus** heard that they had thrown him out,
  he found him and said, "Do **you believe** in the **Son of Man?**"
He answered and said,
  "Who is he, **sir**, that I may believe in him?"
Jesus said to him,
  "You have **seen him**,
  and the one **speaking** with you is **he**."
He said,
  "**I do believe, Lord,**" and he **worshiped** him.]
Then Jesus said,
  "I came into this world for **judgment**,
  so that those who **do not see might** see,
  and those who do see might become **blind**."

Some of the Pharisees who were with him heard this
  and said to him, "Surely we are not also blind, **are we?**"
Jesus said to them,
  "If you **were** blind, you would have no **sin**;
  but now you are saying, 'We see,' so your sin **remains**."

[Shorter: John 9:1, 6–9, 13–17, 34–38 (see brackets)]

left to answer for his new state of existence. No longer a blind beggar, neighbors question his identity and how he came to see. The now visually capable man identifies himself using the language of divine revelation—"I am"—and testifies to Jesus as his healer. Two formal interrogations from the pharisees follow, with an interrogation of the man's parents in between. In contrast to the parents' fear, the man boldly confesses that Jesus healed him. Finally, at the end of the story, Jesus questions the man: "Do you believe in the Son of Man?" This title, taken from Daniel 7:13–14, is a way of speaking about the promised Messiah. When the man asks Jesus for more information about the Son of Man, Jesus reveals himself as such. Ultimately, then, the man gets to profess his faith in Jesus as Lord.

Like the man born blind, whose identity was transformed through an encounter with Christ, those who are baptized into Christ take up a new identity. As adopted children of God, their relationships with God and within their communities change. Herein lies the elect's second scrutiny: Are they prepared to live in the light and act as children of the light, even when facing the questions about their changed identity that will come from their friends, colleagues, associates, and community members? Will they, when finally questioned at their last judgment, profess their faith in Jesus as Lord? E.W.

FIFTH SUNDAY OF LENT

LECTIONARY #35

READING I   Jeremiah 31:31–34

Jeremiah = jayr-uh-Mī-uh

Recall the energized feeling you might have had from a clean bill of health or a new beginning. Proclaim this oracle with the same sense of optimism.
Judah = JOO-duh

Don't use a tone of despair; God has forgiven his people.

God's performative words are incredible: he claims us! Consider familiarizing yourself with this line so that you can deliver it looking directly at the assembly. Emphasis "my" to show possession.

A reading from the Book of the Prophet Jeremiah

The **days** are **coming**, says the Lord,
   when I will make a **new covenant** with the house of Israel
   and the house of **Judah**.
It will not be like the covenant I made with their fathers
   the day I **took** them by the **hand**
   to lead them forth from the land of Egypt;
   for they **broke** my covenant,
   and I had to show myself their master, says the Lord.
But this is the covenant that I will make
   with the house of Israel after those days, says the Lord.
I will place my **law within them** and **write** it upon their **hearts**;
   I will be **their God**, and they shall be my people.
No longer will they have need to teach their friends
      and relatives
   how to **know** the Lord.
All, from **least** to **greatest**, shall **know me**, says the Lord,
   for I will **forgive** their **evildoing** and **remember** their sin
      no more.

There are options for today's readings. Contact your parish staff to learn which readings will be used.

READING I Today's first reading is a centerpiece of "Jeremiah's Book of Comfort" or "Little Book of Consolation," which consists of Jeremiah 30—33. Written amid Judah's downfall, Jerusalem's destruction, and the Babylonia exile, the Book of Jeremiah consists of repeated laments, predictions of destruction, and general expressions of woe. But this small portion conveys a hopeful message. In it, God extends a new promise to the chosen people. God will forge a new covenant with them, despite their having broken the previous covenant, which God forged with them in the Law (Torah) given at Sinai. Like the Sinai covenant's divine legal teaching, this new covenant will consist of God's instruction (torah). However, the new covenant will not be an exterior reality written on tablets that the people will have to internalize through a process of intergenerational teaching and learning. Rather, God will instruct the people directly by writing the law of the new covenant on their hearts. By establishing this new covenant, God will reforge the intimate relationship with the people that was ruptured by their disobedience to the prior instruction. And God rearticulates the nature of that relationship, which corresponds to the old covenant: "I will be their God, and they shall be my people." Yet this new covenant will not be one that perpetuates servitude to sin. Instead, God promises to forgive and forget the sins of the people. Of course, this raises questions about God's justice: How can it be that God gave a just law and

For meditation and context:

RESPONSORIAL PSALM   Psalm 51:3–4, 12–13, 14–15 (12a)

R. Create a clean heart in me, O God.

Have mercy on me, O God, in your
    goodness;
    in the greatness of your compassion wipe
    out my offense.
Thoroughly wash me from my guilt
    and of my sin cleanse me.

A clean heart create for me, O God,
    and a steadfast spirit renew within me.
Cast me not out from your presence,
    and your Holy Spirit take not from me.

Give me back the joy of your salvation,
    and a willing spirit sustain in me.
I will teach transgressors your ways,
    and sinners shall return to you.

Read about Jesus' agony in the garden (Luke 22:39–49) to feel the anguish Paul is referring to.

READING II   Hebrews 5:7–9

A reading from the Letter to the Hebrews

In the days when **Christ Jesus** was in the **flesh**,
    he offered **prayers** and supplications with loud **cries** and **tears**
    to the one who was able to **save** him from death,
    and he was **heard** because of his **reverence**.
Son though he was, he learned **obedience** from what he suffered;
    and when he was made **perfect**,
    he became the **source** of eternal **salvation** for all who
    obey him.

Jesus' perfect obedience is the source of our salvation and becomes our example for the life of discipleship. Proclaim these important words clearly.

GOSPEL   John 12:20–33

A reading from the holy Gospel according to John

Some **Greeks** who had come to worship at the **Passover** Feast
    came to **Philip**, who was from **Bethsaida** in **Galilee**,
    and asked him, "Sir, we would like to **see Jesus**." »

Bethsaida = beth-SAY-uh-duh

Imagine you are asking someone to see Jesus. Who in your life would have taken you to meet him?

---

now would seemingly reject its terms in order to reestablish a relationship with a disloyal people? Recognizing God's profound love for the chosen people cannot negate God's justice; God's forgiveness of the people entails a cost on God's part. That cost comes into view in the subsequent readings.

| READING II | The Letter to the Hebrews consistently appeals to the priestly sacrificial system of the old covenant to understand Christ's life, death, and resurrection. With this sacrificial system as

an interpretive key, Hebrews presents Christ's entire life as a salvific offering to God on our behalf. Today's passage highlights some key elements of that offering. First, it speaks of Christ's "prayers and supplications" and "loud cries and tears" as offerings for our sake. The picture of Christ's prayer here is one of strenuous, heartfelt piety. As Hebrews claims, Christ's prayers were heard because they were uttered in heartfelt reverence or what we might call cautious piety (*eulabeia* in Greek). That is, Christ's mode of prayer, according to Hebrews, was rooted in

thorough-going fear of the Lord. His every appeal to God was understood as a daring act, an appeal to the truly almighty one. The focus of the passage then shifts to Christ's suffering and obedience to the Father. With the Lord's sacrifice on the cross in view, the passage from Hebrews closes by indicating that Christ's passion is the source and cost of our eternal salvation. Made perfect through suffering, "he became the source of eternal salvation for all who obey him." Thus, as we get closer to Holy Week, we are reminded of its meaning —Jesus' sacrifice is our salvation.

"Son of Man" was a Jewish idiom. Read it as one term.

The agrarian community would understand this metaphor.

Emphasize the contrasts: love / hate and loses / preserves.

Bring emotion to the dialogue. Jesus' humanity is seen in his "troubled" state.

Explain the misunderstanding of the crowd using a narrator voice.

"Everyone" will be drawn to Jesus. His words are not only meant for those gathered around him but also for us who hear his word today.

Philip went and **told Andrew**;
   then Andrew and Philip went and told **Jesus**.
Jesus answered them,
   "The hour has come for the **Son of Man** to be **glorified**.
Amen, amen, I say to you,
   unless a grain of **wheat falls** to the ground and **dies**,
   it remains just a grain of wheat;
   but if it dies, it produces much **fruit**.
Whoever **loves** his **life loses** it,
   and whoever **hates** his life in this world
   will **preserve** it for **eternal** life.
Whoever **serves** me must **follow me**,
   and where I am, there also will my **servant** be.
The Father will **honor** whoever serves me.

"I am **troubled** now. Yet what should I say,
'**Father**, **save me** from this hour'?
But it was for this **purpose** that I came to this hour.
Father, **glorify** your name."
Then a **voice** came from **heaven**,
   "I have **glorified** it and will glorify it again."
The **crowd** there **heard** it and said it was **thunder**;
   but others said, "An **angel** has **spoken** to him."
Jesus answered and said,
   "This voice did not come for **my sake** but for **yours**.
Now is the time **of judgment** on this **world**;
   now the ruler of this world will be **driven out**.
And when I am **lifted** up from the **earth**,
   I will **draw everyone** to myself."
He said this indicating the kind of **death** he would die.

GOSPEL On the cusp of Passover, threatened with arrest for capital crimes by religious leaders, anointed in preparation for death, and triumphantly received by a crowd in Jerusalem, Jesus' public ministry dramatically concludes in today's Gospel and his glorification begins. For all the richness of the events leading up to today's Gospel passage and the importance of what follows (the Last Supper and Christ's passion and resurrection), a seemingly innocuous request sparks a fundamental transition in Jesus' mission. The request to see Jesus, which comes from

some Greeks and through disciples with Greek names, symbolizes that the nations of the world now want to see Jesus. So, the time is ripe. The world desires him. His mission is fulfilled. "The hour has come." It is time for him to be glorified by losing his life and making of himself an offering for others. By committing to such self-sacrifice, Christ presents himself as a model for his disciples. At the same time, he reveals the Father to the surrounding crowd by taking up a prayerful conversation in which the Father mysteriously responds. The crowd, however, remains confused, thinking they

hear either thunder or an angel's voice. But Jesus clarifies. His self-offering on the cross will result in judgement of the world and its ruler, and Jesus will draw everyone to himself. Thus, with our Lenten campaign drawing to a close and Holy Week around the corner, we ponder this week the approach of Christ's glorification on the cross, how it reveals the Father, how it introduces the prospect of final judgment and justice, and how it gathers the nations to God. E.W.

FIFTH SUNDAY OF LENT, YEAR A

LECTIONARY #34

READING I   Ezekiel 37:12–14

A reading from the Book of the Prophet Ezekiel

Thus says the LORD God:
  O my people, I will **open** your **graves**
  and have **you rise** from them,
  and bring you **back** to the **land** of **Israel**.
Then you shall **know** that I am the LORD,
  when I open your graves and have you rise from them,
  O my people!
I will **put** my **spirit in you** that you may **live,**
  and I will settle you upon your land;
  thus you shall know that I am the LORD.
I have **promised**, and I will **do** it, says the LORD.

RESPONSORIAL PSALM   Psalm 130:1–2, 3–4, 5–6, 7–8 (7)

R. With the Lord there is mercy and fullness of redemption.

Out of the depths I cry to you, O LORD;
  LORD, hear my voice!
Let your ears be attentive
  to my voice in supplication.

If you, O LORD, mark iniquities,
  LORD, who can stand?
But with you is forgiveness,
  that you may be revered.

I trust in the LORD;
  my soul trusts in his word.
More than sentinels wait for the dawn,
  let Israel wait for the LORD.

For with the LORD is kindness
  and with him is plenteous redemption;
and he will redeem Israel
  from all their iniquities.

Ezekiel = ee-ZEE-kee-uhl

Read Ezekiel 37:1–11 in your Bible to prepare for your proclamation. The image-driven prophecy in today's first reading—graves opening, bodies rising—is preceded by more intriguing happenings as Ezekiel encounters God.

God addresses the people with compassion and love; bring that tone into your proclamation.

Read "promised" with confidence. God will bring new life to the exiled people.

For meditation and context:

TO KEEP IN MIND
On the Third, Fourth and Fifth Sundays of Lent, the readings from Year A are used when the scrutinies—prayers for purification and strength—are celebrated with the elect, those who will be baptized at the Easter Vigil.

There are options for today's readings. Contact your parish staff to learn which readings will be used.

READING I   When the prophet Ezekiel extended a promise from the Lord to the chosen people that their graves will open, that they will rise from them, and that they will return to their homeland, the promise likely seemed impossible and may well have been met with incredulity. The people had been forced to migrate from Israel to Babylon.

For them, the ancient promises made to Abraham, which assured his descendants residence in the land of Israel, a blessed relationship with God, and the delight of abundant offspring, were all threatened, diminished, or seemingly dissolved. Rather than living along the Jordan and the many seasonal rivulets of the land of Israel, God's people were living along rivers in Babylon (Ezekiel 1:1; 3:15; and Psalm 137:1). Adjusting to a new place meant many changes. New weather and agricultural patterns. New ways of obtaining sustenance. Even some of the staples of their diet would have

changed. Moreover, their societal roles, language used in public discourse, and patterns for engaging in commerce and politics would have changed. Exile meant the way of life for God's people changed. In such a context, a new promise from God in which the dead would rise and the whole people—those living and those raised from the dead—would return to the land of promise would have been one more fundamental reality change. This time, though, it was a religious one.

Prior to Ezekiel's message, there is very little evidence suggesting that the

READING II   Romans 8:8–11

A reading from the Letter of Saint Paul to the Romans

Brothers and sisters:
Those who are in the f**lesh cannot please God**.
But **you** are **not** in the flesh;
　on the contrary, you are in the **spirit**,
　if **only** the Spirit of God **dwells** in you.
Whoever does **not** have the Spirit of **Christ** does not **belong**
　　to him.
But if Christ is **in you**,
　although the body is **dead** because of **sin**,
　the spirit is **alive** because of **righteousness**.
If the **Spirit** of the one who **raised Jesus** from the dead dwells
　　in you,
　the **One** who raised Christ from the dead
　will give **life** to your **mortal bodies** also,
　through his Spirit **dwelling** in you.

chosen people sustained a meaningful belief in the resurrection. Death meant burial and descent to Sheol to be among the dead. To live forever was accomplished by establishing offspring who could sustain one's name and reputation into the future. Thus, Ezekiel's message would have called for a significant change in the religious imagination of the people and constituted a difficult concept to grasp, much less accept. Yet, Ezekiel provides a primordial promise of resurrection and for a familiar purpose: to foster knowledge of the Lord. The phrase "that you/they might know that

I am the Lord" appears dozens of times in the Book of Ezekiel and recalls, among other things, God's work in bringing about the Exodus (see Exodus 7:5, 17; 8:22; 10:2; 14:4, 18). So, when Ezekiel uses this phrase in today's passage, however impossible the promise of resurrection may have seemed, it was to be understood as tantamount to the promise that God made good on in the Exodus. Resurrection would assuredly come for God's people. The fulfillment of this promise comes into full view in Christ's actions in today's Gospel reading.

For the elect facing the final scrutiny this weekend, this reading from Ezekiel extends an invitation to reflect more deeply on God's promise of resurrection. This promise, which was originally extended to the chosen people in exile, is extended today to the elect. For their part they are called upon to remove whatever might keep them from being totally open to the hope of resurrection that is fulfilled in God's Incarnate Word, Jesus Christ.

GOSPEL   John 11:1–45

A reading from the holy Gospel according to John

Now a man was ill, **Lazarus** from **Bethany**,
   the village of **Mary** and her **sister Martha**.
Mary was the one who had **anointed** the Lord with **perfumed oil**
   and dried his **feet** with her **hair**;
   it was her **brother** Lazarus who was ill.
So [the sisters **sent word** to **Jesus** saying,
   "Master, the one **you love** is **ill**."
When Jesus heard this he said,
   "This illness is **not** to end in **death**,
   but is for the **glory** of **God**,
   that the **Son** of God may be glorified through it."
Now Jesus **loved** Martha and her sister and Lazarus.
So when he heard that he was ill,
   he **remained** for two **days** in the place where he was.
Then after this he said to his disciples,
   "Let us **go back** to Judea."]
The disciples said to him,
   "**Rabbi**, the Jews were just trying to **stone you**,
   and you want to go back there?"
Jesus answered,
   "Are there not **twelve hours** in a **day**?
If one walks during the day, he does not **stumble**,
   because he sees the **light** of this world.
But if one walks at **night**, he stumbles,
   because the light is not **in** him."
He said this, and then told them,
   "Our friend Lazarus is **asleep**,
   but I am going to **awaken** him." »

Lazarus = LAZ-uh-ruhs

Bethany = BETH-uh-nee

This is a miracle story. Convery the dire situation, the performative words of Jesus, and the reaction of the crowd. Practice so the listener should easily recognize who is speaking or acting.

The disciples are remembering the recent danger (see John 8:59 and 10:31). They do not want to return to it.

Rabbi = RAB-ī

Jesus tries to explain to them, multiple times and in various ways, what is happening. He finally, clearly, explains that Lazarus has died. Still, they cannot anticipate what Jesus' final actions will be in this situation.

READING II   Continuing the focus of our first reading from the prophet Ezekiel, the apostle Paul instructs Christians at Rome, and us, in the life-giving ways of the Spirit of God. As if echoing Ezekiel, Paul highlights how the Spirit of God, which is the same as the Spirit of Christ, transforms those in whom it abides. Contrasting the flesh and the Spirit, Paul instructs us that as dwelling places of God's Spirit we can please God, belong to Christ, and ultimately hope in the promise of a resurrected life in Christ. Paul's discussion here shows that, in raising Jesus from the dead, God has not only fulfilled the promise of resurrection made through the prophet Ezekiel but that the promise has also been extended to followers of Christ through the indwelling of the Spirit. Resurrection is available to us!

That said, Paul's language today is also not presumptive. He uses some important conditional expressions: "if Christ is in you" and "if the Spirit . . . dwells in you." While Paul acknowledges that the promise of resurrection is fulfilled in Christ and is now available for us through the Spirit of God dwelling in us, the effects of the promise are not guaranteed. It remains possible to be closed off to the Spirit and thus not receive the transforming power of the resurrection. Put differently, Paul indicates that, while Christ's resurrection is an entirely unmerited gift, it takes effect in our lives when we respond generously to it. We need to be open to and foster the working of the Spirit in our lives.

As we celebrate the final scrutiny this Sunday, the elect, and we with them, consider those attitudes and dispositions that crowd out, undermine, or reject the Spirit's place and work in our lives. Using Paul's

So the disciples said to him,
    "**Master**, if he is asleep, he will be **saved**."
But Jesus was talking about **his death**,
    while they thought that he meant **ordinary sleep**.
So then Jesus said to them clearly,
    "**Lazarus has died**.
And I am glad for you that I was not there,
    that you may **believe**.
Let us **go** to him."
So **Thomas**, called **Didymus**, said to his fellow disciples,
    "**Let us** also go to **die with him**."

[When **Jesus arrived**, he found that Lazarus
    had already been in the **tomb** for **four days**.]
Now Bethany was **near Jerusalem**, only about **two miles away**.
And many of the **Jews** had come to Martha and Mary
    to **comfort them** about their brother.
[When **Martha heard** that Jesus was coming,
    she went to **meet** him;
    but Mary sat at home.
Martha said to Jesus,
    "**Lord**, **if you had been here**,
    my brother would **not** have **died**.
But even now I **know** that whatever you **ask of God**,
    God will **give** you."
Jesus said to her,
    "Your brother **will rise**."
Martha said to him,
    "I **know** he will rise,
    in the **resurrection** on the **last day**."
Jesus told her,
    "I am the resurrection and the **life**;
    whoever **believes** in me, even if he **dies**, will **live**,
    and everyone who lives and believes in me will **never** die.

Pause for the scene change. Four days after Lazarus has died leaves no room for quibbling about the death; Lazarus was certainly dead.

Read as a complaint but also as a recognition that God is the source of Jesus' power. The complaint will be repeated by her sister.

---

language, we might ask how does the flesh—which cannot please God—continue to hold sway in our thoughts, attitudes, and patterns of decision making and how can we make space for the transforming power of God's resurrecting Spirit?

GOSPEL   The story of the raising of Lazarus is the traditional Gospel reading for the third scrutiny. It constitutes, in story form, a question about ultimate things. Jesus himself effectively poses the question to his friend Martha: "Do you believe that I am the resurrection and the life?" This question presses for an honest, direct profession of faith in Christ's resurrection from the dead and belief in the transforming power of that resurrection. Of course, the story of Lazarus does more than simply place us in a barren terrain of cold, calculated, precise faith claims. It is a story that ushers us gradually but seriously to a moment of decision making, a moment in which we, as listeners, are called upon to give our assent of faith, with Martha, to the power of Christ's resurrection. This story unfolds in stages, each of which merits attention.

The story of the raising of Lazarus begins by introducing Lazarus. He is from Bethany, the brother of Mary and Martha, and facing an illness serious enough for his sisters to send a message to Jesus informing him that "the one you love is ill." By describing their brother as Jesus' beloved (*phileō* in Greek), the sisters connect Lazarus to the core of Jesus' mission from the Father: "For the Father loves [(*phileō* in Greek)] his Son and shows him everything that he himself does" (John 5:20). The sisters' appeal to Jesus, in effect, asks him to act with the same integrity as his heavenly Father.

A powerful statement of faith and acknowledgment of who Jesus is. Let it resonate with your listeners.

Do **you believe** this?"
She said to him, "**Yes**, Lord.
I have come to believe that **you are the Christ**, the Son of God,
   the one who is **coming** into the **world**."]

When she had said this,
   she went and called her sister **Mary secretly**, saying,
   "The **teacher** is here and is **asking** for you."
As soon as she heard this,
   she rose **quickly** and **went** to him.
For Jesus had not yet come into the village,
   but was still where Martha had met him.
So when the Jews who were with her in the house comforting her
   saw Mary get up quickly and go out,
   they **followed** her,
   presuming that she was going to the **tomb** to **weep** there.
When Mary came to where Jesus was and **saw** him,
   she **fell** at his **feet** and said to him,
   "**Lord, if you had been here**,
   my brother would **not** have died."

The Gospel writer makes it clear that Jesus could have handled it differently.

When Jesus saw her **weeping** and the Jews who had come with
    her weeping,
   [he became **perturbed** and deeply troubled, and said,
   "Where have you **laid** him?"
They said to him, "Sir, **come and see**."
And Jesus **wept**.
So the Jews said, "See how he **loved** him."
But some of them said,
   "Could not the one who opened the eyes of the **blind man**
   have **done something** so that this man would not have died?"

"Jesus wept": Read dolefully and pause, letting Jesus' empathy and sadness sink in. Can we be more attentive to those who are suffering loss?

So Jesus, perturbed **again**, came to the tomb.
It was a **cave**, and a **stone lay across** it.
Jesus said, "**Take away** the stone." »

After introducing Lazarus, the story turns to Jesus' initial response. He proclaims that the illness will result in God's glory and then, assured by the narrator that Jesus loved Lazarus, we are told that he waits two days before calling on his disciples to return to Judea to attend to a "sleeping"—that is, dead, Lazarus. The disciples offer multi-faceted resistance, to which we as readers might offer still more. First, the disciples articulate apparent concern for Jesus' well-being. They worry that he will be stoned in Judea. Next, they fail to recognize that Lazarus' "sleeping" means that he

has died. Evidently, they think that Jesus' healing abilities were not necessary for their sick friend. Sleep would rejuvenate him. Jesus makes the matter plain: "Lazarus has died." Finally, their resistance is made plain in Thomas' declaration—return to Judea meant the disciples faced death with Jesus. Their concerns were never for Jesus or Lazarus but for themselves. From our perspective, we can ask why Jesus waited and let Lazarus die. If we recognize that Lazarus was Jesus' beloved friend and that his resurrection glorifies God, we can see in it a prefiguring or preparation for the

resurrection that will unfold and endure in Christ.

Jesus' approach to Bethany follows in two stages. First, Martha comes out to meet him and their exchange is marked by a sequence of faith statements by Martha that are progressively more robust. If Jesus had been present, her brother would not have died, but even in death she trusts in Jesus' power to give life. Then, summoned by Martha, Mary arrives with a cohort of grievers from Jerusalem. Mary makes her own faith claim, but it only amounts to Martha's initial claim: had Jesus

Martha, the dead man's sister, said to him,
  "Lord, by now there will be a **stench**;
  he has been dead for **four days**."
Jesus said to her,
  "Did I not tell you that if you **believe**
  you will **see** the **glory** of **God**?"
So they took away the stone.
And Jesus **raised** his eyes and said,
  "**Father**, **I thank you for hearing me**.
I know that you **always** hear me;
  but because of the **crowd** here I have said this,
  that they may **believe** that you **sent** me."
And when he had said this,
  he cried out in a **loud voice**,
  "**Lazarus**, **come out**!"
The **dead** man came out,
  tied hand and **foot** with **burial bands**,
  and his **face** was **wrapped** in a **cloth**.
So Jesus said to them,
  "**Untie him** and let him **go**."

Now **many** of the Jews who had come to Mary
  and seen what he had done began to **believe** in him.]

[Shorter: John 11:3–7, 17, 20–27, 33b–45 (see brackets)]

Jesus' action of looking up draws our attention to God the Father. Proclaim Jesus' words as if in prayer.

Proclaim Jesus' directives calmly.

been present, he could have prevented Lazarus' death. The anguish of everyone, including Jesus, bubbles up in tears, rendering the crowd of mourners divided. Some see Jesus' compassion, others his ineptitude.

Finally, Jesus requests to be taken to the tomb and commands that it be opened, occasioning Martha's concern about the putrid stench of death and the Lord's reassurance of her need for faith. The Lord's supplication to the Father and loud command raises Lazarus from the tomb. Unbound by members of the crowd,

Lazarus is freed from the bonds of death, and many come to believe in Jesus.

Thus, this Gospel for the third and final scrutiny invites us to move away from our enduring tendency toward self-protection, strive for more robust faith, exercise compassion toward those with weaker faith, and (re-)commit to belief in that most fundamental article of Christian faith, resurrection from the dead. E.W.

PALM SUNDAY OF THE PASSION OF THE LORD

LECTIONARY #37

GOSPEL AT THE PROCESSION   Mark 11:1–10

A reading from the holy Gospel according to Mark

Jesus gives instructions on retrieving a colt. Distinguish between the narrator and the characters' dialogue.

Bethphage = BETH-fuh-jee

Bethany = BETH-uh-nee

When **Jesus** and his **disciples** drew near to **Jerusalem**,
  to **Bethphage** and **Bethany** at the Mount of Olives,
  he sent **two** of his disciples and said to them,
  "**Go** into the village opposite you,
  and **immediately** on entering it,
  you will **find** a **colt** tethered on which **no one** has ever **sat**.
Untie it and **bring it** here.
If anyone should say to you,
  '**Why** are you doing this?' reply,
  'The **Master** has **need of it**
  and will **send it back** here at once.'"

Bring some amazement to the situation. The disciples found everything just as Jesus had foretold.

So they went off
  and **found** a colt tethered at a gate outside on the street,
  and they untied it.
Some of the **bystanders** said to them,
  "**What** are you **doing**, untying the colt?"
They **answered** them just as Jesus had told them to,
  and they **permitted** them to do it.
So they **brought** the colt to Jesus
  and put their cloaks over it.

Pause for the scene change.

And he **sat** on it. »

There are options for today's readings. Contact your parish staff to learn which readings will be used.

PROCESSION GOSPEL **Mark**. The liturgy for Palm Sunday of the Passion of the Lord begins with a proclamation of Jesus' triumphal entrance into Jerusalem. In the Church's liturgical calendar and the schema of Mark's Gospel, this event inaugurates Holy Week. The week concludes with the Lord culminating his salvific work in his passion,

death, and resurrection—the paschal mystery that we celebrate in each liturgy and enter into in a special way during the Triduum.

Anticipating the events at the close of the week, today's entrance Gospel and accompanying procession commemorate the Lord's symbolic entry into Jerusalem. The Gospel of Mark highlights various significant elements and prophetic imagery. The passage begins by describing the setting: Bethphage and Bethany, villages proximate to the Mount of Olives. It is in this area where Jesus makes a temporary

"headquarters" during Holy Week. This setting recalls Zechariah 14:4—a verse in which the prophet predicts a decisive battle won by the Lord against the nations, beginning from the top of the Mount of Olives. As the entrance scene continues, Jesus demonstrates his authority and prophetic capacity by commanding his disciples to "go into the village" and "untie" a colt and "bring it" to him. Jesus' ability to precisely predict that his disciples will find a colt and be questioned about taking it manifests his prophetic nature. His preemptive instructions expand his prophetic

Many **people** spread their **cloaks** on the road,
    and others spread leafy **branches**
    that they had cut from the fields.
Those preceding him as well as those following kept crying out:
    "**Hosanna!**
        Blessed is he who **comes** in the **name of the Lord!**
        Blessed is the **kingdom** of our father **David** that is to come!
    Hosanna in the **highest!**"

Or

This is a noisy scene. The crowds are creating a cacophony of joyful praise. Some of these words are very familiar to us, as we hear them in the Holy, Holy, Holy before the Eucharistic Prayer. Read it boldly; the assembly will hear it anew later when it is sung during Mass.

GOSPEL AT THE PROCESSION   John 12:12–16

A reading from the holy Gospel according to John

When the great **crowd** that had come to the feast heard
    that **Jesus** was **coming** to **Jerusalem,**
    they took palm **branches** and went out to **meet** him,
    and cried out:
        "**Hosanna!**
        Blessed is he who comes in the **name** of the **Lord,**
            the **king** of **Israel.**"
Jesus **found** an **ass** and **sat** upon it, as is written:
    Fear no more, O daughter Zion;
    see, your king comes, seated upon an ass's colt.
His **disciples did not understand** this at first,
    but when Jesus had been **glorified**
    they **remembered** that these things were **written** about him
    and that they had done this for him.

The crowds are shouting. Read the verse with boldness. Some of these words are very familiar to us, as we hear them in the Holy, Holy, Holy before the Eucharistic Prayer. The assembly will hear them anew later when it is sung during Mass.

This quote from Zechariah's prophecy needs the tone of a formal announcement.

The story concludes with a report from the narrator.

nature by highlighting his role as rabbi or teacher. Thus, Jesus is both prophet and teacher as he predicts actions and instructs those involved in his triumphal entry into Jerusalem.

The imagery of the entry itself is royal and priestly. When Jesus mounts the "colt" (*pōlos* in Greek), another prophecy from Zechariah (9:9) comes to mind in which personified Zion/Jerusalem is invited to rejoice as her just and saving king humbly approaches astride a young horse or donkey (a *pōlos* can be either). The fact that no one has sat on the animal seems to high-light the animal's status as sacrificially pure, which marks the event as priestly. Royal equestrian imagery is known from elsewhere in Scripture (Genesis 49:11, Judges 5:10, Judges 10:4). And the provision of cloaks on the animal and the roadway recalls actions of the crowd during Jehu's rise to kingship (2 Kings 9:13). Furthermore, a royal psalm (118:25–26) resounds in the crowd's cries of "Hosanna!" (Hebrew for "save [us], please") and "Blessed is he who comes in the name of the Lord!" Finally, claims about David's coming kingdom emphasize the meaning of the crowd's cries—they regard Jesus' entrance as the coming of the Davidic king.

Mark's account of Jesus' symbolic entry into Jerusalem reveals the Lord to be a prophetic teacher and priestly king. Many biblical prophets performed such acts to communicate God's message. Yet, as the week unfolds, Jesus' many roles take on different meanings. As a prophetic teacher Jesus will anticipate and accept his own demise while supporting his disciples who won't be so accepting. As a priestly king he will reveal his blessedness and offer salva-

LECTIONARY #38

READING I Isaiah 50:4–7

A reading from the Book of the Prophet Isaiah

Isaiah = ī-ZAY-uh

These verses should ring true for those in the ministry of proclamation. The Holy Spirit strengthens us to share the Word of God.

Subdue the first "morning." Conversational tone accents the second mention of a well-known phrase. (Try accenting it the other way around and hear how awkward it sounds.)

Pause after "back", "cheeks," and "face." "I gave" is implied to each action and can be subdued. The meaning is clear with this phrasing.

The Lord **GOD** has **given me**
  a **well-trained tongue**,
that I might know how to speak to the **weary**
  a word that will **rouse** them.
Morning after **morning**
  he opens my **ear** that I may **hear**;
and I have not **rebelled**,
  have not turned **back**.
I gave my **back** to those who beat me,
  my **cheeks** to those who plucked my beard;
my **face** I did not **shield**
  from buffets and spitting.

The Lord GOD is my **help**,
  therefore I am not **disgraced**;
I have **set** my face like **flint**,
  knowing that I shall not be put to **shame**.

For meditation and context:

RESPONSORIAL PSALM Psalm 22:8–9, 17–18, 19–20, 23–24 (2a)

R. My God, my God, why have you abandoned me?

All who see me scoff at me;
  they mock me with parted lips, they wag
    their heads:
"He relied on the LORD; let him deliver him,
  let him rescue him, if he loves him."

Indeed, many dogs surround me,
  a pack of evildoers closes in upon me;
they have pierced my hands and my feet;
  I can count all my bones.

They divide my garments among them,
  and for my vesture they cast lots.
But you, O LORD, be not far from me;
  O my help, hasten to aid me.

I will proclaim your name to my brethren;
  in the midst of the assembly I will
    praise you:
"You who fear the LORD, praise him;
  all you descendants of Jacob,
    give glory to him;
  revere him, all you descendants of Israel!"

tion, but as one who accepts rather than inflicts suffering.

John. The account of Jesus' triumphal entry into Jerusalem in the Gospel according to John contrasts in a few important ways with that of Mark's account. John does not emphasize the Lord's prophetic capacity; he has no need to do so. Prior chapters in the Gospel of John, which are often referred to as the Book of Signs, firmly establish Jesus' prophetic identity. Instead, John's Book of Signs concludes with Jesus entering Jerusalem for a third time in his public career. On this occasion,

the crowd spontaneously praises him. Like Mark's account, the message of Psalm 118:25–26 is on the crowd's lips. They proclaim, "Hosanna! Blessed is he who comes in the name of the Lord." Also like Mark's account, the crowd understands their proclamation to refer to Jesus' kingship. That said, this crowd's proclamation does not simply highlight the Davidic nature of Jesus' kingship. His royal identity is associated with Israel in general. He is hailed as the "king of Israel." Accordingly, Jesus comes across as more than simply a Judean king. The fact that the crowd comes out to him

also signals a broader scope to Jesus' royalty. Hellenistic sovereigns of the time also received preemptive adulation upon visiting the cities they governed. Moreover, when the crowd greets Jesus with branches (*baion* in Greek) from palm trees (*phoinix* in Greek), their action recalls the military reacquisition of Jerusalem (1 Maccabees 13:51) and the purification of the temple during the time of the Maccabees (2 Maccabees 10:7). Thus, for the crowd in John's Gospel, Jesus' final approach to Jerusalem is as a preeminent, victorious royal figure. Jesus responds with a prophetic action—he

Philippians = fih-LIP-ee-uhnz

View the reading in two parts. The first is Jesus' humiliation; he is the subject of the action. The second part is his exaltation by God. Pause just before "Because of this" to begin the second part.

All of creation should acknowledge Christ's lordship. "In heaven and on earth" is a common phrase. Read it as one.

Start your practice early for this lengthy reading. Don't read it as if you know the end of the story. If you are taking a specific part in the narrative, mark your *Workbook* with your lines. Pay attention to the line before yours so you have a timely entrance.

If you are reading solo, pay attention to the many scene changes. Pause between them.

Varying the pace helps listeners determine who is speaking or being acted upon. Varying the inflection helps the assembly comprehend the emotion behind the text. High pitch conveys excitement or exasperation. A low pitch can convey melancholy or contriteness.

READING II   Philippians 2:6–11

A reading from the Letter of Saint Paul to the Philippians

Christ **Jesus**, though he was in the form of **God**,
    did not regard **equality** with God
    something to be grasped.
Rather, he **emptied** himself,
    taking the form of a **slave**,
    coming in **human** likeness;
    and found human in **appearance**,
    he **humbled** himself,
    becoming **obedient** to the point of **death**,
    even death on a **cross**.
Because of this, God greatly **exalted** him
    and **bestowed** on him the **name**
    which is above every name,
    that at the name of Jesus
    every **knee** should bend,
    of those in **heaven** and on **earth** and **under** the earth,
    and every **tongue confess** that
    Jesus **Christ** is **Lord**,
    to the **glory** of God the Father.

GOSPEL   Mark 14:1—15:47

The Passion of our Lord Jesus Christ according to Mark

The **Passover** and the Feast of **Unleavened Bread**
    were to take place in **two days'** time.
So the **chief priests** and the **scribes** were seeking a **way**
    to **arrest** him by **treachery** and put him to **death**.
They said, "**Not** during the festival,
    for **fear** that there may be a **riot** among the **people**."

becomes the king prefigured in Zechariah 9:9. When John notes that the disciples did not understand Jesus' prophetic action, the ordinary pedagogical element of the scene diminishes. According to John, the disciples needed the Lord to be revealed in glory —they needed him to die and rise—to remember these events and make sense of them. For John, Jesus' entry into Jerusalem is only triumphant in light of the paschal mystery. Jesus' royal character is broader than anticipated, but it can only be perceived in light of his death and resurrection.

READING I   Today's first reading, often recognized as one of the "servant songs" in the Book of Isaiah, refers to an anonymous servant who, here and in Isaiah 52:13—53:12, suffers greatly on behalf of others. Because of the anonymity, the servant's historical identity is highly debated. Some think the servant was a collective—all Israel. Others suggest that Jeremiah, Isaiah, or another prophet was in view. Still others suggest that a Judean king (Jehoiachin) was envisaged. But such anonymity also suggests the incompleteness of these suggestions. For various reasons,

each can be rejected. For example, the passage's use of first-person pronouns suggests that an individual is in view: "I gave *my* back to those who beat me." Regardless of who precisely the text is referring to, the servant emerges as an iconic figure whose resilience in the face of suffering becomes palpable. The servant does not flinch from beatings, beard-plucking, or spitting.

The anonymous servant in the Book of Isaiah brings into view the breadth and depth of meaning available in and through suffering. In time, Jesus' revelation of salvation by means of suffering, crucifixion, and

Bethany = BETH-uh-nee

spikenard = SPĪK-nahrd

The woman anointing Jesus foreshadows the anointing of his burial. Read the details carefully. The observers were angry with her. Use the appropriate tone to convey these feelings.

Jesus is equally irritated—but for the opposite reason. Let Jesus' humanity show as he defends the unnamed woman. Change Jesus' tone to that of a teacher as he explains his reasons.

Iscariot = ih SKAYR-ee-uht

Judas changes the dynamics of the story. Pause before the sinister act.

Mark's account begins on the day when the Passover lamb is sacrificed. Don't miss the irony.

When he was in **Bethany** reclining at **table**
in the house of Simon the **leper**,
a **woman** came with an alabaster **jar** of perfumed **oil**,
costly genuine spikenard.
She **broke** the alabaster jar and **poured** it on his **head**.
There were some who were **indignant**.
"Why has there been this **waste** of perfumed oil?
It could have been **sold** for more than three hundred days' wages
and the **money** given to the **poor**."
They were **infuriated** with her.
Jesus said, "Let her **alone**.
Why do you make **trouble** for her?
She has done a **good thing** for me.
The **poor** you will always have **with you**,
and whenever you **wish** you can do **good** to them,
but you will not **always** have me.
She has **done** what she **could**.
She has **anticipated** anointing my **body** for **burial**.
Amen, I say to you,
wherever the **gospel** is proclaimed to the **whole world**,
what she has done will be told in **memory** of her."

Then **Judas Iscariot**, one of the **Twelve**,
went off to the **chief priests** to hand him **over** to them.
When they **heard** him they were **pleased**
and promised to **pay** him **money**.
Then he **looked** for an opportunity to hand him over.

On the first day of the Feast of Unleavened Bread,
when they **sacrificed** the Passover lamb,
his disciples said to him,
"Where do you want us to **go**
and **prepare** for you to **eat** the Passover?" »

death offers a definitive approach to understanding the servant. How can someone not make a sound when beaten, abused, and spit upon? How is it that our ears are opened by God and our tongue trained by the Lord in a manner like that of the servant? We must know the unfathomable wisdom available in suffering—its transformative, redemptive power. In knowing what God has done for us in Christ's suffering and death on the cross, we come to know that power perfectly and definitively. So, when it comes to reflecting on Christ's passion or our own, few Old Testament passages better prepare us than the accounts of the servant in the Book of Isaiah.

READING II In the great Christ hymn from the letter to the Philippians, Paul professes and explores Jesus' status as God's anointed one (Messiah/Christ). As the preeminent human person, Jesus is paradigmatically humble, accepts his call to self-emptying, and unflinchingly obeys God to fulfill the divine plan laid out for him from all eternity. Jesus emerges as the model and fulfillment of God's original plan for humanity. Although made in the divine image and likeness (Genesis 1:26–27), Adam and Eve's "overreach" in Eden, their taking and eating the fruit of the tree of knowledge of good and evil which God had explicitly forbidden, ushered death into the world. By contrast, Christ Jesus, who was from all eternity "in the form of God," accepts all aspects of human existence as they have unfolded from our first parents. Slavery, human appearance, and even death by a grim execution on a cross are things Christ accepts. By humbly accepting the full scope of the

The disciples had many details to take care of. As you prepare this reading during this busy liturgical period, reflect on your attitude toward service.

He **sent** two of his disciples and said to them,
   "Go into the city and a **man** will **meet** you,
   carrying a jar of **water**.
Follow him.
Wherever he **enters**, say to the master of the house,
   'The **Teacher** says, "Where is my guest room
   where I may **eat the Passover** with my **disciples?**"'
Then he will show you a **large** upper room furnished and ready.
Make the **preparations** for us **there**."
The disciples then **went off**, entered the **city**,
   and found it **just** as he had **told** them;
   and they **prepared** the Passover.

When it was **evening**, he came with the **Twelve**.
And as they reclined at table and were **eating**, **Jesus** said,
   "**Amen**, I say to you, **one** of you will **betray** me,
   one who is **eating** with me."
They began to be **distressed** and to say to him, one by one,
   "**Surely** it is not **I?**"
He said to them,
   "One of the Twelve, the one who **dips** with me
      into the dish.
For the **Son of Man** indeed goes, as it is **written** of him,
   but **woe** to that man by whom the Son of Man is betrayed.
It would be **better** for that man if he had never been **born**."

At some point in our lives, each of us has betrayed Jesus with our sinful actions. Read their question with uncertainty.

Elongate "woe" to express what it is implying. In the next line, pause after "better for that man" before delivering the condemnation.

These verbs are very important (take, bless, break, and give). They will be heard again in the Eucharistic Prayer.

While they were eating,
   he **took** bread, said the **blessing**,
   broke it, and **gave** it to them, and said,
   "**Take** it; this is **my** body."
Then he **took** a **cup**, gave **thanks**, and **gave** it to them,
   and they all **drank** from it.
He said to them,
   "This is my **blood** of the **covenant**,
   which will be **shed** for **many**.

human condition and avoiding "overreach," Jesus garners exalted status. He rises from the dead. Following from Jesus' resurrection, this hymn professes that heaven, earth, and the netherworld glorify God by acknowledging Jesus as Lord. Jesus, the hymn proclaims, is the one true God, the God of Israel, who called the chosen people into a unique relationship. Effectively, it conveys in poetic form the deep truth that later councils of the Church would articulate in the creeds—Jesus is fully divine and fully human.

The hymn's claim that Jesus is the paradigmatic glorified human person is very important. Highlighting how Jesus is fully human by means of being humble and obedient to death, the hymn presents Jesus as the model by which Christians, at Philippi and throughout the world, are to act: Christ's humble self-emptying is to be imitated. Our self-sacrificial behavior will not be identical with Christ's offering on the cross—that was uniquely redemptive for all (see Hebrews 10:14). However, Christ's self-offering is to characterize all human interactions, especially those among Christians.

Immediately before appealing to the Christ hymn, Paul exhorts the Philippians to live in a humble, self-sacrificial way (Philippians 2:1–4). His rationale is put forth plainly in the Christ hymn, which recognizes that the fullness of human flourishing and our glorification by God arise from holding the interests and well-being of others before our own. Thus, this hymn (which the Philippians may have previously known) not only highlights what Christ has done for us through his self-emptying, acceptance of low (slave) status, and endurance unto death, it also highlights how we are to act in accord with

Scholars note that Psalms 114—118 would have been used during the Passover celebration. Pray these psalms as part of your preparation for this liturgy.

Give Peter's tone the eager bravado he probably felt in this moment.

Give rise to Peter's emphatic tone. Resume a steady voice for the narrator to add the denials from the others.

Gethsemane = gehth-SEM-uh-nee

Despite what the disciples say about their commitment, Jesus knows differently. Use a weary tone as Jesus tells them to "Sit here . . ." Then his tone reflects his disposition of being "troubled and distressed" as he prays.

Amen, I say to you,
   I shall not **drink** again the fruit of the **vine**
   until the day when I drink it new in the kingdom of **God**."
Then, after **singing** a hymn,
   they went **out** to the **Mount of Olives**.

Then Jesus said to them,
   "**All** of you will have your **faith shaken**, for it is written:
      *I will **strike** the **shepherd**,*
         and the sheep will be dispersed.
But after I have been **raised** up,
   I shall **go** before you to **Galilee**."
Peter said to him,
   "Even though **all** should have their **faith shaken**,
   mine will **not** be."
Then Jesus said to him,
   "Amen, I say to you,
   this very night before the **cock crows** twice
   you will **deny** me **three** times."
But he **vehemently** replied,
   "Even though I should have to **die** with you,
   I will **not deny** you."
And they all spoke similarly.

Then they came to a place named **Gethsemane**,
   and he said to his disciples,
   "**Sit** here while I **pray**."
He took with him **Peter**, **James**, and **John**,
   and began to be **troubled** and **distressed**.
Then he said to them, "My soul is **sorrowful** even to **death**.
Remain here and keep **watch**." ❯❯

that grace first poured out in Christ's death on the cross.

PASSION Accounts of Jesus' passion lie at the heart of each Gospel and show significant correspondence among themselves. They tend to begin with a gathering to celebrate a Passover meal. At that meal Jesus reformulates a familiar Jewish ritual to inaugurate a new covenant with a corresponding new ritual. Jesus' Last Supper is the first Eucharist in the synoptic Gospels (Matthew, Mark, and Luke). In the Gospel according to John, Jesus washes the disciples' feet during the Last Supper to inaugurate the Church's ministry of service. All passion narratives alert us to Judas' looming betrayal and convey a scene in which Jesus faces hardship on the slope opposite Jerusalem. While there, an armed group arrests him and takes him to Judean leaders who put him through a mock trial and find him guilty of blasphemy, which leads to a similar sham inquiry before the local Roman authority, Pontius Pilate. Pilate, seeking to keep peace (or at least avoid a riot), orders Jesus to be executed by crucifixion. Once he is in the hands of Roman soldiers, public mocking and torture of Jesus ensues. He is led out of Jerusalem, stripped of his clothes, and crucified with criminals. In a few hours, Jesus dies on the cross and, due to the approaching Sabbath, is hastily buried in a nearby rock-cut tomb of a local Jewish dignitary.

Alongside these similarities, each passion account has unique features that remind us that the many graces poured out for us in Jesus' passion cannot be conveyed in a single account. Thus, each year we read two passion accounts during Holy

Jesus is prostrate on the ground. Read this section with compassion.

He advanced a little and **fell** to the ground and **prayed**
that if it were **possible** the **hour** might pass by him;
he said, "Abba, Father, **all things** are possible to you.
Take this cup **away** from me,
but not what **I** will but what **you** will."
When he **returned** he found them **asleep**.
He said to Peter, "**Simon**, are you **asleep**?

Read Jesus' question to Peter with incredulity.

Could you not keep watch for **one** hour?
Watch and **pray** that **you** may not **undergo** the **test**.
The **spirit** is **willing** but the **flesh** is **weak**."
Withdrawing **again**, he prayed, saying the same thing.
Then he returned once **more** and **found** them asleep,
for they could not keep their **eyes** open
and did not know what to **answer** him.
He returned a **third time** and said to them,
"Are you **still** sleeping and taking your rest?
It is **enough**. The hour has **come**.
Behold, the **Son of Man** is to be **handed** over to **sinners**.
Get **up**, let us **go**.
See, my **betrayer** is at hand."

Then, while he was still speaking,
Judas, one of the Twelve, arrived,
accompanied by a crowd with **swords** and **clubs**
who had come from the chief **priests**,
the scribes, and the elders.
His betrayer had arranged a **signal** with them, saying,
"The man I shall **kiss** is the one;
arrest him and lead him away **securely**."
He came and immediately went over to him and said,
"**Rabbi**." And he kissed him.
At this they **laid hands** on him and arrested him.

Pause after "Rabbi!" Judas calls him teacher, a sign of respect, and then kisses him, an act of betrayal. Such irony.

Week. On Good Friday, we hear John's passion account, while on Palm Sunday a passion account from one of the synoptic Gospels is proclaimed. Each time, we re-enter the mystery of what God has done for us in Christ's passion and death. Doing so not only renews the graces of those events in us, it also better disposes us to receive the hope of Christ's resurrection, which we celebrate at Easter. This liturgical year we hear the account of the Lord's passion from the Gospel according to Mark.

Mark's passion opens with a notice about the context. It is just prior to the feast of Unleavened Bread and Passover, two Jewish feasts in which devout, able-bodied, first century Jews would visit Jerusalem to ritually celebrate the event of God's deliverance of their ancestors from Egypt (see Exodus 12). Jesus' Last Supper, passion, death, and resurrection transpire simultaneously with these feasts as a fulfillment of them. Accordingly, they result in similar commemorative practices. To celebrate the Eucharist is to participate once more in the saving events of Christ's paschal (or Passover) mystery. As often as we participate in the Eucharist, we participate in Jesus' passion, death, and resurrection. Mark clearly intends for us to recognize the connection between the Jewish feasts and Jesus' passion; in the second part of his opening lines, Mark highlights how Jesus' enemies—the chief priests and scribes—plot to arrest and kill him from the moment he arrives in Jerusalem. Only fear of the crowds supporting Jesus restrains them. Strikingly, Jesus' enemies commiserate in an undisclosed place. They speak ominous words from nowhere. Jesus, by contrast, operates openly, at a very particular place: the house of Simon the leper in Bethany.

One of **the bystanders** drew his **sword**,
  struck the high priest's **servant**, and cut off his **ear**.
Jesus said to them in reply,
  "Have you come out as against a **robber**,
  with swords and clubs, to seize me?
Day after **day** I was with you **teaching** in the temple area,
  yet you did not arrest me;
  but that the Scriptures may be **fulfilled**."
And they **all** left him and fled.
Now a young **man followed** him
  wearing nothing but a linen **cloth** about his body.
They **seized** him,
  but he **left** the cloth behind and **ran** off naked.

They **led** Jesus away to the high **priest**,
  and **all** the chief priests and the elders and the scribes
    came **together**.
Peter followed him at a **distance** into the high priest's courtyard
  and was **seated** with **the guards**, **warming** himself at the fire.
The chief priests and the entire Sanhedrin
  kept trying to obtain **testimony** against Jesus
  in order to put him to **death**, but they found **none**.
Many gave **false** witness against him,
  but their testimony did not **agree**.
Some took the stand and testified falsely against him,
  alleging, "We **heard** him say,
  'I will **destroy** this **temple** made with hands
  and within **three days** I will build **another**
  not made with hands.'"
Even so their testimony did not **agree**.
The high priest rose before the assembly and questioned Jesus,
  saying, "Have you no **answer**?
What are these men testifying against you?"
But he was **silent** and answered **nothing**.
Again the high priest asked him and said to him,
  "Are **you** the Christ, the son of the **Blessed** One?" »

Despite Jesus' predicament, he is still teaching his disciples.

Pause after this short vignette.

The high priest correctly identified Jesus.

In Simon's house, the Lord receives a lavish expression of love. A woman breaks an alabaster jar of precious oil and anoints his head. The container and its contents likely came a great distance (possibly from India), suggesting the event's opulence. A more judicious use of such oil would have meant mixing a small amount with another common (less expensive) aromatic oil. But the scene has a deep meaning. Only Mark notes that Jesus' *head* is anointed, recalling Psalm 23:5—"you anoint my head with oil, my cup overflows." The allusion to this royal hymn makes a powerful yet subtle claim: Jesus, in his death and burial, is the rightful king of God's people.

Judas then departs to commiserate with the chief priests and scribes. The threat again comes from no "place." We do not know where they meet. Moreover, we don't know exactly when their exchange occurs. The mounting threat on Jesus' life unfolds outside of space and time while Jesus remains well-situated in and in control of this world's space and time.

With Passover approaching, Jesus gives detailed instructions that not only inform the disciples about the preparations they are to make, but they also predict what his disciples will find when making their preparations. Jesus, here, is no ordinary teacher—he is a prophet who anticipates the details of pending events. The anointed one is inaugurating the new Passover in a place known by and prepared for him.

The Passover meal follows, with Jesus first predicting his betrayal. The disciples deny the possibility, but tension and turmoil mount as his death looms. Amid these tensions, Jesus institutes the Eucharist by taking, blessing, breaking, and giving the

Then Jesus answered, "**I am**;
    and 'you will **see** the **Son of Man**
        seated at the **right** hand of the **Power**
        and coming with the **clouds** of heaven.'"
At **that** the high **priest tore** his garments and said,
    "What further **need** have we of **witnesses**?
You have **heard** the blasphemy.
What do you **think**?"
They **all condemned** him as deserving to die.
Some began to **spit** on him.
They **blindfolded** him and **struck** him and said to him,
    "**Prophesy!**"
And the guards greeted him with **blows**.

While **Peter** was below in the **courtyard**,
    one of the high priest's **maids** came along.
Seeing Peter **warming** himself,
    she **looked** intently at him and said,
    "You too were with the Nazarene, **Jesus**."
But he **denied** it saying,
    "I neither **know** nor understand what you are talking about."
So he went out into the **outer** court.
Then the **cock crowed**.
The maid **saw** him and began **again** to say to the bystanders,
    "This man is **one** of **them**."
Once **again** he denied it.
A little later the **bystanders** said to Peter once more,
    "Surely you are one of them; for you too are a Galilean."
He began to **curse** and to **swear**,
    "I do not know this man about whom you are **talking**."
And immediately a cock crowed a **second** time.

Prophesy = PROF-uh-sī = (verb) to speak divine foretelling

Read the maid's first statement casually. She is not quite sure of Peter's identity. Increase her tone as she gains confidence in subsequent statements.

Nazarene = NAZ-uh-reen

bread of the festival to his disciples who take and eat it. Doing similarly with the festival wine, Jesus establishes the new covenant in *his blood*. As he replaces the Passover lamb, Jesus substitutes a knowing, willing, and pure sacrifice for an unwitting, unwilling animal sacrifice. The contrast is striking. The Last Supper concludes with Jesus and his disciples singing a hymn before departing for the Mount of Olives—a reminder of the Lord's presence in song.

    As Jesus and the disciples walk by night to the Mount of Olives, Jesus prepares his disciples for the shaking of their faith. Quoting Zechariah 13:7, he says "strike the shepherd, and the sheep will be dispersed." Jesus also promises that, after their faith is shaken, he will go before them to Galilee—a much-debated phrase. In as much as their journey began in Galilee, Jesus seems to promise a new beginning for his disciples upon his resurrection. Unfortunately, the disciples miss the promise and fixate on the prospect that their faith will be shaken. Peter leads a chorus of resistance, but Jesus clarifies the matter when he predicts Peter's three-fold denial by sunrise. Thus, the entire trek to Gethsemane is tinged by Jesus' candid predictions and the disciples' defensiveness and exaggerated sense of faithfulness. They remain closed to the transformative power of Jesus' passion, death, and resurrection.

    Once at Gethsemane, the disciples' weakness emerges quickly as Jesus takes select companions—Simon Peter, James, and John—to pray and keep watch while he engages in some private prayer. Repeatedly caught sleeping, the Lord's "select" disciples cannot fulfill their responsibilities, nor do they respond to reprimands Jesus makes. They symbolically represent the

Pause after "wept."

Then Peter **remembered** the word that Jesus had said to him,
"Before the cock crows twice **you will** deny me three times."
He broke down and **wept**.

Sanhedrin = san-HEE-druhn

[As soon as **morning** came,
the chief priests with the elders and the scribes,
that is, the whole Sanhedrin, **held a council**.
They **bound** Jesus, led him **away**, and handed him **over** to **Pilate**.
Pilate questioned him,
"Are you the **king** of the Jews?"
He said to him in reply, "**You** say so."
The chief priests **accused** him of **many** things.
Again Pilate questioned him,
"Have you no **answer**?
See how many things they accuse you of."
Jesus gave him no further answer, so that Pilate was amazed.

Barabbas = buh-RAB-uhs

Now on the occasion of the **feast** he used to **release** to them
one **prisoner** whom they requested.
A man called **Barabbas** was then in prison
along with the rebels who had committed **murder**
in a **rebellion**.
The **crowd** came forward and began to **ask** him
to do for them as he was **accustomed**.
Pilate answered,
"Do you want me to **release** to you the **king** of the **Jews**?"
For he **knew** that it was out of **envy**
that the chief **priests** had handed him **over**.
But the chief priests **stirred** up the crowd
to have him release Barabbas for them **instead**. »

Pilate is asking a frenzied crowd. Project your voice to make this clear. Subdue your tone to reflect the narrator's observation of Pilate's true knowledge.

weakness and frailty of all Jesus' disciples. As they falter in prayer, Jesus equips himself spiritually through appeals to his heavenly Father. In prayer, Jesus acknowledges a desire to forgo his impending suffering: "Take this cup from me." But he offers an immediate clarification: basically, "not my will, but thy will be done." This characteristic phrase from the Our Father is first alluded to here in Mark's Gospel, suggesting that Jesus' fundamental teaching on prayer comes on the eve of his suffering, rather than during his teaching career.

Equipped for the next stage of his passion, Jesus announces Judas' approach.

Greeting Jesus with a gesture and an expression characteristic of a strong, close, and long-standing disciple-spiritual leader relationship, Judas kisses Jesus and salutes him as "Rabbi" ("teacher" in Hebrew). The greeting should convey deep trust and vulnerability, but, with an armed crowd in tow, we cannot even see a professionally distanced student-teacher relationship typical of today's classrooms. The greeting is duplicitous. It warps the underlying bond into an icon of betrayal. And, typical of

Mark's Gospel, the whole exchange happens swiftly. Judas *immediately* greets Jesus upon his arrival in Gethsemane. Chaos ensues. A servant's ear gets cut off. A young man scampers off naked after squirreling out of his clothes when seized by a member of the crowd. Yet, amid the bedlam, Jesus maintains poise. He calmly and plainly asks a rhetorical question and again predicts his own demise.

The next scene consists of parallel inquiries. In one, Jesus undergoes a bogus trial with multiple witnesses falsely testifying against him until, finally, he affirmatively

Pilate again consults the crowd.

Pilate again said to them in reply,
  "Then **what** do you **want** me to do
  with the man you **call** the king of the Jews?"
They shouted again, "**Crucify** him."
Pilate said to them, "**Why**? What **evil** has he done?"
They only shouted the louder, "**Crucify** him."
So Pilate, wishing to **satisfy** the crowd,
  released Barabbas to them and, after he had Jesus **scourged**,
  handed him **over** to be **crucified**.

praetorium = prih-TOHR-ee-uhm

Mocking Jesus as king is irony the crowd
does not understand. Practice your delivery
of this line looking out at the assembly.
We do believe, with sincere hearts, that
Jesus is king.

The **soldiers** led him away inside the **palace**,
  that is, the praetorium, and assembled the whole cohort.
They **clothed** him in **purple** and,
  weaving a **crown** of thorns, placed it on him.
They began to **salute** him with, "**Hail**, **King** of the **Jews!**"
  and kept **striking** his head with a reed and **spitting** upon him.
They **knelt** before him in **homage**.
And when they had **mocked** him,
  they **stripped** him of the purple cloak,
  dressed him in his **own** clothes,
  and led him out to **crucify** him.

Cyrenian = sī-REE-nee-uhn

They **pressed** into service a passer-by, **Simon**,
  a Cyrenian, who was coming in from the country,
  the father of **Alexander** and **Rufus**,
  to **carry** his **cross**.

Golgotha = GAWL-guh-thuh

They **brought** him to the place of **Golgotha**
  —which is translated Place of the **Skull**—.
They gave him **wine** drugged with **myrrh**,
  but he did not take it.
Then they crucified him and **divided** his **garments**
  by casting **lots** for them to see what **each** should **take**.
It was **nine** o'clock in the morning when they **crucified** him.

answers the direct question: "Are you the Christ, the son of the Blessed One?" His honest testimony immediately agitates his interlocutors, who deem him blasphemous and worthy of death. He is blindfolded, beaten, and mocked for testifying to the truth. The parallel inquiry scene, "below in the courtyard," finds Peter keeping a safe distance and comforting himself by a fire. When questioned about his relationship with Jesus, Peter testifies falsely about himself three times. His physical distance

from Jesus and location ("below" in the courtyard) symbolize his moral state. The man above—Jesus—testifies honestly about himself. The man below—Peter— testifies falsely about himself. The former will die as the Just One for the unjust; the latter will weep in his misery when the cock crows. Along with his physical distance, Peter's tears underline his ruptured relationship with Jesus.

As daylight emerges on the day of Jesus' death, the Jewish authorities

involved in his nighttime trial bind him and bring him to the local Roman authority, Pontius Pilate. Pilate's concerns pertain to temporal rule: "Are you the king of the Jews?" The chief priests also pile up accusations. But Jesus, in Mark's passion account, remains virtually silent. "You say so," are his only words. Jesus' degradation continues as Pilate turns to the crowd gathered for a political "game" on the occasion of the feast—shall a rebellious murderer (Barabbas) or "the king of the Jews" be

In Mark's Gospel, notice that there is no repentant thief. Everyone is mocking Jesus.

"Aha!" and the words following it should have a haughty and mocking tone. They are quoting Jesus' own words back to him as an insult.

Eloi, Eloi, lema sabachthani = ehl-oh-ee, ehl-oh-ee, luh-MAH sah-bahk-tah-nee or ay-loh-ee

Practice the Aramaic phrase until you are comfortable with it. Jesus, despite his weakness as he approached death, "cried out in a loud voice." Deliver the narrator's translation with less intensity.

Elijah = ee-Lī-juh

Raise your volume for Jesus' last effort to cry out, and then subdue "breathed his last."

centurion = sen-TOOR-ee-uhn or sen-TYOOR-ee-uhn

The mood of the assembly will be somber. Use a narrator voice to report what happens next.

The soldier's words should have a tone of awe. He has had an instant change of heart.

The **inscription** of the charge against him read,
   "The **King** of the **Jews**."
With him they crucified two **revolutionaries**,
   one on his **right** and one on his **left**.
Those passing by **reviled** him,
   shaking their **heads** and saying,
   "**Aha**! You who would destroy the temple
   and rebuild it in three days,
   save yourself by coming **down** from the cross."
Likewise the chief **priests**, with the **scribes**,
   mocked him among themselves and said,
   "He **saved others**; he cannot save **himself**.
Let the **Christ**, the **King** of Israel,
   come **down now** from the **cross**
   that we may see and **believe**."
Those who were **crucified** with him **also** kept **abusing** him.

At **noon darkness** came over the whole land
   until **three** in the afternoon.
And at three o'clock **Jesus cried** out in a loud voice,
   "*Eloi, **Eloi, lema sabachthani**?*"
which is translated,
   "My God, my **God**, **why** have you **forsaken** me?"
Some of the **bystanders** who heard it said,
   "**Look**, he is **calling Elijah**."
One of them **ran**, soaked a **sponge** with **wine**, put it on a reed
   and **gave** it to him to drink saying,
   "**Wait**, let us see if Elijah **comes** to take him down."
Jesus gave a loud **cry** and **breathed** his **last**.

[Here all kneel and pause for a short time.]

The **veil** of the **sanctuary** was **torn** in two from top to bottom.
When the **centurion** who stood facing him
   saw how **he** breathed his last he said,
   "**Truly** this man was the **Son of God!**"]
There were also **women** looking on from a distance. »

released for them? Whipped into a frenzy and manipulated, the crowd requests the rebellious murderer. And Pilate presses them about how to treat Jesus. They request crucifixion. Pilate acquiesces and adds scourging to Jesus' punishment.

As he nears the end of his earthly journey, Jesus is silent as soldiers mock, beat, and ridicule him, and as a passerby is made to "serve" him. (Mentioned by name, Simon, Alexander, and Rufus were likely known members of Mark's community.)

At Golgotha—a place designated for executions outside of Jerusalem and later associated with Adam's burial site—Jesus' humiliation is completed. He is stripped bare. Clothing gambled away. Crucified. Mocked with an accusation hanging over his head. Two brigands (*lestai* in Greek) are nailed beside him to face the same fate. Passersby add to the chorus of mocking underway. After Jesus is suspended between heaven and earth for a relatively short time (a few hours), his death is accompanied by a char-

acteristic manifestation of divine withdrawal —the sky darkens (see Job 3; Wisdom 17). And while his last words are the first ones of Psalm 22—"My God, my God, why have you forsaken me?"—confused witnesses think he is calling on Elijah.

After Jesus' loud cry and last breath, the torn sanctuary veil symbolizes the reunion of God, hidden in the heart of the temple, with the world at large. Ironically, the first to profess faith that Jesus was the Son of God by virtue of his death is a

Magdalene = MAG-duh-luhn or MAG-duh-leen

Joses = JOH-seez or JOH-sehz
Salome = suh-LOH-mee

Pause briefly for a scene change.

Arimathea = ayr-ih-muh-THEE-uh

Emphasize "courageous"". To openly associate with someone considered a criminal would be risky.

Report this act of compassion tenderly. Taking care of the details after a beloved has died will resonate with some in the assembly. Grief is intertwined with the practical necessities of burial.

Among them were Mary **Magdalene**,
    Mary the **mother** of the younger **James** and of **Joses**,
        and **Salome**.
These women had **followed** him when he was in **Galilee**
    and **ministered** to him.
There were also many **other** women
    who had come up **with** him to **Jerusalem**.

When it was already **evening**,
    since it was the day of **preparation**,
    the day **before** the sabbath, **Joseph of Arimathea**,
    a distinguished member of the **council**,
    who was **himself awaiting** the kingdom of **God**,
    came and courageously went to Pilate
    and **asked** for the **body** of Jesus.
Pilate was **amazed** that he was already **dead**.
He **summoned** the **centurion**
    and **asked** him if Jesus had already **died**.
And when he **learned** of it from the **centurion**,
    he gave the body to **Joseph**.
Having bought a linen **cloth**, he took him **down**,
    wrapped him in the linen cloth,
    and **laid** him in a tomb that had been **hewn** out of the **rock**.
Then he rolled a **stone** against the **entrance** to the tomb.
Mary **Magdalene** and **Mary** the mother of **Joses**
    watched where he was **laid**.

[Shorter: Mark 15:1–39 (see brackets)]

Roman soldier. The women who accompanied Jesus from Galilee, like Peter earlier, look on at a distance. Only Joseph of Arimathea, a Judean Jewish dignitary, musters the courage to request Jesus' body and see to his burial.

A stone rolled across the rock-cut tomb punctuates Mark's account of Jesus' passion with hollow silence, as watchful but distant eyes of two women from Jesus' party look on. E.W.

EVENING MASS OF THE LORD'S SUPPER (HOLY THURSDAY)

LECTIONARY #39

READING I   Exodus 12:1–8, 11–14

A reading from the Book of Exodus

The LORD said to **Moses** and **Aaron** in the land of **Egypt**,
    "This **month** shall stand at the **head** of your **calendar**;
    you shall reckon it the first month of the year.
Tell the whole community of **Israel**:
    On the tenth of this month every one of your families
        must **procure** for itself a **lamb**, one apiece for each **household**.
If a family is too **small** for a whole lamb,
    it shall **join** the nearest household in procuring one
    and shall **share** in the lamb
    in **proportion** to the number of persons who partake of it.
The lamb must be a year-old **male** and **without blemish**.
You may **take** it from either the **sheep** or the **goats**.
You shall **keep** it until the fourteenth day of this month,
    and then, with the whole **assembly** of Israel present,
    it shall be **slaughtered** during the evening twilight.
They shall **take** some of its **blood**
    and apply it to the two **doorposts** and the lintel
    of every **house** in which they **partake** of the lamb.
That same night they shall **eat** its roasted **flesh**
    with **unleavened bread** and bitter **herbs**. »

Marginal notes:

Exodus = EK-suh-duhs

The prescriptions of the Passover are dictated by God. This is the original event, not the holyday that commemorates it.

This is to be a communal act. No one is to be left out nor anything wasted.

The blood on the doorposts and lintels: a visceral sign of those who keep God's command.

READING I   Exodus describes regulations for the first Passover—such a fundamental event in the lives of God's people that its significance is difficult to exaggerate.

Leading up to the first Passover, God hears Israel's cries under the burden of servitude in Egypt (Exodus 2:23–25) and inaugurates Israel's exodus from Egypt by calling Moses (and his helpful brother Aaron) to lead the Israelites to freedom (see Exodus 3—4). They are instructed by God to go to Pharaoh and ask for the people's release; Pharaoh refuses Moses' request and makes their plight worse (Exodus 5). Moses and Aaron then "preside" over a series of nine wonders or plagues performed by God in Egypt (Exodus 7—10). Pharaoh's magicians "match" the first few wonders but are eventually confounded. Still, Pharaoh does not release the Israelites, and a tenth, final plague is called for: the death of all the first-born in Egypt (Exodus 11). This final catastrophe will soften Pharaoh enough to allow Israel to depart.

To help Israel survive and negotiate the consequences of the catastrophic event, God provides regulations that, when followed, ensure that the plague will pass over them. Israel will survive through a God-given ritual that ultimately distinguishes and (re)defines them as a people. The Passover, first and foremost, results in Israel reckoning time differently. The month of Passover becomes the first on Israel's calendar. Ritual prescriptions follow. A small flock animal (sheep or goat) is to be procured for sacrifice. It should be a single, unblemished year-old male lamb. Each household shall have one, or smaller households can combine their resources and partake in the ritual together. On the

girt = gert = belted

"This is **how** you are to eat it:
　with your loins **girt**, **sandals** on your feet and your **staff**
　　in hand,
　you shall eat **like** those who are in **flight**.
It is the **Passover** of the LORD.
For on this same night I will **go** through **Egypt**,
　striking down every **firstborn** of the land, both man and beast,
　and executing **judgment** on all the **gods** of Egypt—**I**, the LORD!
But the blood will **mark** the houses where you are.

Do not run "pass" and "over" together.

Seeing the blood, I will **pass over** you;
　thus, when I **strike** the land of Egypt,
　no **destructive** blow will come upon you.

The feast celebrates God's intervention in Israel's history. Passover is still celebrated today.

"This day shall be a **memorial feast** for you,
　which all your **generations** shall celebrate
　with **pilgrimage** to the LORD, as a perpetual institution."

For meditation and context:

RESPONSORIAL PSALM   Psalm 116:12–13, 15–16bc, 17–18
(1 Corinthians 10:16)

R. Our blessing-cup is a communion with the Blood of Christ.

How shall I make a return to the LORD
　for all the good he has done for me?
The cup of salvation I will take up,
　and I will call upon the name of the LORD.

Precious in the eyes of the LORD
　is the death of his faithful ones.

I am your servant, the son of your
　handmaid;
　you have loosed my bonds.

To you will I offer sacrifice of thanksgiving,
　and I will call upon the name of the LORD.
My vows to the LORD I will pay
　in the presence of all his people.

chosen day (mid-month), at the chosen time (twilight), the animal is to be slaughtered and its blood used to mark exterior door frames of Israelite houses, thereby signaling that the occupants are protected from the lethal plague. Thus, only the lives of first-born Egyptians would be lost. The animal is then roasted and entirely consumed with unleavened bread and bitter herbs while the members of the household(s) remain standing and dressed for travel. The ritual, therefore, not only protects Israel, it also prepares them for their exodus from Egypt.

The Passover liberated Israel from servitude and protected them from a divinely wrought death-dealing plague. Its accompanying ritual provided a natural means of annually celebrating God's work in the Exodus. It also became the means of commemorating and appropriating the meaning of that work in each new generation. Modern Passover ritual texts instruct each person to view himself or herself as one who was liberated from Egypt. This sentiment also characterizes the Passover celebrated and transformed by Jesus during the Last Supper. On the night before he died,

he offered the bread and wine of the Passover meal as himself, thus instituting the Eucharist. That meal, which commemorates his passion, death, and resurrection as often as we celebrate it for our generation, invites us into Christ's paschal mystery. Thus, as we commemorate this Mass of the Lord's Supper, each of us must now view ourselves as recipients of the grace of Christ's redeeming Passover and participants in his suffering and death, that we might enjoy the hope of his resurrection.

Corinthians = kohr-IN-thee-uhnz

The words of this reading are heard at every Mass, prayed by the priest during the Eucharistic Prayer. Tonight, they will also be proclaimed by you in this reading. Practice until you are familiar enough with the phrases to look up and out at the assembly to deliver the most important lines. Give special attention to the verbs.

Past, present, and future concerns come together in this one short reading.

READING II   1 Corinthians 11:23–26

A reading from the first Letter of Saint Paul to the Corinthians

Brothers and sisters:
I **received** from the **Lord** what I also **handed** on to **you**,
   that the Lord Jesus, on the night he was handed over,
   took bread, and, after he had given **thanks**,
   broke it and said, "This is my body that is for **you**.
Do this in **remembrance** of me."
In the same way also the **cup**, after supper, saying,
   "This cup is the **new covenant** in my blood.
Do this, as **often** as you **drink** it, in remembrance of **me**."
For as **often** as you eat this bread and drink the cup,
   you **proclaim** the **death** of the Lord until he **comes**.

Practice pausing in the long first verse.

A encouraging line before the evil of the betrayal is revealed. Take your time savoring it. The mood quickly changes.

Iscariot = ih-SKAYR-ee-uht

Jesus is not deterred by the betrayal. He has an important lesson to impart to his disciples—and to us.

Listening to music can help one enter into the spiritual meaning of a passage. Listen to "The Servant Song" by Richard Gillard to capture the beauty of Jesus' action.

GOSPEL   John 13:1–15

A reading from the holy Gospel according to John

Before the **feast** of Passover, **Jesus knew** that his **hour** had come
   to **pass** from this **world** to the **Father**.
He **loved** his **own in** the world and he loved them to the **end**.
The **devil** had already induced **Judas**, son of Simon the **Iscariot**,
      to hand him **over**.
So, during supper,
   fully **aware** that the **Father** had **put** everything into his **power**
   and that he had **come** from **God** and was **returning** to God,
   he rose from supper and took **off** his outer garments.
He took a **towel** and tied it around his waist.
Then he poured **water** into a basin
   and began to **wash** the **disciples' feet**
   and **dry** them with the towel around his waist. »

READING II In his first letter to the church at Corinth, Paul provides one of the earliest accounts of the institution of the Eucharist. Three other such institution narratives appear in the synoptic gospels (Matthew 26:26–29; Mark 14:22–25; Luke 22:14–20). Although each account is unique, there is great correspondence among them. At the time ordained for the Passover meal—nighttime—Jesus gathered with his disciples. When they were assembled, Jesus took the Passover bread. Giving thanks, he blessed it. Then he broke the bread and said, "This is my body."

Presumably, he then gave the bread to those gathered, as the synoptic accounts indicate; Paul is not explicit about this action. Likewise, Jesus took a cup of wine at this, his last Passover meal. Presumably, he blessed it with the customary blessing for wine. Again, Paul is silent on this point. In any case, Jesus initiates a new covenant when he identifies this cup of wine with his blood. And, as Paul does makes explicit, the eating and drinking of the Eucharistic bread and wine "proclaim the death of the Lord until he comes." That is, the breaking of the bread is his broken body on the cross,

and his blood poured out in death is the wine. To celebrate this meal, as often as we do, is to celebrate and partake in Christ's self-sacrifice for us.

GOSPEL Unlike accounts of the Last Supper that emphasize the institution narrative, John focuses on Jesus' symbolic washing of the disciples' feet. The disciples, acknowledging Jesus as "teacher" and "master" (*kúrios* in Greek), are confirmed in their address of Jesus by his "I am" (*eimí* in Greek). This language is typical of John's Gospel; it clearly presents

Imagine Peter's indignation and Jesus' calm, fatherly response. To help the assembly grasp the dialogue, consider delivering the words of Peter with a slightly faster pace than Jesus' and a steady, even tone for the narrator.

He **came** to Simon **Peter**, who said to him,
    "**Master**, are you going to wash **my** feet?"
Jesus answered and said to him,
    "What I am doing, you do n**ot understand now**,
    but you **will** understand **later**."
Peter said to him, "You will **never** wash **my** feet."
Jesus answered him,
    "**Unless** I wash **you**, you will have no **inheritance** with me."
Simon Peter said to him,
    "Master, then not **only** my feet, but my **hands** and **head**
        as well."
Jesus said to him,
    "Whoever has bathed has **no need** except to have his
        feet washed,
    for he is **clean** all over;
    so **you** are clean, but not **all**."
For he **knew** who would **betray** him;
    for this reason, he said, "Not all of you are clean."

So when he had washed their feet
    and put his garments back on and reclined at table again,
    he said to them, "Do you **realize** what I have **done** for you?
You call me '**teacher**' and '**master**,' and rightly so, for indeed **I am**.
If I, therefore, the master and teacher, have w**ashed your f**eet,
    you ought to wash one **another's** feet.
I have given you a **model** to follow,
    so that as **I** have done for **you**, you should **also** do."

Use an upward inflection and then pause. Practice so that you can deliver it while looking at the assembly. Jesus is asking his disciples—he is also asking us.

Let these final words of Jesus resound. His actions present us with an image of what Church should look like: he gave of himself completely; we should do likewise.

Jesus claiming his status as the incarnate Lord of the chosen people. He is the Lord worshiped by Abraham, Isaac, and Jacob. He is the One revealed to Moses in the burning bush. The One who descended on the mountain in Sinai, instructed the people, and gave the law that would form, guide, and govern their lives from one generation to the next now washes the disciples' feet. Peter understandably objects. The work is humiliating. The Lord should not do it! When instructed by his divine teacher, Peter vacillates to the opposite extreme; he asks for more washing. Like

any grace, he wants more. Yet Jesus' objective is instruction. Like prophets of old, he has done something that, due to its symbolic nature, requires interpretation. Ultimately, he explains that his actions are meant as a model or example (*húpodeigma* in Greek) for the disciples to follow. He has shown them the scope that their service is to have.

Jesus asks his disciples to do for others as he has done for them. Of course, this includes us today. To follow Jesus is to care for others to the point of accepting humiliating tasks, to do chores that do not garner

honor or cohere with elevated social status. As the noblest of all human beings sets aside his garment to take up a towel and wash dirty feet, so his disciples take up menial tasks that ennoble those served by them. According to John, the memorial of the Last Supper entails accepting a mandate to service, to mission, and to do for others as the Lord has done for us. E.W.

FRIDAY OF THE PASSION OF THE LORD (GOOD FRIDAY)

LECTIONARY #40

READING I   Isaiah 52:13—53:12

A reading from the Book of the Prophet Isaiah

> See, my **servant** shall **prosper**,
>   he shall be **raised high** and greatly exalted.
> Even as **many** were **amazed** at him—
>   so **marred** was his look beyond human **semblance**
>   and his appearance beyond that of the sons of man—
> so shall he **startle** many **nations**,
>   because of him **kings** shall stand **speechless**;
> for those who have **not** been **told** shall **see**,
>   those who have not **heard** shall **ponder** it.
>
> **Who** would **believe** what we have heard?
>   To whom has the arm of the LORD been **revealed**?
> He **grew** up like a **sapling** before him,
>   like a shoot from the parched **earth**;
> there was in him no **stately** bearing to make us **look** at **him**,
>   nor appearance that would **attract** us to him.
> He was **spurned** and **avoided** by people,
>   a man of **suffering**, accustomed to infirmity,
> one of those from whom people **hide** their faces,
>   spurned, and we held him in no esteem. »

Isaiah = ī-ZAY-uh

God is speaking through the prophet Isaiah, foretelling the messiah. The first section describes the disfiguring torture of a righteous man and his triumph to greatness. So unexpected, it renders one to speechlessness. Subdue the parenthetical.

Practice this question so that it can be delivered looking at the assembly. The "Who?" can be appropriated to us.

The servant is rejected by his own people, adding insult to injury.

READING I | Few (if any) Old Testament passages offer more apt imagery for understanding Christ's suffering than the portrayal of the Suffering Servant in Isaiah 52—53. This servant's exalted and elevated state, which is countered by his marred, other-than-human appearance, startles foreign observers, renders kings mute, and begets pondering or contemplation of those who see him. The mere sight of the servant seems to raise incredulity—"Who would believe what we have heard?" His appearance does not garner attention. It is not attrac-

tive. In fact, the servant seems detestable, someone from whom faces are hidden. Yet, his sufferings, his burdens, his God-given afflictions, and his quiet anguish result in the wholeness of those who observe him. The servant's patient endurance, his willing suffering, his dying for others, and his burial among the wicked combine to produce the justification of others and to win pardon for their offenses: "by his stripes we were healed." The servant is ultimately portrayed as one who suffers vicariously for others, especially those who gaze upon and ponder him.

Since the earliest days of the Church, one of the primary means for understanding the Lord's crucifixion has been to appeal to today's first reading. Various New Testament authors quote or refer to portions of this passage from Isaiah. For example, commenting on Jesus' healing ministry, Matthew 8:17 highlights how "He took away our infirmities and bore our diseases." To explain why belief in Jesus after his many miracles (signs) continued to be difficult, John 12:38 refers to Isaiah 53:1, noting, "Lord, who has believed our preaching, to whom has the might of the Lord been

The narrator expresses the traditional way of understanding the servant's plight but quickly changes to acknowledge he had done no wrong. Emphasize "But" and "our" in the following sentence to make sure the assembly hears the correct interpretation.

Use a hushed, slow voice to describe his complete submission—a shocking reaction of one in torture.

This is another opportunity to look directly at the assembly and deliver the question.

Even in death, the servant was humiliated.

"Pleased" because God knows the ultimate outcome of the servant.

Yet it was **our infirmities** that he **bore**,
    our **sufferings** that he endured,
while we thought of him as stricken,
    as one smitten by God and afflicted.
But he was pierced for **our** offenses,
    crushed for our sins;
upon him was the chastisement that makes **us whole**,
    by his **stripes** we were **healed**.
We had all **gone astray** like sheep,
    each following his own way;
but the LORD laid upon him
    the **guilt** of us all.

Though he was **harshly treated**, he **submitted**
    and opened not his **mouth**;
like a **lamb** led to the **slaughter**
    or a sheep before the shearers,
    he was silent and opened not his mouth.
Oppressed and condemned, he was taken **away**,
    and **who** would have thought any more of his **destiny**?
When he was cut **off** from the land of the **living**,
    and **smitten** for the sin of his **people**,
a **grave** was assigned him among the **wicked**
    and a burial place with evildoers,
though he had done **no wrong**
    nor spoken any falsehood.
But the LORD was **pleased**
    to **crush** him in infirmity.

If he **gives** his **life** as an offering for **sin**,
    he shall **see** his **descendants** in a long life,
    and the **will** of the **LORD** shall be **accomplished**
        through him.

Because of his affliction
    he shall see the **light** in fullness of days;

revealed?" Belief in Jesus, according to John's interpretation of the Suffering Servant, was difficult and required divine revelation. By appealing to the same passage in Isaiah, Paul makes a similar argument in Romans 10:16–17. Jesus quotes part of the Suffering Servant passage before departing from the Last Supper and heading for Gethsemane in the Gospel of Luke. In doing so, Jesus shows that he will fulfill Isaiah's prophecy when he is "counted among the wicked" that is, arrested, put on trial, condemned, and executed as a criminal. When 1 Peter 2:19–25 appeals to vari-

ous verses in Isaiah 53, the purpose is to show how, in Jesus, we can understand innocent suffering as commendable. And in Acts 8:32–35, the Ethiopian eunuch is reading the Suffering Servant passage of Isaiah when Philip overhears and begins, from that passage, to share the Good News of Jesus.

As we keep the memorial of the Lord's passion today, we once more turn to the words of the prophet Isaiah and hear them proclaimed in our midst. As they resound amid the community gathered on this Good Friday, they prepare us to hear once more the account of the Lord's suffering, passion,

and death. And so prepared, we are able to enter more deeply into that mystery of Jesus' death, by which we know salvation.

READING II   While Hebrews continues to focus on sacrificial, vicarious offerings made for others, as in the first reading, the focus here broadens. Christ's high priestly status garners initial attention in this reading. Subsequently, Jesus' efficacious self-sacrifice is discussed.

Building on an analogy with the priesthood of Aaron, Hebrews presents Jesus as the "great high priest who has passed

This is good news. We are part of the "many" made righteous.

through his suffering, my **servant** shall **justify many**,
    and their guilt he shall bear.
Therefore I will give him his **portion** among the **great**,
    and he shall divide the spoils with the mighty,
because he **surrendered** himself to death
    and was counted among the **wicked**;
and he shall take **away** the **sins** of **many**,
    and win **pardon** for their **offenses**.

For meditation and context:

RESPONSORIAL PSALM   Psalm 31:2, 6, 12–13, 15–16, 17, 25 (Luke 23:46)

R. Father, into your hands I commend my spirit.

In you, O LORD, I take refuge;
    let me never be put to shame.
In your justice rescue me.
Into your hands I commend my spirit;
    you will redeem me, O LORD,
        O faithful God.

For all my foes I am an object of reproach,
    a laughingstock to my neighbors, and a
        dread to my friends;
    they who see me abroad flee from me.
I am forgotten like the unremembered dead;
    I am like a dish that is broken.

But my trust is in you, O LORD;
    I say, "You are my God.
In your hands is my destiny; rescue me
    from the clutches of my enemies and
        my persecutors."

Let your face shine upon your servant;
    save me in your kindness.
Take courage and be stouthearted,
    all you who hope in the LORD.

READING II   Hebrews 4:14–16; 5:7–9

A reading from the Letter to the Hebrews

Brothers and sisters:
Since we have a great high **priest** who has passed through
    the **heavens**,
    Jesus, the Son of **God**,
    let us **hold** fast to our **confession**.
For we do not have a high priest
    who is unable to **sympathize** with our **weaknesses**,
    but one who has similarly been **tested** in every way,
    yet without **sin**. »

The high priest is Jesus, the one who mediates for us.

The double negatives might make it difficult to hear the positive meaning. Paul is saying that we *do* have a high priest who is *able* to sympathize with us: Jesus. As you proclaim the double negatives, ensure that the positive meaning of them can be heard.

through the heavens." Although similar to the priesthood of Aaron, whose line offers sacrifices for others, our great high priest also differs from them: Jesus is the Son of God. As such, he needs no intermediary. There is no go-between who provides access to or means of traversing the heavens. He, as the Lord of Israel, enjoys direct access to the heavenly realm. Accordingly, we can be confident in our faith that we, in him, enjoy access to the grace that flows from God's heavenly throne. In him we can be bold. In him we can approach God for mercy, grace, and help. At the same time,

we can also be confident that we are known and understood by our high priest. Our frailties are something with which Jesus sympathizes. The tests we face, he also underwent. And he negotiated them without sinning. So we do well to confidently follow the lead of this new high priest who provides offerings in the new covenant with God.

After Hebrews unpacks Jesus' unprecedented yet accessible high priesthood and establishes the confidence we can have in him, it turns our focus back to Jesus' suffering. He faces death in the flesh with

prayers, loud cries, and tears. The reaction is entirely, fully human. Death is scary. The fully and perfectly human Jesus passionately appeals to God for deliverance from death. Yet, he also remains faithful to his identity as the Son of God. For this he suffered (*paschō* in Greek). And through the mystery of suffering, he learned (*manthánō* in Greek) obedience (*hupakoē* in Greek). Put differently, Jesus submits his mind and will to God's plan and will for him. Ultimately, as Christ journeys through suffering, he submits his will and intellect to God and thereby reveals his perfection,

"Confidently" tells you how to read this.

So let us **confidently approach** the throne of **grace**
   to **receive mercy** and to find grace for timely **help**.

In the days when **Christ** was in the **flesh**,
   he offered **prayers** and **supplications** with loud **cries** and tears
   to the one who was able to **save** him from **death**,
   and he was **heard** because of his reverence.
Son though he was, he learned **obedience** from what he suffered;
   and when he was made **perfect**,
   he became the **source** of eternal **salvation** for all who
     obey him.

GOSPEL   John 18:1—19:42

The Passion of our Lord Jesus Christ according to John

Kidron = KID-ruhn

Jesus went out with his **disciples** across the Kidron valley
   to where there was a **garden**,
   into which he and his disciples entered.
Judas his **betrayer** also **knew** the place,
   because Jesus had **often** met there with his disciples.
So Judas **got** a band of **soldiers** and guards
   from the chief **priests** and the **Pharisees**
   and went there with **lanterns**, **torches**, and **weapons**.

The energy of the narrative quickens with the mention of soldiers, weapons, and Jewish authorities.

Jesus is in control: *he* goes out to meet *them* and initiates the dialogue. Use an upward inflection for his question.

Jesus, **knowing everything** that was going to happen to him,
   went out and said to them, "**Whom** are you looking for?"
They answered him, "Jesus the **Nazorean**."
He said to them, "**I AM**."

Here, "I AM" is more than a simple statement of identification; it recalls for us one of the divine names of God in the Old Testament and illustrates Jesus' divinity. The name, so strong on Jesus' lips, causes the people arresting him to fall to the ground. The name is repeated three times, an intentional use by the evangelist. Proclaim it clearly.

Judas his betrayer was **also** with them.
When he said to them, "**I AM**,"
   they turned away and **fell** to the ground.
So he again asked them,
   "**Whom** are you looking for?"
They said, "Jesus the **Nazorean**."

Jesus repeats his question. He remains calm.

---

which is also our way to salvation. Thus, Hebrews argues that the meaning of suffering is revealed in Christ. For our part, as we follow Christ and undergo suffering, we too learn obedience, which is to say, we seek to submit our wills and intellects to God's will and plan for us. It is this dynamic transformation through suffering that we are invited to contemplate as we open ourselves to the passion account proclaimed in the Gospel.

PASSION | Each year on Good Friday, the Church commemorates

what God accomplished for us in Jesus' suffering and death. To commemorate God's work, we proclaim John's account of the Lord's passion. It is the second time in Holy Week that Jesus' passion is proclaimed. The first occurs on Palm Sunday of the Lord's Passion. This past Palm Sunday, we heard Mark's account of Jesus' passion. John's passion account differs in important ways from that of Mark. Accordingly, it provides a valuable complement to what we have already heard this week and invites us to enter the mystery of Christ's passion more deeply. We entrust ourselves, with

deeper faith and greater hope, to God's loving care.

John begins his passion account with Jesus and his disciples crossing the Kidron valley to an unnamed garden, which he had previously frequented with them. The short journey results in an almost immediate encounter with Judas and a band of soldiers and guards. John alone provides the name of the valley, which may subtly refer to David's flight from his son, Absalom, when the latter orchestrated a coup against his father (2 Samuel 15:14, 23). In contrast to the synoptics, John does not explicitly

Multiple times in this reading, the narrator will explain how the Scriptures are being fulfilled. Use a steady, even tone to provide these details.

Impetuous Peter! Read this burst of violence with energy and then return to the narrator voice.

Malchus = MAL-kuhs

scabbard = SCA-b*rd

Annas = AN-uhs

Caiaphas = KAY-uh-fuhs or KĪ-uh-fuhs

Use a hushed tone. They do not want to attract attention.

Peter responds casually; leave room for his denials to escalate in the coming verses.

Jesus answered,
   "I told you that **I AM**.
So if you are **looking** for **me**, let these men **go**."
This was to **fulfill** what he had said,
   "I have not **lost any** of those you gave me."
Then Simon **Peter**, who had a **sword**, **drew** it,
   struck the high priest's slave, and **cut** off his right ear.
The slave's name was **Malchus**.
Jesus said to Peter,
   "Put your sword into its **scabbard**.
Shall I not **drink** the cup that the **Father** gave **me**?"

So the band of soldiers, the tribune, and the Jewish guards
      seized Jesus,
   bound him, and brought him to **Annas** first.
He was the father-in-law of **Caiaphas**,
   who was high **priest** that year.
It was Caiaphas who had **counseled** the **Jews**
   that it was **better** that **one** man should **die** rather than
      the **people**.

Simon **Peter** and **another** disciple **followed** Jesus.
Now the other disciple was **known** to the high priest,
   and he entered the **courtyard** of the high priest with **Jesus**.
But Peter stood at the gate **outside**.
So the other disciple, the **acquaintance** of the high priest,
   went out and **spoke** to the **gatekeeper** and brought Peter in.
Then the maid who was the gatekeeper said to Peter,
   "**You** are **not** one of this man's **disciples**, are you?"
He said, "I am **not**."
Now the slaves and the guards were standing around
      a charcoal **fire**
   that they had made, because it was cold,
   and were **warming** themselves.
Peter was also standing there keeping warm. »

call the place "Gethsemane," nor does he refer to the "Mount of Olives." Yet he alone identifies the location as a garden. Some interpreters associate his reference to a garden with the opening chapters of Genesis and thus consider it a new Eden—a place in which God initiates a renewed relationship with humanity.

   Those with Judas are evidently numerous. The "band of soldiers" (*speira* in Greek) refers to a collection of Roman military figures that typically number in the hundreds. Such a contingent is evidently sent from Pilate. The armed guards or police (*hupēretēs*

in Greek) come from the chief priests and Pharisees. Their number cannot be ascertained, but they come prepared for violence and resistance. Jesus, aware of what is going to happen to him, remains calm and unconcerned. Unlike the account in Hebrews or the witness of the other Gospels, John does not present Jesus as enduring anguished prayer at this time. Neither does Judas brazenly approach Jesus to betray him with a kiss. Instead, *Jesus* approaches the crowd and asks them plainly, "Whom are you looking for?" Not only is Jesus aware of what will happen to

him, he guides and governs the exchange in the garden. The crowd responds to him pedantically—"Jesus the Nazorean." They ask for a man. Jesus responds with a theologically weighty claim: "I am" (*egō eimi* in Greek). This phrase identifies Jesus not simply as the human being sought by the crowd, but as the God of Israel who, revealing himself to Moses in the burning bush, calls himself "I am" (*egō eimi* in Greek, see Exodus 3:14). This is God's name revealed to the chosen people. It is the name that is sacred and powerful. The crowd's response—turning away and falling to the

Jesus speaks calmly; he has no secrets.

The high priest **questioned** Jesus
  about his **disciples** and about his **doctrine**.
Jesus answered him,
  "I have spoken **publicly** to the world.
I have always **taught** in a **synagogue**
  or in the temple area where all the Jews gather,
  and in **secret** I have said **nothing**. Why **ask** me?
Ask those who **heard** me what I said to them.
They **know** what I said."
When he had said this,
  one of the temple **guards** standing there **struck** Jesus and said,
  "Is this the **way** you answer the high **priest**?"
Jesus answered him,
  "If I have spoken **wrongly**, testify to the wrong;
  but if I have spoken **rightly**, why do you **strike** me?"
Then **Annas** sent him **bound** to **Caiaphas** the high priest.

Emphasize "struck" and use a tone of false bravado for the guard's question.

Now Simon **Peter** was standing there keeping warm.
And they said to him,
  "**You** are not one of his **disciples**, **are** you?"
He **denied** it and said,
  "I am **not**."
One of the **slaves** of the high priest,
  a relative of the one whose ear Peter had cut off, said,
  "Didn't I **see** you in the **garden** with him?"
Again Peter **denied** it.
And **immediately** the cock **crowed**.

This is Peter's second denial. Use a little more energy but save the strongest, most defiant tone for the third denial.

Then they brought Jesus from Caiaphas to the **praetorium**.
It was morning.
And they themselves did not **enter** the praetorium,
  in order not to be **defiled** so that they could eat the **Passover**.
So **Pilate came** out **to** them and said,
  "What **charge** do you bring against this man?"

Pause after "crowed." Give the well-known prediction of betrayal time to settle in. It is not just Peter's denial we reflect on, but also on our own denial of Jesus when we fall short in our daily lives.

praetorium = prih-TOHR-ee-uhm

The narrative will alternate the dialogue between Pilate and Jesus, inside, with the crowd, outside. Practice so that the assembly can follow the back-and-forth exchanges and the movement of the characters.

ground—shows the power of the divine name, even if the crowd does not acknowledge Jesus as the incarnate Lord. A second time Jesus initiates an exchange with a question, and the crowd's verbal response is identical. This time, Jesus expands his answer with words that further echo the Lord's mandates in the Exodus. As when Moses, following the Lord's command, tells Pharaoh to let God's people go (see Exodus 5:1), so Jesus commands the crowd to "let these men go." The results of both mandates match. In the garden, as in Egypt, the Lord's company is spared. Strikingly, John

explicitly indicates earlier that Judas is a member of the company that rivals the Lord. The garden scene closes with the familiar skirmish in which a member of the crowd has his ear cut off. John, unique among the Gospel writers, names all parties involved and Jesus, still governing the whole scene, has the final word. He calls for an end to the skirmish and, with a rhetorical question, invites Peter, the perpetrator, to accept Jesus' plight: "Shall I not drink the cup that the Father gave me?"

Seized and bound, Jesus is led by the crowd to Jewish leaders, the high priests

Annas and Caiaphas, in Jerusalem. They will oversee his official interrogation. As with Mark's passion account, a parallel scene unfolds in which Peter, in this case aided by a disciple known to the high priest, makes his way into the high priest's courtyard. Peter seeks to stay close to Jesus, yet at various points during Jesus' official questioning he is recognized as a disciple of Jesus. At the gate, when entering the courtyard, a maid questions him. Twice while warming himself by a fire in the courtyard, slaves grill him. Each time, Peter denies that he is Jesus' disciple. His language

They answered and said to him,
    "If he were **not** a criminal,
    we would not have handed him over to you."
At this, Pilate said to them,
    "Take him **yourselves**, and **judge** him according to your law."
The Jews answered him,
    "We do not have the **right** to **execute** anyone,"
    in order that the word of Jesus might be fulfilled
    that he said indicating the kind of death he would die.
So Pilate went back into the praetorium
    and **summoned** Jesus and said to him,
    "Are **you** the **King** of the Jews?"
Jesus answered,
    "Do you say this on your **own**
    or have **others** told you about me?"
Pilate answered,
    "I am **not** a **Jew**, am I?
Your own **nation** and the chief **priests** handed you over to me.
What have you done?"
Jesus answered,
    "My **kingdom** does not belong to this **world**.
If my kingdom did belong to **this** world,
    my **attendants** would be **fighting**
    to keep me from being handed over to the Jews.
But as it is, my kingdom is not **here**."
So Pilate said to him,
    "Then you **are** a king?"
Jesus answered,
    "**You** say I am a king.
For this I was **born** and for this I **came** into the **world**,
    to testify to the **truth**.
Everyone who **belongs** to the truth **listens** to my voice."
Pilate said to him, "What **is** truth?" »

Pilate distances himself from the Jewish people and their affairs.

A famous line in Scripture; don't rush it.

precisely contrasts with Jesus' testimony in the garden—"I am not" (*ouk eimi* in Greek), says Peter. His false testimony simultaneously reveals his weakness and the important theological reality that is true for all Jesus' disciples: Peter (or any other person then or now) is not Israel's incarnate Lord; that remains true of Jesus alone. Peter's third and last denial of Jesus is punctuated with a cock's crow. While John has long since reported Jesus' prediction of Peter's denial (John 13:38), John seems to associate this cockcrow with a more significant matter—the change of time. It is now the

earliest hour of the morning (just after 3 AM). The day is dawning. Passover begins at sundown.

Jesus, for his part, undergoes a formal inquisition simultaneous with Peter's informal questioning. Annas questions him about his students (disciples) and his teachings. Jesus claims to have taught openly in public places where many heard him teach. He encourages inquiry of those who heard him teach. He calls for witnesses. The proposal earns him a blow from a guard and a rhetorical reprimand. Jesus responds by doubling down on his request for due pro-

cess. He asks for testimony explaining his mistreatment: "If I have spoken wrongly, testify to the wrong; but if I have spoken rightly, why do you strike me?" For John, as opposed to the synoptic accounts, Jesus experienced a miscarriage of justice on the level of procedure. He underwent a hearing without any indication that witnesses were presented for his case or that due process of any kind was followed. Jesus' formal inquisition before Annas is simply and suddenly shifted to the domain of Caiaphas, Annas' relative and probable crony. John reports nothing of what happens in Jesus'

Barabbas = buh-RAB-uhs

The torturing of Jesus is hard to hear. The intensity of the reading is felt by the mob's repeated response.

When he had said this,
    he **again** went **out** to the Jews and said to them,
    "I find no **guilt** in him.
But you have a custom that I **release** one **prisoner** to you
        at Passover.
Do you want me to release to you the **King** of the Jews?"
They **cried** out again,
    "Not this one but **Barabbas**!"
Now Barabbas was a **revolutionary**.

Then Pilate took Jesus and had him **scourged**.
And the soldiers wove a **crown** out of thorns and placed it
      on his head,
    and **clothed** him in a **purple** cloak,
    and they came to him and said,
    "**Hail, King** of the Jews!"
And they **struck** him repeatedly.
Once more Pilate went out and said to them,
    "**Look**, I am bringing him out to **you**,
    so that you may know that I find no **guilt** in him."
So Jesus came out,
    wearing the crown of **thorns** and the purple **cloak**.
And he said to them, "**Behold**, the man!"
When the chief priests and the guards saw him they **cried** out,
    "Crucify him, **crucify** him!"
Pilate said to them,
    "Take him **yourselves** and crucify him.
I find no guilt in him."
The Jews answered,
    "We have a law, and according to that **law** he ought to **die**,
    because he **made himself** the Son of **God**."
Now when Pilate **heard** this statement,
    he became even **more** afraid,
    and went back into the praetorium and said to Jesus,
    "Where are you **from**?"

hearing with Caiaphas. He only signals, at the outset of Jesus' "trial," that Caiaphas had been counseling fellow Jews "that it was better that one man should die rather than the people." Thus, when Jesus appears before Caiaphas, we are to understand that his fate is sealed. Death awaits.

When Jesus is taken to Pilate, the process changes and the nature of his case comes under scrutiny. The procedural problems in Jesus' hearings before Jewish officials give way to concerns about ritual procedure in interactions with Pilate. Pilate must come out to meet Jesus' accusers,

since they want to avoid becoming defiled before Passover by being in Pilate's headquarters. Such defilement would render them unable to partake in the Passover meal later that day. Pilate obliges, upholding procedures of Jewish ritual law. As for the nature of Jesus' case, it becomes a dispute between Jewish and Roman authorities over legal jurisdiction in cases of capital crimes. Which authority in first-century Roman Palestine has the right to handle Jesus' capital case? The matter is subtle, complex, and fraught with challenges and inconsistencies. Roman authori-

ties clearly have the legal prerogative to try and implement capital cases for both Roman citizens and non-citizen residents of provincial regions like Palestine. Still, Jewish authorities in Palestine also have some prerogative to handle capital cases and execute justice accordingly. Thus, Stephen is stoned in Acts 7:58–60 and Paul, seemingly fearing the same fate, avoids a trial in Jerusalem by appeal to the Roman judicial system as a citizen (Acts 25:9–11). So, when John reports that Jewish authorities did not consider themselves able to execute Jesus, their claim seems to signal

Pilate is flaunting his authority. Use an indignant tone.

Jesus did not **answer** him.
So Pilate said to him,
    "Do you not **speak** to **me**?
Do you not **know** that I have **power** to **release** you
    and I have power to **crucify** you?"
Jesus answered him,
    "You would have **no** power over me
    if it had not been **given** to you from **above**.
For this reason the one who handed me over to you
    has the greater **sin**."
Consequently, Pilate **tried** to release him;
        but the **Jews** cried out,
    "If you **release** him, you are not a **Friend** of **Caesar**.
Everyone who makes himself a **king** opposes Caesar."

The crowd, unwilling to accept Pilate's decision, increase the stakes. They use fear to control him.

When Pilate heard these words he **brought** Jesus out
    and seated him on the judge's bench
    in the place called Stone **Pavement**, in Hebrew, **Gabbatha**.
It was **preparation** day for **Passover**, and it was about noon.
And he said to the Jews,
    "**Behold**, your **king**!"
They cried out,
    "Take him **away**, take him **away**! **Crucify** him!"
Pilate said to them,
    "Shall I crucify your **king**?"
The chief priests answered,
    "We have no king but **Caesar**."
Then he handed him over to them to be crucified.

Gabbatha = GAB-uh-thuh

Accent "himself." He alone takes the sins of the world.

Golgotha = GAWL-guh-thuh

So they **took** Jesus, and, **carrying** the cross **himself**,
    he went out to what is called the Place of the **Skull**,
    in Hebrew, Golgotha.
There they **crucified** him, and with him two others,
    one on either side, with Jesus in the middle. »

the nature of Jesus' case. They do not want him tried for blasphemy, at least not initially, but for an infraction of imperial law. Based on Pilate's first inquiry, the accusation against Jesus seems to be insurrection—specifically, that he claims to be the "King of the Jews."

The initial exchange between Pilate and Jesus results in discourses running at cross purposes. Although both men talk of Jesus' kingdom and kingship, their interests differ. Pilate wants juridical clarity and certitude. Jesus wants truth. Pilate cannot grasp Jesus' meaning or find him guilty.

Nonetheless, recognizing the discord it has wrought, he appeals to the custom of releasing a prisoner at Passover. The release of Barabbas, a revolutionary, is requested in place of Jesus' release.

Pilate has Jesus punished. Soldiers scourge, beat, and mock him by crowning him with thorns, clothing him in royal purple, and hailing him as "King of the Jews!" Then, demonstrating the lack of threat Pilate perceives in Jesus, he has him publicly displayed. Beaten and wearing the crown of thorns and purple cloak, Jesus is flaunted before the chief priests and guards

who call for his crucifixion. Pilate finds Jesus not guilty and says that the local authorities should execute him themselves if they so desire.

Suddenly, a new charge is presented. The infraction is of local, Jewish law: Jesus is guilty of blasphemy. He claims to be the Son of God. Again, such a matter would be a capital crime within the purview of local authorities. The legal justification for Jesus' death, in human terms, would shift from being an imperial infraction to a religious one. Yet, hearing this accusation, Pilate interrogates Jesus with renewed fervor

Read the inscription slowly. Reflect on Pilate's choice of words in the context of the back and forth he and the religious authorities and crowds had, as well as his question of "What is truth?"

Pilate also had an **inscription** written and put on the cross.
It read,
"Jesus the **Nazorean**, the **King** of the **Jews**."
Now many of the Jews **read** this inscription,
because the place where Jesus was crucified was near the **city**;
and it was written in **Hebrew**, **Latin**, and **Greek**.
So the chief priests of the Jews said to Pilate,
"Do **not write** 'The King of the Jews,'
but that **he said**, 'I am the King of the Jews.'"
Pilate answered,
"What I have **written**, I have written."

When the soldiers had **crucified** Jesus,
they **took** his **clothes** and divided them into four **shares**,
a share for each **soldier**.
They also took his **tunic**, but the tunic was **seamless**,
woven in one piece from the top down.
So they said to one another,
"Let's not **tear** it, but cast **lots** for it to see whose it will be,"
in order that the passage of Scripture might be **fulfilled**
that says:
They divided my garments among them,
and for my vesture they cast lots.
This is what the soldiers **did**.
Standing by the cross of Jesus were his mother
and his mother's sister, **Mary** the wife of **Clopas**,
and Mary of **Magdala**.
When Jesus **saw** his mother and the **disciple** there whom
he **loved**
he said to his mother, "**Woman**, behold, **your** son."
Then he said to the disciple,
"Behold, **your mother**."
And from that hour the disciple **took** her into his **home**.

The scene changes to those who support Jesus. Use a tone of compassion and admiration. These women are brave. They stand in solidarity and witness Jesus' final moments. Clopas = KLOH-puhs

Despite his agony, Jesus demonstrates his love for his mother and provides for her.

rather than handing him over to Jewish authorities. Jesus remains silent. Only when Pilate threatens Jesus with his "power to crucify" him does Jesus speak up, reminding Pilate that his power does not come from his own authority but is given to him "from above." Jesus refers to God. Pilate, however, likely understands Jesus to refer to the Roman authority over Pilate.

Wishing to release Jesus, Pilate again presents the case before the locals, who now threaten to charge *Pilate* with insurrection. Releasing Jesus would mean

opposing Caesar. Recognizing the direction that the whole affair is taking, Pilate subjects Jesus to a mock public trial. Placing him on the judge's bench, twice Pilate refers sarcastically to Jesus as "your king." In a choreographed response to Pilate's mocking of Jesus' authority, the locals profess their allegiance to Caesar, not their humiliated countryman. Jesus is swiftly condemned to death by crucifixion and promptly led out to the designated place for such executions (Golgotha, the "Place of the Skull").

When he is crucified between two criminals, the legal charge leveled against Jesus is hung over his head. It is an imperial infraction—When he is crucified"The King of the Jews." Local authorities ask to include a religious infraction as well—"I am the King of the Jews." Pilate keeps the charge as written. The show of power is complete. The deed is done.

While he is hanging on the cross, Jesus' seamless tunic is gambled away among soldiers. His mother, some of the women from his cohort, and the disciple whom he

Read slowly and with sadness.

After this, aware that everything was now **finished**,
    in order that the Scripture might be fulfilled,
    Jesus said, "I **thirst**."
There was a vessel filled with common **wine**.
So they put a sponge soaked in wine on a sprig of hyssop
    and put it up to his **mouth**.
When Jesus had **taken** the wine, he said,
    "It is **finished**."
And **bowing** his head, he **handed** over the **spirit**.

[Here all kneel and pause for a short time.]

Now since it was **preparation** day,
    in order that the bodies might not **remain**
    on the cross on the **sabbath**,
    for the sabbath day of that week was a **solemn** one,
    the Jews asked Pilate that their **legs** be **broken**
    and that they be taken **down**.
So the soldiers came and broke the legs of the **first**
    and then of the **other** one who was crucified with Jesus.
But when they came to Jesus and saw that he was **already** dead,
    they did not break **his** legs,
    but one soldier thrust his **lance** into his **side**,
    and immediately **blood** and **water** flowed out.
An eyewitness has **testified**, and his testimony is **true**;
    he knows that he is speaking the truth,
    so that you **also** may come to believe.
For this happened so that the Scripture passage might
        be fulfilled:
    *Not a **bone** of it will be **broken**.*
And again another passage says:
    They will look upon him whom they have pierced. »

loved gather by the cross. In simple phrases reminiscent of an exchange of vows, Jesus entrusts his beloved disciple to his mother and her to the beloved disciple. He acknowledges his thirst, which he slakes with wine provided, symbolically, on hyssop. No longer thirsty, with all things fulfilled, and in full control, Jesus declares: "It is finished." And he dies.

The soldiers, having not noticed Jesus' death, set out to expedite the executions by breaking the legs of those crucified. Jesus, already dead, is pierced through; the

blood and water that flow from his side symbolize the Holy Spirit. They also serve as types of baptism and the Eucharist. Accordingly, this piercing inaugurates a new era in the human community's relationship with God. Christ's death, into which we are baptized, comes with a promise of eternal life. Thus, it is fitting that, when Joseph of Arimathea obtains Jesus' body by Pilate's permission, Nicodemus also helps bury him. Nicodemus, who went to speak with Jesus at night to inquire about Jesus' teaching on eternal life (see

John 3), has learned that being born from above has nothing to do with re-entering our mother's womb but entering into Christ's death, which is made present to us in the baptismal waters.

Finally, the garden of the crucifixion and burial is a direct symbol—in it we have a new Eden, from which new life will emerge. E.W.

Arimathea = ayr-ih-muh-THEE-uh

The conclusion describes many details about the burial process. The inclusion of it here and the way John describes the actions give witness to the fact that Jesus is once again in the company of those who love him: the compassionate handling of the body, the large amounts of oils and spices, and the fresh tomb.

Nicodemus = nihk-uh-DEE-muhs

myrrh = mer

aloes = AL-ohz

We return to a garden at the close of the reading.

After this, Joseph of **Arimathea**,
 secretly a disciple of Jesus for fear of the Jews,
 asked Pilate if he could remove the body of Jesus.
And Pilate permitted it.
So he came and took his body.
Nicodemus, the one who had first come to him at **night**,
 also came **bringing** a mixture of **myrrh** and **aloes**
 weighing about one hundred pounds.
They **took** the **body** of Jesus
 and **bound** it with burial cloths along with the **spices**,
 according to the Jewish burial **custom**.
Now in the place where he had been crucified there was
 a garden,
 and in the **garden** a **new tomb**, in which no one had yet
 been buried.
So they **laid** Jesus there because of the Jewish preparation day;
 for the tomb was close by.

EASTER VIGIL (HOLY SATURDAY)

LECTIONARY #41

READING I Genesis 1:1—2:2

A reading from the Book of Genesis

[In the **beginning**, when **God created** the **heavens** and the **earth**,]
   the earth was a formless **wasteland**, and **darkness** covered
      the **abyss**,
   while a mighty **wind** swept over the waters.

Then God said,
   "Let there be **light**," and there **was** light.
God saw how **good** the light was.
God then **separated** the light from the darkness.
God **called** the light "**day**," and the darkness he called "**night**."
Thus evening came, and morning followed—the **first** day.

Then God said,
   "Let there be a **dome** in the middle of the waters,
   to **separate** one body of water from the other."
And so it happened:
   God made the dome,
   and it separated the water above the dome from the water
      below it.
God called the dome "**the sky**."
Evening came, and morning followed—the **second** day.

Then God said,
   "Let the **water** under the sky be gathered into a single **basin**,
   so that the dry **land** may appear." »

Take note of the many literary patterns throughout this reading. They represent the ordered way in which God creates.

Modern concern for care of creation and its relationship with theology is reinforced by the repeated phrase of God finding his work "good." This acknowledges the inherent worth of creation and acknowledges the genius of God's creation.

Pause in between each of the days.

Proclaim "And so it happened" reverently. God's performative words should bring a sense of awe. They are effortless.

There are options for today's readings. Contact your parish staff to learn which readings will be used.

READING I At the Easter Vigil, the liturgy of the word provides the fullest offering of the Word of God available in any Mass throughout the liturgical year. As many as nine readings may be proclaimed: seven from the Old Testament, one epistle reading, and one Gospel reading. In them we hear and participate anew in foundational events of God's loving plan.

By way of overview, the readings for this holiest of nights begin with an account of creation (Genesis 1) and then progress through a series of events in which God delivers, revives, or instructs his people. Isaac is spared from sacrifice on Mount Moriah (Genesis 22). The Israelites are delivered from the Egyptians at the sea (Exodus 14). The exiles are restored to relationship with God (Isaiah 54). Returning exiles are assured provisions (Isaiah 55). Members of God's people who are dispersed throughout the world are called back to the way of wisdom (Baruch 3).

Exiles are cleansed of impurities and given new hearts (Ezekiel 36). Our baptism, we learn, is a baptism into Christ's death (Romans 6). And finally, in the account of Jesus' empty tomb, we are wondrously reintroduced to the amazing mystery of the resurrection (Mark 16). Each reading invites extended reflection. We begin with the creation account.

The first reading, which begins the Bible, conveys God's stunning capacity to create simply by speaking. "Let there be . . ." is God's daily refrain. And all the elements of creation, great and small, flow

And so it happened:
   the **water** under the sky was gathered into its **basin**,
   and the dry **land** appeared.
God called the dry land "the **earth**,"
   and the basin of the water he called "the **sea**."
God saw how **good** it was.
Then God said,
   "Let the earth bring forth **vegetation**:
   every kind of **plant** that bears seed
   and every kind of fruit **tree** on earth
   that bears fruit with its seed in it."
And so it happened:
   the earth brought forth every kind of plant that bears seed
   and every kind of fruit tree on earth
   that bears fruit with its seed in it.
God saw how **good** it was.
Evening came, and morning followed—the **third** day.

Then God said:
   "Let there be **lights** in the dome of the sky,
   to separate day from night.
Let them **mark** the fixed **times**, the **days** and the **years**,
   and serve as luminaries in the dome of the sky,
   to shed light upon the earth."
And so it happened:
   God made the **two great** lights,
   the greater one to **govern** the **day**,
   and the lesser one to govern the **night**;
   and he made the **stars**.
God set them in the dome of the sky,
   to shed light upon the earth,
   to govern the day and the night,
   and to separate the light from the darkness.
God saw how **good** it was.
Evening came, and morning followed—the **fourth** day.

forth from that phrase. As each day concludes, the narrator announces the day of the week that has transpired. This poetic technique helpfully reminds us where we are in the week of creation, should we find ourselves overtaken by the wonders of creation recounted on any given day. This week of creation begins with a single, simple announcement: "Let there be light." Interestingly, darkness is separated from light, not eradicated. A fundamental distinction is introduced between light and darkness at the outset of creation, but the two exist together.

On the second day, God separates two basic kinds of waters that we perceive during our time on earth: those above (rain, atmospheric moisture) and those below (oceans, seas, lakes, rivers, streams, springs, and so forth). In effect, God's division of water on the second day produces not simply types of waters, but two basic cosmic realms: heaven and earth. Yet, there remain only light and darkness, heaven and earth. On the third day, more distinctions are made as the earthly domain is further parceled out. Water is set aside in some places so the earth can

appear. And then, with a command, vegetation springs forth from the earth. By the end of the third day, the basic elements and domains that we perceive in daily life emerge, and every manner of plant comes into being.

On day four, God's creative work shifts. What God brought into existence on prior days is now refined or populated with life. The luminaries and celestial bodies—sun, moon, and stars—are called into being. That is, lights of various kinds are brought forth. The domain of light is refined, and that refinement provides a means of

God's work is fertile and abundant.

Then God said,
"Let the water teem with an **abundance** of living creatures,
and on the earth let birds fly beneath the dome of the sky."
And so it happened:
God created the great sea **monsters**
and all kinds of swimming creatures with which the
water teems,
and all kinds of winged **birds**.
God saw how **good** it was, and God blessed them, saying,
"Be **fertile**, multiply, and **fill** the water of the seas;
and let the birds multiply on the earth."
Evening came, and morning followed—the **fifth** day.

Then God said,
"Let the earth bring forth all kinds of living **creatures**:
cattle, creeping things, and wild animals of all kinds."
And so it happened:
God made all kinds of wild animals, all kinds of cattle,
and all kinds of creeping things of the earth.
God saw how **good** it was.

Then [**God** said:
"Let us make **man** in **our image**, after our **likeness**.
Let them have **dominion** over the fish of the sea,
the birds of the air, and the cattle,
and over all the wild animals
and all the creatures that crawl on the ground."
God created **man** in **his** image;
in the image of God he created him;
male and female he created them.
God **blessed** them, saying:
"Be **fertile** and multiply;
fill the earth and subdue it.
Have dominion over the fish of the sea, the birds of the air,
and all the living things that move on the earth." »

keeping track of times and seasons. What God produces on this day allows for regulating agricultural and social practices. Crop plantings can be scheduled. Worship and civic calendars can be established. The observation, tracking, and measuring of time, which is so fundamental to human existence and society, becomes possible.

The fifth day finds God populating the waters parceled out on the second day of creation. The seas and rivers are made to teem with fish and other water-borne creatures. The sky, for its part, is populated with birds. On this day we hear, for the first

time, God commanding animals to be fruitful and multiply. They are to fill the domains for which they have been made and in which they have been placed. It would seem that, as remarkable as it is to know that the sky and earth exist as distinct domains, God is not content simply to have such spaces exist. Nor is God content for them only to consist of water or land or vegetation. God desires living things to populate them and abound in them. And, as on other days, God sees such life in abundance as good.

By the sixth day, creation abounds with wonders. Light and darkness. Realms above and below. Earth and sea. Vegetation of all kinds. Birds and aquatic life in abundance. It is fitting that the land should be further populated inasmuch as it has yet to be given its own collection of living beings. And so, on this sixth day, God creates all the many land animals. These Genesis classifies using three basic categories. There are domesticated animals (cattle), insects (crawling things), and non-domesticated (wild) animals. Observing all these animals brought forth simply by divine command,

God also said:

"See, I give you **every** seed-bearing plant all over the earth
and every tree that has seed-bearing fruit on it to be
your **food**;
and to all the animals of the land, all the birds of the air,
and all the living creatures that crawl on the ground,
I give all the green plants for food."
And so it happened.
God looked at everything he had made, and he found it
very good.]
Evening came, and morning followed—the **sixth** day.

Thus the heavens and the earth and all their array
were **completed**.
Since on the **seventh** day God was **finished**
with the work he had been doing,
he **rested** on the **seventh** day from all the **work** he
had undertaken.

[Shorter: Genesis 1:1, 26–31a (see brackets)]

This is a long reading but finish strong. God's action on the seventh day is important to creation and to our lives today. Only when the work was complete did God rest.

For meditation and context:

RESPONSORIAL PSALM   Psalm 104:1–2, 5–6, 10, 12, 13–14, 24, 35 (30)

R. Lord, send out your Spirit, and renew the face of the earth.

Bless the LORD, O my soul!
O LORD, my God, you are great indeed!
You are clothed with majesty and glory,
robed in light as with a cloak.

You fixed the earth upon its foundation,
not to be moved forever;
with the ocean, as with a garment, you
covered it;
above the mountains the waters stood.

You send forth springs into the watercourses
that wind among the mountains.
Beside them the birds of heaven dwell;
from among the branches they send forth
their song.

You water the mountains from your palace;
the earth is replete with the fruit
of your works.
You raise grass for the cattle,
and vegetation for man's use,
producing bread from the earth.

How manifold are your works, O LORD!
In wisdom you have wrought them all—
the earth is full of your creatures.
Bless the LORD, O my soul!

Or:

God declares them good. And, with the earth populated by living beings and determined to be good, we might anticipate that God's creative work would end here as it did with creation on the fifth day, when the waters above and below were populated with living beings. But God's creative work on the sixth day concludes with the creation of a special, entirely superfluous being—the human person. Created male and female in God's image and likeness, God moves beyond the pattern of creation established on prior days. In the creation of humanity, God does not simply refine or

populate an area of creation. That has already been done. Rather, all of creation becomes populated with beings who distinctively reflect and emulate the creator. They are to increase and multiply, which is largely the work God has been doing. Moreover, all of creation is entrusted to their care. And, by God's command, this is so. And it is very good.

With all of creation complete, God rests on the seventh day. Thus, the normative measure of work, the week (a quarter-cycle of the moon), is established by God and punctuated by rest. So, creation comes

about through work. And what that work routinely produces is that which is good. Yet the aim and fulfillment of creation lie in rest or, as it is called in Hebrew, sabbath.

READING II   When we read that God puts Abraham to the test at the outset of Genesis 22, putting that passage in context can help provide some perspective on the nature and meaning of that test. Abraham's story begins in Mesopotamia, the cradle of civilization, but his father uproots him from his homeland when he decides to move his household

For meditation and context:

RESPONSORIAL PSALM Psalm 33:4–5, 6–7, 12–13, 20 and 22 (5b)

R. The earth is full of the goodness of the Lord.

Upright is the word of the LORD,
   and all his works are trustworthy.
He loves justice and right;
   of the kindness of the LORD the earth
   is full.

By the word of the LORD the heavens
   were made;
   by the breath of his mouth all their host.
He gathers the waters of the sea as in a flask;
   in cellars he confines the deep.

Blessed the nation whose God is the LORD,
   the people he has chosen for his own
   inheritance.
From heaven the LORD looks down;
   he sees all mankind.

Our soul waits for the LORD,
   who is our help and our shield.
May your kindness, O LORD, be upon us
   who have put our hope in you.

READING II   Genesis 22:1–18

A reading from the Book of Genesis

[**God** put **Abraham** to the **test**.
He called to him, "Abraham!"
"**Here** I am," he replied.
Then God said:
   "Take your **son Isaac**, your **only** one, whom you **love**,
   and go to the land of **Moriah**.
There you shall offer him up as a **holocaust**
   on a **height** that I will point **out** to you."]
Early the next morning Abraham saddled his **donkey**,
   took with him his son **Isaac** and two of his **servants** as well,
   and with the **wood** that he had cut for the **holocaust**,
   set out for the place of which God had told him.

On the third day Abraham got sight of the place from afar.
Then he said to his servants:
   "Both of you **stay** here with the donkey,
   while the boy and I go on over yonder.
We will worship and then **come back** to you."
Thereupon Abraham took the **wood** for the holocaust
   and laid it **on** his son Isaac's **shoulders**,
   while he himself carried the **fire** and the **knife**. »

Pause for the scene change.

Pause for a scene change. Three days of travel have passed.

This is a very important line. Notice the plural "we" and the indication that they both will return.

The details of the preparation for the sacrifice (wood, the son carrying it, and so on) should bring to mind the accounts of Jesus' passion.

westward (Genesis 11:31). Although they were destined for Canaan, they only make it halfway, settling in Haran (associated with the modern city of Harran on the Turkey-Syria border). In addition to being a migrant and having to negotiate the hardships that entails, Abraham's wife, Sarah is barren from the outset (Genesis 11:30). So, Abraham's story begins with an abandoned homeland and no prospects for future offspring. After his father dies, Abraham's relationship with God begins. God (repeatedly) promises him an abiding relationship filled with blessings, a land that he can call

home (Canaan), and offspring as numerous as the stars or the sand on the shore of the sea. Yet, as Abraham's life unfolds, these promises seem thin. Immediately after the first divine promises, Abraham arrives in Canaan, but it is occupied by long-standing residents. Then, a famine requires Abraham to go to Egypt for food. There he jeopardizes his life and Sarah's by passing her off as his sister for fear of Pharaoh. Although the matter works out to Abraham's benefit, when he returns to the land with his household, he must negotiate a territory conflict with his nephew Lot and conflicts with

kings in Canaan. God renews his promises to Abraham, but the promise of offspring seems less likely to be fulfilled through Sarah. So she offers her maid, Hagar, to Abraham as a concubine. Hagar conceives Ishmael, but the boy is not the one through whom God will extend his promises. Conflict between Sarah and Hagar ensues. Another round of promises is made. A closer encounter with God unfolds. Another, more protracted drama with Lot follows. More wandering. More conflict over Sarah, who even in old age seems to have been a beauty. Eventually, Abraham and Sarah

As the two walked on together, Isaac spoke to his
        father Abraham:
    "**Father**!" Isaac said.
"Yes, son," he replied.
Isaac continued, "Here are the fire and the wood,
    but where is the sheep for the **holocaust**?"
"Son," Abraham answered,
    "God himself will **provide** the sheep for the holocaust."
Then the two **continued** going **forward**.

[When they came to the place of which God had told him,
    Abraham built an **altar** there and arranged the wood on it.]
Next he **tied up** his son Isaac,
    and put him on top of the wood on the altar.
[Then he reached out and took the knife to slaughter his son.
But the LORD's messenger called to him from heaven,
    "Abraham, **Abraham**!"
"Here I am," he answered.
"**Do not** lay your hand on the boy," said the messenger.
"**Do not** do the least thing to him.
I know now how **devoted** you are to God,
    since you did not withhold from me your own beloved son."
As Abraham looked about,
    he spied a **ram** caught by its horns in the thicket.
So he went and took the ram
    and offered it up as a holocaust in place of his son.]
Abraham named the site **Yahweh-yireh**;
    hence people now say, "On the mountain the Lord will see."

[Again the LORD's messenger called to **Abraham** from **heaven**
        and said:
    "I **swear** by myself, declares the Lord,
    that because you **acted** as you did
    in not withholding from me your beloved son,
    I will **bless** you abundantly
    and make your **descendants** as **countless**

Proclaim the angel's call to Abraham with insistence.

Yahweh-yireh = YAH-way-YEER-ay

conceive, and Isaac is born (Genesis 21). But conflict follows immediately in Abraham's household. His two sons (Isaac and Ishmael) get along, which disturbs Sarah, who calls for Hagar and Ishmael to be cast out. God promises to bless and protect them. Finally, conflicts within Abraham's household seem resolved. Then, Abraham makes a few treaties (covenants) with Canaanite leaders, which seemingly forges peace between Abraham's household and the households of resident Canaanites. All, it seems, is at peace in Abraham's life.

Then, as we arrive at today's reading, God calls Abraham. "Abraham!" (Note the exclamation mark.) Abraham, at the ready, says, "Here I am." Then God, in calculated, gradual stages (obscured by the English translation) asks the unthinkable: "Take your son. Your only one. The one who is beloved. Isaac. Go to the land of Moriah. Sacrifice him there on one of the mountains I will show you" (author's translation of the Hebrew text). This test (*nasah* in Hebrew), after everything Abraham has been through, is gut wrenching. It raises questions. How can God ask such a thing,

especially when Abraham's topsy-turvy life has only just settled?

Some ancient Jewish rabbis suggest that Abraham had a dialogue with God as he posed the test. When asked to take his son, Abraham quibbles: "Which? I have two" (referring to Ishmael and Isaac). The apparent clarifier "Your only one" is met with more hedging: "This one (Ishmael) is the only one of his mother (Hagar); that one (Isaac) is the only one of his mother (Sarah)." God's reference to "the beloved" is met with a similar equivocation—each son is Abraham's beloved of the respective

as the stars of the sky and the sands of the seashore;
your descendants shall take possession
of the gates of their enemies,
and in your descendants **all the nations** of the earth shall
    find blessing—
all this because you **obeyed** my command."]

[Shorter: Genesis 22:1–2, 9a, 10–13, 15–18 (see brackets)]

Notice the inclusivity of the Lord's blessing.

For meditation and context:

RESPONSORIAL PSALM   Psalm 16:5, 8, 9–10, 11 (1)

R. You are my inheritance, O Lord.

O LORD, my allotted portion and my cup,
    you it is who hold fast my lot.
I set the LORD ever before me;
    with him at my right hand I shall not
    be disturbed.

Therefore my heart is glad and my
    soul rejoices,
    my body, too, abides in confidence;

because you will not abandon my soul
    to the netherworld,
    nor will you suffer your faithful one
    to undergo corruption.

You will show me the path to life,
    fullness of joys in your presence,
    the delights at your right hand forever.

READING III   Exodus 14:15—15:1

A reading from the Book of Exodus

The **Lord** said to **Moses**, "**Why** are you **crying** out to me?
Tell the **Israelites** to go **forward**.
And you, **lift** up your **staff** and, with **hand outstretched**
    over the **sea**,
    split the sea in two,
    that the Israelites may **pass through** it on dry **land**.
But I will make the **Egyptians** so **obstinate**
    that they will go in **after** them.
Then I will receive **glory** through **Pharaoh** and all his **army**,
    his **chariots** and charioteers.
The Egyptians shall know that **I am** the **Lord**,
    when I receive glory through Pharaoh
    and his chariots and charioteers." »

Exodus = EK-suh-duhs

God's divine presence is manifested in several forms in this reading: the words of God himself, the angel of God, the pillar of cloud and fire, and the movement of the water.

Moses acts as an instrument of God's activity. Although the description of what God will do here is repeated a few verses later in the actual event, don't rush through God's words. The repetition of it later as it comes to pass reinforces our understanding of God's power.

---

mother. When God finally names Isaac, there is no getting away from the request. While this tradition expands the biblical text to make it palatable, Abraham still seems to anticipate the direction things will go. The biblical text is more abrupt. It does not bother with the hedging. God has his way. The patriarch seems to know this and accept it without hesitating. Perhaps he has been through enough in his life. Only Isaac questions what unfolds, asking where the sacrificial animal is. And although Abraham consoles him—*God will provide*— we quickly see Isaac bound, atop the wood

on an altar, and knife aimed at his neck to make of him a bloody sacrifice. The last-minute divine intervention spares Isaac, restores him to his father, and provides an alternate sacrifice.

The whole drama of Abraham's test captures the stakes of ritual sacrifice and prepares us for what God will ultimately reveal in Christ. In him we see another son. A first-born. A beloved. One who carries the wood (cross) of sacrifice and trustingly mounts it that he might be delivered. Yet, in Christ, the sacrifice is completed. This enables deliverance to come *through* him.

Through his death, he shares his deliverance. In this way, Abraham's test prepares us for what God does in Christ.

READING III Although the Old Testament readings for this liturgy are more numerous than those of any other Mass in the liturgical year, only the reading from Exodus *must* be proclaimed. It cannot be omitted, even when circumstances allow for the reduction of the number of Old Testament readings proclaimed. Its absolute necessity is due to the realities

There is a lot of movement occurring here; what the angel does and what the cloud does. Practice these sentences so that the assembly can easily understand what is happening

Moses is obedient to God's commands. What God told Moses at the beginning of the reading is now happening.

The **angel** of God, who had been **leading** Israel's **camp**,
  now moved and went around **behind** them.
The column of **cloud** also, leaving the front,
  took up its place behind them,
  so that it came **between** the **camp** of the **Egyptians**
  and that of **Israel**.
But the cloud now became **dark**, and thus the night passed
  without the rival camps coming any closer together all
    night long.
Then **Moses** stretched out his **hand** over the **sea**,
  and the LORD **swept** the sea
  with a strong east wind throughout the night
  and so **turned** it into dry **land**.
When the water was thus **divided**,
  the Israelites **marched** into the midst of the sea on dry land,
  with the water like a **wall** to their **right** and to their **left**.

The Egyptians followed in **pursuit**;
  all Pharaoh's horses and chariots and charioteers went
    after them
  right **into** the midst of the **sea**.
In the **night** watch just before dawn
  the LORD cast through the **column** of the fiery **cloud**
  upon the Egyptian force a glance that threw it into a **panic**;
  and he so **clogged** their chariot **wheels**
  that they could hardly **drive**.
With that the Egyptians sounded the **retreat** before Israel,
  because the Lord was fighting for them against the Egyptians.

Then the LORD told Moses, "Stretch out your hand over the sea,
  that the water may **flow back** upon the Egyptians,
  upon their chariots and their charioteers."
So Moses stretched out his hand over the sea,
  and at **dawn** the sea flowed back to its normal **depth**.
The Egyptians were **fleeing** head on toward the sea,
  when the LORD **hurled** them into its midst.

it makes present in the liturgy of the word, realities that are central to this liturgy.

The reading from Exodus 14, with its corresponding response from Exodus 15 (likely one of the oldest in Scripture), recalls the conclusion of everything that transpires in the first Passover. Prior to Israel's deliverance from Egypt, they celebrate the ritual sacrifice and accompanying meal prescribed by God for the Passover. These inaugurate Israel's deliverance while also providing a means of memorializing that deliverance throughout subsequent generations. But, as Exodus 14—15 makes clear, God's deliver-

ance at Passover is only initiated with the ritual meal and sacrifice. Full deliverance for God's people must come in God's wondrous deeds, which follow the rituals. First comes the death of the first-born in Egypt. It softens Pharaoh's heart and makes the Egyptians well-disposed toward the Israelites, who are told to depart and given resources (for example, gold) for the journey. As they journey, however, Pharaoh has a change of heart and sends his military after the Israelites to bring them back by force. Then comes the pinnacle of God's saving work in the Passover. Israel, caught

between the sea and the mighty Egyptian army, heads into the sea—which parts for them—on dry land. While Israel passes through the sea unharmed—an image of passing through death to life—Egypt's mighty military cannot complete the same journey. It is destroyed by the waters of the sea. Thus, God's final, full deliverance of Israel comes through the waters of Passover. In this way, Exodus 14—15 portrays the consummation of God's deliverance of the chosen people. God saves them through water.

As the water flowed **back**,
   it **covered** the chariots and the charioteers of Pharaoh's
      whole army
   which had followed the Israelites into the sea.
Not a **single** one of them **escaped**.
But the Israelites had masrched on dry **land**
   through the midst of the sea,
      with the water like a wall to their **right** and to their **left**.
Thus the LORD **saved Israel** on that day
   from the power of the Egyptians.

When Israel saw the Egyptians lying dead on the seashore
   and beheld the great power that the LORD
      had shown against the Egyptians,
      they **feared** the LORD and **believed** in him and in his
         servant Moses.

Then Moses and the Israelites sang this **song** to the LORD:
   I will sing to the LORD, for he is gloriously **triumphant**;
   horse and chariot he has cast into the sea.

The Israelites rightly give God thanks and praise for their deliverance from their oppressors. As you prepare, read through their song of praise in the response that follows—it picks up immediately where this reading ends.

For meditation and context:

RESPONSORIAL PSALM   Exodus 15:1–2, 3–4, 5–6, 17–18 (1b)

R. Let us sing to the Lord; he has covered himself in glory.

I will sing to the LORD, for he is gloriously
   triumphant;
   horse and chariot he has cast into the sea.
My strength and my courage is the LORD,
   and he has been my savior.
He is my God, I praise him;
   the God of my father, I extol him.

The LORD is a warrior,
   LORD is his name!
Pharaoh's chariots and army he hurled
   into the sea;
   the elite of his officers were submerged in
      the Red Sea.

The flood waters covered them,
   they sank into the depths like a stone.
Your right hand, O LORD, magnificent
   in power,
   your right hand, O LORD, has
      shattered the enemy.

You brought in the people you redeemed
   and planted them on the mountain
      of your inheritance—
the place where you made your seat,
   O LORD,
   the sanctuary, LORD, which your
      hands established.
The LORD shall reign forever and ever.

As at the first Passover, when God brings the fullness of Israel's salvation through water, so at the Easter Vigil God completes or fulfills the saving journey of those who enter the waters of baptism this night. The saving act that God mysteriously accomplished for Israel at the conclusion of the first Passover unfolds once more in our midst in this liturgy. Yet, this night, God's salvation through water is a deliverance, a liberation with a more ultimate, cosmic scope. In this liturgy the slavery of sin meets its demise in the saving waters of baptism. Accordingly, Exodus 14 and its accompanying response (Exodus 15), which commemorate God's first saving Passover, cannot *not* be proclaimed this night. With the rite of baptism in view this night, we joyfully and necessarily proclaim what God has done and continues to do in his Passover deeds.

READING IV   Amid the Babylonian exile (587/6–540 BC), God's people found themselves forced out of their homes and homeland. The institutions that ordinarily governed their lives and provided them with stability were obliterated. The closely connected institutions of kingship and prophetic intermediation that provided and governed an organized military, international diplomacy, political discourse, and economic exchange had collapsed. The priestly sacrificial system of worship ended with the destruction of the temple so there was no definitive means of rectifying one's relationship with God. Without homes, land, governance, or a system of worship, the turmoil that God's people faced was nearly total. Accompanying existential questions would have likely been terrifying. Will we continue as a people? Has God

READING IV   Isaiah 54:5–14

A reading from the Book of the Prophet Isaiah

Isaiah = ī-ZAY-uh

The metaphor of a married couple is used to explain God's love and fidelity. Read with conviction so that the assembly feels the depth of God's love.

The One who has become your **husband** is your **Maker**;
    his **name** is the Lord of **hosts**;
your redeemer is the Holy **One** of **Israel**,
    called **God** of all the **earth**.
The LORD calls you **back**,
    like a **wife forsaken** and **grieved** in spirit,
    a wife married in youth and then **cast** off,
    says your God.

Similar to married relationships, the relationship between God and God's people has its ups and downs, moments of anger and times of reconciliation. Look beyond negative biases of male–female balances of power and blame—in this metaphor, the Lord is the husband, but all of Israel, both genders, is the unfaithful wife.

For a brief **moment** I **abandoned** you,
    but with great **tenderness** I will take you **back**.
In an outburst of **wrath**, for a moment
    I **hid** my face from you;
but with enduring **love** I take **pity** on you,
    says the LORD, your **redeemer**.
This is for me like the days of **Noah**,
    when I **swore** that the waters of Noah
    should never **again** deluge the earth;
so I have sworn not to be **angry** with you,
    or to rebuke you.

What an image—even if mountains are no more, God's love remains.

Though the **mountains** leave their place
    and the hills be shaken,
my **love** shall never **leave** you
    nor my covenant of **peace** be shaken,
    says the LORD, who has **mercy** on you.

Read sad, descriptive language slowly. Then, use an upbeat tone to describe the jeweled city the Lord is promising.

carnelians = kahr-NEEL-yuhnz = a type of gemstone

O **afflicted** one, storm-**battered** and **unconsoled**,
    I lay your **pavements** in **carnelians**,
    and your **foundations** in **sapphires**;
I will make your **battlements** of **rubies**,
    your gates of **carbuncles**,
    and all your **walls** of precious **stones**.

carbuncles = KAHR-bung-k*lz = a type of gemstone

God's blessings are not just upon their homes and cities, but upon their children as well.

All your **children** shall be taught by the LORD,
    and great shall be the **peace** of your children.

abandoned us? Will God take up our cause again? Does God care about us? Does God exist?

In the twilight of the exile comes the prophet responsible for conveying God's message in Isaiah 54. The passage attends to the deep fears and concerns of the exiles. It takes them seriously. The prophet, on God's behalf, says "For a brief moment I abandoned you. . . . In an outburst of wrath . . . I hid my face." The sense of abandonment is real. Similar occasions are presented or recalled to elaborate upon the point. A forsaken wife of one's youth is brought to mind. Also, the disastrous, destructive waters of the flood in Noah's day. The imagery and story confirm that the ruptured relationship between God and his people, which is experienced in the exile, is real. But it is not final. As the examples suggest, the wife of one's youth is not forgotten. The flood did not bring all of humanity to an end. So too, the exile will not be the final word for God's people. Not only that, the restoration of God's people after the exile will result in a life more glorious and glowing than it was prior to the exile. Restored Jerusalem will be made of rubies and precious stones of various kinds. And, most important, the peace of God will be restored.

In this liturgy we commemorate similar transformative work wrought by God. Faced with death due to the wages of sin, all of humanity was left to contend with anxieties about our future. Can and will God deliver us from our unavoidable demise? In the revelation of Christ's death and resurrection the ultimate, existential angst meets with a comparably ultimate answer—in Christ we know the promise of resurrection. Not only does God know and

In **justice** shall you be established,
    far from the fear of **oppression**,
    where destruction cannot come **near** you.

For meditation and context:

RESPONSORIAL PSALM   Psalm 30:2, 4, 5–6, 11–12, 13 (2a)

R. I will praise you, Lord, for you have rescued me.

I will extol you, O LORD, for you drew
    me clear
    and did not let my enemies rejoice
      over me.
O LORD, you brought me up from the
    netherworld;
    you preserved me from among those
      going down into the pit.

Sing praise to the LORD, you his
    faithful ones,
    and give thanks to his holy name.
For his anger lasts but a moment;
    a lifetime, his good will.
At nightfall, weeping enters in,
    but with the dawn, rejoicing.

Hear, O LORD, and have pity on me;
    O LORD, be my helper.
You changed my mourning into dancing;
    O LORD, my God, forever will I give
      you thanks.

READING V   Isaiah 55:1–11

Isaiah = ī-ZAY-uh

A prophetic oracle that should be read with compassion. God's invitation is for rich and poor alike. Food and water are basic human needs, yet we are confronted with the sobering awareness that many in our world today do not receive the nourishment they need to survive.

A reading from the Book of the Prophet Isaiah

Thus says the LORD:
All you who are **thirsty**,
    come to the **water**!
You who have no **money**,
    come, receive grain **and eat;**
come, **without paying** and without cost,
    drink **wine** and **milk**!
Why spend your **money** for what is not **bread**,
    your **wages** for what fails to **satisfy**?
Heed **me**, and you shall **eat well**,
    you shall **delight** in rich **fare**.
Come to me heedfully,
    listen, that you may have **life**.
I will **renew** with you the everlasting **covenant**,
    the benefits assured to David. »

---

care about us, he also reaches out to us and enters into our reality in order to call us into eternal life. Our access to assurance of that life comes to us in the sacraments in which the Church participates in this night. Through baptism, confirmation, Eucharist— the sacraments of our initiation—we partake in Christ's death and resurrection and find comfort for the deepest of our worries that emerge on account of the frailty of our human condition.

READING V   At the close of the exile, when God's chosen people

were returning to the chosen land after having been dispersed by the Babylonians, reoccupation of the holy land became an awe-inspiring possibility. The homeland from which God's people had been separated was reopened to them. The fruits of that land were once more made available. The prospect of restoring shattered institutions became a reality. A kingship lost could be revived. Worship restored. The people rejuvenated. And, as the prophet responsible for Isaiah 55 suggests, the price of that restoration seems to have been paid by God.

We know that, historically, the great but short-lived empire of Babylon, where Israel was in exile, came under the rule of Cyrus and, through him, the Persians, without a fight. Cyrus simply, peacefully occupied the capital city of Babylon and promptly proceeded to expand his empire westward to the Mediterranean. He then established policies that facilitated a return to the promised land for God's people. They did not need to engage in contest for their restoration— God provided it freely, abundantly.

In light of the post-exilic context, God's provisions for the chosen people—

As I made him a **witness** to the peoples,
  a **leader** and commander of **nations**,
so shall you **summon** a nation you knew not,
  and nations that knew you not shall **run** to you,
because of the LORD, your **God**,
  the Holy One of Israel, who has **glorified** you.

Seek the LORD while he may be **found**,
  call him while he is **near**.
Let the **scoundrel forsake** his **way**,
  and the wicked man his **thoughts**;
let him **turn** to the LORD for **mercy**;
  to our God, who is generous in forgiving.
For **my** thoughts are not **your** thoughts,
  nor are **your** ways **my** ways, says the LORD.
As high as the **heavens** are above the **earth**,
  so **high** are **my** ways above **your** ways
  and **my** thoughts above **your** thoughts.

For just as from the **heavens**
  the rain and snow come **down**
and do **not return** there
  till they have **watered** the earth,
  making it **fertile** and **fruitful**,
giving **seed** to the one who **sows**
  and **bread** to the one who **eats**,
so shall my **word** be
  that goes forth from **my** mouth;
my word shall not **return** to me **void**,
  but shall **do** my will,
  achieving the end for which I sent it.

These are imperatives: "Seek the Lord" and "call him." As you prepare, listen to "Seek the Lord" by Roc O'Connor and meditate on the assurances of Isaiah's words.

The Lord's ways and thoughts are far beyond ours; they are almost incomprehensible. The prophet attempts to articulate this with natural imagery. Just as rain accomplishes what it is supposed to, so will God's word accomplish its objective. These lines are particularly appropriate to lectors as proclaimers of God's word.

God's acts are always effective. We might not acknowledge them or see them fulfilled, but God is always present and active in our world.

water for the thirsty, food for the poor, wine and milk without cost, words that give life, a restored Davidic covenant—flow in such abundance that unknown nations will seek them out that they might encounter God, the Holy One of Israel. For their part, God's people are called to forsake wickedness and unrighteousness and make their own return to the Lord. They are to recognize the difference between God's ways and theirs. They are to acknowledge the abundant mercy that God extends to all. They are to recognize the effectiveness of God's word in the world.

As we enter more deeply into the mystery of Christ's passion, death, and resurrection in the liturgy of the Easter Vigil, Isaiah 55 presents to us once more the remarkable, transforming power of God's word. The Word that forged all of creation in Genesis 1 also restores it. And God's generative Word is freely given and unmerited by us and all who receive it.

READING VI The Book of Baruch was probably composed in the second century before Christ (c. 150 BC), but its author used a pseudonym to associate it with Baruch, the scribe of Jeremiah (see Jeremiah 36; 45). Associating this book with Jeremiah connects it with a biblical tradition in which wisdom emerges through suffering. Jeremiah was called by God to warn the leaders of Judah and Jerusalem of impending conquest and destruction by the Babylonians. His message was doom. It was roundly rejected. For it, he faced acute suffering, even the prospect of execution for predicting the temple's destruction (Jeremiah 26). Yet, with Baruch's scribal support, Jeremiah was able to communicate with those who considered the

For meditation and context:

RESPONSORIAL PSALM   Isaiah 12:2–3, 4, 5–6 (3)

R. You will draw water joyfully from the springs of salvation.

God indeed is my savior;
    I am confident and unafraid.
My strength and my courage is the LORD,
    and he has been my savior.
With joy you will draw water
    at the fountain of salvation.

Give thanks to the LORD, acclaim his name;
    among the nations make known
        his deeds,
    proclaim how exalted is his name.

Sing praise to the LORD for his glorious
        achievement;
    let this be known throughout all
        the earth.
Shout with exultation, O city of Zion,
    for great in your midst
        is the Holy One of Israel!

READING VI   Baruch 3:9–15, 32—4:4

Baruch = buh-ROOK

A reading from the Book of the Prophet Baruch

Hear, O Israel, the **commandments** of life:
    listen, and **know** prudence!
How **is** it, Israel,
    that you are in the land of your **foes**,
    grown **old** in a foreign **land**,
defiled with the dead,
    accounted with those destined for the **netherworld**?
You have **forsaken** the fountain of **wisdom**!
    Had you walked in the way of God,
    you would have **dwelt** in enduring peace.
Learn where prudence is,
    where **strength**, where **understanding**;
that you may know also
    where are length of **days**, and **life**,
    where light of the **eyes**, and **peace**.
Who has **found** the place of wisdom,
    who has entered into her **treasuries**? »

"Grown old": they have been in exile for a while.

Stress "Learn where" and it will then be applied to "prudence," "strength," and "understanding." This is invitational. We too should search for these virtues.

"Her" refers to wisdom.

prophet a pariah and distanced themselves from him. Moreover, Jeremiah, again with Baruch's aid, could correspond with those displaced during the exile.

Situated in Jeremiah's time, this passage from the Book of Baruch makes an overt appeal to the Bible's wisdom tradition for three purposes. First, it reprimands its audience for not following the way of wisdom. Second, it invites its audience to grow in wisdom and God's grace, especially by pondering God's work in creation. And third, it calls for renewed commitment to the law, which it equates with personified

wisdom. As a whole, the passage provides a pair of biblical traditions—the wisdom tradition and the prophetic—while inviting us to delve further into the mystery of what we encounter in Christ, God's incarnate wisdom.

Beginning by way of reprimand, this passage notes that, had Israel only committed to grow in prudence, strength, and understanding, its members would have avoided exile. They would not have known displacement and could have escaped living among foreigners in a foreign land. If those who went into exile had advanced in

wisdom, they would have enjoyed long life, rather than knowing death. Instead of turmoil, they would have lived in God's enduring peace. For the Jews dispersed throughout the world at the time when Baruch was written, the message is clear: they could access their homeland if they but grew in wisdom.

But Baruch offers more than reprimand here. This passage, in a manner common to the wisdom tradition, presents wisdom as personified: "the One who knows all things knows her [wisdom]." This presentation of wisdom closely associates it

All creation rejoices in God's actions. The author gives creation anthropomorphic (human) qualities.

precepts = PREE-sehpts = commandments

The One who knows **all** things knows **her**;
  he has probed her by his **knowledge**—
the One who **established** the earth for all **time**,
  and **filled** it with four-footed **beasts**;
he who **dismisses** the **light**, and it **departs**,
  calls it, and it **obeys** him trembling;
before whom the stars at their posts
  shine and **rejoice**;
when he calls them, they answer, "Here **we are**!"
  shining with joy for their Maker.
Such is **our** God;
  no other is to be **compared** to him:
he has traced out the whole way of **understanding**,
  and has given her to **Jacob**, his servant,
  to Israel, his beloved **son**.

Since then she has **appeared** on **earth**,
  and moved among **people**.
She is the book of the **precepts** of God,
  the law that endures **forever**;
all who cling to her will **live**,
  but those will **die** who **forsake** her.
Turn, O Jacob, and receive her:
  walk by her light toward **splendor**.
Give not your **glory** to **another**,
  your **privileges** to an alien race.
Blessed are **we**, O Israel;
  for what **pleases** God is known to us!

with God, a common motif in the wisdom tradition. God and wisdom are often partners in creation according to the wisdom tradition. Accordingly, God, in this wisdom idiom, manifests wisdom in creation: "the One who established the earth for all time . . . is our God." To attend to creation, Baruch and the wisdom tradition suggest, promises growth in knowledge of God, who is beyond compare.

Finally, inasmuch as God has given wisdom to Jacob/Israel, the chosen people enjoy access to God. Nowhere is such access clearer, according to Baruch, than

the law. "She [wisdom] is the book of the precepts of God." Accordingly, the author of Baruch counsels his audience, as Jeremiah would before him, to cling to the law that they might have life. The author concludes by acknowledging that Israel is indeed blessed on account of their law, because through the law they know what pleases God.

READING VII For Ezekiel, the exile again looms large. The prophet builds his message based on it. The Lord's people, having been forced to

depart from their homeland because of their unclean worship and idolatry, were driven from their land as a punishment by God. Yet, as the Lord further observes and conveys through the prophet, exiling the people has proven counterproductive for a larger goal. The nations, instead of learning the Lord's name and keeping it holy, are learning from the exiles to profane and defile it. Moreover, the nations to which the exiles go begin to mock and question the Lord's power and place. "These are the people of the LORD, yet they had to leave their land," say the inhabitants of the nations.

For meditation and context:

RESPONSORIAL PSALM   Psalm 19:8, 9, 10, 11 (John 6:68c)

R. Lord, you have the words of everlasting life.

The law of the LORD is perfect,
    refreshing the soul;
the decree of the LORD is trustworthy,
    giving wisdom to the simple.

The precepts of the LORD are right,
    rejoicing the heart;
the command of the LORD is clear,
    enlightening the eye.

The fear of the LORD is pure,
    enduring forever;
the ordinances of the LORD are true,
    all of them just.

They are more precious than gold,
    than a heap of purest gold;
sweeter also than syrup
    or honey from the comb.

READING VII   Ezekiel 36:16–17a, 18–28

A reading from the Book of the Prophet Ezekiel

Ezekiel = ee-ZEE-kee-uhl

God is speaking to Ezekiel.

Do not bring too much angst to the reading. God is using the past tense.

The actions of God's people are observed by other nations, who then draw incorrect conclusions about who God is.

The **word** of the LORD came to **me**, saying:
    Son of man, when the house of **Israel** lived in their **land**,
    they **defiled** it by their **conduct** and deeds.
Therefore I poured out my **fury** upon them
    because of the **blood** that they poured out on the **ground**,
    and because they defiled it with **idols**.
I **scattered** them among the **nations**,
    dispersing them over foreign lands;
    according to their conduct and deeds I judged them.
But when they **came** among the **nations** wherever they came,
    they served to profane **my** holy **name**,
    because it was said of them: "These are the **people** of
        the LORD,
    yet they had to **leave** their land."
So I have **relented** because of my holy name
    which the house of Israel profaned
    among the nations where they came.
Therefore say to the house of **Israel**: Thus says the Lord GOD:
    Not for **your sakes** do I **act**, house of Israel,
    but for the sake of **my** holy name,
    which you profaned among the nations to which you came. »

With Israel as an untrustworthy vessel and means of bringing about global sanctification of the Lord's name, and the nations beginning to taunt God, a heavenly plan is hatched: God will deliver the people. But God's salvation is not for the good of the people. They have not earned it. If anything, they have done more to dissuade him from delivering them. Rather, it is because the Lord is holy and seeks to have that holiness respected that the people are delivered.

Lest we become spiritually proud this night of Easter Vigil, Ezekiel sets us

straight. God does not deliver us because we have earned it or deserve it. Quite the contrary. The deliverance that God extends to us in Christ's passion, death, and resurrection and which he perpetuates for us in the sacraments is entirely gratuitous. It comes to us because God is holy, not because we are. This truth, of course, is not meant to produce spiritual despondency or moral malaise—we remain responsible for acting in accord with truth and justice and right. But holiness is the Lord's, which he extends to us freely, without cost, without merit. We cannot earn the Lord's love or

enjoy and manifest the Lord's holiness without the Lord making it so. Only as he gives to us can we respond in kind. Thankfully, he abounds in unfathomable holiness and generosity. And we are blessed this night and throughout our lives to partake in that holiness.

EPISTLE Paul's message to the Romans lies at the heart of tonight's liturgy of the word and the broader liturgy of this night. Tonight, the baptismal waters are blessed. Tonight, we renew our baptismal promises. Tonight, the elect who

I will prove the **holiness** of my great name, profaned among
    the nations,
        in whose midst you have profaned it.
Thus the nations shall **know** that **I am** the LORD, says the
    Lord GOD,
        when in their sight I **prove** my **holiness** through **you**.
For I will take you **away** from among the nations,
    gather you from all the foreign lands,
    and **bring** you back to your own land.
I will sprinkle **clean water** upon you
    to cleanse you from all your **impurities**,
    and from all your **idols** I will cleanse you.
I will give you a new **heart** and place a new **spirit** within you,
    taking from your bodies your **stony hearts**
    and giving you **natural** hearts.
I will put my spirit **within** you and make you live by my
    statutes,
        careful to observe my decrees.
You shall **live** in the land I gave your fathers;
    you shall be **my people**, and I will be your **God**.

This is a consoling line. God cleanses us from our old ways and makes our hearts new.

Deliver the last line looking at the assembly. God assures us of a mutual relationship. We are his and he is ours. Praise God!

For meditation and context:
Used when baptism is celebrated.

RESPONSORIAL PSALM   Psalm 42:3, 5; 43:3, 4 (2)

R. Like a deer that longs for running streams, my soul longs for you, my God.

Athirst is my soul for God, the living God.
    When shall I go and behold the face
    of God?

I went with the throng
    and led them in procession to the house
    of God,
amid loud cries of joy and thanksgiving,
    with the multitude keeping festival.

Or:

Send forth your light and your fidelity;
    they shall lead me on
and bring me to your holy mountain,
    to your dwelling-place.

Then will I go in to the altar of God,
    the God of my gladness and joy;
then will I give you thanks upon the harp,
    O God, my God!

have been preparing for baptism will be baptized. One life will end, and another will begin. Their journey of initiation will end and their journey in the Christian life will begin as they are incorporated into the Body of Christ. In the waters of baptism, the ambiguity of water emerges: not enough, we die; too much, we die; the right amount and life flourishes.

Throughout tonight's liturgy of the word, waters have proven key. In Genesis, primordial waters, stirred by the Spirit in the form of wind, are the basis from which God's creative word thunders forth and all

that is comes into being. Yet those waters had no power to bring forth life without God's word. They were, at best, inert, lifeless. In the parting of the waters of Exodus, God brings final deliverance to Israel. Their life and liberty are restored as God delivers them through water. Yet assurance of their deliverance comes at a cost. Bodies of dead Egyptians wash ashore to confirm Israel's liberation.

Now, Paul proclaims to the Romans a mystery that is difficult to fathom but one for which we have been prepared. In the baptismal waters, we experience a means

of becoming a new creation and partake in a new Passover, but we do so by entering into Christ's death. As Christ's paschal mystery reveals, death is the way to new, risen life. So when we enter the waters of baptism, we enter into Christ's death. And we do so not to derive pleasure from pain but that we might participate in his resurrection. These waters first bring death. Then they give life.

Baptism's dynamic of life-giving death, as Paul further reminds us, has ramifications for how we live as Christians. It shapes our consciences and moral lives. As children of

For meditation and context:
Option used when baptism is not celebrated.

RESPONSORIAL PSALM　Isaiah 12:2–3, 4bcd, 5–6 (3)

R. You will draw water joyfully from the springs of salvation.

God indeed is my savior;
　I am confident and unafraid.
My strength and my courage is the LORD,
　and he has been my savior.
With joy you will draw water
　at the fountain of salvation.

Give thanks to the LORD, acclaim his name;
　among the nations make known his deeds,
　proclaim how exalted is his name.

Sing praise to the LORD for his glorious
　achievement;
　let this be known throughout all the earth.
Shout with exultation, O city of Zion,
　for great in your midst
　is the Holy One of Israel!

Or:

For meditation and context:
Option used when baptism is not celebrated.

RESPONSORIAL PSALM　Psalm 51:12–13, 14–15, 18–19 (12a)

R. Create a clean heart in me, O God.

A clean heart create for me, O God,
　and a steadfast spirit renew within me.
Cast me not out from your presence,
　and your Holy Spirit take not from me.

Give me back the joy of your salvation,
　and a willing spirit sustain in me.
I will teach transgressors your ways,
　and sinners shall return to you.

For you are not pleased with sacrifices;
　should I offer a holocaust, you would not
　accept it.
My sacrifice, O God, is a contrite spirit;
　a heart contrite and humbled, O God, you
　will not spurn.

EPISTLE　Romans 6:3–11

A reading from the Letter of Saint Paul to the Romans

Brothers and **sisters**:
Are you **unaware** that we who were **baptized** into Christ **Jesus**
　were baptized into his **death**?
We were indeed buried with him through baptism into death,
　so that, just as Christ was **raised** from the dead
　by the **glory** of the **Father**,
　we **too** might live in **newness** of life. »

Let the elect hear what is in store for them; the newness of their baptismal life is almost upon them. Paul's words are also a good reminder for those who have already been baptized. Let us all rejoice!

Adam and Eve, we were born into this world set on a trajectory whose aim and end were death. The wages of sin, Paul will go on to say, is death. Born into the fallen human condition, we are subject to the effects of sin and, vulnerable as we are, we fall into sin. Accordingly, before Christ, our end was death. But to enter into Christ's death as we do in baptism reorients our trajectory. Death remains a part of our journey, but on a cosmic moral plane, we come to enjoy a broader promise—resurrected life. Thus, for Paul, being baptized into Christ's death means we are to think of ourselves as "dead to sin," that is, dead to sin's effects (and ideally its appeal). But also, consequently, as "living for God in Christ Jesus."

GOSPEL　Mark's resurrection account picks up not simply at the end of the passion of Jesus, but where today's first reading left off—sabbath. It is a new week. The eighth day. The day of a new creation. A new beginning. Echoing the first acts of creation, daylight fills the sky. Having rested on the sabbath, in accord with God's final act of creation and Jewish legal custom, the women approach the tomb. Their task and conversation are practical and yet revelatory.

They purchase spices to anoint Jesus' dead body, an important religious and moral act. The act of anointing the deceased was practical but was also a demanding task. The purpose was to reduce the stench of the decaying corpse. The willingness of these women to take up this task for the body of a man they cared about demonstrates their interior strength. We could regard them as moral heroines for their willingness to do it. At the same time, they

For if we have grown into **union** with him through a death
    like his,
    we shall also be **united** with him in the **resurrection**.
We know that our **old** self was **crucified** with him,
    so that our **sinful** body might be done **away** with,
    that we might no longer be in **slavery** to sin.
For a **dead** person has been **absolved** from sin.
If, then, we have **died** with Christ,
    we believe that we shall also **live** with him.
We know that **Christ**, **raised** from the dead, dies no **more**;
    death no longer has **power** over him.
As to his death, he died to sin **once** and for **all**;
    as to his life, he lives for God.
Consequently, you too must **think** of yourselves as being **dead**
    to sin
    and **living** for God in Christ **Jesus**.

Emphasize "once:" Jesus' sacrifice is not repeated yet it is still effective.

For meditation and context:

RESPONSORIAL PSALM   Psalm 118:1–2, 16–17, 22–23

R. Alleluia, alleluia, alleluia.

Give thanks to the LORD, for he is good,
    for his mercy endures forever.
Let the house of Israel say,
    "His mercy endures forever."

The right hand of the LORD has struck
    with power;
    the right hand of the LORD is exalted.

I shall not die, but live,
    and declare the works of the LORD.

The stone which the builders rejected
    has become the cornerstone.
By the LORD has this been done;
    it is wonderful in our eyes.

GOSPEL   Mark 16:1–7

A reading from the holy Gospel according to Mark

When the **sabbath** was **over**,
    Mary **Magdalene**, Mary, the **mother of James**, and **Salome**
    bought **spices** so that they might go and **anoint** him.
Very **early** when the sun had risen,
    on the **first** day of the week, they came to the **tomb**.

A narrator begins the story. Read with an even tone before the dialogue starts.

Salome = suh-LOH-mee

Magdalene = MAG-duh-luhn or MAG-duh-leen

are discussing who they might get to roll back the stone. Mark will explain, momentarily, that the stone is "very large." So their question may concern their limited collective strength. If so, their poor planning could be chalked up to the fog of grief. After all, no one thinks clearly after a loved one dies. These women would be no different. But they do not stop and fetch help when they realize the problem. Moreover, Mark has already reported that these same women watched Joseph roll the stone over the tomb (Mark 15:46–47). Even if he was only the overseer of others who placed the

stone, the women know what they face, and we might presume that they judged themselves *able* to roll the stone since they do not change their plans. But, since they are carrying aromatic spices to anoint the body, their concern may not be their collective strength as much as the anticipated strength of the *stench* they expect to encounter emitting from the corpse in the tomb. The body, presumably, has been decomposing for two nights and the start of a third day! Whatever their aim and concern, it is fair to assume they are attending to practical matters. And it becomes evi-

dent that they do not, in any way, expect to discover anything other than Jesus' dead body in the tomb where they saw it interred just days before.

When they see the stone rolled back, enter the tomb, and spot the young man sitting and clothed in a white robe, they are utterly amazed (*ekthambéō* in Greek). Their amazement reflects the crowd's earlier amazement in Mark 9:15, when they see Jesus after his transfiguration. Perhaps he was radiant like Moses was after seeing God face to face (Exodus 34:29–35). In any case, the women are suddenly silent, all

Use a rising inflection for the women's question.

Entering the tomb and encountering a man in white "amazed" them. Imagine that encounter for yourself—what would your reaction have been?

Use a tender but confident voice to disarm their fear.

This news is not to be kept private. Pause after "go." The women are to be evangelists to the disciples. Your proclamation is doing the same.

They were saying to one another,
  "**Who** will roll **back** the **stone** for us
  from the entrance to the tomb?
When they looked **up**,
  they saw that the stone **had** been rolled back;
  it was very **large**.
On **entering** the tomb they saw a young **man**
  sitting on the right **side**, clothed in a **white robe**,
  and they were utterly **amazed**.
He said to them, "Do **not** be amazed!
You **seek** Jesus of **Nazareth**, the **crucified**.
He has been **raised**; he is not **here**.
Behold the place where they **laid** him.
But **go** and **tell** his disciples and Peter,
  'He is going **before** you to **Galilee**;
  there you will **see** him, as he told you.' "

practicalities put aside. They are struck mute by the cognitive dissonance of what they are seeing: the stone should not be rolled back; the tomb should not be empty. No one should be in it, certainly not someone alive. And the young man's white robe— its color must signal something. His knowledge of the situation and his ability to direct the women through their amazement makes it evident that he is an angelic guide, typical of apocalyptic Jewish literature from this period.

Of course, it is not the women or the young man, but his simple announcement that matters most: "Do not be amazed! You seek Jesus of Nazareth, the crucified. He has been raised; he is not here." The Easter Vigil commemorates and celebrates what this announcement conveys: Christ's resurrection has changed the course of our souls and the aim of the cosmos. E.W.

EASTER SUNDAY
OF THE RESURRECTION
OF THE LORD

LECTIONARY #42

READING I   Acts of the Apostles 10:34a, 37–43

A reading from the Acts of the Apostles

Peter proceeded to speak and said:
   "You **know** what has **happened** all over Judea,
   beginning in Galilee after the baptism
   that John preached,
      how **God anointed** Jesus of **Nazareth**
      with the Holy **Spirit** and **power**.
He went about doing **good**
      and **healing** all those **oppressed** by the **devil**,
      for God was with him.
We are **witnesses** of all that he **did**
      both in the country of the Jews and in Jerusalem.
They put him to **death** by hanging him on a **tree**.
This man God **raised** on the third day and **granted** that he
         be **visible**,
      not to all the people, but to us,
      the **witnesses chosen** by God in advance,
      who ate and **drank** with him **after** he **rose** from the dead.
He **commissioned** us to **preach** to the people
      and testify that he is the one appointed by God
      as **judge** of the **living** and the **dead**.
To him all the **prophets** bear **witness**,
      that everyone who **believes** in him
      will receive **forgiveness** of sins through his **name**."

Paul is teaching the people by telling them the story of Jesus.

Judea = joo-DEE-uh or joo-DAY-uh

Paul testifies to the resurrected Jesus by recounting his eating, a bodily action that cannot be denied. Stress "after" to make this clear.

Jesus commissioned the apostles to preach, to share the Good News; this commission extends to all the baptized.

There are options for today's readings. Contact your parish staff to learn which readings will be used.

READING I It is not an overstatement to say that the readings of Lent and the celebrations of Holy Week all come together in the readings of Easter Sunday. While some of these readings come from contexts that are distant from Easter's historical events, all of the readings reflect on Easter's central mystery:

Christ was raised from the dead and inaugurated a new age of grace.

Today's first reading from the Acts of the Apostles describes the missionary activity and message of the early church following the martyrdom of Stephen. After missionaries had brought the message to Samaria and to an Ethiopian eunuch, Peter brings the Good News to a Gentile in Caesarea named Cornelius. Both Peter and Cornelius had received visions that inspired their meeting. Having entered Cornelius' home, and heard of his vision, Peter proceeds to speak to Cornelius and his house-

hold in the words of today's reading. Peter's words, his final missionary speech, summarize the life and ministry of Jesus as God's chosen one. Most importantly, he describes Jesus' death, resurrection, appearances, and the commission he gave to the disciples to preach. Placing all this detail against the backdrop of salvation history that is now fulfilled in Jesus, Peter interprets Jesus' role as the divinely appointed "judge of the living and the dead," as well as the source of forgiveness of sins for all who believe. This speech is one of the best examples of the core teaching of the early

For meditation and context:

Corinthians = kohr-IN-thee-uhnz

Notice the repeated words in this short reading. Don't overemphasize them; allow the message to come through: seek the things of heaven, our eternal home in Christ. Make eye contact with the assembly and deliver the last line. This is part of our Easter joy!

RESPONSORIAL PSALM   Psalm 118:1–2, 16–17, 22–23 (24)

R. This is the day the Lord has made; let us rejoice and be glad.
or
R. Alleluia.

Give thanks to the LORD, for he is good,
  for his mercy endures forever.
Let the house of Israel say,
  "His mercy endures forever."

"The right hand of the LORD has struck
    with power;
  the right hand of the LORD is exalted.

I shall not die, but live,
  and declare the works of the LORD.

The stone which the builders rejected
  has become the cornerstone.
By the LORD has this been done;
  it is wonderful in our eyes.

READING II   Colossians 3:1–4

A reading from the Letter of Saint Paul to the Colossians

Brothers and **sisters**:
If then **you** were **raised** with **Christ**, **seek** what is **above**,
  where Christ is **seated** at the right **hand** of God.
Think of what is above, not of what is on **earth**.
For you have **died**, and your **life** is hidden with Christ in **God**.
When Christ your **life** appears,
  then you too will **appear** with him in **glory**.

  Or:

Church. The scene is immediately followed by the fourth outpouring of the Holy Spirit in the Acts of the Apostles, with the hearers' response of faith to the message being affirmed by the reception of baptism. This scene also demonstrates the first step in the controversial mission to the Gentiles that is taken up in Acts.

READING II | **Colossians.** Holy Saturday and Easter Sunday's emphasis on baptism makes Paul's letter (written from his imprisonment) to the Colossians an especially relevant reading.

Coming from the very end of Paul's life, or perhaps shortly after his death, Colossians offers a penetrating reflection on the power of baptism as the answer to the community's confusion about external religious influences, such as ascetic practices, repeated rituals, and elements from Jewish folk tradition. Since the community tends to view the world as profoundly evil, Paul assures them that the power of the risen Christ is stronger than the world. Then, in today's reading, Paul pulls the community itself into this powerful mystery. With echoes of Psalm 110:1, Paul declares that

Christ is *now* seated at God's right hand. But there is more! By virtue of their baptism, the Colossians are *now* raised with Christ, their lives are "hidden with Christ in God," and they are destined to "appear with him in glory." Consequently, through the one act of baptism, they are freed from ascetic practices and repeated rituals. Indeed, as Paul declares, they should "think of what is above, not of what is on earth."

1 Corinthians. For Paul, baptism effects a total transformation. While his most powerful image of that transformation is of dying and rising (for example,

Corinthians = kohr-IN-thee-uhnz

Paul is calling us to a new ethical standard. Emphasize "little" and "all."

Paul gets practical. Name the concrete sins of our life slowly ("malice and wickedness"), as well as the virtues we should replace them with ("sincerity and truth").

For meditation and context:

READING II   1 Corinthians 5:6b–8

A reading from the first Letter of Saint Paul to the Corinthians

Brothers and **sisters**:
Do you not **know** that a **little** yeast leavens **all** the dough?
Clear out the **old** yeast,
　　so that you may become a **fresh** batch of dough,
　　inasmuch as **you** are **unleavened**.
For our paschal **lamb**, **Christ**, has been **sacrificed**.
Therefore, let us **celebrate** the feast,
　　not with the old yeast, the yeast of **malice** and **wickedness**,
　　but with the unleavened bread of **sincerity** and **truth**.

SEQUENCE   Victimae paschali laudes

Christians, to the Paschal Victim
　Offer your thankful praises!
A Lamb the sheep redeems;
　Christ, who only is sinless,
　Reconciles sinners to the Father.
Death and life have contended in that
　　combat stupendous:
　The Prince of life, who died,
　　reigns immortal.
Speak, Mary, declaring
　What you saw, wayfaring.

"The tomb of Christ, who is living,
　The glory of Jesus' resurrection;
Bright angels attesting,
　The shroud and napkin resting.
Yes, Christ my hope is arisen;
　to Galilee he goes before you."
Christ indeed from death is risen, our new
　　life obtaining.
　Have mercy, victor King, ever reigning!
　Amen. Alleluia.

TO KEEP IN MIND

Sequences originated as extensions of the sung Alleluia before the proclamation of the Gospel, although they precede the Alleluia now. The Easter Sequence is an ancient liturgical hymn that praises Christ, the paschal victim, for his victory over death. Mary Magdalene recounts her experience at Christ's tomb, proclaiming, "Christ my hope is arisen."

Romans 6:1–11), he uses the image of a fresh batch of dough in today's reading. Addressed to a community in Corinth that he founded, and with which he lived for eighteen months, Paul tackles many difficult ethical issues in this talented but headstrong community. While Paul complained much about their rivalries and divisions, he was especially appalled by their boasting and conceit. Today's reading is part of a larger argument against divisions, boasting, and conceit. In this reading, he accuses the community of tolerating a case of incest in their midst. Not only do they tolerate the

presence of a member engaging in incest, but they are conceited and boastful about it.

In order to emphasize the seriousness of this situation, Paul appeals to their identity as God's holy people. He argues his case by pointing to the Passover meal and the way that it was made holy for Christians at the Last Supper. Just as Jews would cleanse their houses of the old leaven before the yearly celebration of Passover, the Corinthians were to "clear out" the old yeast of sin in order to be made into a new and unleavened batch. Alluding to the sacrifice of the Passover lamb that saved the

Hebrews from the angel of death, Paul reminds the Corinthians that their "paschal lamb, Christ, has been sacrificed." Thus, reminded of their paschal lamb and their vocation as God's holy people and as unleavened bread, the community is to celebrate and act "with the unleavened bread of sincerity and truth." The practical consequence is to remove the offending person from their midst as one clears out old leaven. While the events of this reading are removed in time from the events of Easter, it still offers a powerful reflection on the effects of baptism.

GOSPEL John 20:1–9

A reading from the holy Gospel according to John

On the **first** day of the week,
Mary of **Magdala came** to the **tomb** early in the morning,
while it was still **dark**,
and saw the **stone removed** from the tomb.
So she **ran** and went to Simon **Peter**
and to the **other** disciple whom **Jesus loved**, and told them,
"They have **taken** the **Lord** from the **tomb**,
and **we** don't **know where** they **put** him."
So Peter and the other disciple went **out** and came to the tomb.
They **both ran**, but the **other** disciple ran **faster** than **Peter**
and arrived at the tomb first;
he **bent** down and **saw** the **burial cloths** there, but did **not**
go in.
When Simon Peter arrived after him,
he went **into** the tomb and saw the burial cloths there,
and the cloth that had **covered** his **head**,
not with the burial cloths but rolled up in a **separate** place.
Then the **other** disciple also went **in**,
the one who had arrived at the tomb first,
and he **saw** and **believed**.
For they did not **yet understand** the Scripture
that he had to **rise** from the dead.

Emphasize "first"; it represents a theological statement of a new beginning, a new creation.

This Gospel account doesn't say why Mary came to the tomb. Use the tone of a news report and build speed as the story unfolds.

Mary is frantic with concern as she reports to Peter and the Beloved Disciple.

Mary speaks in the plural. "We" is not explained.

Pause after "saw," and emphasize "believed."

GOSPEL In today's Gospel from John, we find an account of the discovery of the empty tomb. In contrast to the resurrection accounts in other Gospels, where Mary Magdalene and her companions, in the dawning light, encounter an open tomb and there are one or two angelic beings, John has only Mary arrive in the dark to find an open tomb. Not only is it dark, but she remains in the dark as she runs to report this to Simon Peter and the Beloved Disciple. Typical of John's Gospel, the word "dark" refers to more than physical darkness. It is a word that implies a lack of faith. This is clear in Mary's message: she says nothing of resurrection; rather, she is still looking for a dead body and presumes that it has been stolen.

In that same darkness, Peter and the Beloved Disciple run to the tomb. When the Beloved Disciple sees the evidence that death has been overcome—the empty tomb and the empty burial cloths, and especially when he enters after Peter—the darkness begins to lift. This is in no way a repetition of the raising of Lazarus (John 11:1–44), for whom the stone had to be removed, and who emerged from the tomb bound with burial cloths, and with a cloth over his head. The open tomb, the discarded cloth, and the placement of the head covering in separate place all indicate that death has been overcome in an unprecedented manner. Because of these things, we hear that the Beloved Disciple *believed*. Nevertheless, we should note that the darkness does not lift for either Peter or the Beloved Disciple completely. The account of their visit to the empty tomb remarks that they don't fully understand the *necessity* of Jesus' resurrection. Clearly,

Emphasize "first," a theological statement that represents a new beginning, a new creation.

Emmaus = eh-MAY-uhs

The question was so shocking, it needs their full attention. They stop in their tracks. What tone would you use to answer him? Incredulity? Sadness?

Cleopus = KLEE-oh-puhs

At Jesus' continued questioning, they respond. "They" indicates both are responding. Alternate the tone from the one who states the facts to the one who interprets the facts.

Nazarene = NAZ-uh-reen

Their hopes were dashed. Read this with regret.

They hear valuable testimony and then have additional witnesses of the empty tomb, yet they still do not believe.

AFTERNOON GOSPEL　Luke 24:13–35

A reading from the holy Gospel according to Luke

That very day, the **first day** of the week,
　　two of Jesus' **disciples** were **going**
　　to a **village** seven miles from **Jerusalem** called **Emmaus,**
　　and they were conversing about all the things that
　　　　had occurred.
And it happened that while they were conversing and debating,
　　Jesus himself **drew near** and walked **with** them,
　　but their eyes were **prevented** from **recognizing** him.
He asked them,
　　"What are you **discussing** as you walk along?"
They **stopped**, looking **downcast**.
One of them, named **Cleopas**, said to him in reply,
　　"Are you the **only** visitor to Jerusalem
　　who does not **know** of the things
　　that have taken place there in these **days**?"
And he replied to them, "What sort of **things**?"
They said to him,
　　"The things that happened to Jesus the **Nazarene,**
　　who was a **prophet** mighty in **deed** and **word**
　　before **God** and all the **people,**
　　how our chief **priests** and **rulers** both **handed** him **over**
　　to a sentence of **death** and **crucified** him.
But we were **hoping** that he would be the **one** to **redeem Israel;**
　　and besides all this,
　　it is now the **third day** since this took place.
Some **women** from our group, however, have **astounded** us:
　　they were at the tomb early in the morning
　　and did not **find** his **body;**
　　they came back and reported
　　that they had indeed seen a vision of **angels**
　　who announced that he was **alive. »**

there is so much to absorb that this revelation will take time to accept.

| AFTERNOON GOSPEL | The Lukan Gospel assigned

to celebrations of Mass in the afternoon on Easter day, Jesus' appearance to the disciples on the road to Emmaus, has powerful resonances with other appearances of the risen Lord (especially to Mary Magdalene in John 20). These stories demonstrate that recognizing the resurrected Lord was neither simple nor immediate even for those who knew him well. Not only does this say something about resurrection, it also offers insight into the process necessary to accept the very idea of resurrection. As such, it models the process of moving from dejection and incomprehension to faith.

What is particularly striking in this story is the way the two disciples tell and *interpret* what they are telling. Moving away from Jerusalem and fully immersed in their sadness, the two disciples are joined by an unknown stranger to whom they accurately describe the key elements of the Jesus story that will later form the heart of their preaching. But at this point they conclude that it must not have been true, because Jesus was killed. Nevertheless, they puzzle over the contradictory evidence received only that morning from some women of their group: the empty tomb and the proclamation of the angels, all of which was confirmed by other members of the group.

Still blinded to the identity of their unknown companion, they listen as he tells the story again and explains that Moses and the prophets all revealed that the Christ would suffer but also enter into glory. The need for this explanation recalls

Then some of those with us **went** to the **tomb**
and found things **just as** the women had described,
but him they did not **see**."
And he said to them, "**Oh**, how **foolish** you are!
How **slow** of **heart** to **believe** all that the **prophets** spoke!
Was it not **necessary** that the **Christ** should **suffer** these things
and **enter** into his **glory**?"
Then beginning with **Moses** and all the prophets,
he **interpreted** to them what **referred** to **him**
in all the **Scriptures**.
As they approached the **village** to which they were **going**,
he gave the impression that he was going on farther.
But they **urged** him, "**Stay** with us,
for it is nearly evening and the day is almost **over**."
So he went **in** to stay with them.
And it happened that, while he was with them at **table**,
he **took bread**, said the **blessing**,
broke it, and **gave** it to them.
With that their eyes were **opened** and they **recognized** him,
but he **vanished** from their **sight**.
Then they said to each other,
"Were not our **hearts burning** within us
while he **spoke** to us on the way and **opened** the **Scriptures**
to us?"
So they set **out** at **once** and **returned** to Jerusalem
where they found gathered **together**
the eleven and those with them who were saying,
"The **Lord** has truly **been raised** and has **appeared** to **Simon**!"
Then the two **recounted**
what had taken **place** on the **way**
and how he was made **known** to them in the **breaking**
of **bread**.

Jesus is frustrated yet also compassionate; he will go on to explain what they do not yet understand. Read strongly.

Change to a narrator voice.

Read the eucharistic language slowly.

The energy of the narrative intensifies.

Imagine the pace at which they walked away from Jerusalem at the beginning of the reading and the pace at which they returned here.

the Gospel from this morning, in which we heard that even as they left the empty tomb, Peter and the Beloved Disciple still did not understand the Scriptures that predicted the *necessity* of Jesus' suffering. In spite of this explanation, however, the two disciples still cannot "see" the identity of their strange travel companion.

It is only when they invite him to dine with them, and when he takes the bread, blessing it, breaking it, and giving it to them (as he had done the night of the Last Supper), that they come to sight. Jesus' sudden disappearance prompts them to reflect on what was happening in their hearts as they heard Jesus' words, which in turn propels them to return to Jerusalem and share with the other disciples the news of their encounter. This Easter Gospel gives witness to the power of the Eucharistic liturgy, the Mass, as it demonstrates how the Lord is truly present in the story told and the bread broken and shared. S.L.

SECOND SUNDAY OF EASTER (SUNDAY OF DIVINE MERCY)

LECTIONARY #44

READING I Acts of the Apostles 4:32–35

A reading from the Acts of the Apostles

The early community is striving to live in a way that reflects Jesus' teachings.

The apostles, witnesses to the resurrected Jesus, are emboldened by the Holy Spirit to give testimony. So too is your proclamation of the Word of God!

The community of **believers** was of **one heart** and **mind**,
　　and **no** one **claimed** that any of his **possessions** was his own,
　　but they had everything in **common**.
With great **power** the apostles bore **witness**
　　to the **resurrection** of the Lord **Jesus**,
　　and great **favor** was accorded them **all**.
There was no **needy** person among them,
　　for those who **owned** property or houses would **sell** them,
　　bring the **proceeds** of the sale,
　　and put them at the feet of the **apostles**,
　　and they were **distributed** to each according to **need**.

For meditation and context:

RESPONSORIAL PSALM Psalm 118:2–4, 13–15, 22–24 (1)

R. Give thanks to the Lord, for he is good; his love is everlasting.
or
R. Alleluia.

Let the house of Israel say,
　"His mercy endures forever."
Let the house of Aaron say,
　"His mercy endures forever."
Let those who fear the LORD say,
　"His mercy endures forever."

I was hard pressed and was falling,
　but the LORD helped me.
My strength and my courage is the LORD,
　and he has been my savior.
The joyful shout of victory

in the tents of the just.

The stone which the builders rejected
　has become the cornerstone.
By the LORD has this been done;
　it is wonderful in our eyes.
This is the day the LORD has made;
　let us be glad and rejoice in it.

READING I | Throughout the seven weeks of Easter on Sundays and weekdays, we hear from the Acts of the Apostles about the struggles and triumphs of the first followers of Christ. These readings describe how the apostles understood the significance of Jesus' life, death, and resurrection to transform the way they interacted with the world. Thus, over forty-nine days, we hear the central message of the Good News and how the early Church attempted to live it out from a post-resurrection view.

Today's account is the third description in Acts of the early community. The first description (1:13-14) described the community as the apostles with a few women and members of Jesus' family, all dedicated to prayer, while the second (2:42–47) expanded the ranks to those who adhered to the apostles' teaching, lived a communal life, and celebrated the liturgical life with prayers and breaking bread together. Following an account of the community at prayer and how it was filled with the Holy Spirit (4:24–31), today's reading introduces new elements to the communal life. Drawing

on the Greek theme of friendship—*philia*, often described as a oneness of "heart and mind"—the description of the early community details the consequences of this oneness; it renounces individual possessiveness and provides for each person according to need. This is not secular altruism, however. Rather, it flows from the power of the aforementioned apostolic witness, and it leads to an outpouring of divine grace.

READING II 1 John 5:1–6

A reading from the first Letter of Saint John

"Beloved" is a term of endearment. Read it as such.

Beloved:
Everyone who **believes** that **Jesus** is the **Christ** is **begotten**
    by **God**,
    and everyone who **loves** the **Father**
    loves **also** the one begotten by him.
In this way we know that we love the children of God
    when we love God and **obey** his **commandments**.
For the **love** of **God** is **this**,
    that we keep his commandments.
And his commandments are not **burdensome**,
    for **whoever** is begotten by God **conquers** the **world**.
And the victory that conquers the world is our **faith**.
Who indeed is the victor over the world
    but the one who **believes** that Jesus is the Son of **God**?

This reading mentions all three persons of the Trinity. Clearly distinguish which member of the Trinity is being spoken about.

This is the one who came **through water** and **blood**,
    Jesus Christ,
    not by water **alone**, but by water and **blood**.
The **Spirit** is the one that **testifies**,
    and the Spirit is **truth**.

GOSPEL John 20:19–31

A reading from the holy Gospel according to John

Help the assembly hear the different voices—narrator, Jesus, the disciples, and Thomas.

Narrate Jesus' appearance with some surprise; the doors were locked. Then, use a tender tone as Jesus speaks peace to them. Repeat the tone each time Jesus says this.

On the evening of that **first** day of the week,
    when the **doors** were **locked**, where the **disciples** were,
    for **fear** of the **Jews**,
    Jesus came and stood in their midst
    and said to them, "**Peace** be with you."
When he had said this, he **showed** them his **hands** and his **side**. ❯❯

READING II Similar to the prominent role of Acts of the Apostles in the Easter season, 1 John also is heard frequently throughout Easter Time. It provides the second reading for the second to seventh Sundays of Easter, Year B.

1 John echoes themes from John's Gospel in order to guide and help a struggling community. It is the first of three letters sent by "the Elder" of a Johannine community to other members of the same community. As with other early Christian communities, the Johannine community struggled with disunity among its members

regarding practice and core beliefs. Three issues divided the Elder's more orthodox position from a group of secessionists (people who left the community). The secessionists denied that the historical person of Jesus was the Christ who came down from heaven. There was division over following the commandments, specifically the command to love as articulated in John's Gospel. Finally, the Elder complained that the secessionists failed to love their brothers and sisters. In 1 John, the Elder advises the community about how to relate to the secessionists.

Under the rubric of love, today's reading touches upon all three issues by connecting belief in Christ with living out God's love. The foundation of the Elder's argument is that whoever "believes that Jesus is the Christ is begotten by God." This identity and belief leads to love for the Father and the Son, which is demonstrated by the believer's adherence to God's commands. These commands are not a burden; rather, they help believers overcome the world. Finally, the Elder recalls the Gospel witness that from Jesus' pierced side flowed water and blood (John 19:34), with

Joy can be reflected in your words and on the countenance of your face.

The disciples **rejoiced** when they saw the Lord.
Jesus said to them again, "**Peace** be with you.
As the **Father** has **sent** me, so I send **you**."
And when he had said this, he **breathed** on them and said
     to them,
    "**Receive** the Holy **Spirit**.
Whose **sins** you **forgive** are forgiven **them**,
     and whose sins you **retain are** retained."

Elongate "breathed." Let the word become similar to what it represents.

Pause before the next scene.

Thomas, called **Didymus**, one of the **Twelve**,
     was not **with** them when Jesus **came**.
So the other disciples said to him, "**We** have **seen** the Lord."
But he said to them,
    "Unless **I** see the **mark** of the nails in his **hands**
     and put my finger into the nailmarks
     and put my hand into his **side**, I will **not** believe."

Use energy for the disciples' report to Thomas. Despite their testimony, he does not believe. Pause again for the scene change before Jesus' next appearance the next week.

Now a week **later** his disciples were **again** inside
     and **Thomas** was **with** them.
Jesus **came**, although the doors were locked,
     and stood in their midst and said, "**Peace** be with you."
Then he said to Thomas, "Put your **finger here** and see
        my **hands**,
     and bring your hand and put it into my **side**,
     and do not be unbelieving, but **believe**."
Thomas answered and said to him, "**My Lord** and my **God!**"
Jesus said to him, "Have you come to believe because you have
        seen me?
Blessed are those who have **not** seen and **have** believed."

Use energy for the disciples' report to Thomas. Despite their testimony, he does not believe. Pause again for the scene change before Jesus' next appearance the next week.

Now Jesus did many other **signs** in the presence of his disciples
     that are not **written** in this book.
But these are written that you may come to believe
     that Jesus is the **Christ**, the Son of **God**,
     and that through this belief you may have **life** in his name.

---

the Spirit testifying to the truth of these things, echoing the witness of the Beloved Disciple in John 19:35.

GOSPEL If Easter's Gospel traced the movement from unbelief to belief for the Beloved Disciple and Peter, today's account presents a two-act sequel to the unresolved story of the disciples. The first act begins on Easter evening, implying that the events of the morning, Mary Magdalene's testimony, as well as Peter and the Beloved Disciple's experience at the tomb, have had minimal effect.

Ignoring the laws of physics, Jesus appears to ten fearful disciples (minus Thomas), bestows peace, and shows them his hands and side, leading them to rejoice and come to faith. For them to bear witness, however, they need the gift of the Spirit. Thus, Jesus breathes on them and bestows the Spirit. Still part of John's *hour* (of the cross and resurrection), the Spirit-filled disciples can now be for the world as Jesus was for them. This Spirit-filled presence, which is essentially God's work, grounds their ministry to bring God's forgiveness for sins and to uncover all sinfulness.

The second act begins on that same evening when Thomas arrives. Having missed it all, Thomas is in the darkness of unfaith, which he will lay aside only if Jesus meets his conditions. About a week later, Jesus reappears, willing to meet the conditions, but also commanding Thomas to move past them. Thomas forgets his conditions and states his faith: "My Lord and my God!" Jesus' final comments describe two eras of faith: the journey to faith in the physical presence of the risen Jesus and the journey of faith in the absence of Jesus, which applies to all future generations. S.L.

THIRD SUNDAY OF EASTER

LECTIONARY #47

READING I   Acts of the Apostles 3:13–15, 17–19

A reading from the Acts of the Apostles

Emphasize "God" the first time and subdue when repeated. The new information will stand out.

Don't proclaim too harshly; it is not intended to be anti-Semitic. Jesus is the fulfillment of God's promises and offers forgiveness to all who turn to him.

Pause after "witnesses."

Jesus' death and resurrection have salvific consequences and fulfill God's plan from the beginning—let your tone match this Good News.

Peter said to the **people**:
"The **God** of **Abraham**,
   the God of **Isaac**, and the God of Jacob,
   the God of our **fathers**, has **glorified** his servant **Jesus**,
   whom you handed over and **denied** in **Pilate's** presence
   when he had decided to **release** him.
You **denied** the **Holy** and **Righteous** One
   and asked that a **murderer** be released to you.
The author of **life** you put to **death**,
   but God **raised** him from the dead; of this we are **witnesses**.
Now I know, **brothers**,
   that you **acted** out of **ignorance**, just as your **leaders** did;
   but God has thus brought to **fulfillment**
   what he had announced **beforehand**
   through the mouth of all the **prophets**,
   that his Christ would **suffer**.
Repent, therefore, and be **converted**, that your **sins** may be
   wiped away."

READING I   More than other New Testament writers, Luke used speeches to convey early Christianity's *kerygma* (the salvific message of Christ). Throughout the Acts of the Apostles, this powerful message was communicated by Peter, Stephen, and Paul who, through their speeches, interpreted the events of Jesus' life, death, and resurrection and showed how these events fulfilled God's salvific plan.

Today's first reading forms part of Peter's third speech, in which he addresses his fellow Jews who marvel over the healing of a lame man, and who presume that Peter and John have done this by their own power. In response, Peter clarifies that the one at work is none other than the God of their ancestors. Peter then emphasizes his central message: Jesus, whom they and their leaders had handed over and had sentenced to death is, in fact, "the Holy and Righteous One," "the author of life," and the one whom God raised up and glorified. Strikingly, Peter notes that their action came from their ignorance. This fact justifies the current offer of salvation to them (compare this with Jesus' words on the cross in Luke 23:34). To emphasize the enormity of this message, the offer, and their divine origin, Peter declares that these events are the fulfillment of what God had proclaimed through the prophets.

The speech indicates that Jesus' prophetic power is now found in the words and deeds of the apostles. Addressed to the Jewish people of the era, the call to "be converted" offers the promise of being cleansed of their sins, but also the warning that their fate rests in responding to the apostles' prophetic words. It is, of course, as timely a call now as it was then.

For meditation and context:

RESPONSORIAL PSALM Psalm 4:2, 4, 7–8, 9 (7a)

R. Lord, let your face shine on us.
or
R. Alleluia.

When I call, answer me, O my just God,
  you who relieve me when I am in distress;
  have pity on me, and hear my prayer!

Know that the Lord does wonders for his
  faithful one;
  the Lord will hear me when I call
  upon him.

O Lord, let the light of your countenance
  shine upon us!
  You put gladness into my heart.

As soon as I lie down, I fall peacefully asleep,
  for you alone, O Lord,
  bring security to my dwelling.

---

expiation = ehk-spee-AY-shuhn =
making amends

A comforting reading; redemption is
available to the whole world.

"Knowing" is not just about information,
but also about a relationship and action.

READING II   1 John 2:1–5a

A reading from the first Letter of Saint John

My **children**, I am writing this to you
  so that you may not commit **sin**.
But if anyone **does** sin, we have an **Advocate** with the Father,
  Jesus **Christ** the **righteous** one.
He is **expiation** for **our** sins,
  and not for our sins only but for those of the whole **world**.
The way we may be **sure** that we **know** him
  is to keep his **commandments**.
Those who say, "**I know** him," but do not keep
    his commandments
  are **liars**, and the **truth** is not **in** them.
But whoever **keeps** his word,
  the **love** of God is truly **perfected** in him.

Use a steady, even tone to set the context of
the story. As you prepare, read Luke 24:13–
35 to remind yourself of the Emmaus story.

GOSPEL   Luke 24:35–48

A reading from the holy Gospel according to Luke

The two **disciples recounted** what had taken place on the **way**,
  and how **Jesus** was made **known** to them
  in the breaking of **bread**.

READING II 1 John was the first and most important of three letters written by the Elder to his Johannine community to warn them about a group of unorthodox (professing incorrect beliefs) secessionists who question that Jesus is both human and divine, and whose ideas about keeping the commandments and living love are inadequate.

The first half of today's reading emphasizes the reality of sin, even among community members. The author encourages them to avoid sin but then assures them that Jesus Christ, who is the righteous one, is their advocate if they do, in fact, sin. Not only is he their advocate, but he is also the "expiation" for their sins and those of the whole world. It should be noted that referring to Jesus as the advocate, a term we often think of as applying only to the Spirit, is not unusual in the Johannine tradition.

The second half of the reading emphasizes the idea that we come to know God by following his commandments. References to "him" and "his" in this part of the reading are referring to God, and not to Jesus, who was the subject of the first half of the reading. Ultimately, the Elder stresses (in contrast to the ideas of the secessionists) that there is an unbreakable bond between knowing God and keeping the commandments. Indeed, to keep the commandments is the perfection of love.

GOSPEL Understandably, the Gospels of the first weeks of Easter Time focus on the appearances of the resurrected Lord to his disciples. When it comes to such appearances, however, the four Gospels reflect two different traditions: Matthew and Mark point to his appearance to the disciples in Galilee; Luke

Use a gentle tone for Jesus' dialogue. He doesn't want to scare them.

While they were still **speaking** about this,
   he stood in their midst and said to them,
   "**Peace** be with you."
But they were **startled** and **terrified**
   and thought that they were seeing a **ghost**.
Then he said to them, "Why are you **troubled**?
And why do **questions** arise in your **hearts**?
Look at my **hands** and my **feet**, that it is **I** myself.

Still reassuring them, he invites the disciples to confirm for themselves his corporal nature.

Touch me and see, because a ghost does not have **flesh** and **bones**
   as you can see I have."
And as he said this,
   he **showed** them his hands and his feet.
While they were still **incredulous** for **joy** and were amazed,
   he asked them, "Have you anything here to **eat**?"
They gave him a piece of baked **fish**;
   he took it and **ate** it in **front** of them.

Jesus teaches them about himself to help them understand. They (and we) are not left alone to figure everything out by themselves.

He said to them,
   "These are my **words** that I spoke to you while I was still
      with you,
   that everything **written** about me in the law of **Moses**
   and in the **prophets** and **psalms** must be **fulfilled**."
Then **he** opened their **minds** to **understand** the **Scriptures**.
And he said to them,
   "Thus it is written that the **Christ** would **suffer**
   and **rise** from the **dead** on the third **day**
   and that **repentance**, for the forgiveness of **sins**,
   would be **preached** in his name
   to **all** the **nations**, beginning from Jerusalem.

Deliver looking at the assembly. *We* are now the witnesses of "these things."

You are witnesses of these things."

and John focus on appearances in Jerusalem. Today's Gospel is Luke's version of Jesus' appearance to the disciples in Jerusalem.

When the two disciples who encountered Jesus on their way to Emmaus return to Jerusalem to share the Good News with the other disciples, Jesus appears in their midst. In spite of his greeting of peace, they experience mixed emotions: terror, fright, doubt, and disbelief, but also joy and amazement. Elements such as touching his wounds and eating fish may appear to emphasize the physical, but Luke is carefully differentiating Jesus' new mode of

existence from his former presence. This is resurrection, not resuscitation!

Even more important in Luke's account is how Jesus serves as the model interpreter. Just as he "opened their minds to understand the Scriptures," showing them that all that had happened is, in fact, a fulfillment of the law and the prophets, the disciples, who "are witnesses of these things," will be charged to do the same. Their message will be grounded in his message and his manner of interpretation. They too are to open the minds of future believers so that all nations will know that Jesus'

suffering and resurrection lead to repentance and forgiveness of sins. This reading, coming toward the very end of the Gospel of Luke, describes and justifies the mission the disciples will undertake in Luke's second volume, the Acts of the Apostles. S.L.

FOURTH SUNDAY OF EASTER

LECTIONARY #50

READING I Acts of the Apostles 4:8–12

A reading from the Acts of the Apostles

As you prepare, read Acts 4:1–7 to put this reading in context.

Nazorean = naz-uh-REE-uhn

Use confidence. We don't need to look for other options.

Peter, filled with the Holy **Spirit**, said:
    "**Leaders** of the people and **elders**:
    If we are being **examined** today
    about a good **deed** done to a **cripple**,
    namely, by what **means** he was **saved**,
    then all of you and all the people of **Israel** should **know**
    that it **was** in the name of Jesus **Christ** the **Nazorean**
    whom you **crucified**, whom **God raised** from the **dead**;
    in his name this man stands before you **healed**.
He is the *stone **rejected** by you, the **builders**,*
    *which has become the **cornerstone**.*
There is no **salvation** through anyone **else**,
    nor is there any other name under heaven
    given to the human race by which we are to be **saved**."

READING I Today's first reading, from Luke's Acts of the Apostles, features yet another speech from Peter. This fourth speech is the first directed at the leaders and elders of the people, and it addresses the same event as last week: the healing of a man crippled from birth. Whereas last week's speech to the people was explanatory and received a sympathetic hearing (Acts 4:4), this speech is confrontational, and the disciples are met with skeptical questioning.

Having been taken into custody while they were speaking to the people, Peter and John are questioned by the Sanhedrin regarding their authority and their use of the name through which the crippled man was healed. Peter boldly clarifies that it is the power of Jesus Christ, and God who raised him, that saved the crippled man. The use of "saved" echoes Acts 2:21, where Peter declared that "everyone shall be saved who calls on the name of the Lord." As in earlier speeches, Peter states that they (the people and the leaders) had crucified Jesus. But now he goes further. By citing and slightly altering Psalm 118:22 (Psalm 117:22 in the Septuagint), Peter replaces the image of the stone rejected (*apedokimasan* in Greek) with the stone scorned (*exouthenētheis* in Greek), repeating the attitude of the leaders toward Jesus in Luke 18:9. The entire scene echoes Luke 21:13–15, where Jesus predicted that the disciples' opponents would be unable to refute them. In the end, Peter courageously proclaims that salvation can be found only in this name, and none other. Strikingly, the leaders and elders receive no call for conversion at the end.

For meditation and context:

RESPONSORIAL PSALM Psalm 118:1, 8–9, 21–23, 26, 28, 29 (22)

R. The stone rejected by the builders has become the cornerstone.
or
R. Alleluia.

Give thanks to the Lord, for he is good,
    for his mercy endures forever.
It is better to take refuge in the Lord
    than to trust in man.
It is better to take refuge in the Lord
    than to trust in princes.

I will give thanks to you, for you have
    answered me
    and have been my savior.
The stone which the builders rejected
    has become the cornerstone.

By the Lord has this been done;
    it is wonderful in our eyes.

Blessed is he who comes in the name
    of the Lord;
    we bless you from the house of the Lord.
I will give thanks to you, for you have
    answered me
    and have been my savior.
Give thanks to the Lord, for he is good;
    for his kindness endures forever.

READING II 1 John 3:1–2

A reading from the first Letter of Saint John

Beloved:
See what **love** the **Father** has **bestowed** on us
    that we may be called the children of **God**.
Yet so we **are**.
The reason the world does not **know us**
    is that it did not know **him**.
Beloved, we are God's **children** now;
    what we shall be has not yet been revealed.
We do know that when it is revealed we shall be like him,
    for we shall see him as he is.

"Beloved" and "children" can be read tenderly.

Take time to read and understand this passage so your proclamation communicates the way God's infinite love is shared with us.

READING II Today's short reading from 1 John takes a break from the Elder's arguments against the secessionists to reflect upon and ponder what the community has already received: the status of being children of God. In the Johannine tradition, the term "Son" is reserved for Jesus' relationship with the Father, while the term "child" identifies the believer's relationship with God. This identify is affirmed in both verses of this reading.

The reading appears simple and clear, but it is made complex by the unclear use of "he" and "him." Do the pronouns refer to

God the Father or to the Son? Grammatically, there is no way to be absolutely sure, but there is a logical flow to the passage when the pronouns are understood as referring to God the Father. Using God the Father as the lens helps to clarify the texts: the world did not know *God*. And, when "what we shall be" has been revealed, then we will be like *God*, for we shall see *God* as *God* is. In the end, the Elder provides his readers, and us, with confidence in what we already are (children of God), and a revelation of what we will be (like God as God is), thereby

reinforcing the already joyous message of this season.

GOSPEL If the second reading provides a very affirmative understanding of the believer as a child of God, today's Gospel offers an equally affirming image of Jesus as the Good Shepherd, all with a uniquely Johannine flair. Drawn from a section of John's Gospel that describes the end of Jesus' ministry in Jerusalem (John 7:1—10:21) and set during the feast of Booths, John employs the image of the shepherd. Throughout the Old

Visio divina uses art to help us enter more deeply into prayer. As you prepare, pray with a picture of Jesus carrying a lamb.

Jesus is teaching us who he is. Use a fatherly tone. He gently instructs us.

GOSPEL　John 10:11–18

A reading from the holy Gospel according to John

Jesus said:
　"I am the **good shepherd**.
A good shepherd lays down his **life** for the sheep.
A **hired** man, who is **not** a shepherd
　　and whose sheep are not his **own**,
　　sees a **wolf** coming and leaves the sheep and runs **away**,
　　and the wolf **catches** and **scatters** them.
This is because he works for **pay** and has no **concern** for
　　　the sheep.
I am the good shepherd,
　　and I **know mine** and mine know **me**,
　　just as the Father knows me and I know the Father;
　　and I will lay down my **life** for the sheep.
I have **other** sheep that do **not** belong to this fold.
These also I **must** lead, and they will hear my **voice**,
　　and there will be **one flock**, one **shepherd**.
This is **why** the Father loves me,
　　because I lay **down** my **life** in order to take it **up** again.
No one takes it from me, but I lay it down on my own.
I have **power** to lay it down, and power to take it up **again**.
This **command** I have received from my **Father**."

Emphasize the divine name, "I am." We are intimately connected to Jesus the shepherd, and he is intimately connected to God.

Contrast "down" and "up." Jesus is in uncontested control. "No one" can challenge him.

Testament, God was identified as the shepherd of Israel, in contrast to Israel's unfaithful and corrupt leaders (bad shepherds). This led to the expectation of an ideal Davidic shepherd-messiah.

John goes beyond that tradition, however. In contrast to the messianic shepherd, Jesus, the Good Shepherd, will lay down his life for the sheep. This idea of self-giving has no parallel in Israel's messianic texts. This self-gift is contrasted with the actions of the hired worker, who abandons the sheep. Repeating again *"I AM* the good shepherd," Jesus employs one of

seven "I AM" sayings unique to John. They are reminiscent of God's self-identification to Moses—I AM (Exodus 3:13–14)—and clearly connect Jesus' identity to that of God. This connection is deepened through Jesus' use of the word "know." He *knows* his sheep and they *know* him, just as the Father *knows* him and he *knows* the Father. In essence, Jesus surpasses the Davidic shepherd-messiah tradition, and his role as shepherd flows from his oneness with the Father.

Jesus' relationship with the Father, through which he reveals the Father's love, also amazingly and creatively enlarges the

sheepfold. Whereas Israel is the original sheepfold, Jesus' self-gift includes Israel and extends to the world beyond, with the result that he will bring others into the fold to create one flock that has one shepherd. The idea of enlarging is an apt one, for today's readings expand our understanding of God, Jesus, ourselves, our world, and the scope of God's love. S.L.

FIFTH SUNDAY OF EASTER

LECTIONARY #53

READING I Acts of the Apostles 9:26–31

A reading from the Acts of the Apostles

When **Saul** arrived in Jerusalem he **tried** to **join** the **disciples**,
but they were all **afraid** of him,
not **believing** that he was a disciple.
Then **Barnabas** took **charge** of him and **brought** him
to the **apostles**,
and he **reported** to them how **he** had seen the **Lord**,
and that he had spoken to him,
and how in **Damascus** he had spoken out **boldly** in the name
of **Jesus**.
He moved about **freely** with **them** in **Jerusalem**,
and spoke out boldly in the name of the Lord.
He also spoke and **debated** with the **Hellenists**,
but they tried to **kill** him.
And when the **brothers learned** of this,
they took him down to **Caesarea**
and sent him on his **way** to **Tarsus**.

The **church** throughout **all** Judea, Galilee, and Samaria was
at peace.
It was being built **up** and walked in the **fear** of the **Lord**,
and with the consolation of the Holy **Spirit** it grew
in **numbers**.

Read Acts 9:1–25 to set the stage for today's reading and to help you understand why the disciples were afraid of Saul. Saul's name eventually changes to Paul, yet in today's reading it is still Saul.

Barnabas = BAHR-nuh-buhs

Notice the frequent use of masculine pronouns. Practice so that it is clear who they refer to.

Damascus = duh-MAS-kuhs

Caesarea = sez-uh-REE-uh or see-zuh-REE-uh
Tarsus = TAHR-suhs
Pause for the scene change.
Judea = joo-DEE-uh or joo-DAY-uh
Galilee = GAL-ih-lee
Samaria = suh-MAYR-ee-uh

READING I Whereas the previous weeks have focused on understanding the Easter events, and developing ideas about Jesus, the Father, and the early community, the readings this week issue a call to action: to be fruitful. It is not enough to know about the mystery. Rather, one must abide in it and bear fruit.

The reading from the Acts of the Apostles introduces Saul/Paul, who first appeared at the stoning of Stephen (Acts 7:58–8:3). Consistent with earlier descriptions of the Jerusalem community, today's reading describes the community's hesi-

tant acceptance of its former foe in a short passage marked by consistency and paradox. In terms of consistency, Paul's credentials are similar to those of the other apostles: he has seen the Lord, he speaks boldly in the name, and, like the master, he faces opposition even to death. Still, it is paradox that dominates. Saul the persecutor is now Paul the reluctantly accepted apostle. Saul, earlier in league with the Hellenists, is now opposed to and by the Hellenists. Saul, who approved of the Hellenists' killing of Stephen is now the object of their hatred. These paradoxes

fulfill what had been predicted when Saul first saw the Lord: that he would suffer for the name (Acts 9:16).

Finally, Paul's rescue by the believers and his addition to the ranks of the apostles —all linked to geographical expansion and community growth—remind us of the community's active mission. Encouraged by the Holy Spirit, Paul and the apostles boldly preach in the name of Jesus, thus bearing fruit in preparation for the next phase: the outreach to the Gentiles.

167

For meditation and context:

RESPONSORIAL PSALM   Psalm 22:26–27, 28, 30, 31–32 (26a)

R. I will praise you, Lord, in the assembly of your people.
or
R. Alleluia.

I will fulfill my vows before those who fear
   the LORD.
   The lowly shall eat their fill;
they who seek the LORD shall praise him:
   "May your hearts live forever!"

All the ends of the earth
   shall remember and turn to the LORD;
all the families of the nations
   shall bow down before him.

To him alone shall bow down
   all who sleep in the earth;
before him shall bend
   all who go down into the dust.

And to him my soul shall live;
   my descendants shall serve him.
Let the coming generation be told of
   the LORD
   that they may proclaim to a people
      yet to be born
   the justice he has shown.

READING II   1 John 3:18–24

A reading from the first Letter of Saint John

"Children" is a term of endearment.

Children, let us **love** not in **word** or **speech**
   but in **deed** and **truth**.

Note all three members in the Trinity in this reading.

Now this is how we shall **know** that we **belong** to the **truth**
   and reassure our hearts before him
   in whatever our **hearts** condemn,
   for **God** is **greater** than our hearts and knows **everything**.

Deliver confidently, looking at the assembly. We have no need to hide something in our hearts; God is already there. Slight pause after "everything."

Beloved, if our hearts do not **condemn** us,
   we have **confidence** in God
   and **receive** from him whatever we **ask**,
   because we keep his **commandments** and do what
      pleases him.
And his commandment is this:
   we should **believe** in the name of his Son, Jesus **Christ**,
   and **love** one another just as he commanded us.
Those who keep his commandments **remain** in him,
      and he in them,
   and the way we **know** that he remains in us
   is from the **Spirit** he gave us.

READING II | Today's reading from 1 John is best understood as a summation of the Elder's understanding of the Gospel's primary message: "we should love one another" (1 John 3:11). The Elder first reflects on love by condemning the bad behavior of the secessionists (1 John 3:13–17). Then comes today's positive reflection on how love functions in the community's life.

   At its most basic, the Elder emphasizes that their love must be actively expressed in deeds, and not just in words. Mindful that some in the community may

have sinned and repented ("whatever our hearts condemn") and others see themselves as sinless ("our hearts do not condemn us"), the Elder encourages *everyone* to embrace a life of fruitful love expressed in deeds, assured that "God is greater than our hearts." All of this is possible because believers have "confidence in God" and because they keep God's commandments and act in accord with his will.

   Finally, in order to establish this fruitful love, the Elder relates it to the Johannine commandment. If the synoptic Gospels have a two-fold commandment to love God

and neighbor, John's commandment starts with belief in Jesus (for example, 1 John 4:9–10) and moves to the command to imitate it: love one another as Jesus loved us (for example, John 13:34–35). Thus, it is Jesus who perfectly embodies fruitful love.

GOSPEL | Last week we heard Jesus identify himself as the Good Shepherd. It said much about who he is. This week we hear Jesus identify himself differently: I AM the vine. This statement tells us much about him, but it also tells us

There is a lot of repetition in this metaphorical reading. Emphasize the new thoughts as they are presented. Consider recording yourself practicing and listen to the playback.

Pruning is good for plants (and for us). If you aren't familiar with these gardening images, find a video online of someone pruning a plant to give you some context for what Jesus is talking about.

GOSPEL   John 15:1–8

A reading from the holy Gospel according to John

Jesus said to his **disciples**:
   "**1 am** the **true vine**, and my Father is the vine **grower**.
He **takes** away every **branch** in me that does not bear **fruit**,
   and every one that **does** he **prunes** so that it bears **more** fruit.
You are already pruned because of the **word** that I spoke to you.
Remain in me, as I remain in **you**.
Just as a branch cannot bear fruit on its **own**
   unless it remains on the **vine**,
   so neither can **you** unless you remain in **me**.
I am the vine, you are the branches.
Whoever remains in me and I in him will bear **much** fruit,
   because **without** me you can do **nothing**.
Anyone who does **not** remain in me
   will be thrown **out** like a branch and **wither**;
   people will gather them and throw them into a **fire**
   and they will be **burned**.
If you remain in me and my **words** remain in you,
   ask for whatever you want and it will be **done** for you.
By this is my Father **glorified**,
   that you bear much fruit and become my **disciples**."

God is faithful to those who remain in him. This is a comforting image in contrast to what happens to those who do not remain in God.

about ourselves and the fruitfulness expected from us.

Five chapters of John's Gospel are dedicated to Jesus' final comments to his disciples at the Last Supper (John 13—17), and they include two of the seven I AM sayings (John 14:6; 15:1). These powerful sayings reveal to us more of who Jesus is and identify him with the Father by affirming his divinity and their oneness. Running throughout today's Gospel reading is the verb "to remain" (*menein* in Greek), which will be a key to understanding discipleship and its fruitfulness.

The Gospel presents three related images: Jesus as the vine, the believers as the branches, and the Father as the vine grower. Each party has a role to play. Jesus, the vine, is the source for life and fruitfulness. The Father, the vine grower, cares for the well-being and fruitfulness of the vine through a process of pruning. Finally, the believers, the branches, are to remain with Jesus, the vine. This instruction to remain consists of much more than passive existence. The believer is to dwell in a process of pruning by the word that promotes growth and removes whatever is unfruitful.

In the end, believers are to bear much fruit as the branches of the vine. This image invites the believer into a relationship with the Father and Son that is expressed in self-giving love. Since the fruit of the branches is love, we can see how this Gospel joins the other readings for today in emphasizing our vocation to bear a fruitful love. S.L.

SIXTH SUNDAY OF EASTER

LECTIONARY #56

READING I   Acts of the Apostles 10:25–26, 34–35, 44–48

A reading from the Acts of the Apostles

When **Peter** entered, **Cornelius met** him
    and, falling at his feet, paid him **homage**.
Peter, however, raised him **up**, saying,
    "Get up. I myself am also a human **being**."

Then Peter proceeded to **speak** and said,
    "In truth, I see that **God** shows no **partiality**.
Rather, in **every nation** whoever **fears** him and acts **uprightly**
    is **acceptable** to him."

While Peter was still speaking these things,
    the Holy **Spirit** fell **upon all** who were **listening** to the **word**.
The circumcised **believers** who had accompanied Peter
    were **astounded** that the **gift** of the Holy Spirit
    should have been **poured** out on the **Gentiles** also,
    for they could hear them speaking in **tongues** and
        glorifying God.
Then Peter responded,
    "Can anyone withhold the **water** for **baptizing** these **people**,
    who have received the Holy Spirit even as we have?"
He **ordered** them to be baptized in the name of Jesus Christ.

Cornelius = kohr-NEEL-yuhs

Peter's humility corrects the misplaced homage. Deliver with a smile; Peter is not angry.

Emphasize "every." This is an important message. God's saving love is not limited.

God works through your ministry to transform those who hear the word. Let the assembly hear the astonishment in your voice. Can we identify a group that would "astonish" us because they too are included in God's embrace?

READING I Today's readings focus on the consequences of the message of God's love for the growing community, as well as the expectations regarding attitudes and actions on the part of the individual believers.

The first reading, drawn from the story of the Gentile Cornelius, harks back to Easter Sunday, when Peter's message to Cornelius' household was our first reading. If Peter's basic message of who Jesus was and what he did (Acts 10:37–43) was key for understanding the events of Easter, today's first reading is key for understanding an earth-shaking development in the community's notion of who is invited into the life of Christ and community of believers. Three scenes from Cornelius' story focus our attention on the message's transforming effect.

In the first scene, Peter enters Cornelius' home. Although not included in this reading, we know both Cornelius and Peter had earlier experienced impelling visions. Peter's vision had led him to understand that what God created must not be declared unclean. Cornelius, described as someone with devout faith in God, has a vision directing him to send for Peter, leading Cornelius and his family to welcome him. In the second scene, Peter moves beyond the insights from his earlier vision to now understand that being acceptable to God is not based on nationality or observing specific customs, but rather on fear of the Lord and righteousness of life. In the third scene, which follows Peter's preaching (skipped today, but delivered in the first reading on Easter Sunday), the message's consequences are revealed: the Holy Spirit descends on Cornelius and his household, leading them to speak in tongues and glorify God. Meanwhile, Peter's circumcised

For meditation and context:

RESPONSORIAL PSALM   Psalm 98:1, 2–3, 3–4 (2b)

R. The Lord has revealed to the nations his saving power.
or
R. Alleluia.

Sing to the LORD a new song,
   for he has done wondrous deeds;
his right hand has won victory for him,
   his holy arm.

The LORD has made his salvation known:
   in the sight of the nations he has revealed
     his justice.

He has remembered his kindness and his
   faithfulness
   toward the house of Israel.

All the ends of the earth have seen
   the salvation by our God.
Sing joyfully to the LORD, all you lands;
   break into song; sing praise.

READING II   1 John 4:7–10

A reading from the first Letter of Saint John

Beloved, let us **love** one **another**,
   because love is of **God**;
   everyone who loves is **begotten** by God and **knows** God.
Whoever is **without** love does **not** know God, for God **is** love.
In this way the love of God was **revealed** to us:
   God **sent** his **only Son** into the **world**
   so that we might have **life** through him.
In this is love:
   not that we **have loved** God, but that **he** loved **us**
   and sent his Son as **expiation** for our **sins**.

Beloved = bee-LUHV-uhd or buh-LUHV-uhd
Address the assembly with the tenderness "Beloved" implies.

"Knowing" is not about knowledge, it is about relationship and encountering God.

Contemplate the enormity of what God did for us. Practice giving this verse the reverence it deserves.

---

companions are amazed that God also chooses the Gentiles. All that remains is for the community to ratify God's decision ritually through the sacrament of baptism.

READING II   If the first reading reveals the unbounded nature of God's love to all people, the second reading develops the community's inner commandment to love. Last week, 1 John emphasized the fruitfulness of love and we connected it to the Gospel's image of the fruitful branch. This week, 1 John focuses on love's origins, how it is revealed, and what it consists of.

And again, it provides insight into the Gospel.

The reading begins with the affirmation that love (like truth, light, and life) is from God. This is followed by the observation that people come to know God and belong to him through love; without love, we can't know or belong to God. The second half of the reading turns to the way the love of God reveals God's self to us and provides a way for us to know and belong to him. To understand better the core of this message, the phrase "In this way the love of God was revealed *to us*" can be read as

"In this way the love of God was revealed *in us*." This more nuanced reading emphasizes the divine indwelling, "that we might have life through him." Our understanding of God's love in us is further developed when the author points to the incarnation; although divine love has always existed, it was *revealed* at the incarnation of the Son. Finally, the text concludes that true love is God's self-giving love for us, which is expressed in God's sending of the Son, who is "expiation for our sins." These emphases will be repeated in today's Gospel.

The back-and-forth comparisons will be more easily grasped if you practice the parallel expressions. "Love" is repeated nine times. Three relationships are established: God's love for Jesus, Jesus' love for us, our love for others.

Jesus showed us, not just told us about, his love. It is God's love that makes it possible for us to receive and to give love in return.

Look out at the assembly, as you are able, throughout these last lines to help the congregation hear Jesus speaking these words to us today.

GOSPEL   John 15:9–17

A reading from the holy Gospel according to John

Jesus said to his **disciples**:
"As the Father **loves me**, so I also love **you**.
Remain in my love.
If **you** keep **my commandments**, you will **remain** in my love,
   just as I have kept my Father's commandments
   and remain in **his** love.

"I have told you this so that **my joy** may be **in** you
   and **your** joy might be **complete**.
This is **my commandment**: love one **another** as I love you.
No one has **greater** love than this,
   to lay down one's **life** for one's **friends**.
You are my friends if you do what I command you.
I no longer call you **slaves**,
   because a slave does not **know** what his master is **doing**.
I have called you friends,
   because I have told you **everything** I have **heard** from
     my Father.
It was not you who chose **me**, but **I** who chose **you**
   and appointed you to **go** and bear **fruit** that will **remain**,
   so that whatever you **ask** the Father in my name he may
     give you.
This I command you: **love** one another."

GOSPEL | Whereas today's first reading recalls a remarkable transformation in the early community to be open to all who love God and the second reading develops the central role that love plays as the community's identity, the Gospel combines both ideas. As it is tied to the image of the vine and branches from last Sunday, today's Gospel encourages the transformed community, rooted in love, to remain in Jesus' love and be fruitful in that love.

Offering his relationship with the Father as the model, Jesus encourages his disciples to remain in his love and to keep his commandments so as to know the fullness of joy. This opening reflection then leads Jesus to his central argument that is book-ended between verses 12 and 17, which are repetitions of Jesus' command to "love one another as I love you." Surrounded by this command to love, Jesus describes the way the disciples have been transformed by divine love. First, they have acquired a new status: they are no longer "slaves," but rather friends. This new status enables them to love as Jesus loved, by washing one another's feet and even by laying down their lives for others (see John 13:1–38). Second, this transformed status comes not from an act of will or effort on their part but rather because Jesus loved and chose them first. Thus, invited into partnership with the Father and the Son, they are to live out this love and keep returning to the source of that love for all their needs. Reflecting also on the insights of today's second reading, we can say, then, that through our actions as Christians, God's love is revealed *in us*. S.L.

THE ASCENSION OF THE LORD

LECTIONARY #58

READING I   Acts of the Apostles 1:1–11

A reading from the Acts of the Apostles

In the first book, **Theophilus**,
   I dealt with **all** that **Jesus did** and **taught**
   until the day he was **taken** up,
   after giving **instructions** through the Holy **Spirit**
   to the **apostles** whom he had chosen.
He presented himself **alive** to them
   by many **proofs** after he had **suffered**,
   appearing to them during forty **days**
   and **speaking** about the kingdom of **God**.
While meeting with them,
   he enjoined them **not** to **depart** from Jerusalem,
   but to wait for "the promise of the **Father**
   about which you have heard me speak;
   for **John baptized** with **water**,
   but in a few days you will be baptized with the Holy **Spirit**."

When they had gathered together they **asked** him,
   "Lord, are you at this **time** going to **restore**
   the **kingdom** to Israel?" »

Theophilus = thee-AWF-uh-luhs = Lover of God

"I" refers to Luke.

Decide where you are going to take a breath or pause in these long verses. Mark your workbook as you practice.

Increase your volume slightly to make it clear that Jesus is being quoted.

The disciples still think Jesus is going to restore an earthly kingdom. Use an upward inflection for their inquiry. Jesus, forever the teacher, again explains himself. Use a patient tone.

There are options for today's readings. Contact your parish staff to learn which readings will be used.

READING I   As the Easter season winds down, the Gospel tradition faces a logistics problem: how to move from the appearances of the resurrected Lord to a Spirit-charged community engaged in mission. In order for a transformation to take place, two events must first occur: Jesus' appearances must cease, and the community must be animated by the Spirit.

The four Gospels deal with these two events in different ways. Regarding Jesus' departure, there are striking variations. In Matthew, Jesus commissions his disciples on a mountain in Galilee, and promises to stay with them (Matthew 28:16–20). Mark's original Gospel text has no account, although Jesus' ascension is found in Mark's "Longer Ending" (Mark 16:1–20). John's Gospel records a final encounter in Galilee, but it refers to Jesus' return, not his departure (John 21:1–25). Finally, Luke concludes his Gospel (Luke 24:50–53) and begins the Acts of the Apostles (Acts 1:6–12) with two

slightly different descriptions of Jesus' ascension from the outskirts of Jerusalem. Regarding the Spirit, Jesus imparts the Spirit at the Last Supper in John; Matthew and Mark imply that Jesus' "Spirit" remains active among the eleven; and Luke provides the dramatic Pentecost descent of the Spirit in the Acts of the Apostles. It is the first event, Jesus' definitive departure and its consequences, that we celebrate today.

   Our first reading includes Luke's second account (Acts of the Apostles) of Jesus' ascension. The ascension account forms the last part of the book's formal introduc-

The baton for being a witness to Christ is passed to us. The Holy Spirit supports our efforts to proclaim God's Word.

This is amazing. Proclaim it with wonder.

Consider what type of tone you want to give the angels' question as they call the stunned apostles back to the present.

He answered them, "It is not for you to **know** the **times** or seasons
that the Father has established by his own **authority**.
But you will receive **power** when the Holy Spirit comes
upon you,
and you will be my **witnesses** in Jerusalem,
throughout Judea and Samaria,
and to the ends of the **earth**."
When he had said this, as they were **looking** on,
he was lifted **up**, and a cloud **took** him from their **sight**.
While they were looking **intently** at the sky as he was going,
suddenly two **men** dressed in white **garments** stood
beside them.
They said, "Men of **Galilee**,
why are you standing there looking at the **sky**?
This **Jesus** who has been taken up from you into heaven
will **return** in the same way as you have seen him going
into heaven."

For meditation and context:

RESPONSORIAL PSALM   Psalm 47:2–3, 6–7, 8–9 (6)

R. God mounts his throne to shouts of joy: a blare of trumpets for the Lord.
or
R. Alleluia.

All you peoples, clap your hands,
    shout to God with cries of gladness.
For the LORD, the Most High, the awesome,
    is the great king over all the earth.

God mounts his throne amid shouts of joy;
    the LORD, amid trumpet blasts.

Sing praise to God, sing praise;
    sing praise to our king, sing praise.

For king of all the earth is God;
    sing hymns of praise.
God reigns over the nations,
    God sits upon his holy throne.

tion known as the prologue. When we consider the prologue, as found in today's first reading, we find that Luke summarizes his Gospel with amazing brevity, referring to Jesus' teaching, ministerial activity, election of his apostles, suffering, resurrection appearances, eating with the disciples (proof that he is alive), and his instruction that they remain in Jerusalem to await baptism with the Holy Spirit.

Following that whirlwind summary, the narrative slows as a process of transformation and empowerment unfolds. Responding to their question about the res-

toration of the "kingdom to Israel," Jesus gradually moves them from knowledge to mission. Knowledge, we read, is not given to them, and belongs only to the Father. Instead, they will be empowered by the Spirit to give witness to Jesus in Jerusalem and beyond, "to the ends of the earth."

Jesus' response to their question, and the promised gift of the Holy Spirit, leads to a second question. As Jesus departs from the disciples' sight, two men in white appear. This recalls for us other appearances of heavenly beings, at the empty tomb (Luke 24:4–9) and at the transfigura-

tion (Luke 9:28–36). These men now question the disciples: "Why are you standing there looking at the sky?" Here, we can draw parallels between Jesus' ascension and his transfiguration. The two men in white at the transfiguration were Moses and Elijah, who, according to tradition, were taken up into heaven to make way for their successors (Joshua and Elisha, respectively). Similarly, now that Jesus has ascended, his successors (the disciples) can be empowered though the Spirit for their mission to go out into the world to be Jesus' witnesses.

Ephesians = ee-FEE-zhuhnz

Paul's prayer for his readers is that they understand better the mysteries that have already happened. We are intimately connected with Christ's paschal mystery through our baptism.

Emphasize "above" and it will be applied to each of the following realms of power. Nothing is beyond Christ's rule.

The metaphor of the body is used. Christ is the head of the Church.

READING II   Ephesians 1:17–23

A reading from the Letter of Saint Paul to the Ephesians

Brothers and **sisters**:
May the **God** of our Lord Jeus **Christ**, the Father of **glory**,
    give you a Spirit of **wisdom** and **revelation**
    resulting in **knowledge** of him.
May the eyes of your **hearts** be **enlightened**,
    that you may **know** what is the **hope** that belongs to his **call**,
    what are the riches of **glory**
    in his **inheritance** among the **holy** ones,
    and what is the surpassing greatness of his **power**
    for us who **believe**,
    in accord with the exercise of his great might,
    which he **worked** in **Christ**,
    raising him from the dead
    and **seating** him at his right hand in the **heavens**,
    far **above** every **principality**, **authority**, **power**, and **dominion**,
    and every name that is **named**
    not only in this **age** but also in the one to **come**.
And he put all things beneath his feet
    and gave him as **head** over all things to the church,
    which is his **body**,
    the fullness of the one who **fills** all things in every **way**.

Or:

READING II   **Ephesians 1**. The Letter to the Ephesians is often identified as one of Paul's prison letters, although some scholars place the letter after Paul's death. All agree that Ephesians is a letter influenced by liturgical forms such as hymns and poems. Addressed to a predominantly Gentile-Christian community (or communities) that was (were) convinced that the world was dominated by the forces of evil, Ephesians proposes that protection is found in strengthening one's identity in Christ who is the head of the universal church. Ephesians presents Paul's

insights as a new generation of Christians is emerging.

Following the Greco-Roman pattern of Pauline letters, this reading comprises all but the first two verses of the thanksgiving section of Paul's letter. The section begins, naturally, with Paul giving thanks (1:15–16 —not in the lectionary reading), and quickly moves to its next task (as found in our reading for today): developing the theme of the universal church, with an exalted Christ as its head.

In contrast to the distrust of visionary experiences in some churches (for exam-

ple, Colossians 2:8–23), Ephesians shows great interest in visionary wisdom and revelation, and Paul prays that "the eyes of your hearts be enlightened." Paul defines the believer as one filled with knowledge of the triune God and as having enlightenment regarding the hope and inheritance that belong to the holy ones. It is through Christ's exaltation that the final triumph of believers is made possible.

The description of Christ seated at God's right hand in heaven and prevailing over other powers is similar to apocalyptic writings (for example, Daniel 7), where

Ephesians = ee-FEE-zhuhnz

The overarching theme of the reading is unity.

Diversity is a blessing; it need not threaten our unity. Unity is more easily achieved when we practice these virtues.

Emphasize "he gave." Our vocations are not of our own volition, but are given to us as gifts from God. Read the listing slowly and with equal emphasis on each item so the assembly can consider the calling in their own lives; one vocation is not better than another if it is given to us by God.

READING II   Ephesians 4:1–13

A reading from the Letter of Saint Paul to the Ephesians

[**Brothers** and **sisters**,
I, a **prisoner** for the **Lord**,
    urge you to live in a manner **worthy** of the **call** you
        have received,
    with all **humility** and **gentleness**, with **patience**,
    bearing with one another through **love**,
    striving to preserve the **unity** of the **spirit**
    through the bond of **peace**:
    one body and one **Spirit**,
    as you were also called to the one **hope** of your call;
    one Lord, one **faith**, one **baptism**;
    one **God** and **Father** of **all**,
    who is **over** all and **through** all and **in** all.

But **grace** was given to **each** of us
    according to the measure of Christ's **gift**.]
Therefore, it says:
    He ascended on high and took prisoners **captive**;
    he gave **gifts** *to men.*
What does "he **ascended**" mean except that he also **descended**
    into the lower regions of the **earth**?
The one who descended is also the **one** who ascended
    far above all the **heavens**,
    that he might **fill** all things.

[And he **gave** some as **apostles**, others as **prophets**,
    others as **evangelists**, others as **pastors** and **teachers**,
    to equip the holy ones for the work of **ministry**,
    for **building** up the body of **Christ**,
    until we all attain to the **unity** of faith
    and knowledge of the Son of God, to mature **manhood**,
    to the extent of the full **stature** of Christ.]

[Shorter: Ephesians 4:1–7, 11–13 (see brackets)]

---

heavenly exaltation celebrates a triumph over historical authorities and powers. Because the Ephesians are convinced that the "ruler of the power of the air" (Ephesians 2:2) dominates the present age, the letter's potent counterimage is their God, who seats Christ in heaven as head of the Church and who "put all things beneath his feet." The reading concludes by declaring that Christ was given as head over the Church, thus tying the Ephesians' understanding of the Church to their understanding of the exalted Christ. This image of Christ's heavenly role enriches our reflection of his ascension and the work he continues to do after he ascended to the Father.

Ephesians 4. An essential part of any Pauline letter is its ethical exhortation, also known as a paraenesis. Often, after an initial exhortation, Paul followed with the development of a major theme. In this reading, after exhorting the believers to "live in a manner worthy of the call you have received," Paul turns to a his major theme: unity.

Beginning with a poetically worded confessional statement, Paul uses the word "one" to demonstrate the community's oneness of body, Spirit, hope, Lord, faith, baptism, and God and Father. His inclusion of baptism in this description of oneness illustrates its role as a liturgical source of their unity. Paul concludes the poetic description of baptismal unity with the observation that it results in the gift of grace, given to each in a certain measure.

This idea of grace, given "according to the measure of Christ's gift," is developed in two ways, again to emphasize unity. First, Paul quotes from Ps 68:19, a text often interpreted by rabbis as referring to Moses' ascent to Mount Sinai to retrieve the law and then his descent to deliver it to the

GOSPEL   Mark 16:15–20

A reading from the holy Gospel according to Mark

Jesus said to his disciples:
  "**Go** into the **whole world**
  and **proclaim** the gospel to **every creature**.
Whoever believes and is **baptized** will be **saved;**
  whoever does **not** believe will be **condemned**.
These **signs** will **accompany** those who believe:
  in my name **they will** drive out **demons**,
  they will speak new **languages**.
They will pick up **serpents** with their **hands**,
  and if they drink any **deadly** thing, it will not **harm** them.
They will lay hands on the **sick**, and they will **recover**."

So then the Lord Jesus, after he **spoke** to them,
  was **taken** up into **heaven**
  and took his seat at the right hand of **God**.
But they went forth and **preached** everywhere,
  while the Lord **worked with** them
  and **confirmed** the word through accompanying **signs**.

Jesus is giving a commission. Convey confidence in your tone.

Emphasize "whole." God's message is not exclusive.

Emphasize "they will" in this first instance. Let each new sign be the item that is heard in the following lines.

Jesus was raised by another power. Emphasize "taken."

---

people. However, Paul alters the text slightly and uses it to refer to Christ the giver of the gift, that is, grace. In his ascending and descending, Christ is more powerful than any other force (he "took prisoners captive"). Thus, there is but one giver of the gift— Christ. Second, Paul identifies the large number of ministries in the Church that have but one purpose: "building up the body of Christ." Once again, as in the first reading, Christ's exaltation in his ascension emphasizes a Church on mission, united in Christ.

GOSPEL   Mark's original Gospel text presents a conundrum in that there is no resurrection appearance. It appears that the Gospel originally ended with an empty tomb and a message directed to his disciples to meet him in Galilee (Mark 16:1–8). In the second century, this troubling ending was supplemented with several possible endings. Today's Gospel is taken from the second half of one possible ending (the "Longer Ending") and is part of a collection of appearance accounts drawn from other Gospels. In it, there are two distinct parts presented. The first is the commission of the eleven to "proclaim the gospel to every creature." Not only does the text identify the signs that will identify believers (exorcisms, speaking new languages, handling serpents, surviving poison, and healing the sick), but it also specifies that faith and baptism are necessary for salvation. The second is a fulfillment of the commission, in a Luke-inspired version of Christ's ascension and enthronement. We hear that the disciples did go forth, preaching and working signs. Our mission is a continuation of Christ's mission, which he left us to take up after his ascension. S.L.

SEVENTH SUNDAY OF EASTER

LECTIONARY #60

READING I   Acts of the Apostles 1:15–17, 20a, 20c–26

A reading from the Acts of the Apostles

Peter stood up in the midst of the **brothers**
—there was a group of about one hundred and twenty persons
in the one place—.
He said, "My brothers,
the **Scripture** had to be **fulfilled**
which the Holy **Spirit** spoke beforehand
through the mouth of **David**, concerning **Judas**,
who was the **guide** for those who arrested **Jesus**.
He was **numbered** among us
and was allotted a **share** in this **ministry**.

"For it is written in the Book of **Psalms**:
*May **another** take his **office**.*

"Therefore, it is necessary that one of the men
who accompanied us the **whole** time
the Lord **Jesus** came and went among us,
beginning from the baptism of John
until the day on which he was taken up from us,
become with **us** a **witness** to his resurrection."
So **they proposed** two, Judas called **Barsabbas**,
who was also known as Justus, and **Matthias**.

Use a tone of regret. One of their own betrayed them; this is a painful memory.

Project so that it is clear that Peter is quoting the Psalms.

Barsabbas = bahr-SAH-buhs or bahr-SAB-uhs. Practice this name so it is not confused with Barabbas.
Justus = JUS-tuhs
Matthias = muh-THĪ-uhs

READING I   Today's first reading provides us with some context for next week's celebration of Pentecost. Following Luke's description of the ascension in the Acts of the Apostles, we hear that the eleven returned to Jerusalem to await the coming of the Spirit. That first community included the eleven, the women who followed Jesus, and members of Jesus' family, including Mary, his mother, as well as many other followers. As they waited, they prayed. During this period of waiting, Peter delivered his first speech, portions of

which form our first reading. But why is Peter speaking?

Before the Spirit can come upon Jesus' disciples, there is one matter that must be resolved: the number of the twelve apostles (currently at eleven) must be restored to twelve. The number has symbolic meaning, as the twelve, in Luke's understanding, are related to a restoration of the people of Israel (twelve patriarchs and twelve tribes). Such an understanding is confirmed in the opening address, when Peter addresses those gathered for this event as "brothers" (*andres adelphoi* in Greek), twice emphasiz-

ing their maleness, and when he cites Psalm 109:8 (Psalm 108:8 in the Septuagint) to justify replacing Judas, who had abandoned his apostolic office. This restoration will occur only one time. As we later read in Acts of the Apostles, when future members of the twelve die, they are not replaced. Clearly, the need to establish a full contingent of witnesses stretching from Jesus' baptism to his ascension is necessary so that the Spirit can descend upon them. Having prayed and placed the final decision in God's hands (by drawing lots), the community is poised to receive the Spirit.

Pause after "prayed." Shortly, they will cast lots. This is not gambling but an ancient practice of determining God's will.

Then they **prayed**,
"You, **Lord**, who **know** the hearts of **all**,
show which **one** of these two you have **chosen**
to take the place in this apostolic ministry
from which Judas turned **away** to go to his **own** place."
Then they gave **lots** to them, and the lot fell upon **Matthias**,
and he was counted with the eleven **apostles**.

For meditation and context:

RESPONSORIAL PSALM   Psalm 103:1–2, 11–12, 19–20 (19a)

R. The Lord has set his throne in heaven.
or
R. Alleluia.

Bless the LORD, O my soul;
  and all my being, bless his holy name.
Bless the LORD, O my soul,
  and forget not all his benefits.

For as the heavens are high above the earth,
  so surpassing is his kindness toward
    those who fear him.

As far as the east is from the west,
  so far has he put our transgressions
    from us.

The LORD has established his throne
  in heaven,
  and his kingdom rules over all.
Bless the LORD, all you his angels,
  you mighty in strength, who do
    his bidding.

READING II   1 John 4:11–16

A reading from the first Letter of Saint John

Pause after the tender salutation.

Pay attention to the verbs.

Beloved, if **God** so **loved** us,
  we also must love one **another**.
No one has ever **seen** God.
Yet, if we love one another, God **remains** in us,
  and his love is brought to **perfection** in us.

This is how we **know** that we remain in him and he in us,
  that he has **given** us of his **Spirit**.
Moreover, we have **seen** and **testify**
  that the **Father sent** his **Son** as **savior** of the **world**. ≫

READING II In contrast to the first reading, which provides a suitable liturgical context for next week's celebration of Pentecost, the second reading continues our steady progression through 1 John that commenced at the beginning of the season. The fifth and sixth Sundays of Easter took up dimensions of the author's exhortation: "we should love one another" (1 John 3:11). Today's reading builds on and refines those earlier discussions.

The Elder begins by grounding the believer's love in the source of all love: God.

God loved us, so we must love. God's love is an incarnational and active love. In other words, God remains in the one who loves, and thereby brings love to perfection. This is an amazing reciprocity: love is brought to perfection in the disciple when the disciple is brought to perfection in love. For the Elder's community, this is actualized in the commandment to love one another. Placing all in God's hands, the Elder notes that the criterion for God's "remaining" is found, not in the Spirit, but in the fact that *God has given* his Spirit.

The members of the Elder's community came to know this because they correctly understood the relationship between the Father and the Son. In contrast to the secessionists, the Elder's community acknowledges that Jesus, the one who came in the flesh, is the one whom God sent as savior of the world and is the Son of God. This, the community has come to realize, is the embodiment of God's love for them, and it leads them to know it, to believe it, and to remain in God who remains in them.

Love is active. Passivity has no place in the Christian life.

Whoever **acknowledges** that **Jesus** is the Son of **God**,
 God **remains** in him and **he** in God.
We have come to **know** and to **believe** in the love God has for us.

God is **love**, and whoever remains in love
 remains in **God** and God in him.

GOSPEL   John 17:11b–19

A reading from the holy Gospel according to John

The reading has some repetition. Emphasize the new idea and subdue ideas when repeated.

Lifting up his eyes to heaven, **Jesus prayed**, saying:
 "Holy **Father**, **keep** them in your **name** that you have
  given me,
 so that they may be **one** just as **we** are one.
When I was with them I **protected** them in your name that you
  gave me,
 and I guarded them, and **none** of them was **lost**
 except the son of **destruction**,
 in order that the **Scripture** might be **fulfilled**.
But now I am **coming** to **you**.
I **speak** this in the world
 so that they may **share** my **joy** completely.

Let Christ's joy reflect on your face and then go to a neutral expression when recounting the world's hostile response. Be sure to enunciate so that "word" and "world" are heard distinctly.

I gave them **your word**, and the **world hated** them,
 because they do not **belong** to the world
 any more than **I** belong to the world.
I do not ask that you **take** them out of the world
 but that you **keep** them from the **evil** one.
They do not belong to the world
 any more than I belong to the world.
Consecrate them in the **truth**. Your **word** is truth.
As you sent **me** into the **world**,
 so I sent **them** into the world.

There is a reciprocal nature to the dialogue; the Father sends the Son and the Sons sends us.

And I consecrate **myself** for them,
 so that **they** also may be consecrated in truth."

GOSPEL   The Last Supper of John's Gospel is unique among the four Gospels. It begins with a meal where no one eats, but where feet are washed (including those of Judas!), and it runs for five chapters of lengthy discourses. It concludes with chapter 17 (the High Priestly Prayer) where Jesus prays for his own glorification (17:1–8), for his vulnerable disciples (17:9–19), and for future believers who will come to faith through his disciples (17:20–26).

Today's passage comes from the second part of that prayer: for his disciples. The prayer's appeal to inclusion and exclusion is grounded in Jesus' knowledge that all that he is and does flows from his union with the Father. Thus, he prays that just as he kept his disciples safe in "your [God the Father's] name," Jesus and the Father's divine union will lead the Father to keep them safe (inclusion). This is necessary since Jesus' word, which his disciples have embraced, has led the world to hate them, and Satan to seek their destruction (exclu-

sion). Although Jesus does not ask for his faithful ones to be removed from the world, he does ask, because of the faith of the disciples, that the Father to identify the disciples with his design (the truth), and thereby to make them holy (to consecrate them). Thus, just as Jesus was sent and consecrated, so too will his followers be consecrated and sent, and become one with Father and Son. S.L.

PENTECOST SUNDAY: VIGIL

LECTIONARY #62

READING I Genesis 11:1–9

A reading from the Book of Genesis

The whole world **spoke** the same **language**, using the same words.
While the people were **migrating** in the east,
    they came upon a valley in the land of **Shinar** and settled there.
They said to one another,
    "**Come**, let us mold **bricks** and harden them with **fire**."
They used bricks for **stone**, and **bitumen** for mortar.
Then they said, "**Come**, let us **build** ourselves a **city**
    and a **tower** with its top in the **sky**,
    and so make a **name** for ourselves;
    otherwise we shall be **scattered** all over the **earth**."

The LORD **came** down to **see** the city and the **tower**
    that the people had **built**.
Then the LORD said: "If now, while they are **one** people,
    all speaking the same **language**,
    they have **started** to do this,
    nothing will later stop them from doing **whatever** they
        presume to do.
Let us then **go** down there and **confuse** their language,
    so that one will not **understand** what another **says**."
Thus the LORD **scattered** them from there all over the **earth**,
    and they **stopped building** the city. »

Genesis = JEN-uh-sihs

Distinguish between the different voices: the people, the narrator, and the Lord.

Shinar = SHĪ-nahr or SHEE-nahr

Give some energy to the first plan and increase it for the second.
bitumen = bih-TYOO-m*n or bih-TOO-m*n or bĭt-TYOO-m*n = asphalt

Pause slightly after "earth" for a scene change.

Change tone to report what the narrative signifies.

There are options for today's readings. Contact your parish staff to learn which readings will be used.

READING I Easter Time ends with the celebration of Pentecost, the Masses of the vigil (today) and the day (tomorrow). Originally a Jewish pilgrimage festival, Pentecost (the Feast of Weeks [*Shavuot*]) comes seven weeks after the cutting of the first sheaf of grain at Passover. Its Greek name, *Pentecost*, signifies fifty days between the two festivals. For Christians, this is the day when the Holy Spirit descended upon the apostles, resulting in Peter's preaching to Jews from all the nations. The readings for the vigil deepen our understanding of this pivotal event in salvation history.

Coming at the end of the first section of Genesis, which describes the world's primeval history (Genesis 1—11), the story of the tower of Babel acts as a kind of "anti-Pentecost" account, giving us context for why the descent of the Spirit in Acts 2:1–13 was so significant. The primeval history explains why salvation history was needed in the first place. Beginning with stories of creation and structured by frequent genealogies, Genesis 1—11 tells the sad story of alienation between God and humans and between humans and creation, and it identifies a progressive corruption. Even the flood (Genesis 6:5—9:28) was unable to purify the earth of sin and restore original innocence. The progressive corruption reaches a high point in today's first reading about the tower.

After Noah and his sons are told to "fill the earth" (Genesis 9:1), the tower story recalls how the whole world, speaking one

Babel = BAY-b*l or BAB-*l

That is why it was **called Babel**,
     because there the **LORD confused** the speech of all the world.
It was from that place that he scattered them all over the earth.

For meditation and context:

RESPONSORIAL PSALM   Psalm 33:10–11, 12–13, 14–15

R. Blessed the people the Lord has chosen to be his own.

The LORD brings to nought the plans
     of nations;
   he foils the designs of peoples.
But the plan of the LORD stands forever;
   the design of his heart, through all
     generations.

Blessed the nation whose God is the LORD,
   the people he has chosen for his own
     inheritance.

From heaven the LORD looks down;
   he sees all mankind.

From his fixed throne he beholds
   all who dwell on the earth,
He who fashioned the heart of each,
   he who knows all their works.

READING II   Exodus 19:3–8a, 16–20b

Exodus = EK-suh-duhs

This is a theophany, the appearance of God to a human.

A reading from the Book of Exodus

Moses went **up** the mountain to **God**.
Then the LORD **called** to him and said,
   "Thus shall you say to the house of **Jacob**;
   tell the Israelites:
   You have **seen** for yourselves how I **treated** the **Egyptians**
   and how I **bore** you up on eagle **wings**
   and **brought** you **here** to myself.
Therefore, **if** you hearken to my **voice** and keep my **covenant**,
   you shall be my **special** possession,
   dearer to me than all **other** people,
   though **all** the earth **is** mine.
You shall be to me a **Kingdom** of **priests**, a holy **nation**.
That is what you must **tell** the **Israelites**."
So Moses went and **summoned** the **elders** of the people.

Read with authority.

language, determines to settle in one place, build a city, and make a name for itself, so that the peoples would not "be scattered all over the earth." Several terms in today's reading can be understood to allude to other terms that might be more familiar to us. For example, "Shinar" refers to Babylonia in Mesopotamia, "Babel" refers to Babylon, and the "tower" could refer to a ziggurat (an ancient temple tower that proclaimed Mesopotamian greatness and served as a "mountain" where earth and heaven meet). The corruption that shapes this reading is the people's striking deter-

mination to ignore God's will, echoing the Fall in Genesis 3, where the quest for knowledge and equality with God led to profound alienation. The story is divided between humanity's actions (verses 1–4) and God's deliberation and action to avert the progression of corruption (verses 5–9). The people's prideful defiance against God results in the "confusion" (*bll* in Hebrew) of language, playing on the name of the place, "Babel" (*bbl* in Hebrew). In the end, language confusion results in the very scattering they had tried to avoid. While Genesis goes on to describe God's next strategy for

salvation history, blessing the nations through one family (the family of Abraham), Christians celebrate the reversal of Babel in the descent of the Spirit at Pentecost, where Jews of many nations and languages understood the language of the one Spirit.

READING II The Exodus account of Israel at Sinai, with its covenant and commandments, is often seen as the highpoint of the first five books of the Bible. Everything from Genesis and the first part of Exodus leads to this event. Having been set apart as God's chosen

When he set **before** them
all that the **LORD** had **ordered** him to tell them,
the people all answered together,
"Everything the LORD has said, we **will** do."

On the morning of the **third** day
there were peals of **thunder** and **lightning**,
and a heavy **cloud** over the mountain,
and a very loud **trumpet** blast,
so that all the people in the camp **trembled**.
But **Moses** led the people out of the camp to meet **God**,
and they **stationed** themselves at the foot of the mountain.
Mount **Sinai** was all wrapped in **smoke**,
for the LORD came **down** upon it in **fire**.
The smoke **rose** from it as though from a furnace,
and the whole mountain trembled **violently**.
The **trumpet** blast grew **louder** and louder, while Moses
was **speaking**,
and God **answering** him with thunder.

When the LORD came **down** to the top of Mount Sinai,
he **summoned** Moses to the **top** of the mountain.

The people respond with eagerness.

Let the drama of nature be heard. Increase your energy as you proceed.

Moses is chosen to have a momentous encounter with God.

For meditation and context:

RESPONSORIAL PSALM   Daniel 3:52, 53, 54, 55, 56

R. Glory and praise for ever!

Blessed are you, O Lord, the God of
our fathers,
praiseworthy and exalted above
all forever;
and blessed is your holy and glorious name,
praiseworthy and exalted above
all for all ages.

Blessed are you in the temple of your
holy glory,
praiseworthy and glorious above
all forever.

Or:

Blessed are you on the throne of
your Kingdom,
praiseworthy and exalted above
all forever.

Blessed are you who look into the depths
from your throne upon the cherubim,
praiseworthy and exalted above
all forever.

Blessed are you in the firmament of heaven,
praiseworthy and glorious forever.

---

people and given instructions, Leviticus, Numbers, and Deuteronomy move Israel toward its national destiny. But it is the forming of Israel's national and spiritual identity through a covenant with God that is the core of the Exodus account.

While covenants of different types often defined relationships in the ancient world, the covenant between God and the house of Jacob (Israel) in Exodus is without precedent. It begins with an encounter between Moses (Israel's spokesman) and God on the mountain (the place of divine encounter). God proposes a new relation-

ship by describing what has been done for the Israelites. Moving from a historical account ("how I treated the Egyptians") to a powerful poetic image ("I bore you up on eagle wings"), God justifies the new relationship. If Israel agrees to its terms, the Israelites will be God's "special possession" (*sĕgullâh* in Hebrew), becoming "a Kingdom of priests, a holy nation." Embedded in these terms are important insights: Israel will be a sovereign nation, not under the control of other nations, and Israel will have a special role as a holy and priestly nation among other nations, distinctive and set

apart. Without having yet heard the details, the people unanimously agree to the proposal. The account then moves ahead to the third day, when Moses ascends the mountain to receive the commandments (the details of the covenant). The Lord's descent is accompanied by atmospheric upheavals in nature that often describe God's arrival: thunder, lightning, fire, smoke, and clouds, as well as trumpet blasts, marking a royal arrival. The parallels with the arrival of the Spirit on Pentecost are unmistakable: the establishment of a new relationship is marked by the atmospheric

For meditation and context:

RESPONSORIAL PSALM Psalm 19:8, 9, 10, 11

R. Lord, you have the words of everlasting life.

The law of the LORD is perfect,
   refreshing the soul;
The decree of the LORD is trustworthy,
   giving wisdom to the simple.

The precepts of the LORD are right,
   rejoicing the heart;
The command of the LORD is clear,
   enlightening the eye.

The fear of the LORD is pure,
   enduring forever;
The ordinances of the LORD are true,
   all of them just.

They are more precious than gold,
   than a heap of purest gold;
Sweeter also than syrup
   or honey from the comb.

READING III   Ezekiel 37:1–14

A reading from the Book of the Prophet Ezekiel

Ezekiel = ee-ZEE-kee-uhl

This is a cinematic narrative. Practice so that the images are vivid.

The hand of the **LORD** came upon me,
   and he **led** me out in the **spirit** of the LORD
   and set me in the center of the **plain**,
   which was now filled with **bones**.
He made me **walk** among the bones in every direction
   so that I **saw** how many they were on the surface of the plain.
How **dry** they were!
He **asked** me:
   Son of **man**, can these bones come to **life**?
I answered, "Lord GOD, you alone **know** that."
Then he said to me:
   Prophesy over these bones, and say to them:
   Dry bones, **hear** the **word** of the LORD!
Thus says the Lord GOD to these bones:
   See! I will **bring spirit** into you, that **you** may come to **life**.
I will put **sinews** upon you, make flesh **grow** over you,
   cover you with skin, and put spirit in you
   so that you may come to life and **know** that **I am** the LORD.

Use an upward inflection. God is asking a question of faith. Do we think God can bring good to hopeless situations?

prophesy = PROF-uh-sī = verb; to say what will happen (different from "prophecy")

upheaval of wind and fire, indicating that God is once again at work.

READING III The sixth-century BC prophet Ezekiel is one of three major prophets in the Old Testament. Of a priestly family, he was among the Jerusalemites deported to Babylon in the first deportation (597 BC). Dwelling along the Chebar canal in the Babylonian town of Tel Abib, Ezekiel directed his visions and oracles to his fellow Jerusalemites in Babylon and in Jerusalem. Among his most

famous visions is that of the field filled with bones.

The field of bones is a metaphor for the exiled and dispirited people of both the northern (Israel) and southern (Judah) kingdoms. Through its emphasis on the vast number and dryness of the bones, the metaphor recalls the centuries of the nation's undoing, painfully symbolized in the process of degeneration: spirit gives way to skin, giving way to flesh, giving way to sinews, giving way to a skeleton, and, finally, reduced to scattered bones. As Ezekiel prophesies over the bones, the

process is reversed: bone to bone, sinew to skeleton, flesh to sinew, skin to flesh, and, finally, spirit.

The metaphor serves as a response to the nation's threefold despair over its fate: "Our bones are dried up, our hope is lost, and we are cut off." Through the metaphor, Israel is to understand that God is engaging in a similar resurrection/reversal with them. First, God will "open your graves and have you rise from them." Second, God declares, "I will put my spirit in you that you may live." Third, the people will no longer

sinews = SIN-yooz

The sight is amazing. Start to build the energy that culminates when the spirit of life comes into them and they are alive.

Pause slightly to let the image sink in.

Change tone to report what the narrative signifies.

Emphasize "will." We can trust God's word.

I, **Ezekiel**, **prophesied** as I had been told,
    and even as I was **prophesying** I heard a **noise**;
    it was a **rattling** as the bones came **together**, **bone** joining **bone**.
I saw the **sinews** and the flesh **come** upon them,
    and the skin cover them, but there was no **spirit** in them.
Then the Lord said to me:
    Prophesy to the **spirit**, prophesy, son of **man**,
    and say to the spirit: Thus says the Lord God:
    From the four winds **come**, O spirit,
    and breathe into these **slain** that they may come to **life**.
I prophesied as he told me, and the spirit came into them;
    they came **alive** and stood **upright**, a vast **army**.
Then he said to me:
    Son of **man**, these bones are the whole **house** of Israel.
They have been saying,
    "Our bones are **dried** up,
    our **hope** is lost, and we are cut **off**."
Therefore, prophesy and say to them: Thus says the Lord God:
    O **my** people, I will **open** your **graves**
    and have you **rise** from them,
    and bring you **back** to the land of **Israel**.
Then you shall **know** that I am the Lord,
    when I open your graves and have you rise from them,
    O my people!
I will put my **spirit in** you that you may **live**,
    and I will **settle** you upon your **land**;
    thus you shall know that I am the Lord.
I have **promised**, and I **will** do it, says the Lord.

be cut off, because God "will settle you upon your land."

The "spirit" in this text, which is the agent for reanimation and new life, anticipates the experience of the disciples at Pentecost.

READING IV Although little is known of the prophet Joel, or of the book that bears his name, it comes from the post-exilic period when Jerusalem and the temple have been rebuilt, and priests and elders (but no king) serve as the leaders of the nation (late fifth to early fourth

century BC). The first half of the book (1:2—2:27) bemoans a plague of locusts that embodies God's retribution. The second half (4:1–21) describes a future time when Judah's enemies will suffer punishment, even as the land returns to an Edenic state. Between the two halves is today's reading (3:1–5), which is God's promise to pour out the Spirit. The entire book is influenced by the phrase "the day of the Lord," used five times throughout this relatively short book. It describes the day when God, the divine warrior, fights against his enemies.

The first two-thirds of the reading are placed in the mouth of the Lord (beginning with "I will pour"). First, the inhabitants of Judah ("Your sons and daughters") are addressed, declaring that all Israel, regardless of age, gender, or social standing, will become prophetic mouthpieces (oracles, visions, and dreams) just as Moses once hoped (Numbers 11:29). In contrast, the next several lines describe the Lord's "wonders" when the day of the Lord comes, with no specific group being addressed. Finally, in the last third of the reading ("Then everyone shall be rescued . . ."), the prophet

For meditation and context:

RESPONSORIAL PSALM · Psalm 107:2–3, 4–5, 6–7, 8–9

R. Give thanks to the Lord; his love is everlasting. or
R. Alleluia.

Let the redeemed of the LORD say,
  those whom he has redeemed from the
    hand of the foe
And gathered from the lands,
  from the east and the west, from the north
    and the south.

They went astray in the desert wilderness;
  the way to an inhabited city they did
    not find.
Hungry and thirsty,
  their life was wasting away within them.

They cried to the LORD in their distress;
  from their straits he rescued them.
And he led them by a direct way
  to reach an inhabited city.

Let them give thanks to the LORD for
    his mercy
  and his wondrous deeds to the children
    of men,
Because he satisfied the longing soul
  and filled the hungry soul with
    good things.

READING IV   Joel 3:1–5

A reading from the Book of the Prophet Joel

Read the following responsorial psalm as you prepare. The psalmist prays for the same spirit the prophet describes.

prophesy = PROF-uh-sī = verb; to say what will happen (different from "prophecy")

God's power will be manifested in creation. Use a tone of amazement, instead of fear, for the apocalyptic language.

Thus says the **LORD**:
I will **pour** out my **spirit** upon **all flesh**.
  Your sons and daughters shall **prophesy**,
    your old men shall dream **dreams**,
    your young men shall **see visions**;
  even upon the servants and the handmaids,
    in those days, I will pour out my spirit.
And I will work **wonders** in the **heavens** and on the **earth**,
    blood, **fire**, and columns of **smoke**;
  the sun will be turned to **darkness**,
    and the moon to **blood**,
  at the **coming** of the **day** of the **LORD**,
    the great and terrible day.

himself clarifies that those to be rescued are Jews dwelling on Mount Zion and in Jerusalem. Thus, Joel offers words of deliverance, restoration, and vengeance to the chastened remnant in Jerusalem.

This text plays a pivotal role in Peter's Pentecost speech, where he cites almost the entire text to explain the outpouring of the Spirit upon him and the disciples (Acts 2:17–21). In doing so, he alters the text, widening its scope to all diaspora Jews, and then to all people.

EPISTLE   Composed in the late AD 50s, Paul's letter to the Romans is his longest. It is also his theological defense of the Good News he shares. Using many different proofs, Paul argues that the Good News of Jesus Christ has something important to say to the Jews and Gentiles of his time, since all human beings are affected by sin.

In Romans 8:22–27, Paul develops ideas about the Christian life. He argues that Christians live in freedom because they have received the gift of the Spirit. Relying on his conviction that the present age of suffering will be replaced by a future age of glory, Paul cites three witnesses to support his belief: creation, hope, and the Spirit.

First, likely drawing on images from Isaiah's "new heavens and earth" (Isaiah 65:17; 66:22), Paul offers a groaning creation that awaits its own liberation as a counterpoint to Christian suffering in the present age. Each awaits liberation and redemption. Second, describing pagan hope in this world as what is seen (i.e., *not* hope), Paul notes that Christians have hope founded on what is *not seen*: their adoption.

Then everyone shall be **rescued**
  who **calls** on the name of the Lord;
for on Mount **Zion** there shall be a **remnant**,
  as the Lord has said,
and in Jerusalem survivors
  whom the Lord shall call.

For meditation and context:

RESPONSORIAL PSALM Psalm 104:1–2, 24 and 35, 27–28, 29b–30 (see 30)

R. Lord, send out your Spirit, and renew the face of the earth.
or
R. Alleluia.

Bless the Lord, O my soul!
  O Lord, my God, you are great indeed!
You are clothed with majesty and glory,
  robed in light as with a cloak.

How manifold are your works, O Lord!
  In wisdom you have wrought them all—
the earth is full of your creatures;
  bless the Lord, O my soul! Alleluia.

Creatures all look to you

to give them food in due time.
When you give it to them, they gather it;
  when you open your hand, they are filled
  with good things.

If you take away their breath, they perish
  and return to their dust.
When you send forth your spirit, they are
  created,
  and you renew the face of the earth.

EPISTLE Romans 8:22–27

A reading from the Letter of Saint Paul to the Romans

Brothers and **sisters**:
We know that **all creation** is **groaning** in labor pains even
    until now;
  and not only that, but we **ourselves**,
  who have the **firstfruits** of the **Spirit**,
  we also **groan** within ourselves
  as we **wait** for adoption, the redemption of our **bodies**.
For in **hope** we were **saved**.
Now hope that **sees** is not hope. »

Paul is making an urgent appeal. Elongate "groaning." It should be heard with heightened sensitivity to our current climate crises.

Hope is a theological virtue. Paul warns it is not fully realized until the eschaton.

Third, the Spirit itself gives testimony in that it intercedes for the holy ones, who in this age are beset with human weakness. Through "inexpressible groanings," the Spirit ensures that human prayer makes its way to God.

| GOSPEL | John's Gospel, in contrast to the other Gospels, does not follow a strict historical chronology, but rather emphasizes themes through which Jesus' identity is explored. Among those themes are ones associated with certain Jewish feasts such as Sabbath, Passover,

and the Feast of Tabernacles (Booths). In a lengthy section (John 7:1—8:59), Jesus' interactions on the Feast of Tabernacles are developed. Today's Gospel presents three verses that are associated with the last day of the feast.

Whereas water and light played a prominent role during the celebration of the first seven days of the festival, on this "last and greatest day," Jesus identifies himself as the source of water for the thirsty. The text is confusing for two reasons. First, it implies that Jesus is citing from Scripture when, in fact, no known

biblical parallel exists. Two possible references, Ezekiel 47:3–6, 9 and Zechariah 14:8, have been proposed for their imagery. Second, the punctuation is confusing, and likely incorrect, as it implies that the believer, and not Jesus, is the source of the living water. A more accurate reading would be: "And let him drink who believes in me. Just as Scripture says: Rivers of living water will flow from within him." This alternate reading better preserves the sense of the overall reading, with Jesus as the source of living water.

Read with the presumption of agreement. Pause slightly to let the assembly internalize it.

For who hopes for what one **sees**?
But if we hope for what we do **not** see, we wait with **endurance**.

The Spirit gives life to our prayers.

In the same way, the Spirit too comes to the aid of
   our **weakness**;
   for we do not know how to **pray** as we ought,
   but the Spirit himself **intercedes** with inexpressible **groanings**.
And the one who **searches** hearts
   knows what is the **intention** of the Spirit,
   because he intercedes for the holy ones
   according to **God's will**.

GOSPEL   John 7:37–39

A reading from the holy Gospel according to John

Set the scene with a narrator's voice and increase your intensity when Jesus stands and speaks. He speaks with authority. Show that authority to the assembly.

On the last and greatest **day** of the feast,
   Jesus stood up and exclaimed,
   "Let **anyone** who **thirsts come** to me and drink.
As **Scripture** says:
   *Rivers of **living** water will **flow** from within him* who
      believes in me."

Return to the even tone of the narrator for the conclusion.

He said this in reference to the **Spirit**
   that those who came to **believe** in him were to **receive**.
There was, of course, no Spirit yet,
   because Jesus had not yet been **glorified**.

That the text is pointing to Jesus as the source of living water is affirmed in two ways. First, the verbal form "will flow" points to a future event, which admittedly could apply to Jesus or the believer. Second, in the final verse the evangelist explains that this perfect living water is associated with the coming of the Spirit, who cannot arrive until Jesus has been glorified, thus identifying Jesus as the source. Nevertheless, for the sake of reading clarity, the Gospel text should be read as it is printed so that it makes sense grammatically. That includes maintaining the punctuation in the text. Homilists can then emphasize the identity of Jesus as the source of living water, even as they use the ambiguity of the text to imply that believers can channel that living water as well. S.L.

PENTECOST SUNDAY: DAY

LECTIONARY #63

READING I   Acts of the Apostles 2:1–11

A reading from the Acts of the Apostles

When the time for **Pentecost** was fulfilled,
    they were all in one place **together**.
And **suddenly** there came from the sky
    a **noise** like a strong driving **wind**,
    and it **filled** the entire **house** in which they were.
Then there **appeared** to them tongues as of **fire**,
    which **parted** and came to **rest** on **each** one of them.
And they were all **filled** with the Holy **Spirit**
    and began to **speak** in different **tongues**,
    as the Spirit enabled them to **proclaim**.

Now there were devout **Jews** from every **nation** under heaven
    staying in Jerusalem.
At this **sound**, they gathered in a large **crowd**,
    but they were **confused**
    because **each** one **heard** them speaking in his **own** language.
They were **astounded**, and in amazement they asked,
    "Are not all these people who are speaking **Galileans**?
Then **how** does each of us **hear** them in his **native** language?
We are Parthians, Medes, and Elamites,
    inhabitants of Mesopotamia, Judea and Cappadocia,
    Pontus and Asia, Phrygia and Pamphylia, »

The proclamation has auditory and visual descriptors. Present them as if you were there reporting them. Nature is responding to God's intervention in history.

Pause for the scene change. The narrative moves from the inside of the house to the outside.

Use an upward inflection for each question, pausing after each one.
Parthians = PAHR-thee-uhnz
Medes = meedz
Elamites = EE-luh-mīts
Mesapotamia = mes-uh-poh-TAY-mee-uh
Judea = joo-DEE-uh or joo-DAY-uh
Cappadocia = kap-uh-DOH-shuh
or kap-uh-DOH-shee-uh
Pontus = PON-tuhs
Phrygia = FRIJ-ee-uh
Pamphylia = pam-FIL-ee-uh

There are options for today's readings. Contact your parish staff to learn which readings will be used.

READING I Pentecost has rightly been called the birthday of the Church. The interaction between the resurrected Lord and the small band of early disciples was the focus of the Easter season. With Jesus' ascension into heaven, the small band was deprived of his physical presence, but assured that they would receive the gift of his Spirit, a gift that would inaugurate the next phase in salvation history. It is the birth of that next phase and the role of the Spirit that Pentecost commemorates.

With Jesus' ascension, and with the choice of Matthias to bring the number back up to twelve, all is ready for the birth of the Church. This first reading sets the context by mentioning that "the time for Pentecost was fulfilled." Although Pentecost began as an agricultural festival fifty days after Passover, Jews of Luke's time understood it as a covenant renewal ceremony celebrating the giving of Torah at Sinai.

With the scene having been set, the account then is divided into two main parts: the first third of the reading describes the event, whereas the latter two-thirds analyze the observers' response. Three physical phenomena in the first part describe the event: the *sound* of a driving wind, the *appearance* of tongues as of fire (seen only by those in the house), and the *experience* of spoken language. The parallels with the Sinai event (Exodus 19:16–19) when God gave the Law are striking: God's theophany (appearance) in Exodus was marked by thunder, lightning/fire, clouds, a loud voice

Libya = LIB-ee-uh
Cyrene = sī-REEN or sī-REE-nee

Cretans = KREE-tuhns

Egypt and the districts of Libya near Cyrene,
as well as travelers from Rome,
both Jews and converts to Judaism, Cretans and Arabs,
yet we hear them speaking in our **own tongues**
of the mighty **acts** of **God**."

For meditation and context:

RESPONSORIAL PSALM   Psalm 104:1, 24, 29–30, 31, 34 (30)

R. Lord, send out your Spirit, and renew the face of the earth.
or
R. Alleluia.

Bless the LORD, O my soul!
    O LORD, my God, you are great indeed!
How manifold are your works, O LORD!
    The earth is full of your creatures.

If you take away their breath, they perish
    and return to their dust.

When you send forth your spirit,
    they are created,
    and you renew the face of the earth.

May the glory of the LORD endure forever;
    may the LORD be glad in his works!
Pleasing to him be my theme;
    I will be glad in the LORD.

Corinthians = kohr-IN-thee-uhnz

Paul's teaching uses metaphors to explain how the Spirit moves in the lives of believers. It is a timeless message that ministries come in many different forms.

Note the focus on community; the gifts given by the Spirit benefit the community.

The Church is blessed with diversity; we all have an important role to play.

READING II   1 Corinthians 12:3b–7, 12–13

A reading from the first Letter of Saint Paul to the Corinthians

Brothers and **sisters**:
No **one** can say, "Jesus is **Lord**," except by the Holy **Spirit**.

There are **different** kinds of spiritual **gifts** but the same **Spirit**;
    there are different forms of **service** but the same **Lord**;
    there are different **workings** but the same **God**
    who **produces** all of them in everyone.
To each individual the manifestation of the Spirit
    is **given** for some **benefit**.

As a body is **one** though it has many **parts**,
    and all the parts of the body, though many, are one **body**,
    so also **Christ**.

(noise), and wind and smoke. God's message was embodied in the voice/noise and the fire. Thus, in this "new Sinai" event at Pentecost, the disciples experience a theophany (noise/wind and flame/fire) as they are filled with the Holy Spirit. The theophany is experienced by the crowd (an ingathering of Jews from all the nations speaking different languages) through the noise, but especially through the transformation of the disciples. The crowd does not need to see the flames, because they experience the Spirit-infused disciples and their message, each in his own language. Jesus'

earlier promise of the Spirit is fulfilled as the disciples speak of "the mighty acts of God," and the Spirit gives birth to the Church.

| READING II | **1 Corinthians.** Paul's letters often bring his theology to bear on the very real issues facing the communities he founded. In his letter to the community at Corinth, Paul identifies the Spirit as the principle of unity in the face of division caused by diversity.

Paul's relationship with the Christians in Corinth ranged from tenderness to rage, as he strove to support their dynamism

while also keeping them united to one another, to himself, and to the Church. Today's passage employs two strategies in the task. First, Paul associates the Spirit with the Christian vocation when he declares that proclaiming Jesus as Lord means that the Christian is in possession of the Holy Spirit. The Spirit not only makes that proclamation possible, but it is also the unifying origin of the spiritual gifts. Thus, the community benefits from diverse gifts, "forms of service," and "workings," each of which is joined to the others in origin (the Spirit) and purpose ("for some benefit").

For in one Spirit we were all **baptized** into one body,
> whether **Jews** or **Greeks**, **slaves** or free **persons**,
> and we were all **given** to drink of one Spirit.

Or:

READING II   Galatians 5:16–25

A reading from the Letter of Saint Paul to the Galatians

Brothers and **sisters**, **live** by the **Spirit**
> and you will certainly not **gratify** the desire of the **flesh**.
For the **flesh** has desires **against** the **Spirit**,
> and the Spirit against the **flesh**;
> these are opposed to each other,
> so that you may **not** do what you **want**.
But if you are **guided** by the Spirit, you are not **under** the **law**.
Now the **works** of the flesh are obvious:
> **immorality**, **impurity**, **lust**, **idolatry**,
> **sorcery**, **hatreds**, **rivalry**, **jealousy**,
> **outbursts of fury**, **acts of selfishness**,
> **dissensions**, **factions**, **occasions of envy**,
> **drinking** bouts, **orgies**, and the like.
I warn you, as I **warned** you before,
> that those who do such things will not **inherit** the kingdom
> of God.
In contrast, the fruit of the Spirit is **love**, **joy**, **peace**,
> **patience**, **kindness**, **generosity**,
> **faithfulness**, **gentleness**, **self-control**.
Against such there is no **law**.
Now those who belong to Christ Jesus have **crucified** their flesh
> with its **passions** and **desires**.
If we **live** in the Spirit, let us also **follow** the Spirit.

Galatians = guh-LAY-shuhnz

Paul's moral exhortation articulates the tension between vices and virtues. Change your tone between the two lists. Use a stern tone to represent the abhorrent nature of the vices, and let your countenance reflect the love that radiates from the virtues. Read the lists slowly, equal in pace, letting the assembly personally identify with items that hit home. Spread your gaze equally over the congregation, being careful not to rest on any one individual.

Read Paul's warning as fatherly advice. Paul is not threatening, just honest about the consequence of sin.

The advice in this reading is not a one-time examination of conscience. We are continually invited to "live in the Spirit" and be guided to holiness.

Second, Paul employs the image of the body with its many parts. Recalling the body of Christ with its many members, Paul notes that in Christian rituals, the Spirit is the source of unity: in one Spirit, all are baptized; in the Eucharist, all are "given to drink of one Spirit." Thus, in this short reading, Paul verifies the central role that the Spirit plays in the daily life of the Church.

Galatians. Writing a circular letter to Christian communities in Galatia, Paul responds to a challenge to the message of his proclamation of the Good News by a group of outside agitators (likely Jewish Christians from Judea) who teach a different "truth" of the Christian faith. In essence, the agitators tell Galatia's Gentile Christians that to follow Christ they must be circumcised. Because Paul teaches that Christians are free from the requirements of the law (for example, circumcision, dietary regulations, and Sabbath observance), some Galatians conclude that this "law-free Gospel" provides no moral guidance, resulting in community strife and jealousy.

To counter the agitators' teachings, Paul's letter consists of a series of rhetorical proofs focused on a future course of action. His ultimate goal is to eliminate all options except the rejection of circumcision. In the final proof, from which today's reading is drawn, Paul encourages the Galatians to live in the Spirit.

Since the agitators contrast Paul's "law-free Gospel" with the Mosaic Law, Paul turns the tables, stating that those who live the commandment of love as Christ lived it do in fact fulfill the Mosaic Law. To make his point, Paul contrasts two different realms—the realm of the Spirit (that is, the divine Spirit; to dwell in Christ)

TO KEEP IN MIND

Sequences originated as extensions of the sung Alleluia before the proclamation of the Gospel, although they precede the Alleluia now. The Pentecost Sequence, also called the Golden Sequence, is an ancient liturgical hymn praising the Holy Spirit. It is the source of the hymn "Come, Holy Ghost."

SEQUENCE Veni, Sancte Spiritus

Come, Holy Spirit, come!
And from your celestial home
    Shed a ray of light divine!
Come, Father of the poor!
Come, source of all our store!
    Come, within our bosoms shine.
You, of comforters the best;
You, the soul's most welcome guest;
    Sweet refreshment here below;
In our labor, rest most sweet;
Grateful coolness in the heat;
    Solace in the midst of woe.
O most blessed Light divine,
Shine within these hearts of yours,
    And our inmost being fill!

Where you are not, we have naught,
Nothing good in deed or thought,
    Nothing free from taint of ill.
Heal our wounds, our strength renew;
On our dryness pour your dew;
    Wash the stains of guilt away:
Bend the stubborn heart and will;
Melt the frozen, warm the chill;
    Guide the steps that go astray.
On the faithful, who adore
And confess you, evermore
    In your sevenfold gift descend;
Give them virtue's sure reward;
Give them your salvation, Lord;
    Give them joys that never end. Amen.
    Alleluia.

GOSPEL John 20:19–23

A reading from the holy Gospel according to John

On the evening of that **first** day of the week,
    when the doors were **locked**, where the **disciples** were,
    for **fear** of the Jews,
    Jesus came and stood in their **midst**
    and said to them, "**Peace** be with you."
When he had said this, he **showed** them his **hands** and his **side**.
The disciples **rejoiced** when they **saw** the Lord.
Jesus said to them again, "**Peace** be with you.
As the **Father** has **sent me**, so I send **you**."
And when he had said this, he **breathed on them** and said
      to them,
    "**Receive** the Holy **Spirit**.
Whose sins you **forgive** are forgiven them,
and whose sins you **retain** are retained."

Or:

The narrator interjects the response of the disciples. Give a little more energy the second time Jesus offers peace; Jesus wants to share this peace with his disciples (and us).

Read the appearance story as if for the first time. The narrator sets the scene. The disciples are locked in the room and "locked" in fear. Let your tone communicate the astonishment of Jesus' appearance.

and the realm of the flesh (carnal, to dwell in unredeemed humanity). Persons (body and soul) who live in the realm of the flesh produce the works of that realm, which lack freedom ("gratify the desire of the flesh. . . . you may not do what you want"). In contrast, believers (body and soul) who are "guided by the Spirit" are free (no longer "under the law") and produce the fruits of the Spirit. In the end, Paul reminds the Galatians that these realms cannot co-exist and that those who belong to Christ Jesus also "follow the Spirit."

GOSPEL | **John 20.** In contrast to Luke's account of Pentecost, John's Gospel places the event on the "evening of that first day of the week." A longer version of today's Gospel was read on the Second Sunday of Easter, where the focus was placed on the disciples' movement from unbelief to belief in the risen Lord. This shortened version, placed in the Pentecost context, has a different focus.

Having already promised to send "another Advocate" (John 14:16), John's Gospel describes how the resurrected Lord returns to fulfill that promise in two phases.

Similar to Luke's account, where the disciples are gathered in one place, John's first phase describes how Jesus enters the closed and locked room where the disciples are, offers peace, shows the disciples his hands and side, and brings them to joy.

In the second phase, again with some parallels to Luke, Jesus breathes on them, infuses them with the Holy Spirit, transforms them, and gives them a ministry that continues his own. While Luke has a different chronology, the process is similar in John: Jesus breathes on them (in Acts, the strong wind), infuses them with the Holy

GOSPEL   John 15:26–27; 16:12–15

A reading from the holy Gospel according to John

Jesus said to his **disciples**:
  "When the **Advocate** comes whom I will send you
    from the **Father**,
  the Spirit of **truth** that proceeds from the Father,
  he will **testify** to me.
And you **also** testify,
  because you have been **with** me from the beginning.

"I have much **more** to **tell** you, but you cannot **bear** it now.
But when he comes, the Spirit of truth,
  he will **guide** you to all truth.
He will not **speak** on his own,
  but he will speak what he **hears**,
  and will declare to you the **things** that are **coming**.
He will **glorify** me,
  because he will **take** from what is **mine** and **declare** it to you.
Everything that the **Father** has is mine;
  for this reason I told you that he will take from what is mine
  and **declare** it to **you**."

In your Bible, read the verses that are missing from this reading. This reading is part of Jesus' final instruction to his disciples before his passion, warning them of their future trouble, yet assuring them of the Spirit's presence.

Jesus only tells them as much as they are able to handle at this point.

God holds nothing back from us. What generosity!

Spirit (the tongues of flame), transforms them (they speak in other languages), and gives them a ministry (they proclaim God's works). Just as Jesus shared in God's work of forgiveness of sin and laying bare all sinfulness, he identifies this as a fundamental part of his disciples' ministry. As Jesus was sent by the Father, so now they are sent. Their ministry is possible because of the Spirit.

John 15. The lengthy Farewell Discourse (John 14—17) in John's Gospel is Jesus' final will and testament. Among its unique contributions is Jesus' promise to send another Advocate (John 14:16). It is Jesus' development of that promise that is found in this Gospel reading.

The Gospel's mention of another Advocate ties the role intimately to Jesus himself, the first Advocate. Lost from view in today's Gospel is the fact that Jesus is musing on how the world will oppose and hate his disciples (John 16:1–11). Wishing to strengthen them in the face of such hostility, Jesus speaks of the coming Advocate whom he will send from the Father, and who will guide them. This brief passage offers several insights into the Advocate/Spirit. First, he will be an extension of Jesus' presence in their midst. Second, he will be a Spirit of truth, helping them to give testimony. Third, he will guide the disciples to truth (even that which they are not yet able to recognize). Finally, the Advocate is not the ultimate source of truth, but rather speaks what he hears. S.L.

THE MOST HOLY TRINITY

LECTIONARY #165

READING I   Deuteronomy 4:32–34, 39–40

A reading from the Book of Deuteronomy

Deuteronomy = doo-ter-AH-nuh-mee or dyoo-ter-AH-nuh-mee

Moses said to the **people**:
    "**Ask** now of the days of **old**, before your time,
        ever since God created man upon the earth;
        ask from one **end** of the sky to the **other**:
        Did anything so **great** ever happen **before**?

These are rhetorical questions, use an upward inflection.

Pause between questions so the assembly can share in the author's musings.

Was it ever **heard** of?
Did a people ever hear the **voice** of **God**
    speaking from the midst of **fire**, as you did, and **live**?
Or did any god venture to go and **take** a **nation** for himself
    from the midst of **another** nation,
    by **testings**, by **signs** and **wonders**, by **war**,
    with strong **hand** and outstretched **arm**, and by great **terrors**,
    all of which the LORD, your **God**,
    did for you in **Egypt** before your very **eyes**?

After recounting God's amazing deeds, the tone changes to practicality as the author describes what we should do in response.

This is why you must now **know**,
    and fix in your heart, that the LORD is **God**
    in the heavens **above** and on earth **below**,
    and that there is no **other**.
You must **keep** his **statutes** and **commandments** that I **enjoin**
        on you today,
    that you and your **children** after you may **prosper**,
    and that you may have long **life** on the **land**
    which the LORD, your God, is **giving** you **forever**."

READING I The celebration of the Most Holy Trinity, a fundamental Christian teaching, highlights the Christian belief that God's self-revelation is rooted in salvation history. The philosophical definitions, as expressed in the creeds and by Augustine, came centuries after the biblical writings, where believers mused over God's identity as they experienced God's saving action in their midst. Today's readings are among such musings.

Deuteronomy is the final book of the Torah/Pentateuch, bringing to a conclusion the historical period that formed Israel as a nation in covenant relationship with its God. Traditionally, the book is viewed as three discourses delivered by Moses to the people. The people are poised to cross the Jordan to reconquer the land after their long sojourn in Egypt and their wandering in the wilderness. Today's reading comes from the end of Moses' first discourse. Part of the theological heart of the book, Deuteronomy 4 exhorts the Israelites to abide by two basic principles: monotheism and the prohibition of idolatry. The justification for these principles is found in Israel's historical experience, notably, the

exodus and the encounter with God at Horeb (Sinai).

In typical biblical fashion, the text recalls the community's experience of salvation history, such as liberation from Egypt and entry into the covenant at Horeb, and draws conclusions about God's identity. For example, presuming that the all-powerful and omnipresent God is the source and creator of all being ("God created man upon the earth"), Moses declares that Israel's God is stronger than any nation or gods: no other god claimed a people as his own as God "did for you in Egypt." This

For meditation and context:

RESPONSORIAL PSALM Psalm 33:4–5, 6, 9, 18–19, 20, 22 (12b)

R. Blessed the people the Lord has chosen to be his own.

Upright is the word of the Lord,
and all his works are trustworthy.
He loves justice and right;
of the kindness of the Lord the earth
is full.

By the word of the Lord the heavens
were made;
by the breath of his mouth all their host.
For he spoke, and it was made;
he commanded, and it stood forth.

See, the eyes of the Lord are upon those
who fear him,
upon those who hope for his kindness,
to deliver them from death
and preserve them in spite of famine.

Our soul waits for the Lord,
who is our help and our shield.
May your kindness, O Lord, be upon us
who have put our hope in you.

READING II Romans 8:14–17

A reading from the Letter of Saint Paul to the Romans

Brothers and **sisters**:
Those who are **led** by the Spirit of **God** are **sons** of God.
For you did not **receive** a **spirit** of **slavery** to fall back into **fear**,
but you received a **Spirit** of **adoption**,
through whom we cry, "**Abba**, **Father**!"
The Spirit himself bears **witness** with our **spirit**
that we are **children** of God,
and if children, then **heirs**,
heirs of God and **joint** heirs with Christ,
if only we **suffer** with him
so that we may also be **glorified** with him.

Use an encouraging tone to match Paul's message in this reading.

Consider how baptism strengthens us to call out to God as his beloved children.

first realization about God, based on the Exodus, leads to the second. Israel has entered into a covenant (statutes and commandments) with the mightiest and only God. Thus, based on their experience of God's saving power, Israel realizes that God is one (monotheism) and that their future prosperity rests on worshipping only this God (prohibition of idolatry).

READING II In Romans, Paul's longest and most theological letter, Paul reflects on his and other Christians' experience in terms of God's salvific action

through the person of Jesus Christ. Although Paul is an heir of the rich Jewish heritage reflected in the first reading, he realizes that God is doing something radically new in Jesus Christ, which results in a change in salvific situation and status.

In spite of the great benefit of the law as the organizing principle of the covenant between God and Israel, Paul realizes that the resulting relationship is prone to enslavement and distance that only Jesus' death and resurrection can remedy. Consequently, the Spirit of God leads all who believe that Jesus' death and resurrec-

tion liberates one from sin and death into a new salvific situation and status. First, they are freed from "a spirit of slavery" that leads them to "fall back into fear." Second, they receive "a Spirit of adoption." Lacking the precision of philosophical argument, the text poetically argues that, once received, the Spirit leads Christians to adoptive status ("children of God") and establishes a special relationship between Christians and Christ and God, so that they become joint heirs in Christ's suffering and glorification.

GOSPEL   Matthew 28:16–20

A reading from the holy Gospel according to Matthew

The eleven **disciples** went to **Galilee**,
    to the **mountain** to which **Jesus** had **ordered** them.
When they all **saw** him, they **worshiped**, but they **doubted**.
Then Jesus approached and said to them,
    "All **power** in **heaven** and on **earth** has been **given** to **me**.
Go, therefore, and make **disciples** of **all** nations,
    baptizing them in the name of the **Father**,
    and of the **Son**, and of the Holy **Spirit**,
    teaching them to **observe** all that I have **commanded** you.
And behold, I am with **you always**, until the end of the age."

Don't rush Jesus' words. These are his final ones in the Gospel of Matthew.

Recite the names of the Trinity with reverence.

Pause after "you" and make eye contact with the assembly to make Jesus' words personal. Emphasize "always."

GOSPEL Matthew's unique account of the resurrected Jesus' encounter with the eleven on a mountain in Galilee again muses on God's identity based on an experience of unfolding salvation history. These are the final verses of Matthew's Gospel, and this is Matthew's closest parallel to the Ascension and Pentecost.

Keeping in mind the biblical motif of mountains as places of divine revelation, we read that Jesus directed the eleven to an unnamed mountain, where they worship him, even as some of them doubt. If there was any doubt about his identity, Jesus' words provide clarity. Like Israel's God, he is on the mountaintop, he is worshiped, and "all power in heaven and on earth has been given" to him. He who was the authoritative Teacher throughout the Gospel now entrusts his teaching to them, when he commands them to go make disciples and baptize all nations. If Jesus' ministry in the Gospel was directed to Jews, this commission is directed at the nations (including the Gentiles), possibly pointing to a new chapter in salvation history. Jesus' final words, "I am with you always," echo not only the prediction made of him in Matthew 1:23 (Emmanuel—God with us), but also exhibit how Jesus' enduring presence replaces the role of the Spirit as found elsewhere in the New Testament. Once again, the community's experience of salvation forms its understanding of God's identity. S.L.

THE MOST HOLY BODY AND BLOOD OF CHRIST

LECTIONARY #168

READING I   Exodus 24:3–8

A reading from the Book of Exodus

Exodus = EK-suh-duhs

Set the scene with a narrator voice and then change your energy to reflect the crowd's eagerness to do everything the Lord asks of them.

In the second part of the narrative, Moses puts into action the ritual that confirms the covenant the people have agreed to. Describe the preparation with a steady, even tone.

Again, use energy to reflect the crowd's response.

Read "blood of the covenant" distinctly. It will be echoed in the Gospel and in the Eucharistic prayer.

When **Moses** came to the **people**
    and related all the **words** and ordinances of the Lord,
    they all answered with one voice,
    "We **will** do everything that the Lord has told us."
Moses then **wrote** down all the words of the Lord and,
    rising early the next day,
    he erected at the foot of the mountain an altar
    and twelve **pillars** for the twelve **tribes** of Israel.
Then, having sent certain young men of the Israelites
    to offer **holocausts** and sacrifice young bulls
    as **peace** offerings to the Lord,
    Moses took half of the blood and put it in large bowls;
    the other half he splashed on the altar.
Taking the book of the **covenant**, he read it **aloud** to the people,
    who answered, "All that the Lord has said, we **will** heed
        and do."
Then he took the **blood** and sprinkled it on the people, saying,
    "**This** is the blood of the **covenant**
    that the Lord has **made** with you
    in accordance with all these words of his."

READING I The solemnity of the Most Holy Body and Blood of Christ, popularly known as Corpus Christi, evokes images of processions and a consecrated host in a tabernacle. However, today's readings root this celebration in Israel's salvation history, especially the Passover and the covenant ratified at Sinai through bloody sacrifice. These memories and ceremonies help us understand Jesus' sacrifice on the cross and its effects.

Exodus locates the Hebrews at Mount Sinai, after having been rescued from Egypt by the bloody Passover sacrifice of the lambs and God's powerful hand. Moses has received the "words" (concise commands determined by one's individual conscience) and "ordinances" (rules decided by law courts), and he now presents them to the people who unanimously accept them. After the people bind themselves orally, Moses writes down the entire body of law and undertakes the ratification of the covenant through a sacrificial ritual and blood rite.

This ritual begins by creating a sacred setting at the foot of Mount Sinai. The altar symbolizes God's presence, and the twelve pillars represent the tribes entering into the covenant. Two forms of sacrifice follow. The holocausts are entirely burned on the altar as a tribute to God. The peace offerings are partly burned, but also eaten by participants of the sacred, sacrificial meal. Finally, the blood of the sacrificed animals is sprinkled on the altar and the people. As blood was believed to contain the life force that belonged to God alone, sprinkling both the altar *and the people* forges a bond between them. The Hebrews are now bonded to God in a new, covenantal way. Having twice heard the words of the covenant (Exodus 24:3, 7; see also Exodus 19:8)

For meditation and context:

RESPONSORIAL PSALM   Psalm 116:12–13, 15–16, 17–18 (13)

R. I will take the cup of salvation, and call on the name of the Lord.
or
R. Alleluia.

How shall I make a return to the LORD
   for all the good he has done for me?
The cup of salvation I will take up,
   and I will call upon the name of the LORD.

Precious in the eyes of the LORD
   is the death of his faithful ones.

I am your servant, the son of your
   handmaid;
   you have loosed my bonds.

To you will I offer sacrifice of thanksgiving,
   and I will call upon the name of the LORD.
My vows to the LORD I will pay
   in the presence of all his people.

READING II   Hebrews 9:11–15

A reading from the Letter to the Hebrews

Paul's letter has long run-on sentences. Practice pausing.

Brothers and **sisters**:
When **Christ** came as high **priest**
   of the good things that have come to be,
   passing through the greater and more perfect tabernacle
   not made by **hands**, that is, not belonging to this creation,
   he entered once for all into the **sanctuary**,
   not with the **blood** of **goats** and **calves**
   but with his **own** blood, thus obtaining eternal **redemption**.

Make clear the incompleteness of animal sacrifice versus the definitive sacrifice of the blood of Christ.

For if the blood of goats and bulls
   and the sprinkling of a heifer's ashes
   can **sanctify** those who are **defiled**
   so that their flesh is cleansed,
   how much **more** will the blood of Christ,
   who through the eternal Spirit **offered** himself unblemished
     to God,
   cleanse our consciences from dead **works**
   to **worship** the living God.

The concluding paragraph should be read with joy. We are the beneficiaries of the new covenant.

For this reason he is **mediator** of a **new** covenant:
   since a death has taken place for deliverance
   from transgressions under the **first** covenant,
   those who are **called** may receive the promised
     eternal inheritance.

and having been sprinkled by the blood, they are charged to obey and live out all the words of the Lord. This reading focuses our attention on the sacrificial and covenantal nature of today's celebration, as well as its connection with the words of God that are central to the Christian life.

READING II | Few New Testament writings are as enigmatic as the Letter to the Hebrews. Its author is unknown, it is more a homily than a letter, and it was directed to a mixed group of Christians, rather than to Hebrews (Jewish-

Christians). Despite the diverse proposals for understanding the overall work, it is agreed that Hebrews provides profound insights into Christ's priesthood and sacrifice, particularly the ways in which they relate to worship and ministry. Hebrews never mentions the Jerusalem temple but does refer to Israel's sanctuary and Levitical priesthood as described in the Pentateuch, especially Exodus. Through a series of reflections on the unique priesthood of Melchizedek, and contrasting it with Israel's Levitical priesthood, Hebrews aligns Jesus with Melchizedek.

Hebrews states that Jesus did not grasp his high priesthood, but rather he was chosen by the Father. We also read that he embraced human weakness by learning obedience through suffering. Today's account begins with Jesus' arrival in his heavenly destination, "the greater and more perfect tabernacle." In this sanctuary, he will serve forever as priest, and the effects of his priesthood will be discerned by faith. In today's reading, we see contrasts between the Levitical priesthood and Christ's high priesthood. The Levitical sacrifices (animals) sanctified the people in

TO KEEP IN MIND

Sequences originated as extensions of the sung Alleluia before the proclamation of the Gospel, although they precede the Alleluia now. In the thirteenth century, St. Thomas Aquinas composed the hymn that is now the sequence for the Most Holy Body and Blood of Christ.

SEQUENCE Lauda, Sion, Salvatorem

Laud, O Zion, your salvation,
Laud with hymns of exultation,
    Christ, your king and shepherd true:

Bring him all the praise you know,
He is more than you bestow.
    Never can you reach his due.

Special theme for glad thanksgiving
Is the quick'ning and the living
    Bread today before you set:

From his hands of old partaken,
As we know, by faith unshaken,
    Where the Twelve at supper met.

Full and clear ring out your chanting,
Joy nor sweetest grace be wanting,
    From your heart let praises burst:

For today the feast is holden,
When the institution olden
    Of that supper was rehearsed.

Here the new law's new oblation,
By the new king's revelation,
    Ends the form of ancient rite:

Now the new the old effaces,
Truth away the shadow chases,
    Light dispels the gloom of night.

What he did at supper seated,
Christ ordained to be repeated,
    His memorial ne'er to cease:

And his rule for guidance taking,
Bread and wine we hallow, making
    Thus our sacrifice of peace.

This the truth each Christian learns,
Bread into his flesh he turns,
    To his precious blood the wine:

Sight has fail'd, nor thought conceives,
But a dauntless faith believes,
    Resting on a pow'r divine.

Here beneath these signs are hidden
Priceless things to sense forbidden;
    Signs, not things are all we see:

Blood is poured and flesh is broken,
Yet in either wondrous token
    Christ entire we know to be.

Whoso of this food partakes,
Does not rend the Lord nor breaks;
    Christ is whole to all that taste:

Thousands are, as one, receivers,
One, as thousands of believers,
    Eats of him who cannot waste.

Bad and good the feast are sharing,
Of what divers dooms preparing,
    Endless death, or endless life.

Life to these, to those damnation,
See how like participation
    Is with unlike issues rife.

When the sacrament is broken,
Doubt not, but believe 'tis spoken,
    That each sever'd outward token
        doth the very whole contain.

Nought the precious gift divides,
Breaking but the sign betides
    Jesus still the same abides,
        still unbroken does remain.

[Shorter form begins here.]
Lo! the angel's food is given
To the pilgrim who has striven;
    See the children's bread from heaven,
        which on dogs may not be spent.

Truth the ancient types fulfilling,
Isaac bound, a victim willing,
    Paschal lamb, its lifeblood spilling,
    manna to the fathers sent.

Very bread, good shepherd, tend us,
Jesu, of your love befriend us,
    You refresh us, you defend us,
    Your eternal goodness send us
In the land of life to see.

You who all things can and know,
Who on earth such food bestow,
    Grant us with your saints, though lowest,
    Where the heav'nly feast you show,
Fellow heirs and guests to be. Amen.
    Alleluia.

matters related to the flesh but were unable to cleanse consciences or effect redemption. In contrast, Christ's blood (not to be understood as a ransom for sin) cleanses the consciences of believers and redeems them from the power of evil. Levitical sacrifices are completed through fire, but Christ's sacrifice is completed "through the eternal Spirit," which fuses his earthly ministry to his death and exaltation. Thus, Christ's blood points not only to his sacrificial death, but also to his proclaimed message. In this way, Christ's teaching evokes faith and cleanses consciences,

just as his blood proclaims God's grace and mercy.

Finally, echoing Jeremiah 31:31–34, Hebrews identifies Christ as the "mediator of a new covenant." In this new covenantal relationship, Christ's death delivers us "from transgressions under the first covenant" and leads us to the future promise of our eternal inheritance. Identifying Christ's sacrifice with the eternal promises made to Abraham, Hebrews brings atonement, covenant, and promise together.

GOSPEL The Gospel for today's solemnity recalls for us the Last Supper, as described by the Gospel of Mark. Reflecting on this event today, Jesus' final meal with his disciples is read against the backdrop of Passover, the covenant ratification from Exodus, and Hebrews' reflections on Jesus as High Priest. Mark's account of the Last Supper has three parts: preparing for the meal, predictions of Judas' betrayal, and the description of the meal which institutes the Eucharist. Today's reading includes the first and third parts, and eliminates the second.

GOSPEL   Mark 14:12–16, 22–26

A reading from the holy Gospel according to Mark

Use a steady, even tone to set the stage for the narrative.

On the **first** day of the Feast of Unleavened **Bread**,
    when they **sacrificed** the Passover **lamb**,
    Jesus' disciples said to him,
    "**Where** do you want us to go
    and prepare for you to eat the **Passover**?"
He sent two of his disciples and said to them,

Use a stronger, slower tone when reading dialogue.

    "**Go** into the **city** and a man will meet you,
    carrying a jar of **water**.
Follow him.
Wherever he enters, say to the master of the house,
    'The **Teacher** says, "Where is my guest room
    where I may **eat** the Passover with my disciples?"'
Then he will show you a large upper **room** furnished and ready.
Make the **preparations** for us there."

Read with some surprise—Jesus' prediction unfolded with precision.

The disciples then went off, entered the city,
    and found it just as he had told them;
    and they prepared the Passover.

Emphasize all of the verbs.

While they were eating,
    he took **bread**, said the **blessing**,
    broke it, **gave** it to them, and said,
    "**Take** it; this is my **body**."
Then he took a **cup**, gave **thanks**, and gave it to them,
    and they all **drank** from it.
He said to them,
    "This is my **blood** of the **covenant**,
    which will be **shed** for **many**.
Amen, I say to you,
    I shall **not** drink **again** the fruit of the **vine**

Use a tone of regret for Jesus' prediction of his passion and death; Mark's account of this begins soon after this passage.

    until the day when I drink it new in the kingdom of God."
Then, after singing a **hymn**,
    they went out to the Mount of **Olives**.

There is an unsolvable conundrum relating to the Last Supper: was it a Passover meal? Mark, Matthew, and Luke all see the supper as a Passover, whereas John states that Jesus was crucified on the day of preparation for the Passover (John 18:28). Despite Mark's confusing opening sentence, it is clear that he believes that Jesus eats a Passover meal with his disciples. Similar to his entry into Jerusalem, when he sent two disciples to retrieve a colt for him to ride (Mark 11:1–6), Jesus now sends two disciples into the city to make preparations for the Passover.

The description of the meal contains sparse details regarding its Passover elements, but it emphasizes the bread and wine which embody Jesus' sacrificial offering. Significantly, Jesus' words not only rely on the Passover ritual but also draw on the blood of the covenant at Sinai. Just as the first covenant at Sinai was ratified by blood and created a bond between God and the people, so too Jesus' shedding of his blood offers all people a share in the life of the victim. Thus, the sacrifice of Jesus the High Priest establishes a new covenant that will reach fulfillment in the kingdom. S.L.

TENTH SUNDAY IN ORDINARY TIME

LECTIONARY #89

READING I   Genesis 3:9–15

A reading from the Book of Genesis

Genesis = JEN-uh-sihs

Distinguish between the narrator's voice and characters in the story.

God asks three questions. Emphasize "Where," "Who," and "Why." God, of course, knows the answers but gives Adam and Eve the opportunity to verbalize what they have done.

Use an accusatory tone. Adam is passing the blame.

The blame game continues as Eve blames the snake. Nobody is taking responsibility.

After the man, **Adam**, had **eaten** of the tree,
  the Lord **God** called to the man and **asked** him, "**Where** are
    you?"
He answered, "I **heard** you in the garden;
  but I was **afraid**, because I was **naked**,
  so I **hid** myself."
Then he asked, "**Who** told you that you were naked?
You have eaten, then,
  from the tree of which I had **forbidden** you to eat!"
The man replied, "The **woman** whom **you** put **here** with me—
  she gave me fruit from the tree, and so I ate it."
The Lord God then asked the woman,
  "**Why** did you do such a thing?"
The woman answered, "The **serpent** tricked **me** into it,
  so I ate it."

Then the Lord God said to the **serpent**:
  "Because you have done this, you shall be **banned**
    from all the **animals**
    and from all the wild creatures;
  on your belly shall you **crawl**,
    and **dirt** shall you eat
    all the **days** of your life. »

READING I   Today's readings probe the relationship between good and evil and consider the actions surrounding those forces.

Our first reading today reflects on the Fall. In contrast to ancient religions, which proposed that the origin of evil was *metaphysical* (that is, not created), ancient Israel taught that evil had *moral* origins (that is, it originated in human freedom). The story of the Fall develops Israel's teaching on the origin of evil and is set against the backdrop of the goodness of creation. By the end of Genesis 2, we see that human

beings were the summit of God's creation and had been charged with care of the garden and authority over the animal kingdom. The goodness of God's creation was seen in the harmony of creation and its innocence. But this soon changes.

Genesis 3 consists of three parts: the fall into sin, questioning by God, and receiving punishment. Today's reading covers part two and the beginning of part three. The Lord seeks out Adam and Eve, who have hidden themselves. As Adam and Eve speak with God, their words and actions gradually betray their guilt, beginning with

the act of hiding. Even more, their self-awareness that they are naked indicates that something has radically changed from the innocence and harmony of before. Their eyes have indeed been opened, and they know good and evil (Genesis 3:5). Upon further questioning, evil takes deeper hold of them as each shifts the blame to the other. The questions focus on Adam, who had directly received the command not to eat from the tree. Ironically, Adam's excuse for hiding at the sound of God (that "I heard you"), translated differently would

enmity = EN-mih-tee = hostility

> I will put **enmity** between **you** and the **woman**,
>   and between your offspring and hers;
> he will **strike** at your **head**, while you strike at his **heel**."

For meditation and context:

RESPONSORIAL PSALM   Psalm 130:1–2, 3–4, 5–6, 7–8 (7bc)

R. With the Lord there is mercy, and fullness of redemption.

Out of the depths I cry to you, O LORD;
    LORD, hear my voice!
Let your ears be attentive
    to my voice in supplication.

If you, O LORD, mark iniquities,
    LORD, who can stand?
But with you is forgiveness,
    that you may be revered.

I trust in the LORD;
    my soul trusts in his word.
More than sentinels wait for the dawn,
    let Israel wait for the LORD.

For with the LORD is kindness
    and with him is plenteous redemption;
and he will redeem Israel
    from all their iniquities.

Corinthians = kohr-IN-thee-uhnz

READING II   2 Corinthians 4:13—5:1

A reading from the second Letter of Saint Paul to the Corinthians

Brothers and **sisters**:
Since **we** have the same **spirit** of **faith**,
    according to what is written, *I believed, therefore I spoke,*
    we too believe and therefore we speak,
    knowing that the **one** who **raised** the LORD **Jesus**
    will raise us also **with** Jesus
    and **place** us with you in his presence.
Everything indeed is for you,
    so that the **grace** bestowed in abundance on more and
        more people
    may cause the **thanksgiving** to overflow for the glory of **God**.
Therefore, we are not **discouraged**;
    rather, although our **outer self** is wasting away,
    our **inner** self is being renewed day by day.

Elongate "everything" to represent the expansiveness of what it is expressing.

Grace is unmerited divine favor.

Radiate joy. We are saved and can look forward to life with Jesus in heaven despite our current state in our earthly bodies.

---

imply that he obeyed God, which he did not do.

Because they now claim the right to decide for themselves, independent of what God commanded, the transgressors must also accept responsibility for their decisions. The serpent, the woman, and the man are all punished. From the punishments, we see a universal pattern emerge in which the situation of each is negatively altered in terms of his or her nature, and in terms of the fundamental relationships in which he or she participates. In this reading, we only read about the serpent's punish-

ment. Its nature is altered by restricting its manner of movement, and its relationship with humans is permanently marked by enmity. Although we only hear part of the story of the Fall today, we can still see that innocence is lost, humans are identified as perpetrators, and evil enters the human scene.

READING II   The notion that Paul's second letter to Corinth was originally one letter has long faced questions. While scholars agree on Paul's authorship, many consider the letter as we

have it now to be several of his letters (now lost) combined into one. Nevertheless, consistent themes run throughout the letter, one of which we hear in today's reading as Paul reflects on his suffering and eventual glory.

Through the use of richly descriptive images, Paul identifies his present life, one of suffering on behalf of the Good News, as his "outer self [that] is wasting away" through momentary affliction and suffering, a transitory nature, and a being that is earthly. This is contrasted with the glorious life he anticipates, described as his "inner

A reassuring message for the assembly. Our burdens in our earthly life will be nothing compared to our eternal glory.

For this momentary light **affliction**
    is producing for us an eternal weight of **glory** beyond all
      comparison,
    as we look **not** to what is **seen** but to what is unseen;
    for what is seen is **transitory**, but what is unseen is **eternal**.
For we know that if our earthly dwelling, a **tent**,
    should be **destroyed**,
    we have a **building** from God,
    a dwelling not made with **hands**, eternal in heaven.

GOSPEL   Mark 3:20–35

A reading from the holy Gospel according to Mark

Note the different characters involved in this reading.

Jesus came **home** with his disciples.
Again the crowd gathered,
    making it impossible for them even to eat.
When his relatives **heard** of this they set out to **seize** him,
    for they said, "He is out of his mind."
The **scribes** who had come from Jerusalem said,
    "He is possessed by **Beelzebul**,"
    and "By the prince of demons he **drives** out demons."

Beelzebul = bee-EL-zeh-buhl

Slight pause after "demons" for the scene change.

Use a narrator voice as the reader is informed a parable is coming. Slightly increase your volume when Jesus begins his teaching. There are two main lessons: the weakness of a house divided and the reality that even the strong person can be defeated by someone stronger.

Summoning them, he began to speak to them in **parables**,
    "How can **Satan** drive out **Satan**?
If a **kingdom** is **divided** against itself,
    that kingdom cannot **stand**.
And if a **house** is divided against itself,
    that house will **not** be able to stand.
And if Satan has risen **up** against himself
    and is divided, he **cannot** stand;
    that is the **end** of him.
But **no one** can enter a strong man's house to **plunder**
    his property
    unless he **first** ties up the strong man. »

self [that] is being renewed day by day." The implication is that due to evil (sin and death), Paul's present life of faithfulness is one of transitory suffering. However, because of his faithfulness, he will eventually receive the glories of life eternal. Filled with confidence that "the one who raised the Lord Jesus will raise us also with Jesus," Paul identifies reasons for his hope: his present suffering is only temporary, his efforts are producing fruit, and it will all result in eternal glory. Thus, Paul provides a hope-filled perspective on the relationship between good and evil, confident that good will eventually triumph.

| GOSPEL | In line with the previous reflections on the relation-ship between good and evil, today's Gospel reading recounts a disturbing paradox: some people, including some of his family, associate Jesus' behavior with the forces of evil. Employing a unique technique, Mark uses the frame of family (a contrast between Jesus' *natural* family with his *true* one), to enclose an independent story about the charge that Jesus is possessed by Beelzebul.

Having chosen the twelve disciples, Jesus returns home, where his natural family determines that he is "out of his mind" and seeks to seize him. Since such conditions were usually attributed to evil forces, his family's determination sets the tone by implying that he is controlled by evil. This assessment is joined by the opinion of scribes from Jerusalem who say that Jesus "is possessed by Beelzebul," understanding Jesus' exorcistic actions to actually be done in cooperation with the ruler of demons.

The warning of grave consequence needs to be heard. Don't swallow any of it.

Then he can plunder the house.
Amen, I say to you,
all sins and all **blasphemies** that people utter will be **forgiven**
them.
But whoever blasphemes **against** the Holy **Spirit**
will **never** have forgiveness,
but is guilty of an **everlasting** sin."
For they had said, "He has an unclean spirit."

The intercalation ends, and verses about the family of Jesus, mentioned at the beginning of the passage, resume.

His **mother** and his **brothers** arrived.
Standing **outside** they sent **word** to him and **called** him.
A crowd seated around him told him,
"Your mother and your brothers and your sisters
are outside **asking** for you."
But he said to them in reply,
"**Who** are my mother and my brothers?"
And looking around at those seated in the circle he said,
"**Here** are my mother and my brothers.
For **whoever** does the **will** of **God**
is my brother and sister and mother."

"Here are my . . .": Be familiar with the conclusion so that you can look directly at the assembly. Jesus has redefined family and we are part of it.

Jesus cleverly responds with the rhetorical question: "How can Satan drive out Satan?" He continues to undo their argument with two sayings on the unsustainable nature of internal divisions, whether of a house or of Satan himself. Most importantly, he concludes with a brilliant example: the plundering of a strong man's (*ischyros* in Greek) house. Earlier, in Mark 1:7, John the Baptist had identified Jesus as the "mightier" one (*ischyroteros* in Greek). Thus, it is clear that Jesus is no minion of Satan. Rather, he is the stronger one who ties up the strong man (Satan) and plunders his house by establishing God's reign.

Finally, returning to the frame of family and his teaching on true family, Jesus lays the groundwork when he identifies those guilty of the "everlasting sin" as all who interpret God's action through him as a manifestation of evil. (Note that this is in contrast to later Christian generations that view this sin as a refusal to accept God's mercy and forgiveness.) Armed with that insight, Jesus abandons the concept of *natural* family and embraces the idea of *true* family. He is the master of an undivided household, whose family members consist of those who hear him and act on the will of God. S.L.

ELEVENTH SUNDAY IN ORDINARY TIME

LECTIONARY #92

READING I Ezekiel 17:22–24

A reading from the Book of the Prophet Ezekiel

Thus says the Lord GOD:
  I, too, will **take** from the **crest** of the cedar,
    from its topmost branches tear off a tender shoot,
  and **plant** it on a high and lofty **mountain**;
    on the mountain heights of Israel I will plant it.
  It shall **put forth** branches and **bear** fruit,
    and become a **majestic** cedar.
  Birds of every kind shall **dwell** beneath it,
    every winged thing in the shade of its boughs.
  And **all** the trees of the field shall **know**
    that I, the LORD,
  bring **low** the **high tree**,
    lift **high** the **lowly** tree,
  wither up the **green** tree,
    and make the withered tree **bloom**.
  As I, the LORD, have spoken, so **will** I do.

Ezekiel = ee-ZEE-kee-uhl

Read this as an allegory.

Accentuate the verbs. They speak to God's creative action.

Let your tone communicate the expansive effects of God's actions.

God does not go back on his word.

READING I The collected writings of Ezekiel, a priest-prophet, and one of the first deportees from Jerusalem to Babylon, reflect on Judah's political and social destruction, including the destruction of Jerusalem in 586 BC, through long collections of "dooms" or judgement oracles that were received over nearly twenty years (from 593 to 571 BC).

Following a lengthy doom referred to as the Fable of Two Eagles and Two Shoots, today's reading is a prophecy of restoration. The doom, which immediately precedes today's passage, is presented in poetic language and is followed by two interpretations. The doom identifies two eagles as two rulers who were aggressors, Nebuchadnezzar and Pharaoh, and two shoots as Judah's final kings, Jehoiachin and Zedekiah. Although poetic, the doom accurately reflects historical events and clarifies that God used the eagles to vindicate the covenant violated by the shoots. Thus, Ezekiel explains what is happening to Judah and its royal household during his time in history.

Lest this allegory for the relationship between God and Judah end on a hopeless note, however, the prophet concludes with a prophecy of restoration (today's reading), using the same poetic language as in the doom. Providing hope for a future in the midst of Judah's darkest gloom, Ezekiel declares that God, and not the eagles, will pluck a shoot from the cedar (i.e., Babylon) and plant it "on the mountain heights of Israel" where it will prosper and bear fruit. Becoming a "majestic cedar" (i.e., the restored nation of Judah), it will shelter birds of every kind, and all trees shall know of it. This exalted vision of a restored Judah emphasizes that all the nations of the earth

For meditation and context:

RESPONSORIAL PSALM   Psalm 92:2–3, 13–14, 15–16 (2a)

R. Lord, it is good to give thanks to you.

It is good to give thanks to the LORD,
   to sing praise to your name, Most High,
to proclaim your kindness at dawn
   and your faithfulness throughout
      the night.

The just one shall flourish like the
      palm tree,
   like a cedar of Lebanon shall he grow.

They that are planted in the house of
      the LORD
   shall flourish in the courts of our God.

They shall bear fruit even in old age;
   vigorous and sturdy shall they be,
declaring how just is the LORD,
   my rock, in whom there is no wrong.

Corinthians = kohr-IN-thee-uhnz

Proclaim with the courage that Paul
is describing.

A key teaching in this passage.

"All" will be called, but "each" will be judged.

recompense = REK-uhm-pens =
compensation

READING II   2 Corinthians 5:6–10

A reading from the second Letter of Saint Paul to the Corinthians

Brothers and **sisters**:
We are always **courageous**,
   although we know that while we are at home in the **body**
   we are **away** from the **Lord**,
      for we walk by **faith**, not by **sight**.
Yet we are courageous,
   and we would rather **leave** the body and go **home** to the **Lord**.
Therefore, we **aspire** to **please** him,
   whether we are at home **or** away.
For we must **all** appear before the **judgment** seat of Christ,
   so that **each** may receive **recompense**,
      according to what he **did** in the body, whether **good** or **evil**.

---

will recognize that God is sovereign over all nations and that God is the great reverser of national fortunes.

READING II   In today's reading, Paul reflects upon his suffering as an apostle and what gives him hope in the face of it.

Paul begins by comparing two possible states of being which are in tension with one another. His current situation is that he is "at home in the body." Its opposite is to "leave the body and go home to the Lord." Thus, for Paul, being in the body

is a form of suffering because he is away from the Lord. We should not interpret this as negating the incarnational aspect of our faith, but see that it emphasizes what all Christians strive for—eternal life in the presence of God. Although Paul is walking by faith, he is not seeing God face to face. In giving voice to his longing for his true home, Paul describes the destiny of all Christians: being in the body and longing to go home to the Lord.

Thus, Paul concludes that while he and the Corinthians are still in the body, they must do everything possible to please

the Lord. And why? Because our human lives are meaningful. Our choices reflect our faith in the hope of eternal life, and eventually each person will have to give an accounting of what he or she has done in the body. Against the backdrop of this suffering, Paul finds hope in the promise of his and the Corinthians' future home.

GOSPEL   In order to better understand the message of Mark's Gospel, it is important to recall that Mark's original audience was a community of persecuted Christians who needed hope.

GOSPEL   Mark 4:26–34

A reading from the holy Gospel according to Mark

Jesus said to the **crowds**:
   "This is how it is with the kingdom of **God**;
   it is as if a **man** were to scatter **seed** on the land
   and would **sleep** and **rise night** and **day**
   and through it all the seed would **sprout** and **grow**,
   he knows not **how**.
Of its own **accord** the land yields **fruit**,
   first the **blade**, then the **ear**, then the full **grain** in the ear.
And when the grain is **ripe**, he wields the **sickle** at once,
   for the **harvest** has come."

He said,
   "To what shall we **compare** the kingdom of **God**,
   or what **parable** can we use for it?
It is like a mustard **seed** that, when it is sown in the **ground**,
   is the **smallest** of all the seeds on the earth.
But once it is sown, it springs up and becomes the **largest**
      of plants
   and puts forth large **branches**,
   so that the birds of the sky can **dwell** in its shade."
With many such **parables**
   he spoke the word to them as they were able to **understand** it.
Without parables he did not speak to them,
   but to his own **disciples** he **explained** everything in private.

Insert a comma after "rise" so the opposites are emphasized.

Jesus meets people where they are. He spoke to them in the form of a metaphorical story they could wrestle with for themselves. This can be a good model for how we should evangelize others.

Jesus gave additional explanations to his disciples, revealing the meanings of the parables. How can the homily do the same? What might your assembly need to know about who God is, based on this reading?

Read in this light, today's Gospel reading offers encouragement in their work of building up the kingdom of God.

Among Jesus' teachings are parables about the kingdom of God, which often make their point through agricultural images familiar to his audience. Today's Gospel includes two such parables, as well as a note informing us that Jesus often interpreted his parables privately for his disciples.

The parables of the scattered seed and the mustard seed describe the kingdom of God and contain two powerful insights into the nature of that kingdom. There is a contrast between small beginnings (scattered seed and a tiny mustard seed) and their final form (fully grown grain and a large plant). Equally important in this passage is the fact that what at present appears imperceptible will grow in mysterious ways beyond human understanding. The unspoken conclusion is that God is at work.

At the end of today's reading, we hear that although Jesus teaches the crowds in parables, he explains them to his disciples in private. The earlier insight into the slow and mysterious unfolding of the kingdom, as well as the note that Jesus teaches the disciples privately, offers a powerful message of hope in the face of suffering. To Mark's suffering and persecuted community, who were themselves recipients of instruction on the Gospel, Jesus' message offers hope that the seed sown by Christ and through their Christian witness is in fact growing and maturing in mysterious and divinely directed ways toward the fullness of God's kingdom. They need only to hear it, accept it, and patiently allow it to bear fruit. S.L.

TWELFTH SUNDAY
IN ORDINARY TIME

Job = johb

Read the missing verses from today's reading in Job 38 to help set the context for this reading. The questions have an obvious answer; don't proclaim them too harshly. The Lord's reflection on his power over primordial forces is meant to instruct Job (and us).

LECTIONARY #95

READING I Job 38:1, 8–11

A reading from the Book of Job

The **Lord** addressed **Job** out of the **storm** and said:
  Who shut within doors the sea,
    when it burst forth from the womb;
  when I made the clouds its garment
    and thick darkness its swaddling bands?
  When I **set limits** for it
    and fastened the bar of its door,
  and said: **Thus far** shall you come but no **farther**,
    and **here** shall your proud waves be stilled!

For meditation and context:

RESPONSORIAL PSALM Psalm 107:23–24, 25–26, 28–29, 30–31 (1b)

R. Give thanks to the Lord, his love is everlasting.
or
R. Alleluia.

They who sailed the sea in ships,
  trading on the deep waters,
these saw the works of the Lord
  and his wonders in the abyss.

His command raised up a storm wind
  which tossed its waves on high.
They mounted up to heaven; they sank to
  the depths;
  their hearts melted away in their plight.

They cried to the Lord in their distress;
  from their straits he rescued them,
he hushed the storm to a gentle breeze,
  and the billows of the sea were stilled.

They rejoiced that they were calmed,
  and he brought them to their
    desired haven.
Let them give thanks to the Lord for
    his kindness
  and his wondrous deeds to the children
    of men.

READING I In the ancient world of which Israel was a part, people feared the chaos of water and the power of the storm. Like other nations, ancient Israel's writers believed that only God was powerful enough to control such chaos. Power over nature was reserved to God. This conviction can be seen in the first reading, psalm, and Gospel today.

The Book of Job ponders a dilemma faced by many ancient (and modern) people: why do the innocent suffer if God, who is all powerful and all compassionate, is the primary cause for everything? The basic story of Job is based on an ancient folk tale, yet Israel's version of it that we have today reveals important theological questions. The author includes conversations between Job and his friends, in which they dispute Job's innocence. Following these conversations, the Lord engages in dialogue with Job, and Job responds (38:1—42:6). Today's reading is the beginning of the conversation between the Lord and Job.

The Lord's terrifying response to Job comes from the midst of the storm. It speaks of power and divine presence, which cannot be matched by anything else.

Calling to mind Genesis' account of creation, as well as the imagery in today's Psalm 107, we hear a series of questions that demonstrate God's omnipotence. In the face of these powerful acts of the Lord, Job will admit his powerlessness. While the text focuses on God's almighty nature, especially over water, it gives little evidence of God's compassion and justice, which is what we would have expected to hear in response to Job's particular quest for divine justice in the face of suffering. Instead, we are invited to focus on God's power over everything.

Corinthians = kohr-IN-thee-uhnz

Notice the plural pronouns; proclaim in a way that invites the assembly into the reading. Read slowly; the vocabulary is repetitive, which can be confusing.

We should work to see everyone through the eyes of faith, rather than with our human tendency to judge.

READING II   2 Corinthians 5:14–17

A reading from the second Letter of Saint Paul to the Corinthians

Brothers and **sisters**:
The **love** of **Christ impels** us,
    once we have come to the conviction that **one died** for **all**;
    therefore, **all** have died.
He indeed died for all,
    so that those who **live** might **no longer** live for **themselves**
    but for **him** who for their sake died and was **raised**.

Consequently, from now on we regard no one according to
        the **flesh**;
    even if we once **knew Christ** according to the flesh,
    yet now we know him so no longer.
So whoever is **in** Christ is a new **creation**:
    the **old** things have passed **away**;
    behold, **new** things have **come**.

Read the miracle story with the amazement you would have if you were in the stormy scene. Also, look for details you might not have noticed before. For example, "Other boats were with him."

GOSPEL   Mark 4:35–41

A reading from the holy Gospel according to Mark

On that day, as evening drew on, **Jesus** said to his **disciples**:
    "Let us **cross** to the other side."
Leaving the **crowd**, they took Jesus with them in the boat just as
        he was.
And other boats were with him.
A violent **squall** came up and waves were **breaking** over
        the boat,
    so that it was already **filling** up.
Jesus was in the stern, **asleep** on a cushion. **»**

READING II | Continuing the theme of the second readings over the past three weeks, in which Paul reflects on the relationship between his suffering and eventual glory, today's reading places Paul's ministry in the heart of salvation history—the Christ event.

This passage, dense with meaning, unfolds in three steps. First, identifying Christ's salvific act as the love of Christ, which is now the guiding star of his life, Paul unpacks the elements of that event. Second, he describes how the love of Christ has brought Christians to a new way of knowing. Third, he reflects on how those who fully embrace the love of Christ become a new creation.

Echoing the ancient formula, that Christ has died for sins, Paul rewords it: "one died for all." Paul uses his image of Christ who is the New Adam (see Romans 5:6, 12–19) to clarify that Christ's death affects all people in that all can now die to sin. Nevertheless, this gift requires acceptance and response in that "those who live might no longer live for themselves, but for him." The evidence of this acceptance is found in a new way of knowing (which stands in contrast to knowing "according to the flesh") and a new way of being ("a new creation"). This transformation is true for all Christians and aids us in our journey of discipleship.

GOSPEL | Today's Gospel plays a pivotal role in the progression of Mark's Gospel. It is the transition from Jesus' earlier teaching ministry (Mark 3:13—4:34) to a collection of Jesus' mighty deeds (Mark 4:35—8:26). In this text, Jesus expands his ministry from Galilee into Gentile territory. The text also develops

Use a panicked voice to call out, "Teacher."

Jesus speaks with authority and his words are efficacious. Let your tone reflect this.

Jesus knows of their fear, yet he wants them to name it. What tone does he use: disappointment? surprise? Read accordingly.

Read the last line with wonder.

They **woke** him and said to him,
  "**Teacher**, do you not **care** that we are **perishing**?"
He woke up,
  rebuked the wind, and said to the sea, "**Quiet**! Be **still**!"
The wind **ceased** and there was great **calm**.
Then he asked them, "**Why** are you **terrified**?
Do you not **yet** have **faith**?"
They were **filled** with great **awe** and said to one another,
  "**Who** then **is** this whom even wind and sea **obey**?"

discipleship by moving from positive descriptions to critiques of deficient discipleship (as in today's reading when he asks them, "Do you not yet have faith?"). Finally, it further develops Jesus' identity by vesting him with the divine attribute of power over watery chaos.

The transitional nature of this passage is expressed early on in Jesus' instruction to cross to the other side of the sea. With the transition taking place at night, upon water, and in the midst of a storm, the ancient fears of darkness, water, and the chaotic forces of nature are all evoked.

Combined with the images from Job and Psalm 107, the Gospel account reminds us of Israel's conviction that God alone was powerful enough to protect humans from such forces that were often identified with evil, and that relying on God was a necessary act of faith. The final resolution of the danger contributes to our understanding of both Jesus and his disciples.

In terms of Jesus, the account clearly aligns him with divine power over the forces of evil, all metaphorically portrayed by darkness, water, storm, and violent wind. In fact, even Jesus' sleep recalls how

the "Lord awoke as from sleep, . . . He put his foes to flight" (Psalm 78:65–66). Through Jesus' rebuke of the wind and calming of the sea, the disciples are awestruck and terrified because they have seen God at work. Despite Jesus' earlier explanations of his parables in private, the disciples realize that faith is clearly more than the possession of knowledge. Ultimately, this event prompts deeper questions regarding Jesus' identity that will only be answered by the cross (Mark 15:39). S.L.

THIRTEENTH SUNDAY IN ORDINARY TIME

LECTIONARY #98

READING I Wisdom 1:13–15; 2:23–24

A reading from the Book of Wisdom

God's creation is always made for good. Let your tone reflect this goodness; it is encouraging to be reminded of this.

> **God** did not make **death**,
> nor does he rejoice in the **destruction** of the **living**.
> For he **fashioned** all things that they might have **being**;
> and the **creatures** of the world are **wholesome**,
> and there is not a **destructive** drug among them
> nor any domain of the netherworld on earth,
> for **justice** is **undying**.
> For God formed man to be **imperishable**;
> the **image** of his own **nature** he made him.
> But by the envy of the **devil**, **death entered** the world,
> and they who **belong** to his company **experience** it.

Don't lose any of the last line. This is an important warning: evil still lurks in our world. Use a comma after "company."

For meditation and context:

RESPONSORIAL PSALM Psalm 30:2, 4, 5–6, 11, 12, 13 (2a)

R. I will praise you, Lord, for you have rescued me.

I will extol you, O Lord, for you drew
me clear
    and did not let my enemies rejoice
    over me.
O Lord, you brought me up from the
netherworld;
    you preserved me from among those
    going down into the pit.

Sing praise to the Lord, you his
faithful ones,
    and give thanks to his holy name.

For his anger lasts but a moment;
    a lifetime, his good will.
At nightfall, weeping enters in,
    but with the dawn, rejoicing.

Hear, O Lord, and have pity on me;
    O Lord, be my helper.
You changed my mourning into dancing;
    O Lord, my God, forever will I give
    you thanks.

READING I The Book of Wisdom, an anonymous Greek apocryphal work composed between 200 BC–AD 100, is part of the wisdom literature of the Catholic Old Testament. It was written to encourage diaspora Jews to stand firm in their wisdom tradition. Today's reading comes from the first part of Wisdom, which focuses on righteousness (*dikaiosynē* in Greek) and immortality (*athanatos* in Greek). Indeed, Wisdom 1:1 calls the reader to love righteousness and joins it with the assertion in today's reading that "justice is undying." In this passage, the term *dikaiosynē* (justice) reflects the biblical sense of the word—that is, being in right relationship with God and engaging in right behavior toward others. Therefore, it should not be confused with the contemporary judicial term "justice," which can confuse our understanding of this passage.

Working toward the conclusion, then, that right relationship with God is "undying," the reading contrasts death with life. God and the right relationship with God are placed firmly on the side of life, drawing a lesson from Genesis' account of creation, in which God created us in his image. Still, although God is firmly grounded on the side of life, the final verses acknowledge that death is possible. Alluding now to Genesis 3, the story of the Fall, Wisdom notes that Adam and Eve's human sin facilitated the entry of death into the world through "the envy of the devil." This envy, and the death it leads to, stands in stark contrast to God's intention for humankind: to exist, to have a wholesome and imperishable nature, and to be made in God's image. In other words, God created human beings for eternal righteousness.

Corinthians = kohr-IN-thee-uhnz

This is an exhortatory text, a strong urge for compliance. Paul first compliments the people of Corinth before asking for their generous financial support. List the community's virtues slowly.

Proclaim the quote strongly so that the assembly clearly understands that Paul is supporting his exhortation with Scripture.

READING II   2 Corinthians 8:7, 9, 13–15

A reading from the second Letter of Saint Paul to the Corinthians

Brothers and **sisters:**
As you **excel** in **every** respect, in **faith**, **discourse**,
    knowledge, all **earnestness**, and in the **love** we have for you,
    may you excel in this gracious **act** also.

For you know the gracious act of our Lord Jesus **Christ**,
    that though he was **rich**, for your sake he became **poor**,
    so that by his **poverty you** might become **rich**.
Not that others should have **relief** while you are **burdened**,
    but that as a matter of equality
    your **abundance** at the present time should supply their **needs**,
    so that their abundance may **also** supply **your** needs,
    that there may be **equality**.
As it is written:
    *Whoever had **much** did not have **more**,*
    *and whoever had **little** did not have **less**.*

Read the responsorial psalm for today. In this Gospel narrative, Christ's healings do what the psalmist proclaims, changing mourning into dancing.

Jairus = JĪ-ruhs or jay-ī-ruhs

The father's bodily posture shows his desperation. The tone of his request should reflect his anguish.

GOSPEL   Mark 5:21–43

A reading from the holy Gospel according to Mark

[When **Jesus** had crossed again in the boat
    to the **other** side,
    a large **crowd** gathered **around** him, and he stayed **close**
        to the **sea**.
One of the synagogue **officials**, named **Jairus**, came forward.
Seeing him he fell at his **feet** and **pleaded** earnestly
        with him, saying,
    "My **daughter** is at the point of **death**.

READING II 2 Corinthians is well known for Paul's attempts to reconcile with the community. Less well known are the chapters where Paul appeals to the Corinthian community to complete a collection for the community in Jerusalem. Throughout his missionary travels, Paul encourages his communities to show Christian solidarity by collecting money to support the impoverished mother Church in Jerusalem.

Although Paul's correspondence with the Corinthians is often quite heated, regarding the collection he opts for persua-sion rather than confrontation. First, he seeks to persuade them by praising their faith, discourse, and knowledge, and he even recalls his love for them. All of this, Paul says, is reason enough for them to "excel in this gracious act also." He further builds his case by citing the example of Jesus, who was "rich" (divine) and became "poor" (human) for their sake. This image resonates powerfully with Philippians 2:6–11, which portrays Jesus surrendering his divinity to assume poor humanity. This image of the "poor Christ" (in humanity and also in poverty) has long resonated in the Church.

Finally, as if the gifts in which they excel and Jesus' own example are not enough, Paul also states that the collection is a "matter of equality." Recalling Exodus 16:18 at the end of this reading, Paul reminds the Corinthians that in collecting manna in the wilderness, God assured the Hebrews that all would have enough if each took as God directed, so that the needs of all could be supplied. So how should they abide in God? By following the example of the Hebrews in the wilderness and that

Add a slight pause after "come" and "her."

Please, **come lay** your hands on her
  that she may **get well** and live."
He went off with him,
  and a large crowd **followed** him and pressed upon him.]

There was a **woman** afflicted with **hemorrhages** for twelve **years**.
She had **suffered** greatly at the hands of many doctors
  and had **spent all** that she had.
Yet she was not **helped** but only grew **worse**.
She had heard about **Jesus** and came up behind him in the crowd
  and **touched** his **cloak**.
She said, "If I but touch his clothes, I shall be **cured**."
Immediately her flow of blood **dried** up.
She felt in her body that she was **healed** of her affliction.
Jesus, aware at once that **power** had gone **out** from him,
  turned around in the crowd and asked, "**Who** has touched
    my clothes?"
But his disciples said to Jesus,
  "You see how the **crowd** is **pressing** upon you,
  and **yet** you ask, 'Who **touched** me?'"
And he looked around to see who had done it.
The woman, realizing what had happened to her,
  approached in **fear** and **trembling**.
She fell **down** before Jesus and told him the whole **truth**.
He said to her, "**Daughter**, your **faith** has saved you.
Go in **peace** and be **cured** of your affliction."

[While he was still speaking,
  people from the synagogue official's house **arrived** and said,
  "**Your daughter** has **died**; why **trouble** the teacher any **longer**?"
Disregarding the message that was reported,
  Jesus said to the synagogue official,
  "**Do not be afraid**; just have **faith**."
He did **not allow** anyone to **accompany** him inside
  except Peter, James, and John, the brother of James. »

Read "Immediately" with emphasis. Illness is easily—and completely—cured by God's power. Increase your pace slightly to show excitement.

The narrator interprets what Jesus is thinking. Deliver Jesus' question with a surprised, upward inflection.

Deliver the disciples' lines with a slightly scoffing tone. Given the crowd, they think Jesus is wasting his time.

Don't minimize her fear. She has violated religious prohibitions (based on her condition). Her life has consisted of the inability to touch others. Note, this is not moral impurity. Despite the obstacles she faced, her faith remains strong.

Attention is now turned to the ending of the first miracle story. Be clear in your proclamation so that the assembly recognizes the shift between stories.

Deliver "Do not be afraid" with a calm but strong voice. The distraught parents must hear his reassurances.

---

of the poor Christ united with humanity. In other words, the Corinthians should embrace mutual concern as they support their poorer fellow Christians in Jerusalem.

GOSPEL Last Sunday we saw that Mark moved from Jesus' teaching ministry into a more active phase, demonstrating his power over the forces of nature, a power he shared with God. All of this occurred in Gentile territory. While in that same territory, Jesus confronted and vanquished the fierce Gerasene demoniac (Mark 5:1–20), showing yet another aspect

of his divine power. In today's Gospel, Jesus returns to Jewish territory and displays mighty actions in the form of healing two people on the edge of death. His actions point to the divine power of life over death.

The two accounts are presented using a distinctively Marcan technique: intercalation. Intercalation means that there is a story inside of a story. The outer story begins with the appeal from a synagogue official, Jairus. As Jesus is on his way to heal Jairus' daughter, the inner story starts when a woman with hemorrhages touches Jesus' cloak and is healed. The outer story

resumes when Jesus journeys to Jairus' home and heals Jairus' daughter.

While Jesus' healing power is essential in each account, the faith of the woman and of Jairus is a key theological point. Though it is difficult to ascertain exactly what disease afflicts the woman, it is clear that she was not always bleeding, for she would have died. Still, her ongoing bleeding makes her infertile, and also in a constant state of ritual impurity, both of which were serious social liabilities. Furthermore, she is getting worse, perhaps even approaching death. Overcoming the physical barrier of

Use a voice of condemnation. Jesus' response is decisive in the face of their ridicule.

Talitha koum= tal-uh-thuh KOOM
or tah-lee-thah KOOM

Practice the Aramaic phrase until you are comfortable announcing it loudly. A strong commanding voice is needed.

Again, stress "immediately." God's performative words do not get any argument from laws of nature.

When they **arrived** at the **house** of the synagogue official,
    he caught sight of a commotion,
    people **weeping** and **wailing** loudly.
So he went in and said to them,
    "**Why** this commotion and weeping?
The child is **not** dead but **asleep**."
And **they ridiculed** him.
Then he **put** them **all out**.
He took along the child's **father** and **mother**
    and those who were with him
    and entered the room where the child was.
He took the child by the **hand** and said to her, "*Talitha koum*,"
    which means, "Little **girl**, I say to you, **arise**!"
The girl, a child of twelve, arose **immediately** and
        walked around.
At that they were utterly **astounded**.
He gave strict orders that **no one** should **know** this
    and said that she should be given something to eat.]

[Shorter: Mark 5:21–24, 35b–43 (see brackets)]

the crowd, and the religious barrier of ritual impurity, she touches Jesus' clothing and is healed. As both she and Jesus are aware of this healing, she is struck with fear (that is, divine awe) and gives witness to it. Jesus commends her by calling her daughter, praising her faith, sending her away in peace, and declaring her permanently healed. Her faith is paralleled by that of Jairus, who is called to believe despite the sad news from his home. The fact that he accompanies Jesus is a sign of his faith. The story concludes when Jesus enters Jairus' home and heals/raises the girl to life.

The narratives are striking in that they feature two females: a woman suffering for twelve years, and a twelve-year-old girl. Does twelve connect them? In the case of the girl, first called daughter, later, child (*paidion* in Greek), and finally, "little girl"/ young woman (*korasion* in Greek), twelve indicates that she is of marriageable age. Having saved both of these "daughters" from death, perhaps Mark is asserting that Jesus delivers them to life, as both would now be able to bear children, indicating God's favor and blessing. What is clear is that the Gospel affirms that God's power stands on the side of life and rescues the vulnerable from death. S.L.

FOURTEENTH SUNDAY IN ORDINARY TIME

LECTIONARY #101

READING I   Ezekiel 2:2–5

Ezekiel = ee-ZEE-kee-uhl

This is a commissioning story. Look for three parts: God sending, authoritative instruction, and a description of the response.

The prophet's ministry is daunting. However, don't let your tone become too gloomy; God's word strengthens Ezekiel.

A reading from the Book of the Prophet Ezekiel

As the **Lord** spoke to me, the **spirit** entered into me
  and set me on my **feet**,
and I **heard** the one who was speaking say to me:
Son of **man**, I am **sending** you to the **Israelites**,
  rebels who have **rebelled** against me;
they and their ancestors have revolted against me
    to this very **day**.
Hard of face and **obstinate** of heart
  are they to whom I am sending you.
But you shall **say** to them: Thus says the Lord **God**!
And whether they **heed** or **resist**—for they are a
    rebellious house—
  they shall **know** that a **prophet** has been among them.

RESPONSORIAL PSALM   Psalm 123:1–2, 2, 3–4 (2cd)

For meditation and context:

R. Our eyes are fixed on the Lord, pleading for his mercy.

To you I lift up my eyes
  who are enthroned in heaven—
as the eyes of servants
  are on the hands of their masters.

As the eyes of a maid
  are on the hands of her mistress,
so are our eyes on the Lord, our God,
  till he have pity on us.

Have pity on us, O Lord, have pity on us,
  for we are more than sated with
    contempt;
our souls are more than sated
  with the mockery of the arrogant,
  with the contempt of the proud.

READING I   Are prophets born or made? While some prophets like Jeremiah (Jeremiah 1:5) and John the Baptist (Luke 1:15) are called from the womb, others are pressed into the role. Whether born or made, the prophet's mission is daunting. Ezekiel (597–571 BC), the third of the major prophets, was a priest in Babylonian exile who was pressed to serve as God's prophet.

  Writing in the first person ("I"), Ezekiel begins by describing a heavenly vision (1:1–28) that leads to his prophetic commission in today's reading. Once the vision's enthroned figure speaks, Ezekiel is invaded by the spirit (*rûaḥ* in Hebrew; wind, spirit), which sets him on his feet and empowers him to hear the divine voice. Identified as "Son of man" (an epithet for a human person and used frequently to identify Ezekiel), the priest, now become prophet, hears a summary of his mission. He is to inform the Israelites that God has spoken—"Thus says the Lord God!" For their part, the Israelites have rebellion in their blood that is both external ("hard of face") and internal ("obstinate of heart"). In the face of their rebellion against God, the formulaic "Thus says the Lord God" is but the first of many instances where God's message is communicated to them in greater detail. Whether God's message through the priest/prophet is heeded or not, the rebellious Israelites will know that God's prophet and God's Word are present.

READING II   One of Paul's most persistent challenges with the early Christian communities was his need to defend his authority. As today's reading demonstrates, Paul employed sophisticated

READING II   2 Corinthians 12:7–10

A reading from the second Letter of Saint Paul to the Corinthians

Brothers and **sisters**:
That I, **Paul**, might not become too **elated**,
    because of the abundance of the **revelations**,
    a **thorn** in the flesh was **given** to me, an angel of **Satan**,
    to **beat** me, to keep me from being too **elated**.
Three times I **begged** the **Lord** about this, that it might **leave** me,
    but he said to me, "My **grace** is **sufficient** for you,
    for **power** is made perfect in **weakness**."
I will rather boast most gladly of my weaknesses,
    in order that the power of **Christ** may **dwell** with me.
Therefore, I am **content** with **weaknesses**, **insults**,
    hardships, **persecutions** and **constraints**,
    for the sake of Christ;
    for when I am **weak**, then I am **strong**.

Corinthians = kohr-IN-thee-uhnz

Paul acknowledges the gift of his faith.

Paul is not complacent. He does not seek out the "thorn" but acknowledges what the suffering accomplishes.

Deliver the paradox looking directly at the assembly.

GOSPEL   Mark 6:1–6

A reading from the holy Gospel according to Mark

Jesus departed from there and came to his native **place**,
    accompanied by his **disciples**.
When the sabbath came he began to **teach** in the **synagogue**,
    and many who heard him were **astonished**.
They said, "**Where** did this man **get** all this?
What kind of **wisdom** has been **given** him?
What mighty **deeds** are wrought by his hands!
Is he not the **carpenter**, the son of **Mary**,
    and the **brother** of James and Joses and Judas and Simon?
And are not his **sisters** here with us?"
And they took **offense** at him.

Jesus comes as a teacher. They hear, yet they don't (want to) believe. Let the dissonance of the situation come through.

Naming his relatives gives the decriers assurance they have identified the right person. Read with a dismissive tone.
Joses = JOH-seez or JOH-sez

---

rhetorical techniques to convince his Corinthian audience of his authority.

Drawn from the midst of such arguments (2 Corinthians 10—13), chapter 12 begins with Paul's account of his "visions and revelations of the Lord" (2 Corinthians 12:1) and leads to his remarks in today's readings about the "thorn" in his flesh. While all of this is placed in the context of his boasting, Paul cleverly pulls back, giving all of the honor to God's choice (and authority) rather than to himself. Thus, the visions and revelations are not from Paul, nor does he even understand what hap-

pened, and truth demands that he boast only of the giver: the Lord. And lest he rely on having been the recipient of such visions ("being too elated"), God gives him a thorn in the flesh to torment him.

While much speculation surrounds the "thorn" (lust, physical or emotional illness, or even human or demonic opponents), no sure answer is possible. Even more, such speculation obscures Christ's remarkable response: "My grace is sufficient for you." The statement brings the entire account back to boasting and the fact that there is no room for it. While the statement leads

Paul to state that he will "boast most gladly of my weaknesses," he actually places the entire focus on the Lord, who is the true authority and who has extended authority to Paul through vision, thorn, and grace.

GOSPEL   The earliest of the Gospels, Mark's lean account tries to answer the question: Who is Jesus? To answer the question, the first half of Mark records many of Jesus' teachings and actions: healing the blind, deaf, sick, lame; expelling demons; and even raising the

It wasn't that Jesus had no power; it was that he found no faith.

Read with disappointment.

Jesus said to them,
   "A **prophet** is not without **honor** except in his **native** place
      and among his **own kin** and in his own **house**."
So he was **not** able to perform any mighty **deed** there,
   apart from curing a few **sick** people by laying his hands
      on them.
He was **amazed** at their lack of **faith**.

dead. All of it leads to questions about his identity.

Today's Gospel reading emphasizes the fact that those who know Jesus expect nothing extraordinary from him. He is a tradesman, the son of tradesmen. His family members are ordinary and known. Earlier in Mark, Jesus' teaching and actions were deemed threatening to the social order and inappropriate to his status (Mark 3:6). His family determined that he was mentally unstable (Mark 3:21). In today's account, cognitive dissonance reigns! The towns-people know how ordinary Jesus and his family are. Still, the marvels they hear of him lead them to ask disparaging questions and to conclude that he is offensive. Unable to move past their preconceived notions (*Who does he think he is?*), they refuse to believe in him or accept him.

There are two points worth noting. First, Jesus' words and actions (and the example he cites), along with Nazareth's reaction, align him with other Jewish prophets. Unwilling to entertain the prophets' challenging messages, the people neutralized the message by attacking or devaluing the person of the prophet. Jesus will be no different. Second, even if Jesus' family and fellow citizens refuse to believe in him and accept him, there is an emerging group that does: his disciples and those whose lives he has touched. Jesus already identified them as his true family (Mark 3:33–35). Soon he sends them out on mission. S.L.

FIFTEENTH SUNDAY
IN ORDINARY TIME

LECTIONARY #104

READING I   Amos 7:12–15

A reading from the Book of the Prophet Amos

Amaziah, **priest** of **Bethel**, said to **Amos**,
  "**Off** with you, **visionary**, **flee** to the land of **Judah**!
There **earn** your bread by **prophesying**,
  but **never again** prophesy in Bethel;
  for it is the **king's** sanctuary and a royal **temple**."
Amos answered Amaziah, "I was **no** prophet,
  nor have I belonged to a **company** of prophets;
  I was a **shepherd** and a dresser of **sycamores**.
The LORD **took** me from following the flock, and said to me,
  Go, **prophesy** to my people **Israel**."

Amos = AY-m*s
Announce the name of the book carefully.
It is read only once in the Sundays of Year B.

Amaziah = am-uh-ZĪ-uh
Bethel = BETH-*l
Judah = JOO-duh
prophesying = PROF-uh-sī-ing
prophesy = PROF-uh-sī (verb)

Read "never again" with force.

Amos is not self-deprecating or apologetic.
He is explaining himself; he was not a career prophet.

For meditation and context:

RESPONSORIAL PSALM   Psalm 85:9–10, 11–12, 13–14 (8)

R. Lord, let us see your kindness, and grant us your salvation.

I will hear what God proclaims;
  the LORD—for he proclaims peace.
Near indeed is his salvation to those
    who fear him,
  glory dwelling in our land.

Kindness and truth shall meet;
  justice and peace shall kiss.

Truth shall spring out of the earth,
  and justice shall look down from heaven.

The LORD himself will give his benefits;
  our land shall yield its increase.
Justice shall walk before him,
  and prepare the way of his steps.

READING I   Whether prophets or apostles, those who bear challenging messages are often resisted and rejected. Such resistance frequently comes from political and religious leaders, as the prophet Amos discovers. Living in the eighth century BC, Amos, an agriculturalist from Judah (the southern kingdom), was active during the period of the two kingdoms, and challenged the religious and political leadership of Israel (the northern kingdom). Despite the relative economic prosperity of the era, all was not well. As a vassal state to the larger kingdom (Israel), Judah and its population financed Israel's imperial ambitions through heavy taxes and tribute. Three times a year, Judah's people reported to the shrine at Bethel, delivering tribute in spite of the hardships caused by plague and fire. Oppressed like other Judeans, and pressed by God into prophecy, Amos' visit to Bethel led him to deliver fiery oracles against the nations, sermons describing Israel's abuses of the poor, calls to change, and visions of Bethel's future destruction.

Today's reading is a brief biographical narrative from those final visions. It describes Amos' confrontation with Amaziah, the priest of Bethel. The surrounding visions define God's message through Amos: the Lord seeks the removal of Israel's dynasty and its cultic establishment and seeks to restore the house of David over all of Israel. Amaziah, representing king and cult, makes it clear that Amos' message is not welcome in Israel. Indeed, it is seen as treason. For his part, Amos emphasizes the dire nature of things when he notes that he is neither a prophet nor a part of a larger group of prophets. Rather, he is a "shepherd and a dresser of sycamores." In other words, he

Ephesians = ee-FEE-zhuhnz

A lot is packed into this reading. Try reading other Scripture translations to aid in your understanding of the text.

Paul is describing the effects of being followers of Christ: adopted, redeemed, forgiven, have encountered the mystery, chosen. Use energy but don't exhaust the listener. Practice your pacing.

Pay attention to the connections being made between what Christ did and what his actions are doing to us now.

READING II   Ephesians 1:3–14

A reading from the Letter of Saint Paul to the Ephesians

[**Blessed** be the **God** and **Father** of our Lord Jesus **Christ**,
　　who has blessed us **in** Christ
　　with every spiritual **blessing** in the heavens,
　　as he **chose** us in him, before the foundation of the world,
　　to be **holy** and without blemish before him.
In **love** he destined us for **adoption** to himself through
　　　Jesus Christ,
　　in accord with the favor of his **will**,
　　for the praise of the glory of his **grace**
　　that he granted us in the **beloved**.

In **him** we have **redemption** by his blood,
　　the **forgiveness** of transgressions,
　　in accord with the **riches** of his grace that he lavished
　　　upon us.
In all **wisdom** and insight, he has made known to us
　　the **mystery** of his will in accord with his favor
　　that he set forth in him as a plan for the **fullness** of times,
　　to sum up all things in Christ, in **heaven** and on **earth**.]

In **him** we were also chosen,
　　destined in accord with the purpose of the One
　　who accomplishes all things according to the intention
　　　of his **will**,
　　so that we might exist for the **praise** of his glory,
　　we who first hoped in Christ. »

knows the oppression from Israel firsthand, and has been sent by God to testify to it.

READING II Letters are the most common form of writing in the New Testament, and they typically follow the conventions of Greco-Roman letters. Beginning with an opening greeting or salutation, most New Testament letters are then followed by a thanksgiving. However, three letters (2 Corinthians, 1 Peter, and Ephesians) insert a Jewish feature, the blessing. It is the blessing in Ephesians that constitutes today's second reading.

Shaped by some of the liturgical features of blessings (such as frequent repetitions), and consisting of one long sentence, the blessing in Ephesians blesses God and the recipients of God's blessing by describing God's universal plan for salvation that has existed from "before the foundation of the world" and is now fulfilled in Christ. In Christ, the recipients of blessing have been chosen and destined for God. They have received spiritual blessing, adoption, redemption, forgiveness, grace, and wisdom and insight into the mystery of God's will. Most importantly, believers have received the Holy Spirit as the promise of their "inheritance toward redemption."

In addition to its liturgical features, the blessing depicts God as a patron who has released his dependents through his agent (redemption through Christ), reflecting the patron-client relationship of the age. Somewhat uniquely, the blessing emphasizes that this redemption is already experienced now, thus setting believers apart from others in the age, even as it points to future redemptive features.

The purpose of our transformation in Christ is our salvation and our praise of God that flows from it.

In **him** you also, who have heard the word of **truth**,
    the gospel of your **salvation**, and have believed in him,
    were **sealed** with the promised Holy **Spirit**,
    which is the **first** installment of our **inheritance**
    toward redemption as God's **possession**, to the **praise**
      of his glory.

[Shorter: Ephesians 1:3–10 (see brackets)]

GOSPEL   Mark 6:7–13

A reading from the holy Gospel according to Mark

As a refresher, read last week's Gospel, Mark 6:1–6. Just as the disciples would encounter rejection in their proclamation of the Good News, so also did Jesus.

Forgoing provisions takes faith. They must rely solely on hospitality, and God's support, for their mission. Emphasize "nothing."

Jesus summoned the **Twelve** and began to **send** them out
    two by **two**
and gave them authority over unclean **spirits**.
He **instructed** them to take **nothing** for the journey
    but a walking **stick**—
    no food, no sack, no **money** in their belts.
They were, however, to wear **sandals**
    but **not** a second tunic.
He said to them,
    "**Wherever** you enter a house, **stay** there until you leave.
Whatever place does not **welcome** you or **listen** to you,
    leave there and **shake** the dust off your feet
    in testimony against them."
So they went **off** and preached **repentance**.

Deliver looking out at the assembly. "Shake the dust off" is still good advice. Do not let rejection mitigate your zeal for your faith.

Conclude with a narrator voice. Ministering with the Spirit's authority is fruitful.

The Twelve **drove** out many **demons**,
    and they **anointed** with oil many who were sick and
      cured them.

GOSPEL In Mark 6:1–6, last week's Gospel reading, Jesus returned to Nazareth, where he was rejected by his unbelieving fellow towns-folk. While such disbelief did not diminish Jesus' power to heal, it did limit the scope of his healing and teaching. In today's Gospel, after having already chosen the twelve (Mark 3:14–19) and given them the secret of the kingdom of God (4:10–12), Jesus sends them out, warning them that in some places they too will experience a lack of welcome and that some will refuse to hear the message of repentance.

All three synoptic Gospels recall this tradition of sending out the twelve, although minor details differ slightly. For example, in Mark, Jesus permits a staff (a symbol of power and authority) and sandals, whereas Matthew and Luke do not. Beyond such details, Mark's spare account notes that the twelve receive "authority over unclean spirits," they are to preach repentance, and they are advised that some places will not welcome them or listen to their message. Strikingly, although the mystery of the kingdom of God had been revealed to them earlier, they are not explicitly charged with preaching the kingdom. Rather, like Jesus himself, they give concrete witness to the kingdom through their actions, miracles, and messages that flow from acceptance and belief. S.L.

SIXTEENTH SUNDAY IN ORDINARY TIME

LECTIONARY #107

READING I Jeremiah 23:1–6

A reading from the Book of the Prophet Jeremiah

Woe to the **shepherds**
> who **mislead** and **scatter** the **flock** of my pasture,
> says the LORD.
Therefore, thus says the LORD, the God of Israel,
> **against** the shepherds who shepherd **my** people:
> You have scattered my sheep and driven them away.
You have **not cared** for them,
> but I **will** take care to **punish** your evil deeds.
I myself will **gather** the remnant of my flock
> from all the lands to which I have driven them
> and bring them **back** to their **meadow**;
> there they shall **increase** and multiply.
I will **appoint** shepherds for them who **will** shepherd them
> so that they need no longer **fear** and **tremble**;
> and none shall be **missing**, says the LORD.

> Behold, the days are **coming**, says the LORD,
>> when I will raise up a righteous **shoot** to David;
> as **king** he shall reign and govern **wisely**,
>> he shall do what is **just** and **right** in the land.
> In his days **Judah** shall be **saved**,
>> Israel shall dwell in **security**.
> This is the name they give him:
>> "The LORD our **justice**."

Jeremiah = jayr-uh-Mī-uh

"Woe": Do not overdo the emotion you convey here: you don't want to discourage. Rather, call attention to the Lord's disappointment.

There is a price to pay for the neglect of those to whom you have a responsibility.

Emphasize "I." The Lord will provide replacements so that the sheep will be in good hands.

Don't lose the plural of "shepherds"—God's oversight is ongoing.

The new king will succeed where the first kings did not.

READING I Long before Christianity described Jesus as the Good Shepherd, the Hebrew Bible described God as Israel's shepherd, with Israel's kings serving as human shepherds whose task it was to care for the people on God's behalf. However, the image also served as a measure to critique the kings when they misled and failed to care for the sheep.

The prophet Jeremiah was a theological commentator on the final years of the kingdom of Judah, including the destruction of Jerusalem by Babylon in 587 BC, and the deportation of its people into exile in Babylon. Jeremiah mercilessly condemned the failed leadership of the monarchy, even as he offered hints of hope. Today's reading is part of a larger indictment (Jeremiah 22:1—23:8) of the "shepherds" (the kings of Judah/the Davidic monarchy), accusing them of destroying and scattering the "flock" (the people of Judah). In caring only for themselves and their well-being, the kings have roused God to punish their wicked ways.

This pitiable situation leads to some unexpected consequences. First, the Lord himself, and no human agent, will bring the flock back from exile to their meadow, since the kings are not trustworthy. Only after this gathering will new shepherds (that is, restored Davidic kings) be raised up. Second, in an explicitly Davidic promise, Jeremiah gives voice to the exiles' hope that a "righteous shoot" will emerge. This hope is ironic since the last Davidic king's name, Zedekiah, means "righteous" (*tsedaqah* in Hebrew), but he was not. The hope is that the shoot will bear the name "The LORD is our justice," and will embody the reality of that name, doing just and righteous acts.

For meditation and context:

RESPONSORIAL PSALM   Psalm 23:1–3, 3–4, 5, 6 (1)

R. The Lord is my shepherd; there is nothing I shall want.

The LORD is my shepherd; I shall not want.
   In verdant pastures he gives me repose;
beside restful waters he leads me;
   he refreshes my soul.

He guides me in right paths
   for his name's sake.
Even though I walk in the dark valley
   I fear no evil; for you are at my side
with your rod and your staff
   that give me courage.

You spread the table before me
   in the sight of my foes;
you anoint my head with oil;
   my cup overflows.

Only goodness and kindness follow me
   all the days of my life;
and I shall dwell in the house of the LORD
   for years to come.

READING II   Ephesians 2:13–18

Ephesians = ee-FEE-zhuhnz

A reading from the Letter of Saint Paul to the Ephesians

Brothers and **sisters**:
In Christ **Jesus** you who once were **far** off
   have become **near** by the **blood** of Christ.

"Both" refers to Jews and Gentiles.

enmity = EN-mih-tee = hostility

Christ is the one who broke down
the barriers.

For he is our **peace**, he who made both **one**
   and broke down the dividing wall of **enmity**,
     through his flesh,
     abolishing the **law** with its commandments and legal claims,
   that he might create in himself **one** new person in place
     of the **two**,
   thus establishing peace,
   and might **reconcile** both with **God**,
   in one body, through the cross,
   putting that enmity to death by it.

Notice the Trinitarian nature of the
last section.

"Far off" and "near": spatial images describe
the separation that has now been overcome.

He came and preached **peace** to you who were far **off**
   and peace to those who were **near**,
     for through him we **both** have access in one **Spirit**
       to the **Father**.

READING II   Employing many liturgical forms, the letter to the Ephesians is addressed to a predominantly Gentile Christian community in Asia Minor toward the end of the first century. Using metaphors, today's reading explores the unity between human and divine, as well as unity within the community itself. The text is also sensitive to time, relating the pre-Christian past to the current life of the believing community. This is expressed in past actions (for example, "you who once were far off") and the present reality (for example, "have become near").

Using a hymnic form, today's text poetically describes how Christ's blood on the cross reconciled Jews and Gentiles, breaking down the "dividing wall of enmity," which historically was embodied in the partition that separated Gentiles from the inner courts of the Jerusalem temple. Moving past the singularity of Judaism's law, Christ's sacrifice has brought peace, creating one body from the two, and granting "access in one Spirit to the Father."

Still, while unity has been achieved, it needs shoring up. As Gentile Christians increase, they are encouraged to cherish

their shared heritage, since Christ shared his message of peace with both communities and reconciled them to God. Equally important, the new unity has created a new discontinuity: not only is the Church separate from Judaism, but it is also distinct from a threatening outside world, with its hostile society, government, and cosmic powers.

GOSPEL   A central goal of Mark's Gospel is to wrestle with Jesus' identity, especially when many people question his identity and his authority. In line with his deeds of power, his teaching

GOSPEL   Mark 6:30–34

A reading from the holy Gospel according to Mark

The **apostles gathered** together with Jesus
 and **reported** all they had done and taught.
He said to them,
 "**Come** away by yourselves to a **deserted** place and rest
  a while."
People were **coming** and **going** in great **numbers**,
 and they had no opportunity **even** to eat.
So they went **off** in the boat by themselves to a deserted place.
People **saw** them leaving and many came to **know** about it.
They **hastened** there on foot from all the towns
 and arrived at the place **before** them.

When he **disembarked** and saw the vast crowd,
 his heart was moved with **pity** for them,
 for they were like **sheep without** a shepherd;
 and he began to **teach** them many things.

Think of a time when you bubbled over with exciting news. Bring that excitement to the text.

Elongating "coming" and "going" accentuates the hectic nature of the work of evangelization.

Pause after "and." This is a humorous situation. Imagine the disciples arriving at the "deserted" place and finding that the multitude had already *arrived there. Jesus saw their need and couldn't resist helping. That is who he is.*

---

the message of the kingdom, and his prophetic stature, today's reading adds yet one more element to the emerging picture of Jesus' identity: shepherd.

Earlier, in Mark 6, we heard of Jesus' rejection by his own townspeople, as well as the mission of the twelve apostles. Following a brief interlude (Mark 6:14–29) where King Herod's musing over Jesus' identity leads him to revisit the death of John the Baptist, today's Gospel begins with the return of the apostles from the earlier mission. Like Jesus, they have proclaimed conversion and performed power-

ful deeds of exorcism and healing (Mark 6:12–13). And like Jesus, who sought to escape the crowd by seeking refuge in deserted places (Mark 1:45) and using them as a place of prayer (Mark 1:35), Jesus draws the disciples to a deserted place so that they can rest and eat.

The deserted place provides the context for the next revelation of Jesus' identity. His pity at the sight of the large crowd that followed them comes from his awareness that they are "like sheep without a shepherd" (see also Numbers 27:16–17; Ezekiel 34:1–10, 23–24). While Jesus does

not claim the title "Shepherd" here, his compassion links him to shepherd imagery elsewhere in Scripture, as in today's first reading when God cares for the sheep of his flock who have been led astray by mortal shepherd-kings. S.L.

SEVENTEENTH SUNDAY IN ORDINARY TIME

LECTIONARY #110

READING I 2 Kings 4:42–44

A reading from the second Book of Kings

Baal-shalishah = BAY-uhl SHAHL-ih-shuh
or BAH-uhl SHAHL-i-shuh

Elisha = ee-LI-shuh

A man came from Baal-shalishah bringing to **Elisha**,
    the man of **God**,
    twenty **barley loaves** made from the firstfruits,
    and fresh **grain** in the ear.
Elisha said, "**Give** it to the people to eat."
But his **servant objected**,
    "**How** can I set this before a **hundred** people?"
Elisha **insisted**, "**Give it** to the people to eat.
For thus says the LORD,
    'They shall **eat** and there shall be some **left** over.'"
And when they had eaten, there **was** some left over,
    as the LORD had said.

Elisha is a man of God. He has authority and respect. Use the appropriate tone for one in charge.

Use a confident and satisfied tone. The Lord always fulfills what he promises.

For meditation and context:

RESPONSORIAL PSALM Psalm 145:10–11, 15–16, 17–18 (16)

R. The hand of the Lord feeds us; he answers all our needs.

Let all your works give you thanks, O LORD,
    and let your faithful ones bless you.
Let them discourse of the glory of
    your kingdom
    and speak of your might.

The eyes of all look hopefully to you,
    and you give them their food in
    due season;

you open your hand
    and satisfy the desire of every living thing.

The LORD is just in all his ways
    and holy in all his works.
The LORD is near to all who call upon him,
    to all who call upon him in truth.

READING I Through our Christian lens, we often see Jesus' demonstration of power over nature and the gifts of God's creation as proofs that Jesus is God. While they certainly do lead us to this conclusion, it is important to recall other miracles that God has worked through other people in Scripture, as we will read in today's first reading. Yet these other people do not claim divinity. As we reflect on the miracles in the first reading and in the Gospel, we are invited to consider what else God reveals about himself and our life of faith through these actions.

The Books of Kings are a theological interpretation of four hundred years of Israel's history (961 BC–561 BC). While earlier historical books described the way that the people's fate was the result of their own actions, the Books of Kings blame Israel and Judah's destinies on the kings and queens who failed to rule according to the standards of the Book of Deuteronomy.

Today's reading presents a striking contrast between Joram, the idolatrous king of Israel, and the prophet Elisha who is zealous in serving only the Lord. The account is one in a series of miraculous deeds that

include a multiplication of oil, raising a dead child to life, neutralizing poison in food, multiplying barley loaves, curing a leper, and locating a lost axe (see 2 Kings 4:1—6:7). Such deeds are possible because Elisha is "the man of God" whose allegiance is unswervingly dedicated to the Lord and service to him. This focus on God is clear when Elisha explains to his doubting servant that it is the Lord who does the miracle and who will assure that there will be some left over. Elisha may not be divine, but God works powerfully through him,

Ephesians = ee-FEE-zhuhnz

Paul's exhortatory reading uses a persuasive tone. Notice the trinitarian nature of the reading.

The virtues listed promote unity, the overall theme of the reading. Read slowly so the assembly can find virtues that apply to them. What do they already practice? Where do they fall short?

Emphasize "one" the first time and subdue it upon repetition. This will make the words that follow "one" stand out.

READING II   Ephesians 4:1–6

A reading from the Letter of Saint Paul to the Ephesians

Brothers and **sisters**:
I, a **prisoner** for the **Lord**,
   urge you to live in a manner **worthy** of the call
      you have received,
   with all **humility and** gentleness, with **patience**,
   bearing with one another through **love**,
   striving to preserve the **unity** of the spirit through the **bond**
      of peace:
one body and one **Spirit**,
as you were also **called** to the one **hope** of your call;
one Lord, one **faith**, one **baptism**;
one **God** and **Father** of **all**,
who is **over** all and **through** all and **in** all.

Read the name of the book distinctly. We are taking a short break from Mark's Gospel to read from John's Gospel for several weeks.

Galilee = GAL-ih-lee

"signs" = miracles

GOSPEL   John 6:1–15

A reading from the holy Gospel according to John

Jesus went **across** the Sea of Galilee.
A large **crowd** followed him,
   because they saw the **signs** he was performing on the **sick**.
Jesus went **up** on the mountain,
   and there he **sat** down with his **disciples**.
The Jewish feast of **Passover** was near.
When Jesus raised his eyes
   and **saw** that a large crowd was **coming** to him,
   he said to **Philip**,
   "Where can we **buy enough** food for them to **eat**?"
He said this to **test** him,
   because he himself knew what he was going to **do**. »

reminding us that by our faith, we cooperate with the work of God in the world.

READING II Ancient Christian letters often combined theological insight with ethical exhortation. Today's reading from Ephesians centers all ethical activity within the context of baptism, even as it invokes the divine persons and extols the unity the sacrament creates.

Today's short reading can be divided into two parts. First, there is the ethical instruction, which summons the Ephesians to a life "worthy of the call you have received" and which is expressed through dispositions such as humility, gentleness, patience, forbearance, and working for the unity of the Spirit. The text clarifies that it is God's initiative that makes this type of life possible. The second part of the reading consists of a confessional statement that emphasizes that unity is the goal of the dispositions. In beautiful poetry, the confession identifies elements of unity with persons of the Trinity: in the Spirit there is one body and one hope, in the Lord there is one faith and one baptism, and in God the Father we find the one "who is over all and through all and in all." Flowing from baptism, the dispositions lead to unity and peace as the binding elements that will hold the community together against aggression, division, or arrogance. As the Trinity is united in a bond of peace and love, so too is the community.

GOSPEL The miracle of the multiplication of the loaves and the feeding of a great multitude is the only one of Jesus' miracles that is found in all four Gospels. In John, the miracle serves as an entry point into a discourse on the bread from heaven and Jesus as the bread of life.

Read this slowly, with agitation. Make clear the impossibility of the task.

Philip answered him,
"Two **hundred** days' wages worth of food would not be **enough**
for each of them to have a **little**."
One of his disciples,
Andrew, the brother of Simon Peter, said to him,

"Barley loaves" should ring familiar, an echo of the first reading.

"There is a **boy** here who has five **barley** loaves and two **fish**;
but what **good** are these for so **many**?"
Jesus said, "Have the people **recline**."
Now there was a great deal of grass in that place.
So the men reclined, about five **thousand** in number.

This is Eucharistic language. Read reverently. Emphasize "Jesus."

Then **Jesus took** the loaves, gave **thanks**,
and **distributed** them to those who were reclining,
and also as **much** of the fish as they wanted.
When they had had their **fill**, he said to his disciples,

Collecting the fragments was proof positive that a miracle had happened. Notice the concern for not wasting.

"**Gather** the fragments left **over**,
so that nothing will be **wasted**."
So they collected them,
and **filled** twelve wicker baskets with fragments
from the five barley loaves
that had been more than they could eat.
When the people saw the **sign** he had done, they said,
"This is truly the **Prophet**, the **one** who is to come into
the world."

The narrator closes out the story. Jesus withdraws because the crowd still misunderstands who he is.

Since Jesus **knew** that they were going to come and carry
him **off**
to make him **king**,
he **withdrew** again to the mountain **alone**.

Today's account consists of two parts. First, the introduction provides basic information on location, persons, and motives. Second, there is a detailed description of the miracle.

In the first part, John's introduction to the miracle is filled with unique and value-laden details, like the fact that the Passover was near, and that Jesus went up on the mountain (like Moses at Sinai). The detailed description has other distinctly Johannine elements. Only in John does Jesus point out the problem and know what he will do. Jesus' rhetorical question, directed to his disciples, echoes Moses' question of God in

the wilderness: "Where can I get meat to give to all this people?" (Numbers 11:13). The disciples' lack of understanding parallels the lack of comprehension and trust in God's power that Elisha's servant demonstrated in today's first reading. Moving to the second part of the reading, we are invited to look beyond the familiar story to notice how it employs a mix of realism (the number of people is enormous—five thousand men alone!), religious faith (they are instructed to sit on the grass, invoking the memory of Psalm 23:2—"In green pastures he makes me lie down"), and Eucharistic

memory (Jesus taking, giving thanks, and sharing the bread) to communicate the miraculous event. Even the collecting of what is left over interacts with biblical memory (the manna that was collected, but uneaten, would go bad, whereas these fragments, even after all had eaten their fill, will not go bad and are still available). Finally, we read that, in spite of the sign, the people's coming to faith is incomplete. The crowd is looking for a Moses-like prophet with horizons as limited as theirs, and certainly not for the Bread of Life that is come down from heaven. S.L.

EIGHTEENTH SUNDAY IN ORDINARY TIME

LECTIONARY #113

READING I   Exodus 16:2–4, 12–15

A reading from the Book of Exodus

The **whole** Israelite community **grumbled** against **Moses**
    and **Aaron**.
The Israelites said to them,
    "Would that we had **died** at the LORD's hand in the land
        of **Egypt**,
as we sat by our fleshpots and **ate** our **fill** of bread!
But **you** had to **lead** us into this desert
    to make the whole community **die** of famine!"

Then the LORD said to Moses,
    "I will now rain down **bread** from **heaven** for you.
Each **day** the people are to go out and gather their **daily** portion;
    thus will I **test** them,
    to see whether they **follow** my instructions or not.

"I have **heard** the grumbling of the Israelites.
Tell them: In the evening twilight you **shall** eat flesh,
    and in the morning you shall have your **fill** of bread,
    so that you may know that **I**, the LORD, **am** your **God**."

In the evening **quail** came up and **covered** the camp.
In the morning a **dew** lay all about the camp,
    and when the dew **evaporated**, there on the surface
        of the desert
    were fine **flakes** like hoarfrost on the ground. »

Sidebar notes (left margin):

Exodus = EK-suh-duhs

Stress "whole." This was not an isolated individual, but the community at large complaining.

fleshpots = pots of meat

Use an accusatory tone. They have a short memory of what life was like as slaves.

God answers their prayers despite their lack of gratitude.

Pause after "God" before concluding the story.

God's word is dependable.

hoarfrost = HOHR-frawst

READING I   Exodus recounts a scene immediately after God's chosen people cross the Red Sea and finally experience deliverance from Egypt. As they begin their journey to Mount Sinai, where they encounter God directly and receive the law, the Israelites complain about lack of food. Their complaint is well founded. The wilderness is barren. Resources are limited. No obvious source of food appears in their new landscape. Their hunger quickly reveals how accustomed they have become to the abundant food of Egypt. Later, when they make their way from Sinai to the Promised Land, complaining like this will prove detrimental to their relationship with God. At this point, however, these complaints only indicate a potential for growing in relationship with God. The people must learn that God not only provides them with military support to escape Egyptian forces, but God also provides sustenance.

As their needs manifest, God hears the people's grumbling and informs Moses how they will be sustained; quail will be provided for meat at dinner and manna will be given for bread at breakfast. While the Israelites recognize the quail as a source of food, the manna confounds them. In fact, it is so foreign to them that they simply refer to it as "what's-the-stuff?"—which is what "manna" means in Hebrew. Importantly, God provides. By giving the chosen people sustenance in their need, explaining that manna *is* food, and instructing them how to handle it, God is revealed in a new way to the chosen people. God hears their complaints but does not punish them for lack of faith, though that happens during later wanderings in the wilderness (see the book of Numbers). At this point, as the chosen

Give emphasis to the last line Moses speaks so that it is recognized when referred to in today's Gospel reading.

On seeing it, the Israelites asked one another, "**What** is **this**?"
　for they did not **know** what it was.
But Moses told them,
　"This is the **bread** that the LORD has **given** you to eat."

For meditation and context:

RESPONSORIAL PSALM   Psalm 78:3–4, 23–24, 25, 54 (24b)

R. The Lord gave them bread from heaven.

What we have heard and know,
　and what our fathers have declared to us,
we will declare to the generation to come
　the glorious deeds of the LORD and
　　his strength
　and the wonders that he wrought.

He commanded the skies above
　and opened the doors of heaven;
he rained manna upon them for food
　and gave them heavenly bread.

Man ate the bread of angels,
　food he sent them in abundance.
And he brought them to his holy land,
　to the mountains his right hand had won.

READING II   Ephesians 4:17, 20–24

A reading from the Letter of Saint Paul to the Ephesians

Ephesians = ee-FEE-zhuhnz

It is almost as if Paul is making an opening argument in a trial. Take on his certitude in your tone.

Be familiar enough with the text to deliver this line looking out at the assembly.

Subdue the negative traits of the old life. They no longer apply.

Beam with pride, joy, and confidence as you deliver these last lines. We are a new creation!

Brothers and **sisters**:
I **declare** and **testify** in the Lord
　that you must no **longer** live as the **Gentiles** do,
　in the **futility** of their minds;
　that is not **how** you learned Christ,
　assuming that you have **heard** of him and were taught in him,
　as **truth** is in **Jesus**,
　that you should put **away** the old self of your **former** way
　　of life,
　corrupted through deceitful desires,
　and be **renewed** in the spirit of your minds,
　and put on the **new** self,
　created in **God's** way in **righteousness** and holiness of **truth**.

---

people journey with God, the Lord gives them provisions in the wilderness, inviting them to grow in trust and faith. At the same time, this food strengthens them for the journey to the mountain and their direct encounter with God.

READING II | Continuing in our reading of Ephesians, we find Paul using strong legal rhetoric to persuade the Church in Ephesus to forgo living as Gentiles. By this he means two things. First, their engagement in the life of the mind must be transformed. He reminds them

that it is Christ who makes truth accessible, not the thought of some learned community or esoteric philosophy. To the extent that they cling to the latter, their minds are not yet converted to Christ. Second, their way of life must match their transformed minds. Encountering the fullness of truth in Christ should lead spontaneously to upright actions and habits of living. Baptized into Christ, we, like the Ephesians, are to recognize ourselves as new creations: new "Adams" and new "Eves." Made new persons in and through Christ, we can follow God's ways. We can abide in truth both in

our thoughts and in our deeds. With transformed minds and wills, we can take up habits of thought and action that give evidence to our righteousness and holiness and thus become signs of God's ongoing work in the world.

GOSPEL | During this liturgical year (Year B of the lectionary cycle), the Gospel according to Mark is typically proclaimed. Last Sunday, however, we began hearing from the sixth chapter of John's Gospel, a section which is often called the "Bread of Life Discourse." We will

GOSPEL   John 6:24–35

A reading from the holy Gospel according to John

When the crowd **saw** that neither **Jesus** nor his disciples
　　were there,
　　they themselves got into boats
　　and came to Capernaum **looking** for Jesus.
And when they **found** him across the sea they said to him,
　　"**Rabbi**, **when** did you get here?"
Jesus answered them and said,
　　"Amen, **amen**, I say to you,
　　you are looking for me not because you **saw** signs
　　but because you **ate** the loaves and were filled.
Do not **work** for **food** that **perishes**
　　but for the food that **endures** for eternal life,
　　which the Son of **Man** will give you.
For on him the **Father**, **God**, has set his **seal**."
So they said to him,
　　"What can we **do** to accomplish the **works** of God?"
Jesus answered and said to them,
　　"This is the work of God, that you **believe** in the one he sent."
So they said to him,
　　"What **sign** can you do, that we may **see** and **believe** in you?
What can you **do**?
Our ancestors **ate** manna in the desert, as it is written:
　　He gave them bread from heaven to eat."
So Jesus said to them,
　　"**Amen**, amen, I **say** to you,
　　it was not **Moses** who gave the bread from heaven;
　　my Father gives you the **true** bread from **heaven**.
For the bread of God is that which comes down from heaven
　　and gives **life** to the world." »

Capernaum = kuh-PER-nee-*m
or kuh-PER-nay-*m or kuh-PER-n*m

The question is inconsequential but calling Jesus "Rabbi" is not. They are tracking Jesus down so that they can dialogue more with him. They yearn for him, but do they do so for the right reasons?

Physical satiation is fleeting; spiritual food is everlasting.

The crowd asks three questions. Each time, use an upward inflection. The first question asks what they can do; the second and third ask what Jesus can do for them. Read the pronouns carefully so the meaning of the exchange is captured.

Emphasize "my." Jesus' answer corrects the people. All credit belongs to God, not Moses.

---

hear this discourse through the Twenty-First Sunday in Ordinary Time and, in doing so, we have the opportunity to explore in greater depth the mystery hidden in the food that the Lord provides. To situate today's Gospel passage, it helps to recall the Gospel passages from the previous two Sundays.

On the Sixteenth Sunday in Ordinary Time, we heard in the Gospel according to Mark the return of Jesus' disciples from missionary work. They are excited yet exhausted and in need of food and rest to recuperate. Jesus attempts to have them

withdraw to a deserted place so they can have this rest. But crowds follow and Jesus pities them because "they were like sheep without a shepherd" (Mark 6:34).

Then, last Sunday, as we began John 6, we heard the story of Jesus miraculously feeding a multitude with five loaves and a couple of fish—a similar scene would have transpired had we continued reading Mark's Gospel. In John 6, however, the crowd interprets the feeding as an indicator that they should make Jesus their king. But Jesus withdraws to the mountain alone, which is

reminiscent of Moses communing with God at Sinai.

Today, Jesus and his disciples, having returned clandestinely to Capernaum, face the crowd fed by Jesus. The crowd begins to dialogue with Jesus, honoring him with the title "Rabbi" and seeking to determine his mysterious travel practices: "When did you get here?" (read John 6:16–23 to learn what transpired). But Jesus takes control of the conversation. He explains that they only seek him for a superficial reason: he sated their hunger with bread and fish. It is worth recalling that, during the ancient

So they said to him,
 "Sir, **give** us this bread **always**."
Jesus said to them,
 "**I am** the bread of life;
 whoever comes to me will never **hunger**,
 and whoever **believes** in me will never **thirst**."

monarchy, the king was to secure sufficient sustenance for the population. So, when the crowd sought to make Jesus king, we can assume they were attuned to their biblical heritage.

At the same time, Jesus challenges them to see beyond the connection between providing food and the monarchy. He tells them to work for food (i.e., bread) "that endures for eternal life," which the Son of Man provides. The crowd faintly grasps his meaning and asks about the work they must do, which entails believing in the one sent by God. The crowd starts to

catch Jesus' meaning better. He is talking about himself and pointing to something more primordial than the monarchy. In an attempt to understand Jesus in light of a story from earlier in salvation history, the crowd turns to Moses and the manna provided in the desert (as we read in today's first reading). The story seems to match that of Jesus. He too provided food in a deserted place. So, the crowd cautiously considers whether Jesus might be a new Moses, but they want him to perform a sign, also like Moses did when the people were enslaved in Egypt. Importantly, the

crowd follows Jesus' logic, but he continues to look deeper. He points out that Moses was not the one who actually provided the food or worked the wonders in Egypt. He was only an instrument of God, the heavenly Father of Jesus. Seemingly brought to clear understanding, the crowd begs Jesus for the everlasting bread of the Father. With that, today's Gospel passage closes on a cliffhanger: Jesus identifies himself with this bread. Will the people understand? If so, will they accept? And what would it mean to do so? E.W.

NINETEENTH SUNDAY IN ORDINARY TIME

LECTIONARY #116

READING I 1 Kings 19:4–8

A reading from the first Book of Kings

Elijah went a day's journey **into** the **desert**,
    until he came to a broom **tree** and sat beneath it.
He **prayed** for **death**, saying:
    "This is **enough**, O **LORD**!
Take my **life**, for I am no **better** than my fathers."
He lay **down** and fell asleep under the broom tree,
    but then an **angel** touched him and ordered him
        to get **up** and eat.
Elijah looked and there at his head was a hearth **cake**
    and a jug of **water**.
After he ate and drank, he lay down **again**,
    but the angel of the LORD came **back** a second time,
    touched him, and ordered,
    "Get up and eat, else the journey will be too **long** for you!"
He got up, ate, and drank;
    then **strengthened** by that food,
    he walked **forty days** and forty **nights** to the
        mountain of God, Horeb.

Elijah = ee-LĪ-juh

Read Elijah's request, "This is enough," with staccato to show this is no idle threat.

The appearance of angels usually brings fear. Read with surprise that food has "appeared."

This divine food calls to mind the Eucharist, which strengthens us for our journey of discipleship.

Horeb = HOHR-eb

READING I Reminiscent of last Sunday's reading from Exodus, in which the Israelites found themselves needing food in the wilderness on the way to the mountain of God, today we hear of Elijah journeying into the desert toward God's mountain (here called Horeb), only to run short of food and strength. However, unlike the Israelites who, when we encountered them last week, had just been delivered from Egyptian forces, Elijah is being actively pursued by the henchmen of Jezebel and Ahab for having killed the prophets of Ba'al with the sword (1 Kings 19:1–3). He is a force to be reckoned with, yet Elijah is fleeing for his life. The prophet's strength and daring, which enabled him to engage in a grim but righteous feat, have dried up. His courage and resolve give way to fear. Elijah, catapulted into a life-threatening flight into the wilderness, faces an acute lack of resources and sustenance. As Elijah sinks beneath the shade of a tree, the famished fugitive considers himself no better than his ancestors who also wandered in the wilderness. But instead of begging God for food, Elijah begs God for death. The Lord of life will have none of it. Twice God sends a messenger (an angel) with bread, water, and a message: "Get up and eat." This message will echo in Christ's repeated mandate to those whom he raises from illness and death. Ultimately, strengthened by heavenly sustenance, Elijah continues his journey to God's mountain and his broader prophetic mission. Like last week's first reading, this account of God's chosen one languishing in the desert prepares us for Jesus' message today in the Gospel.

For meditation and context:

RESPONSORIAL PSALM   Psalm 34:2–3, 4–5, 6–7, 8–9 (9a)

R. Taste and see the goodness of the Lord.

I will bless the LORD at all times;
    his praise shall be ever in my mouth.
Let my soul glory in the LORD;
    the lowly will hear me and be glad.

Glorify the LORD with me,
    let us together extol his name.
I sought the LORD, and he answered me
    and delivered me from all my fears.

Look to him that you may be radiant
    with joy,
    and your faces may not blush with shame.
When the afflicted man called out, the
    LORD heard,
    and from all his distress he saved him.

The angel of the LORD encamps
    around those who fear him and
    delivers them.
Taste and see how good the LORD is;
    blessed the man who takes refuge in him.

READING II   Ephesians 4:30—5:2

Ephesians = ee-FEE-zhuhnz

A reading from the Letter of Saint Paul to the Ephesians

Brothers and **sisters**:
Do not **grieve** the Holy **Spirit** of God,
    with which you were **sealed** for the day of **redemption**.
All **bitterness**, **fury**, **anger**, **shouting**, and **reviling**
    must be **removed** from you, along with all **malice**.
And be **kind** to one another, **compassionate**,
    forgiving one another as God has forgiven **you** in **Christ**.

So be **imitators** of God, as **beloved** children, and live **in love**,
    as Christ loved us and handed himself over for us
    as a sacrificial **offering** to God for a fragrant aroma.

The first list is what grieves the Spirit. Read slowly so listeners can find themselves. The second list is what it means to imitate Christ. Similarly, read at a measured pace so that the assembly can recognize these good qualities within themselves.

Use a soft and gentle tone. The same forgiveness extended to us should be extended to others.

READING II | Ephesians exhorts its audience to recognize what God has done in Christ and to put aside thoughts and actions not aligned with life in Christ. By saying that the Holy Spirit operates in the life of the faithful as a seal "for the day of redemption," Ephesians recalls an ancient biblical tradition known as the "day of the Lord." Common in prophetic literature, this "day" was an imagined, divinely sanctioned upheaval that supplanted all wrongdoing, injustice, and injury with God's justice and righteousness. The unavoidability of such a "day" invites acting in accord with God's ways and seeking the Lord's protection. For the Ephesians, and for us, abiding in an upright relationship with the Holy Spirit is paramount, for the Spirit protects against that "day." To maintain our relationship with the Holy Spirit, avoidance and removal of certain internal states is in order. Anger and malice in all its forms cannot be given quarter—these are directly contradictory to the Spirit. Rather, kindness, compassion, mutual forgiveness, a life lived in love, and willingness to sacrifice oneself for others mark a life lived in the Spirit. Where such attitudes prevail, not only does the Spirit rejoice, but also the "fragrant" sacrifice of Christ continues to be offered to God. The figurative language here is reminiscent of sacrificial food offerings, which invites us to consider the offering we make of ourselves as we approach the Eucharistic banquet. To what extent is our self-offering a delightful "aroma" to the Lord?

GOSPEL | As we continue to hear the Bread of Life Discourse, concerns emerge among Jesus' audience. This Jewish community in Galilee knows

---

GOSPEL John 6:41–51

A reading from the holy Gospel according to John

The Jews **murmured** about Jesus because he said,
    "I am the **bread** that came down from **heaven**,"
    and they said,
    "Is this not **Jesus**, the son of **Joseph**?
Do we not know his father and mother?
Then **how** can he say,
    'I have come down from heaven'?"
Jesus answered and said to them,
    "Stop **murmuring** among yourselves.
No one can come to me unless the Father who sent me
      draw him,
    and I will **raise** him on the last **day**.
It is written in the prophets:
    *They shall all be **taught** by **God**.*
Everyone who **listens** to my Father and **learns** from him
      comes to me.
Not that anyone has **seen** the Father
    except the one who is **from** God;
    he has seen the Father.
Amen, **amen**, I say to you,
    whoever **believes** has eternal **life**.
I am the **bread** of life.
Your ancestors ate the **manna** in the desert, but they **died**;
    this is the bread that comes down from heaven
    so that one may eat it and **not** die.
I am the **living** bread that came down from heaven;
    whoever eats **this** bread will live **forever**;
    and the bread that I will **give** is my **flesh** for the **life**
      of the world."

Margin notes:

A rhetorical question. They are confirming an assumption.

Use a comma after "come to me." "Unless" doesn't need a comma in this sentence.

"Flesh" points us to the Eucharist but also reminds us of the truth of Jesus' nature, that he is divine *and* human.

Jesus. They know his family. They know he is not someone important, not a man of high status. He is just another Galilean Jew like them. Yet they have heard him refer to himself as the bread of life and say that he is food and drink that, once consumed, will remove all hunger and thirst forever. He has called himself heavenly bread, and he didn't mean it metaphorically. Their murmuring recalls the complaints of the chosen people during their initial wanderings in the wilderness, complaints heard in the first reading last Sunday. Here, as in the wilderness and when Elijah sat parched under a shade tree, the Lord shows compassion on the people. He grasps and understands their concerns.

Responding to their complaints, Jesus continues teaching his audience by appealing repeatedly to Scripture. He freely cites Isaiah 54:13 to remind them that the prophetic tradition promised that God would attract and teach all people. Thus, they are drawn to his words for a reason. Then, turning to a still more primordial source—the Pentateuch—he points to the story of manna in the wilderness. In that situation, food was a temporary solution to the people's concern. However, in Jesus, the soul-deep hunger and parched spirit that the whole human community knows meets satisfaction. Anticipated in the angelic bread that nourished Elijah for a protracted desert journey, Jesus sustains the weary and murmuring beyond all precursors. He is the bread of life. But will his audience accept his claim? E.W.

THE ASSUMPTION OF THE BLESSED VIRGIN MARY: VIGIL

LECTIONARY #621

READING I   1 Chronicles 15:3–4, 15–16; 16:1–2

A reading from the first Book of Chronicles

David assembled **all** Israel in Jerusalem to bring the **ark** of
    the LORD
    to the place that he had **prepared** for it.
David also called together the **sons** of **Aaron** and the **Levites**.

The Levites **bore** the ark of God on their shoulders with poles,
    as Moses had ordained **according** to the word of the LORD.

David commanded the chiefs of the Levites
    to appoint their kinsmen as **chanters**,
    to play on musical instruments, harps, lyres, and cymbals,
    to make a **loud** sound of **rejoicing**.

They brought in the ark of God and set it within the **tent**
    which David had pitched for it.
Then they **offered** up **burnt** offerings and **peace** offerings to God.
When David had **finished** offering up the burnt offerings and
        peace offerings,
    he **blessed** the **people** in the name of the LORD.

Chronicles = KRAH-nih-k*ls
Announce the book's name clearly; it is not often heard from.

The mention of instruments and song creates a sense of joyous cacophony. Read with a countenance of joy.

We leave the sense of hearing and move to the senses of smell and sight. Envision incense and smoke rising. The ark is a symbol of God's revelation to human beings, and David's lavish ceremony is a sign of thanksgiving to God.

READING I | Scripture recalls how God prepared the people to perceive the Lord's handiwork in Mary by first entrusting to them the ark of the Lord. This relatively small but elaborate container housed the tablets of the Ten Commandments, which are also called the decalogue or "ten words" of God. Accordingly, the ark was the first house of the Lord's word. Chronicles recounts the pomp and pageantry that surrounds the ark when David restored it its proper place in the meeting tent in Jerusalem after it had been taken by Philistines. (This event happens prior to Solomon building the temple; hence the ark returns to the tent.) And yet, the celebration hinges on the ark's contents: the fundamental importance of God's words in the life the people.

As we celebrate Mary in this liturgy, we give her high praise, for she is a new ark. She is one in whom God has done great things. Yet, as a new ark, her contents differ slightly. She carries the *eternal* Word of God, Jesus Christ. Accordingly, since her contents cannot pass away, neither can she. So today we celebrate the new ark's assumption into eternity for it is fitting that she who bore the eternal Word should herself receive the first fruits of the promised resurrection.

READING II | In this reading, to the Corinthians closes, Paul confronts the topic of death with the hope of resurrection. For the apostle, to abide in Christ Jesus is to experience the hope of resurrection, and that hope has bearing on this present life as we face its joys and challenges. Using imagery of clothing (which recalls baptism), Paul explains that we know ourselves to be embodied beings and

For meditation and context:

RESPONSORIAL PSALM   Psalm 132:6–7, 9–10, 13–14 (8)

R. Lord, go up to the place of your rest, you and the ark of your holiness.

Behold, we heard of it in Ephrathah;
  we found it in the fields of Jaar.
Let us enter into his dwelling,
  let us worship at his footstool.

May your priests be clothed with justice;
  let your faithful ones shout merrily
    for joy.

For the sake of David your servant,
  reject not the plea of your anointed.

For the Lord has chosen Zion;
  he prefers her for his dwelling.
"Zion is my resting place forever;
  in her will I dwell, for I prefer her."

Corinthians = kohr-IN-thee-uhnz

READING II   1 Corinthians 15:54b–57

A reading from the first Letter of Saint Paul to the Corinthians

Brothers and **sisters**:

When that which is **mortal** clothes itself with **immortality**,
  then the word that is **written** shall come about:

> **Death** is swallowed up in **victory**.
> **Where**, O death, is **your** victory?
> Where, O death, is your **sting**?

Emphasize "written" so that the assembly understands Paul is quoting lines from Hosea. Familiarize yourself with the quoted lines so that you can deliver the hypothetical and ironic questions looking out at the assembly. Paul quotes Hosea with confidence.

Conclude with an upbeat and excited tone of praise.

The sting of death is **sin**,
  and the **power** of sin is the **law**.
But thanks be to **God** who **gives** us the victory
  through our Lord Jesus **Christ**.

GOSPEL   Luke 11:27–28

A reading from the holy Gospel according to Luke

While **Jesus** was speaking,
  a woman from the crowd **called** out and said to him,
  "**Blessed** is the **womb** that **carried** you
  and the **breasts** at which you **nursed**."
He replied,
  "Rather, blessed are those
  who **hear** the **word** of **God** and **observe** it."

This short reading is the crux of today's feast. Make sure the assembly is ready before you begin to read.

Who better than Mary exemplifies a person of faith who completely and fully hears and responds to the word of God?

thus mortal. Yet, in Christ, we have been clothed anew with immortality. Once clothed in Christ's immortality through baptism, the promise of a share in his resurrection becomes ours. With that promise, death's potential victory or sting, death's power, meets its end. On this solemnity of Mary's assumption, we celebrate with great assurance that hope in the resurrection is not in vain, for Christ has begun to share it with those who abide in him, beginning with his mother.

GOSPEL   In a brief exchange between Jesus and a nameless woman in a crowd, Luke captures the twofold nature of Mary that we celebrate in today's solemnity. The woman praises Mary's material contribution to the incarnation by proclaiming a celebratory blessing of Mary's maternal body. Her womb, which carried Christ, and her breasts, which suckled him, are declared blessed. Celebrating Mary's assumption, we too celebrate the blessedness of this body, which God brought up into heaven. At the same time, Jesus amplifies the woman's claim. More

than blessing his mother's carnal nature, he speaks of a still-deeper truth seen in her response to the word of God. Mary, above all others, hears the word of God and acts upon it. Because of Mary's attentive ears and observant will, the Lord will bless her with more than the grace of being the vehicle of his incarnation. Assumed into heaven, Mary becomes the first to follow her son into the promise of resurrection glory where she is both mother of the Word incarnate and observant listener of God's Word. E.W.

THE ASSUMPTION OF THE BLESSED VIRGIN MARY: DAY

LECTIONARY #622

READING I Revelation 11:19a; 12:1–6a, 10ab

A reading from the Book of Revelation

God's **temple** in heaven was **opened**,
  and the ark of his **covenant** could be **seen** in the temple.

A great **sign** appeared in the **sky**, a **woman** clothed with the **sun**,
  with the **moon** under her **feet**,
  and on her **head** a crown of twelve stars.
She was **with** child and **wailed** aloud in **pain** as she **labored**
    to give birth.
Then another sign appeared in the sky;
  it was a huge red **dragon**, with seven **heads** and ten **horns**,
  and on its heads were seven **diadems**.
Its **tail swept** away a third of the stars in the sky
  and **hurled** them down to the earth.
Then the dragon **stood** before the woman about to give **birth**,
  to **devour** her child when she gave birth.
She gave birth to a **son**, a male child,
  destined to **rule all** the nations with an iron **rod**.
Her child was **caught** up to **God** and his throne.
The woman herself **fled** into the desert
  where she had a place **prepared** by God.

Read this vision narrative with such energy that the assembly can visualize it.

Use heightened intensity for "wailed," "pain," and "labored." Though much of the narrative is symbolic, for many in the assembly this description has been their reality of giving birth. Pause after "give birth" to mark the shift to the next cosmic vision.

diadem = Dī-uh-dem = royal crown

Use a slight pause after "tail," then swiftly describe the sweeping and hurling.

Read with joy. The mood changes from the fantastical to one of wonder—the child is safely "caught up to God."

This is a good thing; the desert is a place of escape.

READING I Christ's resurrection promises to all who enter into and abide in relationship with Jesus the hope of our future resurrection. Mary, the mother of God, fittingly became the first recipient of that promised grace. Raised to glory by Christ in her assumption, the Church celebrates this solemn feast because it assures us that God keeps the promise of resurrection made in Christ.

Today's liturgy of the word for Mass begins, fittingly, with the vision of the woman clothed with the sun in Revelation 12. The vision is framed within a broader vision in which the heavenly temple is opened, and the ark of the covenant housed within it appears. Moreover, the vision of the woman concludes with a proclamation from the heavenly realm announcing God's power and Christ's authority. These framing elements recall Old Testament scenes in which God was present, in mysterious ways, to the chosen people prior to being fully revealed in Christ. At Mount Sinai, the heavens opened. God spoke to the people in thunderous proclamation. God etched the law on tablets, gave instructions for the ark in which those tablets were to be kept, and directed the people to build a tent to house the ark. God was to be mysteriously present with the people through multiple layers of mediation. Under the direction of Moses, the people followed God's commands. They received the law. They built that ark and its tent. Later, Solomon replaced the tent with the temple. So, seeing the heavens, the temple, the ark, and the covenant in this vision in Revelation, we recall the layered symbols through which God's presence was mysteriously mediated to the chosen people. And yet, today's reading shows those layers peeled back, so

Use a loud voice as directed.

Then I heard a loud **voice** in heaven say:
"Now have **salvation** and **power** come,
    and the **Kingdom** of our God
    and the **authority** of his **Anointed** One."

For meditation and context:

RESPONSORIAL PSALM   Psalm 45:10, 11, 12, 16 (10bc)

R. The queen stands at your right hand, arrayed in gold.

The queen takes her place at your right hand
    in gold of Ophir.

Hear, O daughter, and see; turn your ear,
    forget your people and your
        father's house.

So shall the king desire your beauty;
    for he is your lord.

They are borne in with gladness and joy;
    they enter the palace of the king.

READING II   1 Corinthians 15:20–27

Corinthians = kohr-IN-thee-uhnz

A reading from the first Letter of Saint Paul to the Corinthians

Brothers and **sisters**:
Christ has been **raised** from the **dead**,
    the **firstfruits** of those who have fallen **asleep**.

Try to bring to the verse the amazement
you might feel if you were hearing this
good news for the first time.

For since **death** came **through** man,
    the **resurrection** of the dead came **also** through man.
For just as in **Adam** all die,
    so too in **Christ** shall all be brought to **life**,
    but each one in proper **order**:
    Christ the **firstfruits**;
    then, at his coming, those who **belong** to Christ;
    then comes the end,
    when he hands **over** the Kingdom to his God and Father,
    when he has **destroyed** every **sovereignty**
    and every authority and power.

Adopt a tone of authority; no one will usurp
God's position. His reign is unchallenged.

For he must **reign** until he has put all his **enemies** under
        his feet.
The last enemy to be destroyed is **death**,
    for "he subjected everything under his feet."

---

to speak, to reveal the great cosmic drama that unfolds in a new way in Christ and in his Church.

The woman symbolizes the chosen people, which has now expanded to become the Church. This people, as woman, labors to bring forth Christ (the child) into the world. But, like a vicious dragon, the world threatens both the woman and the child. God must protect them. The child—Christ—God snatches up to heaven. The woman—again symbolizing the Church—flies to the desert, where God has prepared a place for her. This cosmic imagery

depicting the relationship between the Church and Christ naturally correlates with Mary, the mother of God and the mother of the Church. As model and guide, Mary exemplifies how we, the Church, are to bring forth Christ into the world and follow where God leads, even into deserted places, trusting that God provides.

READING II | Toward the end of his first letter to the Corinthians, Paul recalls the mystery of Christ's resurrection and reflects on its place in the broader context of salvation history. For

Paul, Christ's resurrection is the centerpiece of salvation history. He is the first fruits, the initial harvest of many to come. Fundamentally, Paul recognizes that Christ's glorious resurrection is not a grace unique to the Lord; it will be shared. It is meant for all who have died and will die. Thus, Paul recognizes that the resurrection makes Christ a new Adam, the new primordial human person. For Adam, as the first primordial human person, ushered death into human experience. Conversely, in Christ, the new primordial human person, life reigns through the resurrection. The old,

GOSPEL   Luke 1:39–56

A reading from the holy Gospel according to Luke

Mary set **out**
> and traveled to the hill country in **haste**
> to a town of Judah,
> where she entered the house of **Zechariah**
> and greeted **Elizabeth**.

When Elizabeth **heard** Mary's greeting,
> the **infant leaped** in her womb,
> and Elizabeth, **filled** with the Holy **Spirit**,
> cried out in a loud voice and said,
> "**Blessed** are **you** among **women**,
> and blessed is the **fruit** of your **womb**.

And **how** does this happen to **me**,
> that the **mother** of my **Lord** should **come** to me?

For at the **moment** the sound of your greeting reached my ears,
> the infant in my womb **leaped** for **joy**.

Blessed are you who **believed**
> that what was spoken to you by the Lord
> would be **fulfilled**."

And **Mary** said:

> "My **soul** proclaims the **greatness** of the **Lord**;
>> my **spirit rejoices** in God my **Savior**
>> for he has with **favor** on his lowly **servant**.
>
> From this day **all** generations will call me **blessed**:
>> the Almighty has done **great** things for me
>> and **holy** is his Name.
>> He has **mercy** on those who fear him
>> in every generation.
>
> He has shown the **strength** of his arm,
>> and has **scattered** the **proud** in their conceit.

Say the familiar lines from the Hail Mary and then pause.

Use an upward inflection to show Elizabeth's slight confusion.

Some in the assembly might be familiar with Mary's Magnificat and may be saying it internally with you as you proclaim the reading. Don't rush it.

Emphasize the verbs. God's generous deeds effect change.

death-tainted Adamic order is supplanted by the new, life-imbued Christ-touched order. The trajectory established by Adam is redirected by Christ. Our sad history becomes a hopeful future.

Along with Paul, we can ponder how the grace of the resurrection will continue to be shared as God completes the story of salvation. Although details are sparse, Paul indicates that the grace of resurrection glory will be distributed in an orderly manner. Christ, the first to rise, is naturally first. Then "those who belong to Christ" will be glorified. Then the end of all things will

come about and the cosmic contest between good (Christ) and evil (Christ's enemies) will conclude. This trajectory by which God distributes the grace of the resurrection, which Paul perceived, is known with greater precision thanks to the historical vantage point the Church now enjoys. Christ, of course, remains the first to rise. But of those who belong to Christ, the saints, more can be said. We know that saints have come to enjoy heavenly glory. Queen among them, Mary enjoys the fullness of resurrection glory, having been assumed body and soul into heaven. What

was begun in Christ's resurrection is shared fully by Mary in her assumption.

GOSPEL   If the first and second readings invite us to ponder the grace of Mary's assumption within the context of a cosmic contest between good and evil and the cosmic distribution of resurrection grace, respectively, today's Gospel invites us to contemplate Mary's assumption within the context of her everyday life in the Judean hill country. This Gospel passage follows immediately after Gabriel's announcement to Mary that she is to bear

He has **cast down** the **mighty** from their thrones,
 and has **lifted up** the **lowly**.
He has **filled** the **hungry** with good things,
 and the **rich** he has sent away **empty**.
He has come to the **help** of his **servant** Israel
 for he has **remembered** his promise of **mercy**,
 the promise he made to our **fathers**,
 to Abraham and his children for ever."

Mary remained **with** her about three months
 and then returned to her **home**.

Jesus and that Elizabeth is pregnant with John. Mary, having pondered the matter in the angel's presence, wastes no time when Gabriel departs. She hastens to Elizabeth. Mary's presence alone—as the ark of the new covenant—stirs the spirits of both Elizabeth and John, who is in utero. A spirit-filled Elizabeth repeatedly blesses Mary and the child she is carrying, Jesus. The inspired Elizabeth also questions: "how does this happen to me, that the mother of my Lord should come to me?"

The blessings and question pave the way for Mary to declare her praise of the Lord for all that has been done for her. In her Magnificat, Mary proclaims the Lord's greatness and her own lowliness. Her role in the cosmic contest and the cosmic distribution of grace is not denied. Rather, Mary repeatedly emphasizes that the grace to be the mother of the Lord—Elizabeth's title for Mary—has everything to do with God's strength and care for the lowly and God-fearing. Mary makes the matter absolutely clear: her motherhood is pure gift, pure grace from God. Moreover, God's abundant mercy and grace showers down on all like her. So, if Elizabeth recognizes that she is blessed to receive the mother of her Lord, this too is grace. For one so open to God's grace and so able to understand it, it is little wonder that Mary would, in time, come to share in the outpouring of God's grace given in Christ's resurrection. Thus, God would bear her up to heaven in the assumption. E.W.

TWENTIETH SUNDAY
IN ORDINARY TIME

LECTIONARY #119

READING I   Proverbs 9:1–6

A reading from the Book of Proverbs

> **Wisdom** has **built** her **house**,
> she has **set** up her seven columns;
> she has **dressed** her meat, **mixed** her wine,
> yes, she has **spread** her table.
> She has **sent** out her **maidens**; she **calls**
> from the heights out over the city:
> "Let whoever is **simple** turn in **here**";
> to the one who lacks **understanding**, she says,
> "**Come**, **eat** of my food,
> and **drink** of the wine I have mixed!
> **Forsake** foolishness that you may **live**;
> **advance** in the way of **understanding**."

Wisdom is personified as a female and acts on her own volition. Accenting the verbs gives a sense of active preparation.

This is a lavish feast.

Read the responsorial psalm. "Tasting" the Lord's goodness echoes Wisdom's invitation to satisfy the hunger for wise and righteous living.

For meditation and context:

RESPONSORIAL PSALM   Psalm 34:2–3, 4–5, 6–7 (9a)

R. Taste and see the goodness of the Lord.

I will bless the LORD at all times;
  his praise shall be ever in my mouth.
Let my soul glory in the LORD;
  the lowly will hear me and be glad.

Glorify the LORD with me,
  let us together extol his name.
I sought the LORD, and he answered me
  and delivered me from all my fears.

Look to him that you may be radiant
  with joy,
  and your faces may not blush with shame.
When the poor one called out, the
  LORD heard,
  and from all his distress he saved him.

READING I Aimed at training individuals as future public servants —that is, as educated aids for (Judean) royal court officials—the book of Proverbs opens with nine chapters that explore the potential pitfalls and delights of such service. Proverbs 9 concludes the initial section of the book with a flurry of robust imagery that figuratively depicts personified wisdom orchestrating a sumptuous, well-prepared banquet. The imagery blends elements from the life of learning undertaken by future public servants with the ultimate promise their study, dining at the table of the king. The passage poses a multi-faceted alure for young, would-be scholars interested in public service. Wisdom herself is appealing. She knows how to party in a refined, orderly manner. She establishes a refined context (the seven columns) and presents the finest cuisine. She also offers much in the way of intangibles: understanding, elegance, decorum, and the means of ridding oneself of foolishness. In sum, she offers maturity. Wisdom also has attendants, servants of her own, who are well-mannered and oblige their mistress. They follow her direc-tives by inviting people to Wisdom's feast. Thus, both Wisdom and her attendants, courteous and refined, know their way around all levels of society, which is repre-sented by the city and its heights. To dine, metaphorically, at Wisdom's feast is to grow in maturity, to develop knowledge and understanding, and to learn how to put that knowledge and understanding to the best possible use for the good of others. This reading, therefore, uses banquet imagery to speak of how growth in refine-ment (maturity) comes about. Accordingly, it makes for a robust context in which to

READING II   Ephesians 5:15–20

A reading from the Letter of Saint Paul to the Ephesians

Brothers and **sisters**:
Watch **carefully** how you **live**,
    not as **foolish** persons but as **wise**,
    making the **most** of the opportunity,
    because the days are **evil**.
Therefore, do not continue in **ignorance**,
    but try to **understand** what is the **will** of the Lord.
And do not get **drunk** on wine, in which lies **debauchery**,
    but be **filled** with the **Spirit**,
    addressing one another in **psalms** and **hymns** and
        spiritual **songs**,
    singing and **playing** to the Lord in your **hearts**,
    giving **thanks** always and for **everything**
    in the name of our Lord Jesus **Christ** to God the **Father**.

Ephesians = ee-FEE-zhuhnz

Paul has an urgency to this text. He lays out instructions to maximize every opportunity.

debauchery = dih-BAW-chuh-ree
Notice the Trinitarian nature of the reading.

Display a joyful countenance to evoke the sense of "singing and playing."

GOSPEL   John 6:51–58

A reading from the holy Gospel according to John

Jesus said to the **crowds**:
    "I am the **living bread** that came down from **heaven**;
    whoever **eats** this bread will live **forever**;
    and the bread that I will **give**
    is my **flesh** for the life of the world."

The Jews **quarreled** among **themselves**, saying,
    "How can this **man** give us his flesh to **eat**?" ≫

The Bread of Life Discourse continues. Reread the Gospel readings from the last two or three Sundays to gain a better context for this week's reading.

Jesus restates his claim multiple times; he is very clear. Don't rush through his words. They draw our attention to the Eucharist that will be celebrated later during Mass.

The people discussed Jesus' claim among themselves. Deliver the question deliberately and with an upward inflection to convey their confusion.

ponder the meaning and implications of today's passage from Ephesians and Christ's claims in the Gospel.

READING II Last Sunday, Ephesians called for imitating God by loving and being loved by others. This Sunday a similar exhortation comes by way of a call to act cautiously. Living out Christian love involves avoiding foolishness and taking every opportunity to live wisely. In order to act in this manner, Christians must seek to understand the Lord's will. That is, living in Christian love entails thoughtfully discerning God's actions in our lives and his desires for our lives. We must apply our minds to the work of learning the Lord's mind. At the same time, Ephesians also points out that we must practice virtues. By acting with prudence and applying caution, our behaviors stand to align with and direct us toward our pursuit of the Lord. A life of excess, exemplified in the reading by drunkenness, leads away from the Lord. Instead, Ephesians calls for being filled with the Spirit. When our desire for nourishment is sated by the Spirit, we then naturally overflow with love for others.

This, Ephesians imagines, pours forth from us in songs of praise for the Lord and all he has done. If Proverbs uses banquet imagery to draw its audience into human maturity, Ephesians does likewise to call forth spiritual maturity. The former might manifest in social acumen, the latter in abundant thanksgiving to the Lord.

GOSPEL When Jesus announces, "I am the living bread that came down from heaven; whoever eats this bread will live forever," he confounds his audience by further specifying this banquet

Jesus clarifies, though he doesn't answer their question of "how"; instead he focuses on "why."

Jesus describes the intimate connections between God the Father, Jesus himself, and us. You may need to slow down to ensure that all of these relationships are clearly articulated. These relationships are enduring.

Jesus said to them,
    "Amen, **amen**, I say to you,
    unless you **eat** the flesh of the Son of Man and **drink**
        his blood,
    you do **not** have **life** within you.
Whoever eats my flesh and drinks my blood
        has **eternal** life,
        and I will **raise** him on the last day.
For my flesh is **true** food,
        and my blood is **true** drink.
Whoever eats my flesh and drinks my blood
        remains in me and I **in** him.
Just as the living **Father sent** me
        and I have life **because** of the Father,
        so **also** the one who feeds on me
        will have life because of **me**.
This is the bread that came down from **heaven**.
Unlike your **ancestors** who ate and still **died**,
        whoever eats **this** bread will live **forever**."

imagery: "the bread that I will give is my flesh for the life of the world." The demand of what Jesus' teaching means immediately catapults his audience into a squabble. Jesus avoids their questions and doubles down on his claim. His audience is to consume his flesh and blood, which are true food and true drink. The emphasis on wisdom in today's other readings invites focusing on the word "true." What does the Lord mean when he calls his flesh and blood "true"? Appeal to the manna eaten by the ancestors in the wilderness illuminates his point. That food, although divinely provided, did not spare the people from death. To consume something provided *by* God is not enough to attain eternal life. More is needed. Life eternal calls for consuming God. Jesus is speaking of ultimate things. The wisdom of the banquet of his body and blood, therefore, is not simply about human nourishment. His "true" food does not simply fill our mouths and stomachs for meaningful social interaction (as at Wisdom's meal in Proverbs). Nor is the Lord's body and blood solely spiritual food, though it does fill us with the Spirit to give thanks to the Lord (as in Ephesians). The banquet of Jesus' body and blood—the true food and true drink of God—draws us through death into resurrection and the fullness of eternal life. To be filled with his body and blood is to be filled with life eternal, to experience lasting nourishment within, to enjoy the promise of resurrection, and to remain in him. E.W.

TWENTY-FIRST SUNDAY IN ORDINARY TIME

LECTIONARY #122

READING I Joshua 24:1–2a, 15–17, 18b

A reading from the Book of Joshua

Joshua gathered together all the **tribes** of Israel at Shechem,
    summoning their **elders**, their **leaders**,
    their **judges**, and their **officers**.
When they stood in ranks before **God**,
    Joshua addressed **all** the people:
    "If it does **not** please you to **serve** the Lord,
    decide today whom you **will** serve,
    the gods your fathers served beyond the **River**
    or the **gods** of the **Amorites** in whose country you are
        now **dwelling**.
As for **me** and my **household**, we will serve the Lord."

But the people answered,
    "Far be it from us to **forsake** the Lord
    for the service of **other** gods.
For it was the Lord, **our** God,
    who brought us and our fathers up out of the land of **Egypt**,
    out of a state of **slavery**.
He performed those great **miracles** before our very eyes
    and **protected** us along our entire journey
    and among the peoples through whom we passed.
Therefore we also **will** serve the Lord, for he is **our** God."

Shechem = SHEK-uhm

This moment was so important that all the leaders were summoned.

Three options are given to how they will answer Joshua's question: the Lord God, their past gods, or the gods of others. Joshua made his choice, now others must as well.

Amorites = AM-ehr-ītz

Deliver Joshua's choice with conviction.

The climactic points of their history are held up for admiration. God is personally involved in their lives. Notice how the people use personal and relational language in describing God's actions (us, we, our, and so on).

READING I The word "crisis" can refer to a critical moment in which a choice is made and decisive action taken. Such crisis moments arise at various points in life and occur fairly regularly in our relationship with God. Today's reading from Joshua highlights the power of crisis moments in our journey with God. The scene transpires at the end of Joshua's life. He has led the people of God into the land promised to them. He has guided them through the conquest. He orchestrated the renewal of the covenant between the people and God at Shechem in accord with God's command. Under Joshua's care, the land has been apportioned to each tribe and boundaries established among them. Cities of refuge have also been set up for those who have unintentionally killed others. Joshua has accomplished all that he has been asked to do. He is at the end of his life. Gathering the whole people of Israel again at Shechem—their primordial place of worship—he reminds them of their covenantal relationship with the Lord and, once more, he calls upon them to renew that covenant. This time, Joshua presents the matter as a crisis moment. They have options. They can serve other gods like their ancestors did or like the previous inhabitants of the promised land had. But, after laying out their options, Joshua boldly makes a public decision on behalf of his household: they will serve the Lord. When faced with witnessing Joshua's public commitment to serve the Lord, the people find courage to remember the many things the Lord had done for them and accordingly echo Joshua's commitment.

Similarly, sacraments mark and celebrate crisis moments in our journey with God. Baptism and confirmation celebrate

For meditation and context:

RESPONSORIAL PSALM   Psalm 34:2–3, 16–17, 18–19, 20–21 (9a)

R. Taste and see the goodness of the Lord.

I will bless the LORD at all times;
    his praise shall be ever in my mouth.
Let my soul glory in the LORD;
    the lowly will hear me and be glad.

The LORD has eyes for the just,
    and ears for their cry.
The LORD confronts the evildoers,
    to destroy remembrance of them from
        the earth.

When the just cry out, the LORD hears them,
    and from all their distress he
        rescues them.
The LORD is close to the brokenhearted;
    and those who are crushed in spirit
        he saves.

Many are the troubles of the just one,
    but out of them all the LORD delivers him;
he watches over all his bones;
    not one of them shall be broken.

READING II   Ephesians 5:21–32

Ephesians = ee-FEE-zhuhnz

A reading from the Letter of Saint Paul to the Ephesians

Try not to let your contemporary sensibilities react too strongly to the idea of subordination in the context of marriage. This reading is making a theological point about the intimate relationship between Christ and the Church and the way our human relationships image this.

[**Brothers** and **sisters:**]
Be **subordinate** to one another out of reverence for **Christ**.
Wives should be subordinate to their husbands as to the Lord.
For the husband is head of his wife
    just as **Christ** is **head** of the **church**,
    he himself the **savior** of the body.
As the **church** is **subordinate** to Christ,
    so wives should be subordinate to their husbands
        in everything.

Convey the tenderness of Christ's actions for the Church, his bride, in this passage.

[**Husbands**, **love** your **wives**,
    even as **Christ** loved the **church**
    and handed himself **over** for her to **sanctify** her,
    cleansing her by the bath of water with the word,
    that he might present to himself the church in **splendor**,
    without spot or wrinkle or any such thing,
    that she might be **holy** and **without** blemish.
So also husbands should love their wives as their **own** bodies.
He who loves his wife loves himself.]

our initiation into the Church, which establishes us in a new relationship with God. Marriage and ordination mark out our vocations. Anointing of the sick and reconciliation sanctify times of weakness and frailty. The Eucharist, too, is a kind of routine crisis moment in which we are called upon to discern God's real presence in the Eucharistic species and give our assent in the "amens" of the liturgy. We then respond with decisive actions; after receiving the Lord in the Eucharist, we are sent out from Mass to share him with the world.

READING II   In a protracted reflection on the deep, mysterious relationship between Christ and the Church, Ephesians appeals to the most fundamental, intimate human relationship—marriage—to explain the bond between Christ and the Church. Using the model of household codes, which served as a paradigm for organizing ancient Greco-Roman households, Ephesians transforms the language of those codes to talk about the relationship of Christ and the Church as a household built on mutual love and service. While contemporary readers might focus on elements of inequity in this passage of Ephesians, it aims to highlight the mutual service that is part and parcel of the most robust spousal relationships. Like a husband willing to die for his bride, Christ sanctifies the Church by offering himself. As a husband might wash his wife and clothe her in fine attire with the utmost affection, so Christ speaks his cleansing word to his bride, the Church, with the greatest affection. Moreover, Christ sanctifies the Church by wrapping her in the spotless and wrinkle-free "garment" of his loving word.

For no one **hates** his **own** flesh
>   but rather **nourishes** and **cherishes** it,
>   even as **Christ** does the **church**,
>   because we are **members** of his body.
>   *For this reason a man shall leave his father and his mother*
>   *and be joined to his wife,*
>   *and the two shall become one flesh.*
This is a great **mystery**,
>   but I speak in reference to Christ and the church.

[Shorter: Ephesians 5:2a, 25–32 (see brackets). This shorter version adds 2a as the first line: "Live in love, as Christ loved us."]

Christ humbled himself, became human, to be joined to us so that we could be joined to him.

Christ's self-sacrificing love should be made manifest in marriage relationships. We can better embody this when we enter into the mystery of Christ's paschal love.

GOSPEL   John 6:60–69

A reading from the holy Gospel according to John

Many of **Jesus'** disciples who were listening said,
>   "This saying is **hard**; **who** can **accept** it?"
Since Jesus **knew** that his disciples were **murmuring** about this,
>   he said to them, "Does this **shock** you?
What if you were to **see** the Son of Man **ascending**
>   to where he was before?
It is the **spirit** that gives **life**,
>   while the **flesh** is of no **avail**.
The words I have spoken to you are Spirit and life.
But there are some of you who do **not** believe."
Jesus knew from the **beginning** the **ones** who would not believe
>   and the one who would **betray** him.
And he said,
>   "For this reason I have told you that no one can **come** to me
>   unless it is **granted** him by my **Father**." »

Jesus' claim that believers must eat his flesh and drink his blood scandalizes his followers. A shocking way to begin; responding to this claim of Jesus is at the heart of this reading.

Jesus doesn't diminish his claim, he compounds it with more unbelievable details—his ascension.

Building on this imagery, Ephesians claims that everyone, fundamentally, cherishes and cares for their own flesh. Presumably all readers understand and live by this principle, which, in many respects, remains in force today. We see to our basic physical needs by obtaining food, clothing, and shelter. But Ephesians extends the claim. The care we provide in obtaining our own basic needs is to be applied to spouses. Love of one's spouse is to be considered tantamount to caring for one's own body. There ought not be a conceptual distinction between caring for oneself and caring for one's spouse. Such selfless care and mutual giving between spouses typify Christ's giving of himself for and to the Church. As such, the relationship between Christ and the Church provides the paradigm of the Christian household, wherein mutual subordination to the needs of the other should reign.

GOSPEL   Since the Seventeenth Sunday in Ordinary Time, we have heard from the Bread of Life Discourse in John 6. This protracted exchange between Jesus and his fellow Galilean Jews began with Jesus feeding a hungry crowd. He then fled from them because they mistook his actions for that of royalty and wanted to make him king. When the crowd caught up with him, he began to teach them to seek food that would bring eternal life rather than ordinary food. Next, he proclaimed that he is the bread of life which they ultimately seek. And he went on to instruct them that consuming his flesh and blood as true food and true drink promises resurrection and life eternal. Today we hear the conclusion of this discourse. The talk ends, and the time for decision making

Make this question personal. Look directly at the assembly and deliver, "Do you also want to leave?"

Peter, taking the lead, speaks up. We too can respond to Jesus' question with a wholehearted "no." Pause slightly after each statement of faith that Peter makes.

As a result of this,
  many of his di**sciples returned** to their former way of life
  and no longer **accompanied** him.
Jesus then said to the Twelve, "Do you also **want** to **leave**?"
Simon **Peter** answered him, "Master, to **whom** shall we go?
You have the **words** of eternal life.
We have come to **believe**
  and are convinced that you are the Holy One of **God**."

arrives. Jesus' audience must decide if they are going to believe his teaching and act on it.

As before, they begin with a question in which they recognize (grumble about, really) the difficulty of his teaching: "who can accept it?" In this question a shift can be discerned. Last week the people's question focused on Jesus: "How can this man give us his flesh to eat?" (John 6:52). Now their question focuses on themselves. They recognize that a decision about Jesus is at hand; it is a crisis moment. As before, Jesus responds to their question by amplifying

the matter. He points out that still more startling realities will transpire for those who follow him. For example, they will see him ascend to heaven. But he also points out that his message appeals to them because his words are Spirit and life. Moreover, they are already receiving God's grace because they are drawn to him. They only need to continue accepting the grace that drew them to him in the first place. But at this crisis moment, a division arises. Many disciples return to their former ways of life. His teaching about his flesh being true food and his blood being true drink is

too hard for them. But when Jesus presses the Twelve about their loyalty to him, they echo God's chosen people's response to Joshua. With Simon Peter speaking on their behalf, they respond with faith to Jesus' entire Bread of Life Discourse: "You have the words of eternal life." Hearing this exchange, we face our participation in the Eucharist as a crisis moment as well, and are left to offer our own response. E.W.

TWENTY-SECOND SUNDAY IN ORDINARY TIME

LECTIONARY #125

READING I   Deuteronomy 4:1–2, 6–8

A reading from the Book of Deuteronomy

Moses said to the people:
    "Now, **Israel**, **hear** the **statutes** and **decrees**
    which I am **teaching** you to observe,
    that you may live, and may **enter** in and take possession
        of the land
    which the LORD, the God of your fathers, is **giving** you.
In your **observance** of the commandments of the LORD,
        your God,
    which I enjoin upon you,
    you shall not **add** to what I command you nor **subtract** from it.
Observe them carefully,
    for thus will you give **evidence**
    of your **wisdom** and intelligence to the **nations**,
    who will **hear** of all these statutes and say,
    'This **great** nation is truly a wise and intelligent people.'
For what great nation is there
    that has **gods** so **close** to **it** as the LORD, **our** God, **is** to **us**
    whenever we **call** upon him?
Or **what** great nation has **statutes** and **decrees**
    that are as **just** as this whole law
    which I am setting before you today?"

Deuteronomy = d<u>oo</u>-ter-AH-nuh-mee
or dy<u>oo</u>-ter-AH-nuh-mee

statutes = STACH-<u>oo</u>ts

Emphasize "hear." Moses' exhortative language reveals the significance of the proclamation.

The commandments do not need editing. Divine revelation is just that: divine.

Make sure to contrast the plural "gods" with the singular "God."

Conclude with an upbeat tone. The law is a gift, not a burden.

READING I Highlighting the theme of wisdom and its connection with God's law, Deuteronomy presents Moses, the divinely sanctioned lawgiver, as a commentator on God's laws. In this discourse given at the end of his life, Moses provides some final instruction to the people before he goes the way of all flesh. He who once heard and received the laws from God on the people's behalf now highlights what it means for them to follow those laws. First, he notes that, due to their divine origin, these laws are not to be altered. Expanding on them or doing away with them would undermine the message they communicate to the world, namely, that the God of Israel abides with the chosen people. Second, they are to diligently keep God's laws. To do so will imbue them with the Lord's wisdom and show the nation's wisdom to the whole world. If the people actually follow the law of God, not only will the nations of the world come to know their wisdom and, through them, God's wisdom, but also foreign nations will be able to perceive the intimate bond that the Lord forges with the chosen people through the law. A corollary here is that, by following the law, Israel will enjoy the assurance of a close relationship with the Lord. Put differently, to keep the law given by God is to remain engaged in the intimate relationship that God desires and fosters with the people by virtue of giving the law. Unfortunately, despite their best efforts, Moses' comments eventually show that keeping the law exceeds the people's ability. The Lord's law will need to become incarnate (in the person of Jesus) in order for it to be entirely kept and fulfilled.

For meditation and context:

RESPONSORIAL PSALM   Psalm 15:2–3, 3–4, 4–5 (1a)

R. The one who does justice will live in the presence of the Lord.

Whoever walks blamelessly and does justice;
   who thinks the truth in his heart
   and slanders not with his tongue.

Who harms not his fellow man,
   nor takes up a reproach against
   his neighbor;

by whom the reprobate is despised,
   while he honors those who fear the LORD.

Who lends not his money at usury
   and accepts no bribe against the
   innocent.
Whoever does these things
   shall never be disturbed.

READING II   James 1:17–18, 21b–22, 27

A reading from the Letter of Saint James

Announce the name of the book clearly. This is the first of multiple weeks we will hear from James.

This is an exhortatory text on ethical conduct, yet there is an underlying joy in the acknowledgement that all our gifts come from God.

Dearest **brothers** and **sisters**:
All good **giving** and every perfect gift is from **above**,
   coming down from the **Father** of lights,
   with whom there is no **alteration** or shadow caused by change.
He willed to give us **birth** by the word of **truth**
   that we may be a kind of **firstfruits** of his creatures.

Humbly **welcome** the **word** that has been planted **in** you
   and is able to **save** your souls.

Be **doers** of the word and not **hearers** only, deluding yourselves.

Deception happens when what you say and do don't align. Ask yourself: If you are not a "doer of the word," have you really heard it?

Religion that is **pure** and undefiled before God and the Father
      is this:
   to care for **orphans** and **widows** in their affliction
   and to keep oneself **unstained** by the world.

GOSPEL   Mark 7:1–8, 14–15, 21–23

A reading from the holy Gospel according to Mark

Pharisees = FAYR-uh-seez

When the **Pharisees** with some **scribes** who had come
      from Jerusalem
   gathered around Jesus,

READING II   This Sunday, we begin reading the letter of James, who was probably a relative of Jesus, the first leader of the church in Jerusalem, and martyred in the early 60s. According to James 1:1, the audience is "the twelve tribes in the dispersion," which refers to Jews outside of first-century Roman Palestine. Generally speaking, this text repeatedly exhorts its audience to live morally upright lives, especially through various practical means. Only its initial greeting suggests that it is a letter. A better category for James might be wisdom literature.

This Sunday's passage begins by focusing on gift-giving. James associates the whole dynamic of gift-giving with grace. Any and all good gifts originate in the heavenly "Father of lights" who gives the word of truth. This "word of truth" recalls the law of God celebrated in and commented on in today's first reading and points toward the incarnate word of truth—Jesus—who further imparts God's true word in the Gospel. This word, if welcomed and received openly and with docility, has the power to give life. It is like a seed planted in the soul that can bear fruit. Reception of the word,

for James, amounts to undertaking practical deeds: caring for orphans and widows and remaining "unstained by the world." In this turn of phrase, James uses stereotypical biblical categories to call his audience to care for any and all who experience needs due to social inequity. He equates actions that care for those in need with true religion. Thus, the one who seeks life through the power of the word seeks to care for those overburdened by social injustice.

Jesus wants the Pharisees to move beyond a legalistic understanding of God's law. Read their questions with an accusatory tone. This would explain Jesus' abrupt answer.

Read this slowly and with sadness. Jesus laments those who are far from God.

Pause after "tradition." Jesus turns his attention away from the scribes and Pharisees and back to the crowds. Use an authoritative tone. Jesus wants to clarify an important point.

Read the list slowly so the assembly can take to heart the actions and attitudes that should be avoided. It is almost like an examination of conscience.

they observed that some of his disciples **ate** their meals
　　with **unclean**, that is, unwashed, hands.
—For the Pharisees and, in fact, **all** Jews,
　　do **not** eat without **carefully** washing their hands,
　　keeping the **tradition** of the elders.
And on coming from the marketplace
　　they do not eat without **purifying** themselves.
And there are many other things that they have
　　　traditionally **observed**,
　　the **purification** of cups and jugs and kettles and beds.—
So the Pharisees and scribes questioned him,
　　"**Why** do your disciples not **follow** the tradition of the elders
　　but instead eat a meal with **unclean** hands?"
He responded,
　　"**Well** did **Isaiah** prophesy about you **hypocrites**, as it
　　　is written:
*This people **honors** me with their **lips**,*
　　*but their **hearts** are **far** from me;*
*in **vain** do they worship me,*
　　teaching as doctrines human precepts.
You **disregard** God's **commandment** but cling to
　　human tradition."
He summoned the crowd **again** and said to them,
　　"**Hear** me, all of you, and understand.
Nothing that enters one from **outside** can **defile** that person;
　　but the things that come out from **within** are what defile.

"From within people, from their **hearts**,
　　come evil thoughts, **unchastity**, **theft**, **murder**,
　　adultery, **greed**, **malice**, **deceit**,
　　licentiousness, **envy**, **blasphemy**, **arrogance**, **folly**.
All these evils come from **within** and **they** defile."

GOSPEL As we return to the Gospel of Mark today, we see Jesus facing a new audience: Pharisees from Jerusalem. Up to this point he has been addressing fellow Galilean Jews. Similar to the Bread of Life Discourse in John 6 (which we have heard from the last few Sundays), Jesus' audience resists his teaching. Mark reports that they were accustomed to various cleansing rituals in their everyday lives, especially ritual hand-washing. Such rituals had their logic. They aimed at keeping the Jewish people pure and holy amid a world that was governed by laws that differed from their own God-given laws. Customary ritual washing set them apart, which seemingly sanctified them. In other words, these rituals were thought of as ways to keep the law of Moses and live wisely, objectives outlined in today's first two readings.

Therefore, when the Jerusalemites observe Jesus' disciples eating without ritually washing up, they are surprised. How can a righteous teacher permit his disciples to relinquish customs that seem to assure sanctity and the keeping of the law? The question occasions a strong response.

Jesus cites the prophet Isaiah to explain that their ritual cleansing practices are human innovations, explicitly forbidden by Moses in today's first reading. Jesus then gathers the local Galilean crowd to teach them what it truly means to keep one's sanctity undefiled. As Jesus explains, defilement is not about what we take in from the outside world. Rather, a list of vices shows clearly that defilement comes out from within. So, we do well to ask, what are we putting out into the world? E.W.

TWENTY-THIRD SUNDAY IN ORDINARY TIME

LECTIONARY #128

READING I   Isaiah 35:4–7a

A reading from the Book of the Prophet Isaiah

Thus says the LORD:
    Say to those whose hearts are **frightened**:
      Be **strong**, fear **not**!
    Here is **your** God,
      he comes with **vindication**;
    with divine **recompense**
      he comes to save you.
    Then will the **eyes** of the blind be **opened**,
      the **ears** of the deaf be **cleared**;
    then will the **lame leap** like a stag,
      then the **tongue** of the mute will **sing**.
    Streams will **burst** forth in the desert,
      and rivers in the steppe.
    The burning sands will become **pools**,
      and the **thirsty** ground, springs of water.

Isaiah = ī-ZAY-uh

Accent "your." God is personal.

Practice so you can deliver the line looking directly at the assembly. Pause slightly to let the beauty of the promise soak in. Use energy and build some speed as the list of good things and miracles promised tumble out with enthusiasm. Bring attention to the verbs; they illustrate a joyous renewal.

Steppe = step = grassland

READING I   Isaiah addresses those "whose hearts are frightened" (*lenimharēy-lēv* in Hebrew), a potentially misunderstood phrase for contemporary English speakers. For Isaiah, the heart is a place of intellect rather than emotions, meaning that it is best understood as the "mind." Moreover, Isaiah's verb (*mahar* in Hebrew) connotes swift movement—like flowing water—and is often translated "to hasten" or "to act quickly." So, Isaiah addresses the "hasty of mind." Centuries later, Greek translators render Isaiah's expression as "*oligópsuchoi tē dianoia*," meaning "those who are dispirited of mind" or "those whose minds have little motivating spirit." Thus, ancient Greek speakers understood Isaiah to be addressing those with troubled minds, not those with negative feelings (e.g., fear). Accordingly, Isaiah's message is about healing mental wounds more than emotional ones. Yet thoughts and emotions are closely connected, and the ancients understood this. Indeed, ancient Hebrew speakers would have understood Isaiah to be calling for the kind of care needed when thinking through the emotion of panic (i.e., hasty thinking), while Greek-speaking audiences took Isaiah to be highlighting the care needed when thinking through discouragement (i.e., slow thinking). Either way, Isaiah calls for healing emotionally wounded minds by emphasizing God's might and divine recompense. A divine leveling of justice would come. Moreover, God will heal and provide abundant resources, even in places where resources are limited. The blind will see. The lame will leap. The mute will sing. Waters and streams will spring forth in the desert. Put simply, God

For meditation and context:

RESPONSORIAL PSALM   Psalm 146:6–7, 8–9, 9–10 (1b)

R. Praise the Lord, my soul! or R. Alleluia.

The God of Jacob keeps faith forever,
    secures justice for the oppressed,
    gives food to the hungry.
The Lord sets captives free.

The Lord gives sight to the blind;
    the Lord raises up those who were
    bowed down.

The Lord loves the just;
    the Lord protects strangers.

The fatherless and the widow the
    Lord sustains,
    but the way of the wicked he thwarts.
The Lord shall reign forever;
    your God, O Zion, through all
    generations. Alleluia.

READING II   James 2:1–5

A reading from the Letter of Saint James

In this passage, James is calling the community to task for their un-Christian behavior.

After giving an example of what was happening, James points out why their behavior is problematic.

My **brothers** and **sisters**, show no **partiality**
    as you **adhere** to the faith in our glorious Lord Jesus **Christ**.
For if a man with gold **rings** and fine **clothes**
    comes **into** your assembly,
    and a **poor** person in **shabby** clothes **also** comes in,
    and you pay **attention** to the one wearing the fine clothes
    and say, "Sit **here**, please,"
    while you say to the poor one, "Stand **there**,"
        or "Sit at my **feet**,"
    have you not made **distinctions** among yourselves
    and become **judges** with evil designs?

Despite their behavior, James maintains his care for the community, adding the endearment "beloved" (not found in the initial address).

The preferential option for the poor is not a new, contemporary social justice teaching but a teaching from Jesus, exemplified in his ministry. Do our lives demonstrate this priority?

Listen, my **beloved** brothers and sisters.
Did not God **choose** those who are **poor** in the world
    to be **rich** in faith and heirs of the kingdom
    that he promised to those who **love** him?

---

will wipe away all reason for doubt and restore faith among the chosen people.

READING II   James addresses economic inequality and favoritism in the early Church. The dilemma, according to James, does not lie in the existence of such inequality but in the community's response to it. James does not call for doing away with economic inequity by demanding that the rich become poor or that the community work strenuously to increase the wealth of the less fortunate. Therefore, James seems to consider eco-

nomic inequality an unavoidable reality of life. Evidently, some members of the early Church enjoyed wealth and possessions while others did not. However, James is perfectly clear about how a disciple of Jesus should appropriately respond to such economic inequality. Disciples of Christ must avoid giving greater deference and care to those with economic means. They must also avoid neglecting or shunning those of lesser means or lower economic status. Instead, comparable care and attention must be given to all members of the community regardless of economic sta-

tus. For James, Jesus' disciples might accept the economic inequality as an inevitable reality of life, but they cannot rightly appeal to it as grounds for treating members of the community differently. The rationale and the wisdom of the proper behavior Christians should take springs from God's care for people. As James points out, when God shows favoritism, the preference lies with the poor. After all, God chose the poor to be "heirs of the kingdom," and it is the poor whom God enriches with faith. Where Isaiah speaks of God restoring interior deficiencies, James

GOSPEL   Mark 7:31–37

A reading from the holy Gospel according to Mark

Again **Jesus** left the district of **Tyre**
    and went by way of Sidon to the Sea of **Galilee**,
    into the district of the Decapolis.
And people **brought** to him a **deaf** man who had a
        speech impediment
    and begged **him** to lay **his** hand on **him**.
He took him off by himself **away** from the **crowd**.
He put his **finger** into the man's **ears**
    and, **spitting**, touched his **tongue**;
    then he **looked up to heaven** and **groaned**, and said to him,
    "*Ephphatha*!"—that is, "Be **opened**!"—
And **immediately** the man's ears **were** opened,
    his speech impediment **was** removed,
    and he **spoke** plainly.
He ordered them **not** to tell anyone.
But the **more** he ordered them not to,
    the more they proclaimed it.
They were exceedingly **astonished** and they said,
    "He has done all things **well**.
He makes the **deaf hear** and the **mute speak**."

Sidebar notes:

Tyre = tīr
Sidon = SĪ-duhn
Decapolis = dih-KAP-uh-lis

Practice so all of the masculine pronouns make sense and you can clearly distinguish who is acting.

Jesus prays and acts. Do not cringe at the tactile and bodily aspects of the cure (finger in ear, spit).
Ephphatha = EF-uh-thuh

"Immediately" shows God's word is effective and powerful. Proclaim this miracle story as if hearing it for the first time.

Let "exceedingly astonished" be heard.

---

focuses on God's (and Christians') care for exterior matters.

GOSPEL Today's Gospel passage recounts Jesus' healing of a man who was unable to hear or speak. Given that Mark is the shortest Gospel, we get a somewhat surprisingly detailed description of Jesus' healing, including the distinctive manner by which he performs the deed, as well as the instruction he provides once the man is restored. Notably, the term used by Jesus—"*ephphatha*"—is Aramaic rather than Greek (which is the primary language of the New Testament). By preserving this word in its original language, Mark points to the veracity of the account and may highlight an early tradition of the Church that used this word in ritual healing ministry. Of course, at the heart of such ministry in the Church is the sacrament of baptism, which heals our primordial woundedness and restores us to right relationship with God. In the Roman Catholic tradition an (optional) ephphatha rite is preserved in the current order of baptism. This rite entails the celebrant praying for the opening of the ears and mouth of the newly baptized, that they might hear and proclaim the Gospel like the man from the Decapolis so many years ago. In this way, the Church's liturgical tradition continues Jesus' healing ministry. Like the deaf-mute man, we too, through baptism, can come to hear the Gospel and proclaim it openly. Moreover, through this ministry of "opening," we recognize that Jesus accomplishes both internal and external restoration, thereby fulfilling the messages of both Isaiah and James in today's first and second readings. E.W.

TWENTY-FOURTH SUNDAY IN ORDINARY TIME

LECTIONARY #131

READING I Isaiah 50:5–9a

A reading from the Book of the Prophet Isaiah

> The Lord **GOD opens** my ear that I may **hear**;
>> and I have not **rebelled**,
>> have not turned **back**.
> I gave my back to those who **beat** me,
>> my **cheeks** to those who **plucked** my beard;
> my face I did **not** shield
>> from **buffets** and **spitting**.
>
> The Lord GOD is my **help**,
>> therefore I am not **disgraced**;
> I have set my face like flint,
>> **knowing** that I shall **not** be put to shame.
> He is near who **upholds** my right;
>> if **anyone** wishes to oppose me,
>> let us appear **together**.
> Who disputes my **right**?
>> Let that man **confront** me.
> See, the Lord GOD is my **help**;
>> **who** will prove me wrong?

Isaiah = ī-ZAY-uh

The readiness to hear is attributed to God, not our own volition.

buffets = BUF-ihts = hitting

The Lord sustains us; "help" needs emphasis.

Despite the humiliation, there is no shame.

God is our advocate. The speaker challenges any that dispute his claim. Use an upward inflection and leave the question hanging in the air.

READING I The book of Isaiah repeatedly refers to a servant whose identity remains intentionally vague. In four so-called Servant Songs (Isaiah 42:1–4 [or 42:1–9], 49:1–6, 50:4–11, 52:13—53:12) this servant is the primary agent. Today's first reading is part of one of those songs. In it we hear of the close relationship that the Lord forges with the servant. God has opened the servant's ears—a remarkable grace that is to be celebrated! This language of "opening" continues a message from last week's Gospel in which Jesus opened a deaf man's ears to hear by touching them. At the same time, Isaiah advances last week's message. By pointing out the ramifications of having ears opened to God's message and remaining loyal to (or at least not rebelling against) God's message, Isaiah shows that loyalty to God can lead to great suffering. The servant endures beatings, beard-pluckings, and spitting. Yet, through all these indignities the servant endures with God's help. In fact, by remaining loyal to God through suffering, the servant's resolve strengthens. No one can rightly bring a dispute against him or his case. And he knows it! Fully convinced that God will support him if a case or a trial is brought against him, the servant repeatedly taunts potential contenders, daring them to confront him and his cause. In the servant, then, we see that being loyal to God may mean suffering. At the same time, we also recognize in the servant that suffering-hardened loyalty can beget courage and boldness of the highest order.

READING II With strong rhetoric similar to that of the passage from Isaiah, the reading from James poses a series of demanding questions to its

253

For meditation and context:

RESPONSORIAL PSALM   Psalm 116:1–2, 3–4, 5–6, 8–9 (9)

R. I will walk before the Lord, in the land of the living.
or
R. Alleluia.

I love the Lord because he has heard
   my voice in supplication,
because he has inclined his ear to me
   the day I called.

The cords of death encompassed me;
   the snares of the netherworld seized
     upon me;
   I fell into distress and sorrow,
and I called upon the name of the Lord,
   "O Lord, save my life!"

Gracious is the Lord and just;
   yes, our God is merciful.
The Lord keeps the little ones;
   I was brought low, and he saved me.

For he has freed my soul from death,
   my eyes from tears, my feet
     from stumbling.
I shall walk before the Lord
   in the land of the living.

READING II   James 2:14–18

A reading from the Letter of Saint James

The author puts the thesis statement first and then uses examples and arguments to demonstrate his point.

What good is it, my **brothers** and **sisters**,
   if someone **says** he has faith but does not have **works**?
Can that faith **save** him?
If a brother or sister has **nothing** to wear
   and has **no** food for the day,
   and one of you says to them,
   "**Go** in **peace**, keep warm, and eat well,"
   but you do not give them the **necessities** of the body,
   what good **is it**?
So also faith of itself,
   if it does not have works, is **dead**.

Let these final lines ring out. Belief in the propositions of faith is not enough; it must be embodied. At the end of every Mass, we are invited to go forth and share Christ with the world. Listen for the closing prayer this Sunday.

Indeed someone might say,
   "**You** have faith and **I** have works."
Demonstrate your faith to me without works,
   and I will demonstrate **my** faith to you **from** my works.

---

audience: What good is faith without works? Can that faith save? What good is such a faith? With these questions the author points to a demanding and ancient concern with which all Christians must contend: What difference does our faith in God make? It may be worth noting that the question emerging here is not "Where does our faith in God come from?" That is, James is not saying that faith *comes* from works, as if to counter the claim that faith is a freely given gift from God, a grace. James is well aware that faith in God is an unmerited gift. No one could earn faith in God by their

works. However, for James, if someone claims to possess faith, the legitimacy of their claim could be tested. And, should questions about one's faith arise, should a disciple of Christ have to endure suffering and interrogation like Isaiah's servant, support for claiming to have faith in Christ is found, according to James, in actions that match that claim. By providing for the daily needs of those who would otherwise go without, Christ's disciples embody the faith they freely receive from God. We know also that through such works Christians make Christ present in the world. Thus, by engag-

ing in acts of care rooted in faith, the deeds of Christians demonstrate their faith. This is James' point, and with it comes the unflappable confidence of Isaiah's servant—no claim against such a one can be sustained.

GOSPEL   Jesus' words in today's Gospel test his disciples' commitment. To begin, he asks a question that assesses their listening skills and invites them to consider his importance in their lives. At first, they are able to hide behind the thoughts of others. A second question removes the protective barrier

GOSPEL   Mark 8:27–35

A reading from the holy Gospel according to Mark

Jesus and his **disciples** set out
    for the villages of Caesarea **Philippi**.
Along the way he asked his disciples,
    "**Who** do people say that **I am**?"
They said in reply,
    "John the **Baptist**, others **Elijah**,
    still others one of the **prophets**."
And he asked them,
    "But **who** do **you** say that I am?"
Peter said to him in reply,
    "You are the **Christ**."
Then he warned them **not** to **tell** anyone about him.

He began to **teach** them
    that the Son of **Man** must **suffer** greatly
    and be **rejected** by the **elders**, the chief **priests**, and the **scribes**,
    and be **killed**, and **rise** after three days.
He spoke this **openly**.
Then Peter took him aside and began to **rebuke him**.
At this he turned around and, looking at his disciples,
    rebuked **Peter** and said, "**Get behind me**, **Satan**.
You are thinking **not** as **God** does, but as human **beings** do."

He summoned the **crowd** with his disciples and said to them,
    "Whoever wishes to come **after** me must **deny** himself,
    take up his **cross**, and **follow** me.
For whoever wishes to **save** his life will **lose** it,
    but whoever **loses** his life for **my** sake
    and that of the gospel will **save** it."

Caesarea = sez-uh-REE-uh
or see-zuh-REE-uh

Philippi = fih-LIP-ī

Read this question looking directly at the assembly so they can appropriate it to themselves. Give a slight pause for their internal voice to answer.

Elijah = ee-Lī-juh

Repeat the direct gaze the second time Jesus asks, making it even more personal with the added "you."

The narrator voice reports the content of Jesus' teaching.

Increase your intensity as the narrator voice ends and the character dialogue begins again.

The cost of discipleship is such an important lesson that Jesus addresses the disciples *and* the crowd.

Use a strong voice for Jesus' instruction. Practice so that the inverse relationship is clear: save/lose and loses/save.

and compels the disciples to weigh the implications of following Jesus. If Jesus is another prophet, they could be loyal from a distance and avoid potential suffering. But if Jesus is the Christ—God's anointed—then following him at a distance is not a real option since Jesus would be the supreme authority in the cosmos. Wherever they go, loyally following such a force would inevitably mean facing conflicts with would-be competing powers. To say that Jesus is the Christ is to state where one's fundamental loyalties will lie: with God or somewhere else. Therefore, Jesus does more than draw

out a correct answer from his disciples. He imparts a deeper lesson: following God entails inevitable conflict and suffering because there are always those who would compete with God's rightful claim to ultimate authority.

For Peter, the deeper lesson is too difficult to bear. Faithfulness to God and discipleship of Jesus should not entail such suffering. And for this position Jesus rebukes him. Jesus affirms that to believe in him as God's anointed and to follow him as such is to anticipate suffering in this world because worldly authority has been

corrupted. So, as with Isaiah's servant and James' audience, Jesus highlights that his disciples can anticipate hardship and suffering because their actions must reflect their faith in him. But suffering-laden discipleship also entails an unparalleled promise: to lose one's life for the Gospel means salvation. E.W.

TWENTY-FIFTH SUNDAY IN ORDINARY TIME

LECTIONARY #134

READING I   Wisdom 2:12, 17–20

A reading from the Book of Wisdom

The **wicked** say:
  Let us **beset** the just one, because he is **obnoxious** to us;
    he sets himself **against** our doings,
  reproaches us for **transgressions** of the law
    and charges us with **violations** of our training.
  Let us **see** whether his words be **true**;
    let us **find** out what will **happen** to him.
  For **if** the just one **be** the son of **God**, God will **defend** him
    and **deliver** him from the hand of his **foes**.
  With **revilement** and **torture** let us put the just one to the test
    that we may have proof of his **gentleness**
    and **try** his **patience**.
  Let us condemn him to a shameful **death**;
    for according to his own **words**, God will take **care** of him.

Make sure everyone is settled before you begin. It is important that the assembly hears the opening line, which explains that the reading is told from the perspective of the wicked.

beset = harass or threaten

reproaches = rih-PROHCH-uhz

This is a malicious plan to test God.

The last line is taunting and insincere. The speaker doesn't care and doesn't believe God will take care of the just one.

For meditation and context:

RESPONSORIAL PSALM   Psalm 54:3–4, 5, 6 and 8 (6b)

R. The Lord upholds my life.

O God, by your name save me,
  and by your might defend my cause.
O God, hear my prayer;
  hearken to the words of my mouth.

For the haughty have risen up against me,
  the ruthless seek my life;
  they set not God before their eyes.

Behold, God is my helper;
  the Lord sustains my life.
Freely will I offer you sacrifice;
  I will praise your name, O LORD,
    for its goodness.

READING I   In an attempt to instruct its audience about the challenges faced when striving after justice and righteousness, the author of the Book of Wisdom articulates a hypothetical reflection on justice from the perspective of those who are wicked or godless. The goal is to imagine how such people think about justice by indicating how they go about responding to those who seek it. The picture is unflattering, even intimidating for someone who would pursue justice and righteousness. For the wicked, the just and righteous ones maintain a commitment to the law that calls forth the accountability of everyone—the just and unjust. That accountability is unbearably annoying for the wicked. In their injustice, the wicked hatch nefarious plans in response. They recognize that the just one is gentle and they plan to torture him. The goal in this action is to undermine the patience of the just one and compromise his ability to endure hardship. Their fiendish hope is that, if he cannot maintain his position in gentleness, he will respond by lashing out and thus act as the wicked do. If he does, they will have shown him to be like them. Ultimately, then, the wicked aim at contending not simply with the just one's behavior and right thinking, but with his fundamental identity. They mean to contend with the just one's status as a child of God. The contrast is stark and the picture disturbing. And while Wisdom may present the wicked in a hypothetical way, the example of Christ's passion and death demonstrate the truth it reveals. At the same time, even the wicked recognize the confidence that underlies the gentleness of those who are just: God ultimately cares for them.

This is a wisdom teaching.

Read the vices with a sad tone. Change to a peaceful countenance to recount the virtues. This will sharpen the distinction between the behavior of the wicked and that of the upright.

Wisdom is a gift from God, not simply the result of life experiences.

James uses rhetorical questions to begin this section on the ways of the wicked. He describes sin from the abstract to the concrete. Read the accusatory questions, pause, and then continue with the ending that is heightened by the repeated use of the word "you."

READING II   James 3:16—4:3

A reading from the Letter of Saint James

Beloved:
Where **jealousy** and **selfish** ambition exist,
    there is **disorder** and every foul practice.
But the **wisdom from above** is first of all **pure**,
    then **peaceable**, **gentle**, **compliant**,
    full of **mercy** and good **fruits**,
    without **inconstancy** or **insincerity**.
And the fruit of righteousness is sown in **peace**
    for those who **cultivate** peace.

Where do the **wars**
    and where do the **conflicts** among you come **from**?
Is it not from your **passions**
    that make **war** within your members?
You **covet** but do not **possess**.
You **kill** and **envy** but you cannot **obtain**;
    you **fight** and wage war.
You do not **possess** because you do not **ask**.
You ask but do not **receive**,
    because you ask **wrongly**, to spend it on your **passions**.

READING II | Today's second reading from James continues to attend to contrasts between those who are wicked and those who are wise. The wicked associate with envy and selfish ambition. By contrast, the wise enjoy a gift "from above." And the fruits of the wisdom that comes from above are ample, distinctive, and desirable. Wisdom begets purity, peace, gentleness, docility, mercy, goodness, consistency, and sincerity. It is a lengthy list of fruits worthy of meditation. But for James there is still more. Righteousness begets righteousness. As James puts

it, "the fruit of righteousness is sown in peace for those who cultivate peace."

Unfortunately, the wicked also reap what they sow. As James points out, for the wicked, conflicts and wars are born of their unintegrated desires, which he calls passions. These unholy longings of the wicked ultimately result in fruitlessness. They fight to obtain what they desire, but they cannot come to possess it. Their longings overtake them. Their energies get spent on fighting and waging war, and what they really want remains out of reach. Sadly, what they desire is only a request away. But the

wicked are unable or unwilling to humbly ask for or openly receive what they desire. Accordingly, they are left to live with unmet desires. The contrast with the wise, who receive fruits in abundance, cannot be more pointed. Wisdom brings forth copious blessings; wickedness begets only war and conflict. Thus, the wise are praiseworthy models, while the wicked prove pitiable and in need of an antidote. And for that we must look to the Gospel.

GOSPEL   Mark 9:30–37

A reading from the holy Gospel according to Mark

Jesus and his **disciples left** from there and began a journey
    through Galilee,
  but he did **not** wish **anyone** to **know** about it.
He was **teaching** his disciples and telling them,
  "The Son of **Man** is to be handed **over** to men
  and they will **kill** him,
  and three days after his death the Son of Man will **rise**."
But they did not **understand** the saying,
  and they were **afraid** to **question** him.

They came to **Capernaum** and, once inside the house,
  he began to **ask** them,
  "What were you **arguing** about on the way?"
But they remained **silent**.
They had been discussing among themselves on the way
  who was the **greatest**.
Then he **sat** down, called the Twelve, and said to them,
  "If anyone wishes to be **first**,
  he shall be the **last** of all and the servant of all."
Taking a **child**, he placed it in their midst,
  and putting his **arms** around it, he said to them,
  "Whoever **receives** one **child** such as this in my **name**,
    receives **me**;
  and whoever receives me,
  receives **not** me but the **One** who **sent** me."

Begin with an even, steady tone for the narrator.

Notice how Jesus teaches the disciples apart from everyone else. This is a hard teaching, and even his closest followers do not grasp its meaning yet.

Capernaum = kuh-PER-nee-*m or kuh-PER-nay-*m or kuh-PER-n*m

The change in geography indicates a new section. Pause slightly before starting.

Insert a comma after "not me."

GOSPEL Today's Gospel recalls Jesus' secret journey through Galilee in the northern part of the Holy Land. During this journey, he tries to teach his disciples that he must suffer, die, and rise, but they fail to understand him. Evidently, they were too preoccupied with concerns of their own grandeur to grasp his message. After all, what does suffering and death have to do with greatness? So, when they return to their home base in the village of Capernaum, Jesus asks them about the argument they were having during their journey. Like scolded children, they remain silent. They seem to recognize that their squabble over which one might be the greatest was not in keeping with their master's message or mission. They had been embodying the wickedness described in Wisdom and James. Their infighting and arguing made them unable to peaceably receive a new teaching from Jesus. They were rendered closed off by ambition and swallowed up by bickering. So, before he could meaningfully teach them about his coming suffering, death, and resurrection, he would have to rid them of their wickedness and selfish ambition. To do so, Jesus sits them down and shows them that to receive him, his teaching, and, ultimately, the One who sent him, they must employ the same gentleness and openness applied when embracing a child. The message becomes clear: fighting for God's grace is futile. Instead, fostering an open, docile spirit is the antidote to selfish ambition and wicked desires. Christ's way, the way of wisdom and holiness, means striving for meekness, not power. E.W.

TWENTY-SIXTH SUNDAY IN ORDINARY TIME

LECTIONARY #137

READING I   Numbers 11:25–29

A reading from the Book of Numbers

The LORD came **down** in the cloud and spoke to **Moses**.
Taking some of the **spirit** that was **on** Moses,
    the LORD bestowed it on the seventy **elders**;
    and as the spirit came to **rest** on them, they **prophesied**.

Now **two** men, one named **Eldad** and the other **Medad**,
    were not in the gathering but had been **left** in the camp.
They too had been on the **list**, but had not gone **out** to the tent;
    yet the spirit came to rest on them **also**,
    and they **prophesied** in the camp.
So, when a young man quickly told Moses,
    "Eldad and Medad are prophesying in the camp,"
    Joshua, son of **Nun**, who from his youth had been
        Moses' aide, said,
    "Moses, my lord, **stop them**."
But Moses answered him,
    "Are you **jealous** for **my** sake?
Would that **all** the people of the LORD were **prophets**!
Would that the LORD might **bestow** his spirit **on** them all!"

The mention of the cloud indicates God's presence.

prophesy = PROF-uh-sī

Eldad = EL-dad

Medad = MEE-dad

God's revelation is not limited to a specific site. Where do we see God working outside of the "box" we might place him in?

Emphasize "stop them" to convey how frantic the situation is.

Ask the question gently. If the tent of meeting was the typical ritual place of divine encounter, it was natural that the alternative location was suspect. Moses sets them straight.

READING I As the Israelite people began their journey away from the wilderness of Sinai and toward the promised land, Moses, with the aid of Joshua, led them. They had witnessed God descending on the mountain and had received the law. Now, as Numbers recounts, the Lord dispersed the prophetic spirit, which had been imparted on Moses, to seventy elders among the Israelites. Interestingly, despite the fact that in previous chapters in the Book of Numbers lengthy concerns over protocols and procedures for the people to follow are articu-

lated, this scene constitutes a procedural misstep. Two elders are left in the camp while the others join Moses and Joshua outside the camp to engage in uttering prophecies. Still more interesting, the Lord acts among the people despite their procedural misstep and no harm is incurred because of it. Quite the contrary, in fact. Moses rebukes Joshua for wanting to stop the out-of-place elders turned prophets. For Moses, the event is bolstering the relationship between God and the people, while for Joshua, Moses' unique position within the community needs defending.

Yet, unlike Joshua, Moses knows the role and responsibility of the prophetic endeavor very well at this point, and he sees the Lord's dispersion of the prophetic spirit on two elders within the camp as a glimmer of an unrealized ideal in which all the people might be the Lord's prophets. Thus, far from being a detrimental infraction of some divine law, the two wayward elders prophesying in the camp become icons of an ideal to be looked for in the future: the Lord's people prophesying (that is, sharing the Lord's message) in the world.

For meditation and context:

RESPONSORIAL PSALM   Psalm 19:8, 10, 12–13, 14 (9a)

R. The precepts of the Lord give joy to the heart.

The law of the LORD is perfect,
     refreshing the soul;
the decree of the LORD is trustworthy,
     giving wisdom to the simple.

The fear of the LORD is pure,
     enduring forever;
the ordinances of the LORD are true,
     all of them just.

Though your servant is careful of them,

very diligent in keeping them,
yet who can detect failings?
     Cleanse me from my unknown faults!

From wanton sin especially, restrain
     your servant;
     let it not rule over me.
Then shall I be blameless and innocent
     of serious sin.

READING II   James 5:1–6

A reading from the Letter of Saint James

Come now, you rich, **weep** and **wail** over your
     impending **miseries**.
Your wealth has rotted away, your clothes have become
     moth-eaten,
     your gold and silver have **corroded**,
     and that corrosion will be a testimony **against** you;
     it will **devour** your flesh like a **fire**.
You have **stored** up treasure for the last **days**.
Behold, the **wages** you **withheld** from the workers
     who harvested your fields are **crying** aloud;
     and the cries of the harvesters
     have **reached** the ears of the **Lord** of hosts.
You have **lived** on earth in **luxury** and pleasure;
     you have **fattened** your **hearts** for the day of slaughter.
You have **condemned**;
     you have murdered the **righteous** one;
     he offers you **no resistance**.

Rather than using an accusatory tone against the rich, use a tone that helps the assembly learn a lesson about the way wealth (monetary or otherwise) can be fleeting and can negatively impact others depending on the way it is gained or used.

This is hyperbole; gold and silver do not rust.

The text now moves from personal greed to the impact greed has on others.

Think beyond monetary wealth; what is it that you are rich in that might be having a negative impact upon your relationship with God?

READING II   When James vehemently scolds "rich people" in today's second reading, it can be tempting to think that his audience is a wayward group of Christians who have become overly interested in acquiring wealth through fraudulent means. But this approach misses the more likely reality that James' audience was comprised of mostly poor individuals whose livelihoods would have been threatened by wealthy figures ready to cheat them out of wages. Moreover, since James' audience was early Christians who understood themselves to be united with Christ in their dealings with unjust employers, they probably associated with the righteous one who was condemned and murdered by the "rich people." Accordingly, James' reprimand and condemnation of the rich is best understood as a prophetic oracle aimed at figures who, if not enemies, were at least hostile toward the early Christian community. James' message for such an audience would have been deeply consoling. He would have been seen as a prophet who spoke (and wrote) boldly against economic inequity and injustice. What is more, through his words, the Christian community could have confidence that all who oppressed the Lord's flock through fraudulent acquisitions and covetous hoarding of wealth would receive their comeuppance from God. And so it is that prophetic messages like that of James indicated that the prophetic spirit, which first rested on Moses and the seventy elders, was coming to rest on the Christian community. As in the days of old, God was at work amid his people strengthening them for their sojourn in a new wilderness of oppression.

GOSPEL   Mark 9:38–43, 45, 47–48

A reading from the holy Gospel according to Mark

At that time, **John** said to **Jesus**,
  "**Teacher**, we saw someone **driving** out demons in **your** name,
  and we tried to **prevent** him because he does not follow **us**."
Jesus replied, "Do **not** prevent him.
There is no one who performs a mighty **deed** in my **name**
  who can at the same time speak **ill** of me.
For whoever is not **against** us is for us.
Anyone who **gives** you a cup of **water** to drink
  because you **belong** to **Christ**,
  amen, I say to you, will surely not **lose** his reward.

"Whoever causes one of these **little** ones who believe in me
    to **sin**,
  it would be better for him if a great **millstone**
  were put around his **neck**
  and he were **thrown** into the sea.
If your **hand** causes you to **sin**, **cut** it off.
It is better for you to **enter** into life **maimed**
  than with **two** hands to go into **Gehenna**,
  into the unquenchable fire.
And if your **foot** causes you to **sin**, **cut** if off.
It is **better** for you to enter into life **crippled**
  than with **two** feet to be thrown into **Gehenna**.
And if your **eye** causes you to sin, **pluck** it out.
Better for you to enter into the kingdom of God with **one** eye
  than with **two** eyes to be thrown into Gehenna,
  where 'their worm does **not die**, and the **fire** is not **quenched**.'"

Use a slightly accusatory tone.

Unlike the first reading, where the reader is told that God's spirit descends upon the two who were not at the tent, we do not know if God's presence is with this "someone" here. However, Jesus knows the hearts of all.

Giving drink to the thirsty is a corporal work of mercy.

This is not a threat, but a warning. Read with firmness.

Jesus uses hyperbole to indicate the seriousness of the eternal consequences of our actions.

Gehenna = geh-HEN-nah

The graphic nature of eternal punishment is haunting. Read solemnly.

GOSPEL With exaggerated (hyperbolic) rhetoric, Jesus drives home a lesson for his disciples in today's Gospel: do not hinder supporters, regardless of where they appear. The passage begins with John reporting to Jesus that someone was driving out demons in Jesus' name and that he tried to stop the individual. With this scene in mind, we recall Joshua's complaint to Moses in today's first reading from Numbers and Peter's resistance to Jesus' impending suffering in the Gospel passage from two weeks ago. In John, Joshua, and Peter we encounter examples of strident supporters who, attempting to support and protect their master's work and reputation, unwittingly undermine his mission. Recalling that jealousy means protecting what rightly belongs to someone, the jealousy of these men goes too far. They are overly protective because of their zeal for their master.

To match this zeal, Jesus hyperbolically counters—it would be better to be sent to the bottom of the sea or chopped apart if one's zeal for the Lord hinders the belief and discipleship of another. Jesus does not wish harm on any of his disciples, nor does he mean to prescribe such behavior among his followers. Rather, he makes his point in a rhetorical register that can disrupt and clarify his disciple's confusion. Putting his lesson in a positive, less exaggerated way, he states simply, "whoever is not against us is for us." Put differently, when following Jesus brings divergent claims and forces together, the Lord calls for discernment and recognition that non-threats are really potential friends and allies. E.W.

TWENTY-SEVENTH SUNDAY IN ORDINARY TIME

LECTIONARY #140

READING I Genesis 2:18–24

A reading from the Book of Genesis

The LORD **God** said: "It is **not** good for the **man** to be **alone**.
I will make a suitable **partner** for him."
So the LORD God **formed** out of the **ground**
  various wild **animals** and various **birds** of the air,
  and he **brought** them to the man to see what he would
    call them;
  whatever the man called each of them would **be** its name.
The man **gave** names to all the **cattle**,
  all the **birds** of the air, and all wild **animals**;
  but **none** proved to be the suitable **partner** for the man.

So the LORD God cast a deep **sleep** on the man,
  and while he was asleep,
  he **took** out one of his **ribs** and closed up its place with flesh.
The LORD God then **built** up into a **woman** the rib
  that he had taken from the man.
When he brought **her** to the man, the man said:
    "**This one**, at **last**, is bone of my **bones**
      and flesh of my **flesh**;
    this one shall be **called** 'woman,'
      for **out** of 'her man' this one has been **taken**."
That is **why** a man **leaves** his **father** and mother
  and clings to his **wife**,
  and the two of them become **one** flesh.

Genesis = JEN-uh-sihs

Try to maintain the poetic nature of the text. Using volume and tone, distinguish between the narrator of the story and God's dialogue.

Naming was very important to the ancients. It established relationship and authority. Consider the importance of this in light of our faith and current concerns for ecological issues.

Adam had no knowledge of what God had in store for him.

Bring joy to the text. God's perfect design is brought to fruition and should be celebrated.

READING I To aim humanity toward the good, the Lord makes us for partnership. In the first instance, all of creation provides us with a host of animate companions; however, that partnership is largely one-sided. God does the molding, humanity the naming. A more fitting partnership is possible.

With figurative language, Genesis conveys the potential closeness that God fashions into the bond between men and women. By forming one from the other, God establishes an exchange between them. The man, drawn to the woman as the most fitting of all animate partners, will forgo familiar bonds with parents, home, and kin, to enter a new relationship with a new horizon. Intense attraction matches the close fittingness. Adam's enthralled exclamation, "This one, at last, is bone of my bones and flesh of my flesh," expresses the primordial sentiment that motivates partnership bonds between men and women. By fashioning bonds of partnership between men and women into creation itself, God establishes a primordial institution (marriage) with which he promises to perpetuate the species. With exquisite narrative artistry, Genesis signals the depth and meaning of human partnership, the intensity of interpersonal attraction, and the goal toward which God has ordered these: humanity's ultimate good. Accordingly, the account of humanity's creation in Genesis is a fundamental touchstone for reflecting on the theological nature, meaning, purpose, and goal of humanity and one of its most fundamental institutions—marriage.

READING II As the lectionary switches from a semi-continuous reading of the letter of James to that of

For meditation and context:

RESPONSORIAL PSALM Psalm 128:1–2, 3, 4–5, 6 (5)

R. May the Lord bless us all the days of our lives.

Blessed are you who fear the LORD,
    who walk in his ways!
For you shall eat the fruit of your handiwork;
    blessed shall you be, and favored.

Your wife shall be like a fruitful vine
    in the recesses of your home;
your children like olive plants
    around your table.

Behold, thus is the man blessed
    who fears the LORD.
The LORD bless you from Zion:
    may you see the prosperity of Jerusalem
    all the days of your life.

May you see your children's children.
    Peace be upon Israel!

READING II Hebrews 2:9–11

A reading from the Letter to the Hebrews

The author's Christology here focuses on Jesus' humanity, how he became fully human and suffered for the sake of our salvation.

Lower your voice for the parenthetical.

Brothers and **sisters**:
He "for a little while" was made "**lower** than the **angels**,"
    that by the **grace** of **God** he might **taste** death for **everyone**.

For it was fitting that he,
    for whom and through whom **all** things exist,
    in bringing many **children** to **glory**,
    should make the **leader** to their **salvation** perfect
        through **suffering**.
He who **consecrates** and those who are **being** consecrated
    all have one **origin**.
Therefore, he is not **ashamed** to call them "**brothers**."

Neither should we be ashamed to proclaim this. Read with firm intention.

GOSPEL Mark 10:2–16

A reading from the holy Gospel according to Mark

Jesus is being tested. What tone do you think he uses in his reply? Apply that to your proclamation.

[The **Pharisees** approached **Jesus** and asked,
    "Is it **lawful** for a **husband** to **divorce** his **wife**?"
They were **testing** him.
He said to them in reply, "**What** did **Moses** command you?" »

Hebrews this week, our attention is directed to familial bonds once again. Instead of attending to marriage, Hebrews focuses on the bonds between parents and children and the bonds among siblings. These familial bonds comprise the nature of the relationship that God establishes with and among the faithful in Christ. Hebrews highlights that Christ's suffering paves the way for believers to enter into the divine family. Through Jesus' self-offering, through his willingness to be "made 'lower than the angels'" and to "taste death for everyone," God brings many children to glory. Put differently, through Christ's death for us—which we enter into through baptism—God incorporates us into the divine family. We become God's children. By accepting his suffering and death, Jesus, the author of life, transforms the bonds of death. Prior to and apart from Jesus, death is something all humanity endures as an experience that draws us away from God and one another. However, in and through Christ's suffering and death, the fundamental ground of our relationship with God and others is forged anew. Because Christ suffered and died, death itself becomes a means to life, and through it we become siblings of the Son of God. So it is with great joy that we hear the conclusion of the reading from Hebrews today, which reminds us that, in his passion and death, Jesus is pleased to have obtained familial status for us with God and unabashedly call us his siblings.

GOSPEL | Jesus' teaching on marriage and family was and remains one of his most demanding lessons. Pharisees, in today's Gospel, test him on the topic of marriage and divorce. Jesus

They replied,
  "Moses **permitted** a husband to write a bill of divorce
  and **dismiss** her."
But Jesus told them,
  "Because of the **hardness** of your hearts
  he wrote you this commandment.
But from the **beginning** of creation, *God made* them *male*
    and *female*.
*For this reason a man shall **leave** his father and mother*
  *and be **joined** to his wife,*
  *and the **two** shall become **one** flesh.*
So they are no **longer** two but one flesh.
Therefore what God **has** joined together,
  no human being must **separate**."
In the house the disciples **again** questioned Jesus about this.
He said to them,
  "Whoever **divorces** his wife and marries another
  commits **adultery** against her;
  and if **she** divorces her husband and marries another,
  she commits adultery."]

And people were bringing **children** to him that he might
    touch them,
  but the disciples **rebuked** them.
When **Jesus** saw this he became **indignant** and said to them,
  Let the children **come** to me;
  do not **prevent** them, for the kingdom of God **belongs** to such
    as these.
Amen, I say to you,
  whoever does not **accept** the kingdom of God like a **child**
  will not **enter** it."
Then he **embraced** them and **blessed** them,
  placing his **hands** on them.

[Shorter: Mark 10:2–12 (see brackets]]

Pause slightly before beginning the new section. Time has passed.

Pause slightly for another new section.

"Rebuke" and "indignant" are strong words. Give them the power they represent.

"Amen" shows the earnestness of Jesus' dialogue.

Use a tender, slow tone. Let the assembly savor the image of Jesus picking up their children or grandchildren, embracing them, and blessing them.

---

counters with a question, establishing himself as the superior teacher. At the same time, he points them to the tradition of Moses, which challenges the Pharisees to read Scripture well. To know Mosaic teaching on marriage and divorce would require them to know both the mandates of Torah and the meaning of its stories. The Pharisees know only the mandates. Moses, they say, permitted a bill of divorce. Jesus acknowledges this fact (see Deuteronomy 24:1–4). But this, he explains, was a compromise. Moses was pitying hardened hearts. Divorce, Jesus goes on, is

not in keeping with God's initial plan. By referring to today's first reading from Genesis, Jesus looks beyond Torah mandates to unpack the key story on the topic. Genesis tells of humanity's primordial origins and our God-given call to bonds of partnership. As Jesus shows, Genesis conveys the full meaning and depth of the bond of marriage: the two become one flesh, so that they are no longer two but one. Thus, what God joins in marital union, no one may separate.

After his exchange with Pharisees, Jesus' disciples revisit this teaching, indi-

cating its demanding nature even for Jesus' earliest followers. Jesus responds to them by expanding his position into a mandate that Moses may have given had he not faced the hardness of human hearts: to marry someone who is divorced is adulterous. As Mark's account continues, further basis for Jesus' teaching emerges. The kingdom of God belongs to children, and these the Lord embraces. Since marriages beget children, marriage itself becomes a font for the expansion of God's kingdom. Accordingly, it merits demanding instruction. E.W.

TWENTY-EIGHTH SUNDAY IN ORDINARY TIME

LECTIONARY #143

READING I   Wisdom 7:7–11

A reading from the Book of Wisdom

> I **prayed**, and **prudence** was given me;
>   I **pleaded**, and the spirit of **wisdom** came to me.
> I preferred **her** to scepter and throne,
> and deemed riches **nothing** in comparison with her,
>   nor did I liken any priceless **gem** to her;
> because all **gold**, in view of her, is a little **sand**,
>   and before her, **silver** is to be accounted **mire**.
> Beyond **health** and **comeliness** I **loved** her,
> and I **chose** to have **her** rather than the **light**,
>   because the **splendor** of her never yields to sleep.
> Yet **all** good things together **came** to me **in** her company,
>   and countless riches at her hands.

RESPONSORIAL PSALM   Psalm 90:12–13, 14–15, 16–17 (14)

R. Fill us with your love, O Lord, and we will sing for joy!

Teach us to number our days aright,
   that we may gain wisdom of heart.
Return, O Lord! How long?
   Have pity on your servants!

Fill us at daybreak with your kindness,
   that we may shout for joy and gladness all
      our days.
Make us glad, for the days when you
      afflicted us,
   for the years when we saw evil.

Let your work be seen by your servants
   and your glory by their children;
and may the gracious care of the Lord our
      God be ours;
   prosper the work of our hands for us!
   Prosper the work of our hands!

READING I   The wisdom that comes from the Spirit is, first and foremost, a gift. To accept it we must pray. By repeatedly mentioning that he prayed and pleaded for wisdom, the author of the Book of Wisdom indicates that receiving the Spirit's gift of wisdom calls for a habit of intercessory prayer. Asking once is not enough. Just as repeating any behavior makes us better at it and more inclined to do it, repeating our requests for wisdom makes us more receptive to it and enhances our ability to embrace it. In addition to becoming more receptive of wisdom by repeatedly praying for it, such repetition makes us more *appreciative* of this gift. The author of Wisdom shows us this truth by stating that, once wisdom came to him, he preferred it above all other things. Power, wealth, health, light, and even sleep became pale in comparison to wisdom for him. But preferring wisdom to the things that others might consider valuable does not leave the author of Wisdom destitute. Quite the opposite. All good things come to him on account of keeping company with wisdom. Thus, wisdom is a gift that ushers in other gifts and should therefore be prioritized above those things that are passing.

READING II   Words, while invisible, are powerful. They point beyond themselves to truths and realities outside the material universe. With words we can take on a new status, enter into new states of being, or disclose who we are and what we are about. To profess marriage vows, for example, transforms us into married persons. Through them we take on a new status within the community of the baptized. At the same time, when threats,

For those who proclaim God's Word during Mass, this short pericope is especially meaningful. The author is teaching us the performative power of the Word of God. We have a great privilege and responsibility.

Notice all of the parallel constructions: living/effective, soul/spirit, joints/marrow, reflections/thoughts. Keep them together.

READING II　Hebrews 4:12–13

A reading from the Letter to the Hebrews

Brothers and **sisters**:
Indeed the **word** of **God** is **living** and **effective**,
　　sharper than any two-edged **sword**,
　　penetrating even between **soul** and **spirit**, **joints** and **marrow**,
　　and able to **discern** reflections and thoughts of the **heart**.
No creature is **concealed** from him,
　　but everything is **naked** and **exposed** to the eyes of him
　　to whom we must render an account.

Give some excitement to the opening scene: ran, knelt, asked. The man is breathless and excited to ask Jesus for his wisdom. He is unnamed; he could be any of us.

Emphasize "not" once and then subdue it when it is repeated. The words that follow "not" will stand out.

Let the tenderness of Jesus "looking" and "loving" come through in your proclamation. Be familiar enough with this line to deliver it looking out at the assembly.

Pause after "come." Notice that even his followers will have difficulty understanding Jesus' teaching.

GOSPEL　Mark 10:17–30

A reading from the holy Gospel according to Mark

[As **Jesus** was setting out on a **journey**, a man **ran** up,
　　knelt down before him, and **asked** him,
　　"**Good teacher**, what must I **do** to inherit eternal **life**?"
Jesus answered him, "**Why** do you call me **good**?
No one **is** good but God **alone**.
You **know** the commandments: *You shall **not kill**;*
　　*you shall not **commit adultery**;*
　　*you shall not **steal**;*
　　*you shall not **bear false witness**;*
　　*you shall not **defraud**;*
　　*honor your **father** and your **mother**."*
He replied and said to him,
　　"**Teacher**, all of these I have **observed** from my **youth**."
Jesus, **looking** at him, **loved** him and said to him,
　　"You are **lacking** in one thing.
Go, **sell** what you have, and **give** to the poor
　　and you will have **treasure** in heaven; then **come**, **follow** me."

decorum, or confidentiality call for restrained speech, words permit us to conceal and protect others or ourselves. Such protective use of words governs the seal of confession. So, when Hebrews announces that God's word is living and powerful, we get a sense of what is meant simply by looking to everyday uses of words in our lives. Still, when the word belongs to God, the scope of its power is greater and more precise. As Hebrews notes, God's word penetrates to the depths of our being—"between soul and spirit, joints and marrow"—to the core of our heart, to our innermost thoughts.

When God speaks, we are made totally vulnerable, unable to hide, and faced with an unavoidable reality: we must render an account for ourselves to God. If the Book of Wisdom invites us to invoke God for the gift of wisdom and learn to appreciate wisdom above all other gifts, Hebrews places us in awe before the power of God's word, which conveys God's wisdom to us.

GOSPEL　When an ardent student throws himself at Jesus in an attempt to obtain eternal life, he shows himself to be knowledgeable of the law and

an avid follower of it. As Jesus recites various commandments governing murder, adultery, theft, perjury, fraud, and parental honor, the man confidently professes to have followed God's commands on all these matters from his youth. In his profession, the man tacitly claims to be a good, loyal son, which was itself a matter of legal concern (see Leviticus 20:9; Deuteronomy 21:18–21). Thus, we sense from the man's fervent behavior—*running* up to Jesus, *kneeling* down before him, *honoring* him with the title "Good Teacher"—and his habit of legal obedience that this man will

At that statement his face **fell**,
  and he went away **sad**, for he had **many** possessions.

Jesus looked around and said to his **disciples**,
  "How **hard** it is for those who have **wealth**
  to enter the kingdom of **God**!"
The disciples were **amazed** at his words.
So Jesus **again** said to them in reply,
  "**Children**, how **hard** it is to enter the kingdom of **God**!
It is easier for a camel to pass through the eye of a needle
  than for one who is rich to enter the kingdom of God."
They were **exceedingly** astonished and said among **themselves**,
  "Then **who** can be **saved**?"
Jesus **looked** at them and said,
  "For human beings it is **impossible**, but **not** for God.
All things **are** possible for God."]
Peter began to say to him,
  "We have **given** up **everything** and **followed** you."
Jesus said, "**Amen**, I say to you,
  there is no one who has given **up** house or brothers or sisters
  or mother or father or children or lands
  for **my** sake and for the sake of the **gospel**
  who will not receive a **hundred** times more now in this
    present age:
  houses and brothers and sisters
  and mothers and children and lands,
  with **persecutions**, and eternal **life** in the age to **come**."

[Shorter: Mark 10:17–27 (see brackets)]

They ask each other, yet Jesus responds.

Peter "began," as if interrupted. Read his defensive response hurriedly and then return to Jesus' calm teaching voice.

stop at nothing to obtain eternal life. His investment makes him admirable. He is more than a student of God's will. He does it. So, based on his behavior and his testimony, we anticipate that whatever Jesus might demand of him, he will do it. But something else happens. When Jesus looks at the man, loves him, and invites him to sell all his possessions, give the money to the poor, and then follow Jesus on his journey, the man becomes somber (*stugnazo* in Greek) and departs in sorrow (*lupeo* in Greek). He abandons his quest for eternal life on account of having many possessions.

In the context of the Bible's wisdom tradition, which the first two readings highlight, Jesus' teaching on possessions can be difficult to grasp. In this tradition, wisdom is something this man has likely acquired through his commitment to the law. Moreover, such wisdom was not incommensurate with wealth. In fact, as the first reading suggests, wisdom gives rise to wealth. So, the man's many possessions may well have indicated his vast wisdom. And, with such wisdom, he would have already made significant advances on the path to eternal life. Thus, when the Lord

claims that it is hard for the rich to enter the kingdom of God, the man and Jesus' disciples are flummoxed. If not the rich, then who? Echoing the first reading's reminder that wisdom is, first of all, a gift, Jesus reminds his disciples that salvation too is a gift. Entry into God's kingdom can be sought, but it is ultimately unearned. Instead, it is freely given by God. E.W.

TWENTY-NINTH SUNDAY IN ORDINARY TIME

LECTIONARY #146

READING I   Isaiah 53:10–11

Isaiah = ī-ZAY-uh

Do not say the beginning lines too harshly, even though they convey a violent image. There is a lot going on in this short reading, and it is best understood in the context of the other readings for today.

He endures so others can be justified.

A reading from the Book of the Prophet Isaiah

The LORD was **pleased**
   to **crush** him in **infirmity**.

If he **gives** his **life** as an **offering** for sin,
   he shall see his **descendants** in a long **life**,
   and the **will** of the LORD shall be **accomplished**
      through him.

Because of his **affliction**
   he shall **see** the light in fullness of days;
through his suffering, my **servant** shall justify **many**,
   and their **guilt** he shall **bear**.

For meditation and context:

RESPONSORIAL PSALM   Psalm 33:4–5, 18–19, 20, 22 (22)

R. **Lord, let your mercy be on us, as we place our trust in you.**

Upright is the word of the LORD,
   and all his works are trustworthy.
He loves justice and right;
   of the kindness of the LORD the earth
      is full.

See, the eyes of the LORD are upon those
      who fear him,
   upon those who hope for his kindness;
to deliver them from death
   and preserve them in spite of famine.

Our soul waits for the LORD,
   who is our help and our shield.
May your kindness, O LORD, be upon us
   who have put our hope in you.

READING I Suffering, as a mystery, points beyond itself to a deeper meaning, to an alternate, more vibrant reality. With its uneven and unpredictable distribution, suffering generates sentiments of anguish. As such, suffering can beget suffering, perpetuate and expand itself into all dimensions of life—physical, social, psychological, spiritual. In this way, suffering can take on a life of its own. Still, attaining life's greatest goods tends to call for suffering. Obtaining success often calls for hardship. Securing justice tends to involve equitable injury. And bringing forth new life means birth pangs. The mystery and deep truths that lie at the heart of suffering are topics of contemplation raised by this Sunday's readings.

In the first reading, which is part of the so-called Suffering Servant Song (Isaiah 52:13—53:12), the servant incurs great suffering as an expression of the Lord's will. Crushed in infirmity, the servant's life is given as an offering for sin. That the Lord would bring about such a state of affairs reminds us that suffering is not beyond the purview of God's providence, and in fact may be a constitutive part of it at times.

Still, the servant's anguish and affliction do not simply bring about his end. Darkness and hopelessness are not where his story concludes. Rather, his suffering proves vicarious. It brings life for him and his descendants. Many are justified on his account; their guilt is borne by him through what he suffers. In this way we see that suffering rectifies infractions and ushers in new horizons. Thus, the first reading highlights how suffering can have various meanings and serve a variety of functions in our lives and in the broader scope of salvation history.

READING II   Hebrews 4:14–16

A reading from the Letter to the Hebrews

Brothers and **sisters**:
Since we have a great high **priest** who has **passed** through
    the heavens,
    Jesus, the Son of **God**,
    let us hold fast to our **confession**.
For we do **not** have a high priest
    who is **unable** to **sympathize** with our weaknesses,
    but **one** who has similarly been **tested** in every way,
    yet **without** sin.
So let us **confidently** approach the throne of **grace**
    to **receive** mercy and to **find** grace for timely **help**.

Take the negatives out of this section ("we do have . . . who is able") to help you comprehend what is being said. With renewed understanding, return to the lectionary text as written.

Use the "confidence" that the author speaks of.

GOSPEL   Mark 10:35–45

A reading from the holy Gospel according to Mark

James and **John**, the sons of **Zebedee**, came to **Jesus** and said
    to him,
    "**Teacher**, we want **you** to do for us **whatever** we **ask** of you."
He replied, "**What** do you wish me to **do** for you?"
They answered him, "Grant that in your **glory**
    we may **sit** one at your **right** and the other at your **left**."
Jesus said to them, "You do not **know** what you are **asking**.
Can you drink the cup that **I** drink
    or be **baptized** with the baptism with which I am baptized?"
They said to him, "**We can.**"

Zebedee = ZEB-uh-dee

Names need to be stated boldly so we know who the characters are. When pronouns occur, the assembly can readily recall to whom they are referring.

Use an upward inflection after "drink" and pause.

They have enthusiasm.

READING II When Hebrews reflects on the glory obtained by Jesus as the risen Son of God in this Sunday's second reading, it aims to help its audience connect with the unfathomable "throne of grace" that Christ has attained in rising from the dead. Recognizing and celebrating Jesus as a "great high priest who has passed through the heavens" highlights the means by which Jesus' high priesthood has bearing on his followers and the human community in general. Put simply, Jesus' glory is accessible and meaningful to us because he can "sympathize with our weaknesses" and he knows what it means to be tested. As the glorified, sinless high priest, Jesus provides us with access to heaven. Through his experience of human frailty, he serves as our conduit to heavenly glory. As the one who suffered the common human experience of weakness and endured the human condition, Jesus came to know the anguish of human limitation. But he also took this condition up into heaven, becoming a heavenly intercessor who grasps the fullness of the human experience. Thus, he made enduring human frailty the means by which we too might obtain heavenly glory. Now, because he suffered and endured the human condition and elevated it to the heavens, we can be confident as we approach God in and through him. His suffering offers us a share in heavenly glory.

GOSPEL Like students testing a teacher's authority, James and John come to Jesus with a completely open-ended demand: "we want you to do for us whatever we ask of you." The request is laughable. No reasonable teacher would respond with an unclarified affirmative.

Again, the names are important. You don't want the assembly to think that the ten are indignant with Jesus for his response, but indignant at those who posed the question.

Jesus said to them, "The cup that I drink, you **will** drink,
    and with the **baptism** with which I am baptized, you will
      be **baptized**;
    but to sit at my **right** or at my **left** is not **mine** to give
    but is for those for whom it has been **prepared**."
When the ten **heard** this, they became **indignant** at **James**
    and **John**.
[Jesus **summoned** them and said to them,
    "You know that those who are recognized as **rulers** over
      the **Gentiles**
    lord it **over** them,
    and their **great** ones make their authority over them **felt**.
But it shall **not** be so among you.
Rather whoever wishes to be **great** among you will be
      your **servant**;
    whoever wishes to be **first** among you will be the slave of **all**.
For the Son of **Man** did not **come** to be **served**
    but **to** serve and to give his life as a ransom for many."]

[Shorter: Mark 10:42–45 (see brackets)]

Put a slight comma pause after "great among you" and again after "first among you."

Naturally, Jesus asks them to articulate their request. And they come out with it—they want Jesus to share with them the highest honor, the greatest glory in his kingdom. Interestingly, their request is not rebuked out of hand as self-ambition. Rather, Jesus invites them to consider what they would be willing to suffer for such an honor. Will they drink the cup he will drink, or be baptized with the baptism that he will face? That is, are they willing to accept suffering to join him in glory? They say they are, and Jesus affirms that they will. But, in a cosmic bait and switch, Jesus explains that the honors they request are not his to give. They have been prepared for others. The exchange flusters the other ten, who become angry with James and John. Evidently, they do not grasp that a share in the cup and baptism of Jesus amounts to suffering for the sake of the kingdom. Ultimately, the whole affair leads Jesus to call them all together and instruct them on the nature of leadership and greatness among his followers. For his disciples, greatness will be marked by being others' servant (*diakonos* in Greek) or slave (*doulos* in Greek), or by dying as a ransom for others. For Jesus, true greatness lies not in what one person can make another do but in what one can either do or endure in order to make another free. Whether it is service, slavery, or death, in the mind of Christ greatness amounts to accepting any suffering for the sake of others. E.W.

THIRTIETH SUNDAY IN ORDINARY TIME

LECTIONARY #149

READING I   Jeremiah 31:7–9

A reading from the Book of the Prophet Jeremiah

Thus says the LORD:
Shout with **joy** for **Jacob**,
 exult at the head of the nations;
 proclaim your **praise** and say:
The LORD has **delivered** his people,
 the remnant of Israel.
Behold, I will **bring** them **back**
 from the land of the north;
I will **gather** them from the **ends** of the world,
 with the **blind** and the **lame** in their midst,
the **mothers** and those with **child**;
 they shall **return** as an immense **throng**.
They departed in **tears**,
 but I will **console** them and **guide** them;
I will lead them to **brooks** of water,
 on a level **road**, so that none shall **stumble**.
For I am a **father** to Israel,
 Ephraim is my **first**-born.

Jeremiah = jayr-uh-Mī-uh

The opening lines ring out joy: shout, exult, and praise. Let your countenance be one of happiness.
exult = ehg-ZUHLT

Pause slightly after "Israel" to introduce how he will deliver his people.

This is a list of the most vulnerable. The Lord has a preferential option for the poor.

Ephraim = EE-fray-ihm or EF-r*m = a tribe of Israel

READING I Today's reading from Jeremiah stands out in contrast to the rest of the tone of the prophetic book. Jeremiah's prophecies predominantly resonate with doom and gloom, yet in this passage we find language of hope and rejoicing. In these verses, Jeremiah anticipates the future restoration of Israel. This is clearly a moment of divine triumph as the "remnant of Israel," those who survived the exile, return to their homeland. God does not simply restore the people of Israel to their lands. He consoles them as they journey back, providing fresh drinking water and a smooth road to ease their tears and burdens.

Among those returning, Jeremiah draws special attention to the blind and lame, as well as expectant mothers. These are groups of people who are vulnerable or marginalized in society. In contrast to past injunctions that kept them apart from the rest of Israelite society (for example, Leviticus 21:18 and 2 Samuel 5:8), they are included in the pilgrimage, rejoicing in their restoration to the Israelite community as well as to their homeland. Thus, God's salvation is open to everyone, including the vulnerable. They are included with the rest of Israel when God declares himself "a father to Israel."

The reference to Ephraim is two-fold. First, it refers to the central power base of the northern kingdom of Israel that fell to the Assyrian invasion and exile. Thus, it is first-born as a power base. Second, the tribe of Ephraim are descendants of Joseph's younger son of the same name. As he lay dying, Jacob conferred the blessing of the first-born on Ephraim even though Joseph's elder son, Manasseh, should have received it (Genesis 48:8–20). This reversal

For meditation and context:

RESPONSORIAL PSALM   Psalm 126:1–2, 2–3, 4–5, 6 (3)

R. The Lord has done great things for us; we are filled with joy.

When the LORD brought back the captives
    of Zion,
    we were like men dreaming.
Then our mouth was filled with laughter,
    and our tongue with rejoicing.

Then they said among the nations,
    "The LORD has done great things
    for them."
The LORD has done great things for us;
    we are glad indeed.

Restore our fortunes, O LORD,
    like the torrents in the southern desert.
Those that sow in tears
    shall reap rejoicing.

Although they go forth weeping,
    carrying the seed to be sown,
they shall come back rejoicing,
    carrying their sheaves.

READING II   Hebrews 5:1–6

A reading from the Letter to the Hebrews

Brothers and **sisters**:
Every high **priest** is **taken** from among **men**
    and made their **representative** before **God**,
        to **offer** gifts and sacrifices for **sins**.
He is able to deal **patiently** with the **ignorant** and **erring**,
    for he **himself** is beset by **weakness**
        and so, for this reason, must **make** sin offerings for **himself**
        as well as for the **people**.
No one **takes** this honor upon himself
    but only when **called** by God,
        just as **Aaron** was.
In the **same** way,
    it was **not** Christ who glorified himself in becoming
        high **priest**,
    but rather the **one** who said to him:
        *You are **my** son:*
            *this day I have **begotten** you;*
    just as he *says* in **another** place:
        *You are a priest **forever***
            according to the order of Melchizedek.

The first part of this reading outlines the qualities of a high priest; the second part invites us to apply those qualities to Jesus.

The title of "Christ" means "the anointed one." Jesus is anointed, like the high priest.

"Son" draws attention to the relationship between Jesus and the Father. Read tenderly and with pride.

begotten = bee-GAW-t*n

Melchizedek = mehl-KEEZ-uh-dehk
or mehl-KIZ-uh-dehk

---

of expectations coincides with the reversal of the expectations of the marginalized referred to in this passage.

READING II This reading from Hebrews connects Jesus' priesthood with the characteristics of Israelite high priests. The first characteristic is his patience toward the weak and sinners. Through his incarnation, Jesus understands the weaknesses of the flesh, although he himself did not err. His compassion makes him a fitting high priest who offers sacrifice to purify God's people from their sins.

The second characteristic of a high priest is his humility in never seeking or taking for himself the honor of being a high priest. Instead, he takes it up "only when called by God." Thus, all honor and glory belong to God alone. We see an example of this in the person of Christ, when, in John's Gospel, Jesus' death on the cross is actually a moment of divine triumph, the glorification/exaltation of the cross.

Another point of humility lies in recognizing that Jesus' high priesthood comes from God the Father. The two royal psalms (Psalm 2:7; 110:4) quoted in today's reading

highlight Jesus' nature as Son of God as well as his priesthood. While the psalmist's adoption as God's son is figurative, in Jesus the reference is literal. And as God's Son, Jesus obeys the Father's will and his role in the salvific plan. Unlike Aaron and Melchizedek, Jesus is a "priest forever."

These characteristics of Jesus as high priest are a motive for us to rejoice as the restored remnant of Israel are called to do in the first reading. Just as the vulnerable and marginalized are especially comforted, so should all humanity find comfort in Jesus' understanding of our weaknesses.

GOSPEL   Mark 10:46–52

A reading from the holy Gospel according to Mark

As **Jesus** was leaving **Jericho** with his disciples and
    a sizable crowd,
  Bartimaeus, a **blind** man, the son of **Timaeus**,
sat by the roadside **begging**.
On **hearing** that it was Jesus of **Nazareth**,
  he began to **cry** out and say,
  "Jesus, son of **David**, have **pity** on me."
And **many** rebuked him, telling him to **be silent**.
But he kept calling **out** all the more,
  "Son of David, have pity **on me**."
Jesus stopped and said, "**Call** him."
So they **called** the blind man, saying to him,
  "Take **courage**; get up, Jesus is calling you."
He **threw** aside his cloak, **sprang** up, and **came** to Jesus.
Jesus said to him in reply, "What do you **want** me to do
    for you?"
The blind man replied to him, "**Master**, I want to **see**."
Jesus told him, "**Go** your way; your faith has **saved** you."
Immediately he **received** his **sight**
  and followed him on the way.

Jericho = JAYR-ih-koh

This is a miracle story. Proclaim as if you are witnessing it firsthand.

Bartimaeus = bahr-tih-MAY-uhs or bahr-tih-MEE-uhs

Timaeus = tih-MAY-uhs or tī-MEE-uhs

Imagine that you are the blind beggar. What tone of voice would you use as you call out to Jesus?

Read with breathlessness. "Threw," "sprang," and "came" give the sense of immediacy.

Bartimaeus experienced great joy. What can we do to help someone be set free from their bondage?

Although we are weak and vulnerable, we are rescued and restored through Jesus' sacrifice on the cross.

GOSPEL In today's Gospel reading, we have an example of Jesus' salvific activity. This passage describes Jesus' last miracle before entering Jerusalem and his passion. Today's first reading speaks of the rejoicing of the blind as they are restored. Here in Mark's Gospel, we have the restoration of sight of a blind man named Bartimaeus. He calls to Jesus using the messianic title "Son of David."

Although Bartimaeus is blind, he "sees" Jesus for who he really is: the Messiah who has the power to heal the blind and the lame. Jesus commends his faith and heals him, telling him to "Go."

Upon being restored, Bartimaeus immediately obeys Jesus, following Jesus "on the way." It is important to note that "the way" is a major theme in Mark's Gospel. It is Jesus' journey to Jerusalem and his passion. It also indicates the road of discipleship that leads to the cross. After his healing, Bartimaeus becomes a disciple of Jesus and accompanies him on the way.

In the verses immediately following this passage, Jesus reaches Jerusalem at last, where he fulfills his role as the perfect high priest and perfect sacrifice described in today's second reading.

Today's readings invite us to rejoice in God's salvific action in our lives. At the same time, we can imitate Bartimaeus and ask the Lord to heal us of any "blindness" that keeps us from seeing the path that leads to God's heart or from accepting the crosses that come along "the way." M.B.

ALL SAINTS

LECTIONARY #667

READING I   Revelation 7:2–4, 9–14

A reading from the Book of Revelation

I, **John**, saw another **angel** come up from the East,
    holding the **seal** of the living **God**.
He cried out in a **loud** voice to the **four** angels
    who were given power to **damage** the **land** and the **sea**,
    "Do **not** damage the land or the sea or the trees
    until we put the **seal** on the foreheads of the servants
        of our God."
I **heard** the number of those who had been marked with the seal,
    one **hundred** and forty-four **thousand** marked
    from every **tribe** of the children of **Israel**.

After this I had a **vision** of a great **multitude**,
    which no one could count,
    from **every** nation, race, people, and tongue.
They stood before the **throne** and before the **Lamb**,
    wearing white **robes** and holding **palm** branches in
        their hands.
They **cried** out in a loud voice:

"**Salvation** comes from our **God**, who is seated on the throne,
and from the Lamb."

All the **angels** stood **around** the throne
    and around the elders and the four living creatures.
They **prostrated** themselves before the throne,
    worshiped God, and exclaimed:

This highly descriptive reading brings the end of time to our attention. Let your proclamation paint a picture of the events. Follow the lead of the text when it says "loud."

Build the excitement as you read through the list. They can't say enough, fast enough. Praise is bursting forth.

READING I   Today's first reading presents John's two visions of God's people dealing with the before and after of their trials and persecution. The verses in Revelation immediately preceding today's reading speak of the opening of the sixth seal and the wrath that awaits the wicked. In today's reading, we have the opposite side of the coin with a depiction of the fate of those who remain faithful to God.

In the first vision, before the intended wrath falls upon the wicked of the world, the faithful receive God's seal, setting them apart from the rest of the world. In this way

they are made holy, set apart for God. The number one hundred and forty-four thousand (twelve times twelve times a thousand) is significant within the Book of Revelation. This figure represents inclusion within the Church, with the twelve tribes of Israel in the Old Testament and the twelve apostles in the New Testament coming together, forming a unified whole.

The second vision further reinforces the universal character of the Church by the use of four terms that are slightly synonymous: nation, race, people, and tongue. In this description, we see that the saints in

heaven include people from all nations and backgrounds, united in their worship of God. They are also all clothed in white robes. In Revelation, white represents victory and resurrection. As the elder explains toward the end of today's reading, those clothed in white survived the trials and tribulations of this world. Survival in this instance does not refer to staying physically alive; rather, it refers to remaining faithful to God despite outside pressures and concerns.

The most significant aspect of this great multitude of saints is their continual

"**Amen. Blessing** and **glory**, **wisdom** and **thanksgiving**,
  honor, **power**, and **might**
    be to our God **forever** and **ever. Amen.**"

Then one of the **elders** spoke up and said to me,
  "**Who** are these wearing white robes, and **where** did they
    come from?"
I said to him, "My **lord**, you are the one who **knows**."
He said to me,
  "These are the ones who have **survived** the time
    of great distress;
  they have **washed** their robes
  and made them **white** in the Blood of the **Lamb**."

This is a rhetorical question.

Recall the lives of the saints, persisting in their faith despite trial and tribulation.

For meditation and context:

RESPONSORIAL PSALM   Psalm 24:1bc–2, 3–4ab, 5–6 (6)

R. Lord, this is the people that longs to see your face.

The LORD's are the earth and its fullness;
  the world and those who dwell in it.
For he founded it upon the seas
  and established it upon the rivers.

Who can ascend the mountain of the LORD?
  or who may stand in his holy place?

One whose hands are sinless, whose heart
    is clean,
  who desires not what is vain.

He shall receive a blessing from the LORD,
  a reward from God his savior.
Such is the race that seeks him,
  that seeks the face of the God of Jacob.

READING II   1 John 3:1–3

A reading from the first Letter of Saint John

Beloved:
See what **love** the **Father** has **bestowed** on us
  that we may be called the **children** of **God**.
Yet so we are.
The reason the world does not **know us**
  is that it did not know **him**.
Beloved, we **are** God's children **now**;
  what we **shall** be has not yet been **revealed**. »

"Beloved," "love," and "children" call to mind a tender, loving relationship. Express God's love for us in your tone.

The saints are children of God and so are we. How do you embody this identity in your ministry?

---

act of worship. They hold palm branches, a symbol of victory as well as an allusion to Jesus' triumphant entry into Jerusalem. They are joined by the angels, the elders, and the four living creatures in worshipping God. In Revelation, the number seven represents divine perfection/completeness. Hence the acclamation of a seven-fold doxology ("Blessing and glory, wisdom and thanksgiving, honor, power, and might") by the angels, elders, and living creatures marks the perfect worship that is due to God the Father and that honors the Lamb.

READING II Today's reading from 1 John stresses God's love for humanity while at the same time bolstering a community suffering persecution. This passage underscores the reality that we are children of God by the grace of God's love for us. During times of trials and tribulations, this love may not seem evident. For this reason, today's reading reminds us that any persecution we undergo comes from the world's inability to recognize God's love. If they do not recognize God's love, they cannot recognize God, who is love. Consequently, they cannot recognize God's

love in us, leading to their rejection of God and us, and to our subsequent persecution.

And yet this persecution is not the final word. There is a real sense of justice that awaits both the wicked and the righteous. It is in this justice that we are called to have hope, hope that God will make right the wrongs we suffer. Perhaps we will not witness this justice while we are on earth. If that is the case, then we will witness and receive justice when we are with God in heaven. We are purified as we hold onto this hope. This purification is similar to that which the saints in heaven underwent, as

We **do** know that **when** it is revealed we shall be **like** him,
for we shall **see** him as he **is**.
Everyone who has this **hope** based on him makes **himself pure**,
as he is pure.

GOSPEL   Matthew 5:1–12a

A reading from the holy Gospel according to Matthew

When **Jesus** saw the **crowds**, he went up the **mountain**,
and after he had **sat** down, his disciples **came** to him.
He began to **teach** them, saying:

> "**Blessed** are the poor in **spirit**,
>   for **theirs** is the **Kingdom** of **heaven**.
> Blessed are they who **mourn**,
>   for they will be **comforted**.
> Blessed are the **meek**,
>   for they will **inherit** the land.
> Blessed are they who **hunger** and **thirst** for **righteousness**,
>   for they will be **satisfied**.
> Blessed are the **merciful**,
>   for they will be shown **mercy**.
> Blessed are the **clean** of heart,
>   for they will **see** God.
> Blessed are the **peacemakers**,
>   for they will be called **children** of God.
> Blessed are they who are **persecuted** for the sake
>   of **righteousness**,
>   for theirs **is** the Kingdom of heaven.
> Blessed are **you** when they **insult** you and **persecute** you
>   and utter every kind of evil against you **falsely** because
>   of me.
> **Rejoice** and be **glad**,
>   for your **reward** will be **great** in **heaven**."

There are options for the style of your proclamation of this reading. You could emphasize the first "blessed" and subdue it as you continue. This will make the new idea that follows each "blessed" stand out. Or, if you want to highlight the poetic nature of the text, emphasize "blessed" each time, and exaggerate the comma in each sentence.

Notice the change from "they" to "you."

The last verse, an imperative, breaks the pattern. Deliver these lines with the joy and confidence it speaks of.

described in today's first reading. And then, with those saints, we will be able to offer proper worship to God for eternity.

GOSPEL Today's Gospel reading comes from the Sermon on the Mount, which teaches us what it takes to be a disciple of Jesus. Matthew's concerns deal predominantly with the spiritual struggles of those who seek to follow Christ. The emphasis on the spiritual realm is evident in the first Beatitude, with the reference to the "poor in spirit" and not simply about the materially poor.

The Beatitudes listed are a source of both encouragement and solace to the oppressed and an exhortation to work towards sanctity. As in the reading from 1 John, this passage manifests a preoccupation with divine justice. Ultimately, people want to know that their suffering has a purpose. Those in the early Church suffered much persecution with the very real threat of martyrdom hanging over them. Today's reading provides reassurance that injustices here on earth will be made right in heaven. Their great reward consists of inheriting God's kingdom, where they will receive divine mercy and see God face to face. As heirs to the kingdom, they are now called "children of God." Those currently undergoing persecution can therefore rejoice and be comforted now, in the midst of their trials, in anticipation of their heavenly reward. By adopting the attitudes described in the Beatitudes, as the saints did, all the faithful are encouraged to remain steadfast in their trust in God, in whatever situation they may face, and to give him continual praise and glory. M.B.

THE COMMEMORATION OF ALL THE FAITHFUL DEPARTED (ALL SOULS' DAY)

LECTIONARY #668

READING I   Isaiah 25:6, 7–9

Isaiah = ī-ZAY-uh

Notice the inclusivity of the Lord's providence.

A reading from the Book of the Prophet Isaiah

On this **mountain** the L ORD of hosts
    will **provide** for **all** peoples.
On this mountain he will **destroy**
    the **veil** that veils all peoples,
The web that is woven over all nations;
    he will **destroy death** forever.

Imagine the Lord wiping the tears from all the broken-hearted. Read slowly and tenderly; someone in the assembly might need to hear this message of God's love and care.

Use the exclamation marks! Raise your voice, smile, and show joy, don't just read joy.

The Lord **G OD** will **wipe** away
    the **tears** from all **faces**;
The **reproach** of his people he will **remove**
    from the whole earth; for the L ORD has **spoken**.
    On that day it will be said:
"Behold **our** God, to whom we looked to **save** us!
    This is the L ORD for whom we **looked**;
    let us **rejoice** and be glad that **he** has saved us!"

There are options for today's readings. Contact your parish staff to learn which readings will be used.

READING I   This reading from Isaiah points towards the opening of salvation to all humanity. During the end of days, God will remove the veil from everyone's eyes that they might clearly see his glory and might. His glory is evidenced by his salvific action on behalf of humanity. Additionally, all the nations will witness God's power when he overcomes death.

Though not described in today's reading, Isaiah prophesies the destruction of the kingdom of Judah if the people, especially the king, do not mend their ways and turn to God. The people will lose all they have as they are sent into exile. Yet mixed with the prediction of doom and gloom, there are passages like today's reading, in which Isaiah also declares God's intent to restore them and reveal himself as the God of all the nations, not just the God of Israel. Thus, in the midst of suffering and death, God comforts them and there remains the hope of salvation, a reason for rejoicing.

As we commemorate the souls of the faithful departed, we too receive this prophecy of comfort and hope. While loved ones have passed away and left us with grief and sorrow in our hearts, we also rejoice in knowing that Christ has already conquered death. Thus, we can rest assured that God wipes away our tears and comforts us by assuring us of his continued providence over all of humanity, both the living and the dead.

For meditation and context:

RESPONSORIAL PSALM   Psalm 23:1–3a, 3b–4, 5, 6 (1)

R. The Lord is my shepherd; there is nothing I shall want.
or
R. Though I walk in the valley of darkness, I fear no evil, for you are with me.

The LORD is my shepherd; I shall not want.
    In verdant pastures he gives me repose;
beside restful waters he leads me;
    he refreshes my soul.

He guides me in right paths
    for his name's sake.
Even though I walk in the dark valley
    I fear no evil; for you are at my side
with your rod and your staff
    that give me courage.

You spread the table before me
    in the sight of my foes;
you anoint my head with oil;
    my cup overflows.

Only goodness and kindness follow me
    all the days of my life;
and I shall dwell in the house of the LORD
    for years to come.

READING II   1 Corinthians 15:51–57

Corinthians = kohr-IN-thee-uhnz

A reading from the first Letter of Saint Paul to the Corinthians

Brothers and **sisters**:
Behold, I tell you a **mystery**.
We shall not all fall **asleep**, but we will all be changed,
    in an **instant**, in the blink of an eye, at the last **trumpet**.
For the trumpet will **sound**,
    the dead will be raised **incorruptible**,
    and we shall be **changed**.

Notice the opposites: corruptible/incorruptible and mortal/immortality.

For that which is **corruptible must** clothe itself with
        incorruptibility,
    and that which is **mortal must** clothe itself with **immortality**.
And when this which is corruptible clothes itself with
        incorruptibility
    and this which is mortal clothes itself with **immortality**,
    then the word that is written shall **come** about:

Pause after "come about," before reading the quotations.

Use a confident upward inflection for the questions. Christ's paschal mystery is the answer! Pause to let the assembly consider the question.

> *Death* is *swallowed* up in *victory*.
> *Where*, O death, is *your* victory?
> *Where*, O death, is your *sting*?

READING II In this passage from the first letter to the Corinthians, Paul addresses the concerns of the community regarding who will benefit from the resurrection at the end of time. Paul stresses that *everyone* who believes in Christ benefits from the resurrection. He states that "the dead will be raised incorruptible" and the "corruptible," that is, the living, will also clothe themselves with incorruptibility. Both the living and the dead are transformed through the resurrection of Christ. It is through their faith and their

baptism in the Lord that Christians pass from death into life.

Paul also presents here the resurrection of Christ as fulfillment of a compilation of Old Testament passages. The first line, "Death is swallowed up in victory," paraphrases a verse from today's first reading from Isaiah: "he will destroy death forever." The rest of the quote comes from Hosea 13:14, although Paul seems to interpret this verse as portraying God's redemptive actions on Israel's behalf.

Paul makes a further theological connection between death and sin using a sub-

tle metaphor, where sin is the deadly stinger of a scorpion. For Paul, sin leads to death. The perhaps confusing relation between law and the power of sin seems to point toward sin being even more deadly when you know you are going against the law of God.

However, sin and death no longer hold sway over us thanks to Jesus' defeat of them by his own death and resurrection. In a special way today, we rejoice in Christ's victory over sin and death and the promise of the resurrection for all, both the living and the dead.

The sting of death is **sin**,
　　and the **power** of sin is the **law**.
But thanks be to **God** who **gives** us the victory
　　through our Lord Jesus **Christ**.

GOSPEL　John 6:37–40

A reading from the holy Gospel according to John

Jesus said to the **crowds**:
"**Everything** that the **Father** gives me **will** come to me,
　　and I will not **reject anyone** who comes to me,
　　because I came down from **heaven** not to do my **own will**
　　but the will of the one who **sent** me.
And this is the will of the one who sent me,
　　that I should not **lose anything** of what he **gave** me,
　　but that I should **raise** it on the last day.
For this is the will of **my** Father,
　　that everyone who **sees** the **Son** and **believes** in him
　　may have eternal **life**,
　　and I shall **raise** him up on the **last** day."

Be inviting in your proclamation. Jesus holds nothing back; he came to bring us to the Father.

Notice the two different uses of the word "will."

These last lines sum up our belief in the saints, and the hope of our future with God.

GOSPEL　Today's Gospel reading comes from the Bread of Life Discourse in John 6. The crowd has just heard that Jesus will remove their hunger and thirst forever, yet Jesus also tells them that he knows that they do not believe in him. Jesus' words in today's Gospel highlight that while the people reject Jesus and his words, he himself does not reject anyone who comes to him. If he were to reject anyone, he would be acting contrary to the Father's will.

Instead, there are two things, two commissions as it were, that comprise the Father's will. One commission is that Jesus must not lose anything, or anyone, entrusted to him by the Father. An important theme in John's Gospel is that Jesus does not judge or condemn anyone, rather a person condemns themselves when they reject Jesus. The reason it is considered self-condemnation is that in rejecting Jesus, they are in actuality rejecting the Father who sent him.

Jesus' second commission is to raise from the dead those entrusted to him. This commission reveals the Father's love for humanity. The Father so loves the world that he wants all of humanity to share in the resurrection and in eternal life. In order to partake in this promise, one needs to "see" Jesus and believe in him.

Today we celebrate and rejoice that, through Jesus Christ, God the Father continually extends an invitation for us to accept and reciprocate his love for us. We can accomplish this by rejoicing in the midst of grief, rejoicing that those who have gone before us partake in eternal life and the promise of salvation. M.B.

THIRTY-FIRST SUNDAY IN ORDINARY TIME

LECTIONARY #152

READING I Deuteronomy 6:2–6

A reading from the Book of Deuteronomy

Moses spoke to the people, saying:
    "**Fear** the LORD, your God,
    and **keep**, throughout the days of your lives,
    all his **statutes** and **commandments** which I enjoin on you,
    and thus have **long** life.
Hear then, Israel, and be careful to **observe** them,
    that you may **grow** and prosper the more,
    in keeping with the **promise** of the LORD, the God of
        your fathers,
    to give you a land flowing with **milk** and **honey**.

"**Hear**, O Israel! The LORD is our God, the LORD **alone**!
Therefore, you shall **love** the LORD, your God,
    with **all** your **heart**,
    and with all your **soul**,
    and with all your **strength**.
Take to **heart** these words which I **enjoin** on you today."

Deuteronomy = d<u>oo</u>-ter-AH-nuh-mee
or dy<u>oo</u>-ter-AH-nuh-mee

"Fear" is best understood here as awe and reverence, rather than as being terrified and afraid.

"Hear" calls the people to attention to make sure they are listening. Today, we might say, "Listen up." This implies a message of importance is coming.

This is not a suggestion, but an imperative.

READING I Today's reading follows the restatement of the Ten Commandments in Deuteronomy 5:6–21. Moses provides two reasons for keeping the commandments. First, doing so instills reverence for God. Second, the commandments enjoin correct action on the part of the Israelites. To follow the law is to revere God in all aspects of life. Furthermore, if they keep God's commandments, they will prosper and inherit the promised land.

The last section of the passage elaborates upon the first commandment to have no other gods, connecting it with the way this is to be lived out. Beginning with "Hear, O Israel," the passage presents what is referred to as the *Shema*, taken from the imperative of the Hebrew word *shema'* ("hear"). The *Shema* is the cornerstone of Jewish worship. Likewise, it is the central theme of Deuteronomy. The terms of the *Shema* present the obligations of those who enter into the covenant with God. In return, prosperity will come to those who adhere to the terms of the covenant.

The central verb of the *Shema* is "love." This is the first time in the Bible that we see a reference to loving God. The act of loving does not refer to an emotional attachment; rather, it reveals a proper attitude toward God that manifests itself through actions. To love God is to remain loyal to him. The *Shema* exhorts the people to remain undivided in their devotion to God.

There are three terms used to express how the people should love God: "heart," "soul," and "strength." While there are nuances distinguishing the terms, they each convey the sense of the entire person. The use of all three terms here encapsulates every aspect of the human person.

For meditation and context:

RESPONSORIAL PSALM 18:2–3, 3–4, 47, 51 (2)

R. I love you, O Lord, my strength.

I love you, O Lord, my strength,
   O Lord, my rock, my fortress,
     my deliverer.

My God, my rock of refuge,
   my shield, the horn of my salvation,
     my stronghold!

Praised be the Lord, I exclaim,
   and I am safe from my enemies.

The Lord lives! And blessed be my rock!
   Extolled be God my savior,
you who gave great victories to your king
   and showed kindness to your anointed.

READING II Hebrews 7:23–28

A reading from the Letter to the Hebrews

Brothers and **sisters**:
The levitical **priests** were **many**
   because they were **prevented** by **death** from remaining
      in **office**,
   but **Jesus**, because he remains **forever**,
   has a **priesthood** that does **not** pass away.
Therefore, he is always able to **save** those who **approach** God
      through him,
   since he lives forever to make **intercession** for them.

It was fitting that we should have such a **high** priest:
   holy, **innocent**, **undefiled**, **separated** from sinners,
   higher than the **heavens**.
He has no **need**, as did the **high priests**,
   to offer **sacrifice** day after **day**,
   first for his **own** sins and then for those of the **people**;
   he did that **once** for all when he offered **himself**.
For the **law** appoints men subject to **weakness** to be high **priests**,
   but the word of the **oath**, which was taken **after** the law,
   appoints a son,
   who has been made **perfect** forever.

---

levitical = lih-VIT-ih-k*l =
related to the tribe of Levi

Highlight the contrast. The former type of priesthood is fleeting, while Jesus' office is neither provisional nor temporary.

This is an important message to communicate to the assembly; we can always approach God through Jesus. Read the attributes slowly.

Again, highlight the contrast between Jesus and the human high priests.

"He" and "himself" refer to Jesus.

READING II Today's second reading focuses on priesthood. On one hand, there are the Levitical priests, who are like any other human being in that they eventually die. On the other hand, we are presented with Jesus' permanent priesthood, as he lives forever. Because of his divine nature, his actions are eternally efficacious in his defeat of sin and death through his perfect nature and salvific offering.

Hebrews presents a description of Jesus' priesthood, listing five aspects in this passage. He is "holy, innocent, undefiled, separated from sinners, [and] higher than the heavens." These aspects present a contrast to the list of characteristics ascribed to Melchizedek in Hebrews 7:3. Not only is Jesus' priesthood permanent, but it also exceeds the priesthood of Melchizedek. The reference to "the word of the oath" that appoints Jesus is an allusion to Psalm 110:4: "The Lord has sworn and will not waver: 'You are a priest forever in the manner of Melchizedek.'" It is clear that the letter to the Hebrews views Jesus' priesthood as a fulfillment of Psalm 110:4.

In the first reading, God's people are exhorted to act lovingly toward God. In contrast, today's second reading demonstrates God's loving activity toward us. Jesus offered himself as a sacrifice on our behalf. As the perfect and permanent high priest, Jesus tendered the perfect sacrifice, himself, such that there is no longer a need for any other offering. This salvation becomes the fundamental motivation for rendering worship to God. Our worship is both an internal and external expression of our love of God, as described in the first reading.

GOSPEL   Mark 12:28b–34

A reading from the holy Gospel according to Mark

One of the **scribes** came to **Jesus** and asked him,
    "**Which** is the **first** of all the commandments?"
Jesus replied, "The first is this:
    Hear, O Israel!
    *The Lord our **God** is Lord **alone**!*
    *You **shall** love the Lord your God with **all** your **heart**,*
    *with all your **soul**,*
    *with all your **mind**,*
    *and with all your **strength**.*
The second is this:
    *You shall love your **neighbor** as **yourself**.*
There is no **other** commandment **greater** than these."
The **scribe** said to him, "Well said, **teacher**.
You are **right** in saying,
    'He is **One** and there is no **other** than he.'
And 'to love him with all your **heart**,
    with all your **understanding**,
    with all your **strength**,
    and to love your **neighbor** as **yourself**'
    is **worth** more than all **burnt** offerings and sacrifices."
And when Jesus saw that he answered with **understanding**,
    he said to him,
    "You are not **far** from the kingdom of **God**."
And no one **dared** to ask him any more questions.

Read the question with sincerity. As we will see, this scribe is not trying to trap Jesus but is genuinely seeking a deeper faith.

These lines are well known. Read them reverently.

There is repetition here. Slow down at the end of the scribe's reply when new information is offered, at "worth more."

Why do you think the others were hesitant to inquire further?

GOSPEL   The reading from Mark's Gospel presents the *Shema* we heard in the first reading. The scribe's question stems from a sincere desire to understand the commandments. There are 613 commandments in the Torah, the Jewish name for the first five books of the Old Testament. Jesus answers the scribe's question by reciting the *Shema*, but he goes a step further. He also presents a form of the "golden rule" (as we call it now) as the second greatest commandment. Together, the *Shema* and the command to love one's neighbor as oneself are the foundation of the Ten Commandments. The *Shema* captures the significance of the first three commandments, while the command to love one's neighbor does the same for the other seven commandments.

Jesus teaches the scribe that love of God is inseparable from love of neighbor. In the *Shema*, "love" is a verb. Thus, people must take action in order to be true to the *Shema*. Devotion to God is action, not a sentiment. Likewise, love of neighbor entails actively seeking their good, not simply remaining neutral or doing them no harm.

An interesting development in the dialogue between Jesus and the scribe is the scribe's added observation that the commands are more important than burnt offerings and sacrifice. With this inclusion, the scribe demonstrates that action in and of itself is not sufficient to live out these commandments. Empty actions that check boxes but do not have real love motivating them is not what God wants from his people. Thus, one's disposition is important in living out the two great commandments. We must be genuine in acting out our love for God and neighbor. M.B.

THIRTY-SECOND SUNDAY IN ORDINARY TIME

LECTIONARY #155

READING I   1 Kings 17:10–16

A reading from the first Book of Kings

In those days, **Elijah** the prophet went to **Zarephath**.
As he arrived at the entrance of the city,
    a **widow** was gathering sticks there; he **called** out to her,
    "Please **bring** me a small cupful of **water** to drink."
She left to get it, and he called out after her,
    "Please bring along a bit of **bread**."
She answered, "As the LORD, your **God**, lives,
    I have **nothing** baked; there is only a **handful** of flour
        in my jar
    and a **little** oil in my jug.
Just now I was collecting a **couple** of sticks,
    to go in and **prepare** something for **myself** and my **son**;
    when we have **eaten** it, we shall **die**."
Elijah said to her, "Do not be **afraid**.
Go and do as you **propose**.
But **first** make me a little **cake** and bring it to **me**.
Then you can **prepare** something for yourself and your son.
For the LORD, the **God** of Israel, says,
    'The **jar** of flour shall not go **empty**,
    nor the **jug** of oil run **dry**,
    until the **day** when the LORD **sends** rain upon the earth.'"
She left and **did** as Elijah had said. »

Reading 1 Kings 17:1–10 will provide a context for you as you prepare this reading.
Elijah = ee-LĪ-juh
Zarephath = ZAYR-uh-fath

Elijah is not asking for much, just a "small cupful of water" and a "bit of bread," yet we quickly see it is a great amount to the widow.

A widow at this time was quite disadvantaged. Her plight is exacerbated by the dire circumstances she is in. She remains unnamed.

The action she is being called to will take great faith on her part. Read Elijah's words with comfort and assurance.

Quote the Lord with great confidence. The narrative ends with the prophecy being fulfilled.

READING I   In this reading from 1 Kings, Elijah comes to the widow of Zarephath during a time of drought. This drought is of divine origin, brought about by the wickedness of King Ahab, who married the non-Israelite Jezebel, worshiped Baal, and seemingly engaged in child sacrifice at the cost of two of his sons (see 1 Kings 16:29–34). As is typical in the royal narrative, the transgressions of the king are visited upon the people of Israel. Elijah calls down a drought upon the entire nation as a result of Ahab's sins.

During the drought, God orders Elijah to go to the widow of Zarephath, a Gentile, for nourishment. Elijah obeys God's command and finds the widow just as she is down to the last handful of flour and drops of oil. The widow does not immediately jump at the chance to hand over the last of her food to a stranger, especially considering that she has a son to care for. However, she believes Elijah when he tells her that God will continue to provide for her and her son until the drought ends.

The faith of the widow of Zarephath is remarkable, even more so when we recall that she is a Gentile. Her heritage does not include Israel's history of God's providential care, such as the giving of manna in the wilderness. Yet in obeying Elijah, she implicitly acknowledges the authority of the God of Israel who, through Elijah, brought salvation of an earthly kind to her family.

READING II   A major concern in Hebrews is asserting and elaborating on the permanent priesthood of Jesus. Jesus is the perfect high priest who offers the perfect sacrifice of himself for the salvation of humanity. As the high priest

She was **able** to **eat** for a year, and he and her son as well;
> the jar of flour did **not** go empty,
> **nor** the jug of oil run dry,
> as the LORD had **foretold** through Elijah.

For meditation and context:

RESPONSORIAL PSALM   Psalm 146:7, 8–9, 9–10 (1b)

R. Praise the Lord, my soul!
or R. Alleluia.

The LORD keeps faith forever,
> secures justice for the oppressed,
> gives food to the hungry.
The LORD sets captives free.

The LORD gives sight to the blind;
> the LORD raises up those who were
> bowed down.

The LORD loves the just;
> the LORD protects strangers.

The fatherless and the widow he sustains,
> but the way of the wicked he thwarts.
The LORD shall reign forever;
> your God, O Zion, through all generations.
> Alleluia.

READING II   Hebrews 9:24–28

A reading from the Letter to the Hebrews

Christ did not **enter** into a sanctuary made by **hands**,
> a copy of the true one, but heaven itself,
> that he might **now** appear before **God** on **our** behalf.
Not that he might offer himself **repeatedly**,
> as the high **priest** enters **each** year into the sanctuary
> with **blood** that is not his **own**;
> if that were so, he would have had to suffer repeatedly
> from the foundation of the world.
But now **once** for **all** he has appeared at the end of the ages
> to take away sin by his sacrifice.
Just as it is appointed that **human** beings **die once**,
> and after this the **judgment**, so also Christ,
> offered once to **take** away the sins of many,
> will appear a **second** time, not to take away sin
> but to bring **salvation** to those who **eagerly** await him.

This passage needs to be taken slowly. The author is contrasting repeatable cultic practices with Jesus' once and for all salvific sacrifice.

Emphasize "not" so that the claim of what Jesus didn't do is made clear.

The passage ends with good news; use an uplifting tone. Those who have accepted the offer of salvation will be rewarded when Jesus comes again.

---

entered the sanctuary of the temple each year to offer sacrifice on behalf of the people, so Jesus entered the heavenly sanctuary, offering his very blood for the redemption of humanity.

There is a significant difference between Jesus' sacrifice and that of past high priests. Since Jesus is the perfect sacrifice, there is no need for any other sacrifices. Jesus' priesthood transcends the Levitical priesthood, offering more in a more permanent fashion. Likewise, Jesus' sacrifice is not limited to the people of Israel but extends to all of humanity.

Drawing parallels between the first and second readings, we see how God's actions through Jesus are in keeping with his saving character yet also extend far beyond the small glimpse of it we see in the first reading. In the same way that God provided for the widow of Zarephath in the first reading, he provides for all of humanity through Jesus' sacrificial offering. In this case, instead of a drought on the earth, the drought is a spiritual deficit brought about through sin. Jesus' death and resurrection overcome death, bringing life to God's people, who are made new. Just as the widow

of Zarephath experienced salvation, so does all humanity receive salvation. Yet this salvation Jesus offers is everlasting, for Jesus offered the perfect sacrifice "once for all" for the forgiveness of sins. As the widow of Zarephath gave away that which would sustain her and her son, Jesus also held nothing back. He gave everything, including his body and blood, for the salvation of the world.

GOSPEL   Today's Gospel continues the themes of God's providence and true faith. The first half of the

GOSPEL   Mark 12:38–44

A reading from the holy Gospel according to Mark

In the course of his **teaching Jesus** said to the **crowds**,
   "**Beware** of the scribes, who like to go around in long **robes**
   and **accept** greetings in the marketplaces,
   seats of **honor** in **synagogues**,
   and places of **honor** at banquets.
They devour the houses of **widows** and, as a **pretext**
   recite **lengthy** prayers.
They will receive a very **severe** condemnation."

[He sat down opposite the **treasury**
   and **observed** how the crowd **put** money **into** the treasury.
Many **rich** people put in **large** sums.
A poor **widow** also came and put in two **small** coins worth
      a few cents.
Calling his **disciples** to himself, he said to them,
   "**Amen**, I say to you, this poor widow put in **more**
   than **all** the other **contributors** to the treasury.
For they have all contributed from their **surplus** wealth,
   but she, from her **poverty**, has contributed **all** she had,
   her whole livelihood."]

[Shorter: Mark 12:41–44 (see brackets)]

Place a comma after "teaching."

The long robes call attention to the scribes but for the wrong reason. Slightly elongate "long" so that it sounds like what it represents.

Clearly proclaim Jesus' mention of the widows so that the assembly can make a connection with the widow in the first reading. Do likewise later in the reading.

Imagine Jesus observing the scene at the temple.

Instead of teaching a larger crowd here (as in the first half of the reading), Jesus now teaches his disciples.

Read with a tone of approval for the actions of the widow.

---

reading presents an example of false piety. The scribes go about seeking earthly recognition and respect while neglecting their spiritual lives. They recite lengthy prayers to attract the attention of those around them, seeking to appear pious and earn the respect of humans. They do not pray in order to glorify God or as a means of working on and improving upon their relationship with God.

Jesus accuses the scribes of devouring widows' houses. Widows were among the most vulnerable of society because they had limited means of income and did not always have someone to advocate for them if they were being taken advantage of. There are many injunctions in the Old Testament against exploiting widows (for example, Isaiah 10:1–2; Jeremiah 7:6; Ezekiel 22:7), yet this is what the scribes are doing. Jesus assures the crowds that such people will eventually receive divine justice for their actions.

The second half of today's Gospel presents an example of true piety. Jesus reveals his supernatural knowledge of what lies in the hearts of people when he tells his disciples that the poor widow gave "all she had," withholding nothing from God. She could have kept one coin back for herself, but instead she gave it all to the Lord. She is like the widow of Zarephath from the first reading, withholding nothing, although in this instance there is no promise of continued provision.

Today's readings invite us to examine our lives. Do we give everything over to God, not just financially, but also our time, our worries, our joys, our prayer life? Do we accept Jesus' all-giving sacrifice in our daily lives, sharing his love with others? M.B.

THIRTY-THIRD SUNDAY IN ORDINARY TIME

LECTIONARY #158

READING I   Daniel 12:1–3

A reading from the Book of the Prophet Daniel

In those days, I, **Daniel**,
   heard this **word** of the Lord:
"At that time there shall arise
   Michael, the great **prince**,
   guardian of your people;
it shall be a time **unsurpassed** in **distress**
   since nations began until that time.
At that time your people shall **escape**,
   everyone who is found written **in** the book.

"**Many** of those who **sleep** in the dust of the earth shall **awake**;
   some shall **live** forever,
   others shall be an **everlasting horror** and **disgrace**.

"But the **wise** shall **shine** brightly
   like the splendor of the **firmament**,
and those who **lead** the many to **justice**
   shall be like the stars **forever**."

This apocalyptic reading repeats "at that time." No need to increase the volume on the repetition.

Notice how this passage uses highly descriptive language to describe the time of judgement.

In contrast to "unsurpassed in distress" and "everlasting horror and disgrace," the reading ends on a joyful note.

READING I | In today's first reading, we hear of God's justice and the reward of those who remain faithful to him. The apocalyptic imagery and language of Daniel appear again in the Book of Revelation. The term "apocalypse" is not synonymous with doom and gloom and the destruction of the world, although the end of this world is often described in apocalypses. In reality, "apocalypse" refers to the unveiling of heavenly mysteries, especially as they pertain to human history. The imagery and symbolism utilized are a code understood by insiders but remain incomprehensible to those who persecute them.

In this passage, we find one of the first references to Michael, Israel's guardian, in the Bible. His presence in the midst of persecution brings solace and hope to God's people. The book referred to here is likely the "book of truth" in Daniel 10:21, in which future events are recorded.

Today's reading also contains one of the few Old Testament references to the resurrection of the dead as well as the final judgment and the afterlife. The concept of resurrection here is not exactly the same as that found in the New Testament. It states that "many of those who sleep" will experience resurrection, which gives the impression that not everyone will be resurrected on the last day. Of those who are resurrected, some will be rewarded and others will be punished. Herein lies the hope of future divine justice. After the resurrection, injustices will be made right and the wicked will be punished. In contrast, the wise and those who lead others to justice are compared to stars in the sky, likely a reference to angels. Thus, the faithful will

286

For meditation and context:

RESPONSORIAL PSALM Psalm 16:5, 8, 9–10, 11 (1)

R. You are my inheritance, O Lord!

O Lord, my allotted portion and my cup,
  you it is who hold fast my lot.
I set the Lord ever before me;
  with him at my right hand I shall not
    be disturbed.

Therefore my heart is glad and my soul
    rejoices,
  my body, too, abides in confidence;

because you will not abandon my soul to the
    netherworld,
  nor will you suffer your faithful one to
    undergo corruption.

You will show me the path to life,
  fullness of joys in your presence,
  the delights at your right hand forever.

READING II Hebrews 10:11–14, 18

A reading from the Letter to the Hebrews

Brothers and **sisters**:
Every **priest** stands **daily** at his **ministry**,
  offering **frequently** those same **sacrifices**
  that can **never** take away **sins**.
But **this** one offered **one** sacrifice for sins,
  and took his seat **forever** at the right hand of **God**;
  now he **waits** until his **enemies** are made his footstool.
For by one offering
  he has made **perfect** forever those who are being **consecrated**.

Where there is **forgiveness** of these,
  there is no longer **offering** for sin.

Notice the contrast between the human priest and Jesus' priestly identity.

Add a comma after "one," which is the pronoun used for Christ. The second "one" is numeric.

Jesus' sacrifice is complete and perfect.

be accorded glory akin to that of the angels in heaven.

READING II This reading from Hebrews repeats what we have heard for the past few Sundays concerning Jesus' priesthood. His priesthood is perfect and permanent, which negates the need for any future sacrifice for the forgiveness of sins. What is new in this passage is the reference to daily offerings. These daily offerings were never intended for taking away sin; however, the sacrifices consisted of lamb and wine. Thus, the reference to daily offerings taps into the images of lamb and wine to point to Jesus as the perfect sacrifice, the Lamb of God who spilled his blood to take away the sins of the world.

This passage views Jesus' sacrifice as the fulfillment of the Old Testament. It refers to Psalm 110:1, which begins with God appointing a ruler over Israel who is both king and priest. Jesus fulfills this psalm since he is both king and high priest. We also see in the passage the fulfillment of the first reading, in that wrongs are made right after the resurrection of the dead. With Jesus' resurrection, sins are taken away so that we might enter into a proper relationship with God.

Continuing this focus, the last sentence of the reading alludes to Psalm 40:7, which states that God does not want sacrifice and sin-offering but rather he wants there to be an interior disposition that is properly oriented toward him. Through Jesus' perfect sacrifice, there is no need to revert to animal sacrifices. Instead, humanity is consecrated and set apart for God with hearts inscribed with the new covenant (see Jeremiah 31:33–34) ratified by Jesus' blood. As such, Christians now join

GOSPEL   Mark 13:24–32

A reading from the holy Gospel according to Mark

Jesus said to his **disciples**:
"In those days **after** that **tribulation**
    the sun will be **darkened**,
        and the **moon** will not give its **light**,
    and the **stars** will be **falling** from the sky,
        and the **powers** in the heavens will be shaken.

"And then they will see the 'Son of **Man** coming in the clouds'
    with great **power** and **glory**,
    and then he will **send** out the **angels**
    and **gather** his **elect** from the four winds,
    from the end of the earth to the end of the sky.

"**Learn** a lesson from the fig tree.
When its branch becomes **tender** and sprouts **leaves**,
    you **know** that summer is near.
In the same way, when you **see** these things happening,
    know that he is **near**, at the gates.
Amen, I say to you,
    this **generation** will not pass away
    until **all** these things have taken place.
Heaven and **earth** will pass away,
    but my **words** will **not** pass away.

"But of that **day** or hour, **no** one knows,
    neither the **angels** in heaven, nor the **Son**, but only
        the **Father**."

Start with a solemn tone for the cosmic occurrences.

Pause slightly before changing the tone to awe in the next section. Christ's return is majestic.

Pause before beginning the parable of the fig tree.

Emphasize "near." Despite seeing some warning signs, the exact time will remain unknown.

The message is timely for us today. We must be prepared for Jesus' second coming.

---

in the priestly life of their baptismal vocation, offering a "sacrifice of praise" described later in Hebrews (13:15–16).

GOSPEL Today's Gospel continues the theme of cosmic upheaval. Unlike the reading from Daniel, the stars here refer to creation rather than to angels. The power of the Son of Man extends to all of creation, "from the end of the earth to the end of the sky." Jesus often refers to himself as the "Son of Man," as a representative human (who redeems the rest of humanity) and as the revealer of

heavenly things and judge since he is divine.

There are several possibilities for what brings about this cosmic upheaval. It could represent the fall of Jerusalem and the destruction of the temple that occurred in AD 70. Another interpretation sees this passage as pointing toward Jesus' passion and death on the cross when "darkness came over the whole land" (Mark 15:33). Finally, the cosmic chaos could be a result of the arrival of the end times. The "day or hour" at the end of the reading could refer to the timing of any these events.

Jesus then tells his disciples to learn from the fig tree. On one level, the meaning is explained within the context of the verses that follow. One should pay attention to the signs all around so as not to be caught off guard when the day/hour arrives. On another level, it reminds the disciples of the withered fig tree cursed by Jesus in Mark 11:12–14, 20 when he found it bore no fruit. The reference to the fig tree here could be understood as a warning not to be barren like the fig tree when the day/hour comes. M.B.

OUR LORD JESUS CHRIST, KING OF THE UNIVERSE

LECTIONARY #161

READING I   Daniel 7:13–14

A reading from the Book of the Prophet Daniel

As the **visions** during the night continued, I **saw**
    one like a Son of **man coming**,
        on the **clouds** of heaven;
    when he reached the **Ancient** One
        and was **presented** before him,
    the one like a Son of man received **dominion**, **glory**,
        and **kingship**;
    all peoples, nations, and **languages** serve him.
His dominion is an **everlasting** dominion
    that shall **not** be taken away,
    his kingship shall **not** be destroyed.

RESPONSORIAL PSALM   Psalm 93:1, 1–2, 5 (1a)

R. The Lord is king; he is robed in majesty.

The LORD is king, in splendor robed;
    robed is the LORD and girt about with
    strength.

And he has made the world firm,
    not to be moved.
Your throne stands firm from of old;
    from everlasting you are, O LORD.

Your decrees are worthy of trust indeed;
    holiness befits your house,
    O LORD, for length of days.

Imagine the scene. Use a tone in your proclamation that paints a picture for the listener and invites them into the epic vision.

Do not rush the list of gifts that God enjoys.

The permanence of God's reign is made clear. The use of negatives makes the statement definitive.

For meditation and context:

READING I   Today's first reading focuses on the prophet Daniel's description of the "Son of man." In the Old Testament, the title "son of man" is mostly used as a generic term for man/humanity/mortal. Ezekiel uses it with this sense around seventy times. However, in today's reading, Daniel seems to attribute a different sense to the phrase.

This passage from Daniel depicts the son of man's heavenly descent. Furthermore, this figure is described as having received dominion, glory, and kingship. This first reading emphasizes the universality of the son of man's kingship which encompasses "all peoples, nations, and languages." Furthermore, his kingship is perpetual, withstanding all trials and tribulations. The son of man reflects God's sovereignty over all of humanity.

The question remains of who, then, is meant by the "Son of man" in this reading. There are several possible contenders, including the faithful community, the angel Michael, the angel Gabriel, Judas Maccabeus, Daniel himself, or simply a generic human being. There is no clear answer to the question, though it seems less likely to refer to a generic person in this instance.

Both Old Testament senses of "Son of man" appear in the New Testament. While at times the phrase seems to refer to humanity in general, it is used in Acts 7:56 to refer to Jesus standing at the right hand of God. Likewise, in Revelation 1:13 and 14:14 Jesus appears as the glorified Christ reminiscent of the "Son of man" in this passage.

READING II   This Sunday we recognize and worship Jesus Christ as king of the universe. Today's second reading

Notice the different ways Jesus Christ is described. Proclaim them with praise!

READING II   Revelation 1:5–8

A reading from the Book of Revelation

Jesus **Christ** is the faithful **witness**,
  the **firstborn** of the dead and **ruler** of the kings of the earth.
To him who **loves** us and has **freed** us from our sins by
    his blood,
  who has made **us** into a **kingdom**, priests for his God
    and Father,
  to him be **glory** and **power forever** and **ever**. Amen.

  Behold, he is **coming** amid the clouds,
    and **every** eye will **see** him,
    even those who **pierced** him.
  All the peoples of the earth will **lament** him.
    Yes. Amen.

"**I am** the **Alpha** and the **Omega**," says the Lord **God**,
  "the one who **is** and who **was** and who is to **come**,
    the **almighty**."

Be familiar enough with the Lord's words in the last lines to deliver them looking directly at the assembly.

reminds us that his rule is rooted in the great love he has for us, and it outlines the extent of his kingship. He conquered death, making him "the firstborn of the dead." Christ's rule stands above and beyond all others as he is declared king of kings, confirming his kingship over all the peoples of the world.

Having described the extent of Christ's kingdom, this passage next reveals the kind of king he is. He is a loving, sacrificial king who freed humanity from the bondage of sin by means of his very blood. His salvific love is transformative, creating a royal and priestly people, a kingdom, for God the Father. The letter to the Hebrews explains that the people express their priestly function in offering a sacrifice of praise (13:15–16).

Finally, the last lines in today's reading contain God's direct speech, in which he depicts his transcendent nature as "the Alpha and the Omega" who is, was, and is to come. Since "alpha" and "omega" are the first and last letters of the Greek alphabet, their combined use as a divine title indicates God's authority over all history. In Isaiah 41:4 and 44:6, God describes himself as "the first" and "the last," indicating his role as Israel's liberator and the true God of Israel. The same authority is attributed to Christ when the title "the Alpha and Omega" is applied to him in Revelation 22:13.

It is noteworthy that the description of Jesus coming from the clouds echoes the description of the "Son of man" in the first reading. Thus, the Book of Revelation answers the question of the identity of the "Son of man" in Daniel 7:13 in a final and complete sense: he is Jesus Christ, triumphant king of the universe.

GOSPEL   John 18:33b–37

A reading from the holy Gospel according to John

Pilate said to **Jesus**,
  "Are **you** the King of the **Jews**?"
Jesus answered, "Do you say this on your **own**
  or have **others** told you about me?"
Pilate answered, "I am not a **Jew**, am I?
Your own **nation** and the chief **priests handed** you over to **me**.
What have you **done**?"
Jesus answered, "My kingdom does not **belong** to this world.
If my kingdom **did** belong to this world,
  my attendants would be **fighting**
  to **keep** me from being handed over to the Jews.
But as it is, my kingdom is not **here**."
So Pilate said to him, "Then you **are** a king?"
Jesus answered, "**You** say I am a king.
For **this** I was **born** and for **this** I came into the **world**,
  to **testify** to the truth.
Everyone who belongs to the truth **listens** to my voice."

Distinguish between the two characters in dialogue.

Is Pilate curious or accusatory? Perhaps both?

Jesus is not flustered. He has truth on his side.

Proclaim Jesus' last line with sincerity. His words apply to us today.

| GOSPEL | John's Gospel presents a stark contrast between an earthly king and the divine kingship of Jesus. Previously in John's Gospel, those who called Jesus a king (1:49; 6:15; 12:13) fell far short of the reality of Jesus' identity because they were expecting a messiah to establish his reign and restore the kingdom of Israel through military force. They failed to recognize Jesus' true messianic kingship because they could not see beyond their own expectations.

Likewise, Pilate struggles to understand if Jesus is truly a king. Jesus insists that his kingdom is not of the world and, for Pilate, the world is the only possible realm for reigning as king. He does not recognize that Jesus' kingdom belongs to the heavenly realm. Like the other people in John's Gospel, Pilate cannot see who Jesus truly is because Jesus' kingship goes beyond his expectations.

Furthermore, Jesus' kingship encompasses all of humanity since the invitation to join him in his kingdom is open to all. It requires listening to Jesus' voice, as the sheep heed the voice of the shepherd. In so doing, they recognize the truth to which Jesus testifies and are drawn into that truth. Through baptism, we receive the new, spiritual life that makes us children of God nd heirs to the kingdom.

Today's reading reminds us that as heirs of the kingdom, we too are not of this world (John 17:16). During our earthly life, we remain a part of the world, otherwise we cannot evangelize effectively. Yet, at the same time, we should keep in mind that we work for a kingdom that transcends earthly concerns and for a king who willingly shed his blood that we might live. M.B.